Dennis Swann

The Economics of the
Common Market

Sixth Edition

Penguin Books

To Barbara Claire

PENGUIN BOOKS

Published by the Penguin Group
Penguin Books Ltd, 27 Wrights Lane, London W8 5TZ, England
Viking Penguin, a division of Penguin Books USA Inc.
375 Hudson Street, New York, New York 10014, USA
Penguin Books Australia Ltd, Ringwood, Victoria, Australia
Penguin Books Canada Ltd, 2801 John Street, Markham, Ontario, Canada L3R 1B4
Penguin Books (NZ) Ltd, 182–190 Wairau Road, Auckland 10, New Zealand

Penguin Books Ltd, Registered Offices: Harmondsworth, Middlesex, England

First published 1970
Second edition 1972
Third edition 1975
Fourth edition 1978
Reprinted with revisions and Addendum 1981
Fifth edition, published in Pelican Books, 1984
Sixth edition 1988
Reprinted in Penguin Books 1990
10 9 8 7 6 5 4 3 2

Copyright © Dennis Swann, 1970, 1972, 1975, 1978, 1981, 1984, 1988
All rights reserved

Printed in England by Clays Ltd, St Ives plc
Filmset in 9 on 11 pt Monophoto Times

Contents

Preface to Sixth Edition

On 25 March 1957 the governments of France, West Germany, Italy, the Netherlands, Belgium and Luxembourg signed the Rome Treaty. In so doing they agreed to create what is now known as the Common Market, or, more accurately, the European Economic Community. The latter title indicates that the arrangement is an economic one although, of course, the political aspect is also of the highest importance. This statement is not likely to give rise to any dispute. A former President of the European Economic Community Commission, Dr Walter Hallstein, once said: 'We are not in business at all; we are in politics.' The political nature of the Community is evidenced by the fact that it has political organs such as the European Parliament and the Council of Ministers. The latter makes binding decisions on matters which were formerly a national prerogative, as in the case of agricultural policy. Moreover, although the Community is primarily concerned with economic integration, the ultimate aim of those who have been in the vanguard of the 'European movement' has always been that close economic ties would eventually lead to political unity.

However, the main burden of this book will be related to the economic aspect of Community policy. This should not be taken as a further indication of the British preoccupation with the economic, as opposed to the political, nature of the 'European movement'. Rather, it is a consequence of the need to achieve some specialization in the analysis of Community policy.

As the title emphasizes, the focus of attention in this book is the European Economic Community. The more important aspects of policy in the European Coal and Steel Community are also discussed. Euratom is dealt with, although only in passing.

The book has two overriding aims. One is to discuss some of the economic principles underlying the decision to create the Common Market and the policies which the Community has been following since its inception. The second is to discuss the nature of these policies critically. It will, of course, be appreciated that many of the subjects treated in this book could be the themes of separate monographs. Because of this, the book seeks to introduce the most important economic features of particular areas of policy, and a reading list is provided for those who wish to delve deeper.

In writing this book I have once more been able to avail myself of the courteous and efficient assistance provided by the London Office of the European Community. I am greatly indebted to my secretary, Mrs Brenda Moore, who has again rendered a great service by getting the manuscript into a fit state for the publisher, to David Allen of the Department of European Studies at the Loughborough University of Technology who has once more been a generous source of stimulating ideas and useful information, and to my colleagues David T. Llewellyn and Chris Milner who have kindly read through particular chapters and made most helpful suggestions relating to the argument and its presentation.

1 The Evolution of the European Community

European unity in history

Although the actual steps which have been taken to achieve economic and political unity in Europe are mostly, if not all, post 1945 in origin, the idea of such a coming together is not unique to the last forty or so years. Quite the contrary: history is littered with proposals and arrangements which were designed to foster European unity.

As early as the fourteenth century the idea of a united Christendom prompted Pierre Dubois to propose a European confederation to be governed by a European Council of 'wise, expert, and faithful men'. In the seventeenth century Sully proposed to keep the peace in Europe by means of a European army. In 1693, William Penn, the English Quaker, suggested 'a European Diet, Parliament, or State' in his *Essay towards the Present and Future Peace of Europe*. In the nineteenth century Proudhon was strongly in favour of European federation. He foresaw the twentieth century as opening an era of federations and prophesied disaster if such developments did not occur. It was only after the 1914–18 war that statesmen began to give serious attention to the idea of European unity. Aristide Briand – a Prime Minister of France – declared that part of his political programme was the building of a United States of Europe.

The achievement of a lasting peace has been the chief motivating factor behind the drive for unity. However, economic advantage also played a role. The free-trade tradition, and Adam Smith's dictum that 'the division of labour is limited by the extent of the market', was a contributing element. The idea that European nation states were no longer large enough to hold their own in world markets was put forward by the German thinker Friedrich Naumann in 1915.

Despite the fact that there was no shortage of plans to create a united Europe, it was nevertheless not until after 1945 that there occurred a combination of new forces together with an intensification of old ones, which compelled action. In the first place, Europe had been the centre of yet another devastating war arising out of the unbridled ambitions of nation states. Those who sought, and still seek, a united Europe, have always had at the forefront of their minds the desire to prevent any further outbreak of war in Europe. By bringing the nations of Europe closer together it has always been hoped that such a contingency would be rendered unthinkable. The 1939–45 war also left Europe economically exhausted. This engendered the view that if Europe were to recover, it would require a conjoint effort on the part of European states. The war also soon revealed that for a long time Western Europe would have to face not only a powerful and politically alien USSR, but also a group of European states firmly anchored within the Eastern bloc. An exhausted and divided Europe (since the West embraced co-belligerents) presented both a power-vacuum and a temptation to the USSR to fill it. Then again the ending of the war soon revealed that the war-time Allies were in fact divided, with the two major powers – the US and the USSR – confronting each other in a bid for world supremacy. It was therefore not surprising that 'Europeans'[1] should feel the need for a third force – the voice of Europe. The latter would represent the Western European viewpoint and could also act as a bridge between the Eastern and Western extremities.

Europe – the East–West division

The Economic Commission for Europe (ECE) was one of the first experiments in European regional action. It was set up in Geneva in 1947 as a regional organization of the United Nations (UN), and was to be concerned with initiating and participating in concerted measures aimed at securing the economic reconstruction of Europe. The aim was to create an instrument of cooperation between all the states of Europe – Eastern, Central and Western. Unfortunately, by the time it began to operate, the Cold War had become a reality and the world had been divided into two camps. In the light of future developments in Europe, this was a turning-point. Economic cooperation over the whole of Europe was doomed. Thereafter, Western Europe followed its own path of economic and political unity, and Eastern Europe likewise pursued an

---

1. 'Europeans' – members of the 'European movement' – sought to break away from systems of inter-governmental cooperation and to create institutions in Europe which would lead to a federal arrangement in which some national sovereignty would be given up.

independent course. This in due course led to two blocs in Europe – the Common Market or European Economic Community (EEC) and the European Free Trade Association (EFTA) on the one hand, and the Council for Mutual Economic Assistance (Comecon) on the other. Any attempt to build bridges between the Western and Eastern blocs therefore implies trying to break down a division which began to manifest itself in 1947.

The political division of Europe was further revealed in 1948 by the emergence of the Brussels Treaty Organization. The Brussels Treaty was signed by the UK, France, Belgium, the Netherlands and Luxembourg, and was designed to establish a system of mutual assistance in time of attack in Europe. Clearly the Western European states had the USSR and its satellites in mind. This organization in turn took on an Atlantic shape in 1949 when, in order to provide a military defence organization, the North Atlantic Treaty Organization (NATO) was created by the five states just mentioned, together with the US, Canada, Denmark, Norway, Portugal, Iceland and, significantly, Italy, which had been an Axis power.[1]

Division in Western Europe – the beginning

The creation of the Organization for European Economic Cooperation (OEEC) in 1948 and the Council of Europe in 1949 marked the beginning of a division between the UK and some of the countries later to become members of EFTA, and the Six[2] who subsequently founded the EEC.

The division was founded in large measure on the fact that the UK was less committed to Europe as the main area of policy than the six Continental powers. During the second half of the 1950s the UK was still a world power. She had after all been on the victorious side and had been a major participant in some of the fateful geo-political decision-making meetings such as Yalta. Moreover, she still had the Empire to dispose of. British foreign policy was therefore bound to be based on wide horizons. Relations with Europe had to compete with Commonwealth (and Empire) ties and with the 'special relationship'

1. Greece and Turkey joined in 1952 and West Germany in 1955.
2. The Six were, of course, France, West Germany, Italy, the Netherlands, Belgium and Luxembourg. In discussing divisions between Western and Eastern Europe, and within Western Europe, it should be remembered that the Six were also members of the European Coal and Steel Community (ECSC) and members of the European Atomic Energy Community (Euratom).

with the US. In addition, the idea of a politically united Europe (in some eyes the goal was a United States of Europe) was strongly held on the Continent – particularly in France and Benelux [1] – but, despite the encouraging noises made by Winston Churchill both during the 1939–45 war and after, it was not a concept which excited British hearts.

The difference between British and Continental thinking about the political nature of European institutions was revealed in the discussions and negotiations leading up to the establishment of the OEEC and the Council of Europe.

The war had left Europe devastated. The year 1947 was particularly bleak. Bad harvests in the previous summer led to rising food prices, whilst the severe winter of 1946–7 led to a fuel crisis. The Continental countries were producing relatively little, and what was produced tended to be retained rather than exported, whilst import needs were booming. Foreign exchange reserves were therefore running out and it was at this point that the US entered upon the scene and presented the Marshall Plan. General George Marshall proposed that the US make aid available to help the European economy to find its feet and that European governments get together to decide how much assistance was needed. The US did not feel it fitting that it should unilaterally decide on the programmes necessary to achieve this end. Although it seemed possible that this aid programme could be elaborated within the ECE framework, the USSR felt otherwise. Russian reluctance was no doubt based on the fear that if her satellites participated, this would open the door to Western influence.

A conference was therefore convened, and a Committee for European Economic Cooperation (CEEC) was established. The attitude of the US was that the CEEC should not just provide the US with a list of needs. The latter had in mind that the aid it was to give should be linked with progress towards European unification. This is a particularly important point since it indicates that from the very beginning the 'European movement' has enjoyed the encouragement and support of the US.

The CEEC led in turn to the creation of an aid agency – the OEEC. Here the conflict between Britain and other Western European countries, particularly France, came to a head over the issue of supra-nationalism. France in particular – and she was supported by the US – wanted to

1. Belgium, the Netherlands and Luxembourg agreed to form a customs union in 1944; it came into effect in 1948 and is called Benelux.

inject a supra-national element into the new organization.[1] We should perhaps at this point pause to define what is meant by supra-nationalism. It can refer to a situation in which international administrative institutions exercise power over, for example, the economies of the nation states. Thus the High Authority of the European Coal and Steel Community (ECSC)[2] was endowed with powers over the economies of the Six and these powers were exercised independently of the Council of Ministers. Alternatively, it can refer to a situation in which ministerial bodies, when taking decisions (to be implemented by international administrations), work on a majority voting system rather than by insisting on unanimity.

The French view was not shared by the British. The latter favoured a body which was under the control of a ministerial council in which decisions should be taken on a unanimity basis. The French on the other hand favoured an arrangement in which an international secretariat would be presided over by a Secretary General who would be empowered to take policy initiatives on major issues. Significantly, the organization which emerged was substantially in line with the UK's wish for a unanimity rule. This was undoubtedly a reflection of the UK's relatively powerful position in Europe at the time. In the light of subsequent events it is also interesting to note that the US encouraged the European countries to consider the creation of a customs union. Although this was of considerable interest to some Continental countries, it did not attract the UK. In the upshot the OEEC Convention merely recorded the intention to continue the study of this proposal. For a variety of reasons, one of which was the opposition of the UK, the matter was not pursued further.

The creation of the Council of Europe also threw into high relief fundamental differences in approach between the countries who later formed the Common Market on the one hand and the British and Scandinavians on the other. The creation of the Council was preceded by the Congress of Europe at The Hague in May 1948. The latter was a grand rally of 'Europeans' which was attended by leading European statesmen including Winston Churchill. The Congress adopted a resolution which called for the giving up of some national sovereignty prior to the accomplishment of economic and political union in Europe. Subsequently a proposal was put forward, with the support of the Belgian and French Governments, calling for the creation of a European Parliamentary Assembly in which resolutions would be passed by majority

1. It is, of course, ironic that whereas France was then in the vanguard of the supra-national movement she subsequently became a dedicated opponent.
2. Created under the Paris Treaty of 1951.

vote. This was, of course, contrary to the unanimity rule which was then characteristic of international organizations. A Committee of Ministers was to prepare and implement these resolutions. Needless to say, the UK was opposed to this form of supra-nationalism and in the end the British view largely prevailed. The Committee of Ministers, which is the executive organ of the Council of Europe, alone has power of decision and generally decisions are taken on the unanimity principle. The Consultative Assembly which came into existence is a forum – its critics would call it a debating society – and not a European legislature. In short, the British and Scandinavian functionalists, who believed that European unity, in so far as it was to be achieved, was to be attained by inter-governmental cooperation, triumphed over the federalists who sought unity by the more radical method of creating European institutions to which national governments would surrender some of their sovereignty. The final disillusionment of the federalists with the Council of Europe as an instrument of federal unity in Europe was almost certainly marked by the resignation of Paul-Henri Spaak from the Presidency of the Consultative Assembly in 1951.

The Six set forth – success and failure

The next step in the economic and political unification of Europe was taken without the British and Scandinavians. It took the form of the creation in 1951 of the ECSC by the Six, and this creation marks a parting of the ways in postwar Europe – a parting which by 1959 was to lead to the creation of two trading blocs.

The immediate precipitating factor was the revival of the West German economy. The passage of time, the efforts of the German people and the aid made available by the US all contributed to the recovery of the German economy. Indeed the 'Economic Miracle' was about to unfold. It was recognized that the German economy would have to be allowed to regain its position in the world, and that Allied control of coal and steel under the International Ruhr Authority could not last indefinitely. The fundamental question was how the German economy in the sectors of iron, steel and coal (the basic materials of a war effort) could be allowed to re-attain its former powerful position without endangering the future peace of Europe. The answer was a French plan, elaborated by Jean Monnet and put forward by Robert Schuman in May 1950. The Schuman Plan was essentially political in character. It sought to end the historic rivalry of France and Germany and to do this by making a war between France and West Germany not only 'unthinkable but materially impossible'. This was to be done in a way which ultimately would have the result of bringing about that 'European federation which is indispensable to peace'. The answer was not to nationalize nor indeed to internationalize the ownership of the means of production in coal, iron and steel, but to create, by the removal of customs duties, quotas and so forth, a common market in these products. Every participant in the common market would have equal access to the products of these industries wherever they might be located, and, to reinforce this, discrimination on grounds of nationality was to be forbidden.

The plan had a number of attractive features. It provided an excellent basis for solving the Saar problem. The handing back of the Saar to West Germany was more likely to be palatable to the French if West Germany was firmly locked in such a coal and steel community. It was also extremely attractive to the Germans since membership of the Community was a passport to international respectability – it was the best way of speeding up the ending of occupation and of avoiding the imposition of dampers on German economic expansion. It was also attractive to the federalists who had found the OEEC as inadequate to their aspirations as the Council of Europe. The OEEC unanimity rule, and the fact that no powers could be delegated to an independent commission or commissariat, were extremely frustrating. Not only that, but the prospects for the OEEC were not good, since by 1952 the four-year period of the Marshall Plan would be over, and the UK attitude was that thereafter its budget should be cut and some of its functions passed over to NATO. As it emerged, however, the Community was much more to the federalists' taste since, as already indicated, the High Authority was endowed with substantial direct powers which could be exerted without the prior approval of the Council of Ministers.

The Schuman Plan met with a favourable response from West Germany, France, Italy, the Netherlands, Belgium and Luxembourg. The UK was invited to join but refused. The Prime Minister, Clement Attlee, told the House of Commons:

We on this side are not prepared to accept the principle that the most vital economic forces of this country should be handed over to an authority that is utterly undemocratic and is responsible to nobody. (Quoted in Palmer *et al.*, 1968, p. 258)

However, the Six were undeterred, and in April 1951 the Treaty of Paris was signed. The ECSC was brought into existence and the Community embarked on an experiment in limited economic integration.

The next episode in the development of European unity was also connected with West Germany. When the Korean War broke out in

1950 the response of the US was to suggest that West Germany be re-armed. However, this proposal was opposed by France, which was equally opposed to West Germany becoming a member of NATO. But the French approach to this problem was not a negative one. Instead, the French Prime Minister – René Pléven – put forward a plan. This envisaged that there would be no German army as such but there would be a European army to which each participating state, including West Germany, could contribute.

The UK was not opposed to the idea but did not itself wish to be involved. The Six were positively enthusiastic and discussion began in 1951 with a view to creating a European Defence Community (EDC). It was envisaged that there would be a Joint Defence Commission and a Council of Ministers. In addition, there was to be a Parliamentary Assembly and a Court of Justice parallel to those created in connection with the ECSC. The Six made rapid progress in the negotiations and the EDC Treaty was signed in May 1952.

Having gone so far, there seemed to be a number of good reasons for proceeding yet further. The pooling of defensive and offensive capa-bilities inevitably reduced the possibility of independent foreign policies. It was therefore logical to follow integration in the field of defence with measures which would serve to achieve political integration as well. Other forces were also at work. One was the desirability of establishing a system whereby effective democratic control could be exercised over the proposed European army. The other was the Dutch desire that progress in the military field should be paralleled by more integration in the economic sphere. The foreign ministers of the Six therefore asked the ECSC Assembly, in conjunction with coopted members from the Consultative Assembly of the Council of Europe, to study the possi-bilities of creating a European Political Authority. In 1953 a draft of a European Political Community (EPC) was produced. It proposed that, after a transition period, the institutions of the ECSC and the proposed EDC be subsumed within a new framework. There would then be one European Executive responsible to a European Parliament (the later would consist of a People's Chamber elected by direct universal suffrage, and a Senate elected by National Parliaments). In addition, there would be one Council of Ministers and one European Court to replace the parallel bodies created under the ECSC and EDC Treaties.

This was undoubtedly a high-water mark in the history of the 'Euro-pean movement'. The Six had already successfully experimented in limited economic integration in the fields of coal and steel. They had now signed a treaty to integrate defence and were about to go further and create a Community for the purpose of securing political unity. Not only that; the draft treaty proposed to push economic integration still further since it called for the establishment of a general common market based on the free movement of goods and factors of production.

However, on this occasion the success which had attended the Six in the case of coal and steel was not repeated. Five national Parliaments approved the EDC Treaty, but successive French Governments felt unable to guarantee success in asking the French Assembly to ratify. Finally, the Mendès-France Government attempted to water down the Treaty but failed to persuade the Five. The Treaty as it stood was therefore submitted to the French Assembly. The latter refused to consider it and in so doing killed the EPC also.

An amalgam of motives lay behind the refusal of the French Assembly to consider the Treaty. One was opposition to the supra-national element which it contained. Another was the refusal by the French Left to countenance the re-armament of West Germany and the refusal of the French Right to have the French army placed under foreign control. British aloofness was also a contributory factor. One of the arguments employed by those who were against the Treaty was that France could not take part in the formation of a European army with West Germany if Britain was not a member.

It is perhaps worth noting that the failure of the EDC was followed by a British initiative also aimed at dealing with the problem of re-arming West Germany in a way acceptable to the French. A series of agreements was reached in 1954 between the US, UK, Canada and the Six. Under these agreements, the Brussels Treaty Organization was modified and extended. West Germany and Italy were brought in and a new inter-governmental organization – Western European Union (WEU) – was formed. The agreements also related to the termination of the occupation of West Germany and the admission of the latter into NATO. As a counterbalance to the West German army, the UK agreed to maintain specified forces on the Continent. As has been pointed out, the main purpose of the agreement

was to provide a European framework in which Germany could be re-armed and become a member of NATO, while providing also for British military participation to relieve French fears that there would be no check or balance to possible German predominance. (Palmer *et al.*, p. 32)

It should also be noted that the response of Eastern Europe to those agreements was a further hardening of the East–West division in the shape of the formation of the Warsaw Pact.

The *relance*

1954 had been a bad year for European unity. The supra-nationalist cause had suffered a reverse and the creation of WEU – an organization cast more in the traditional inter-government mould – had thereafter held the centre of the stage. However, such then was the strength of the 'European movement' that by 1955 new ideas were again being put forward. The relaunching initiative came from the Benelux states. They produced a memorandum calling for the establishment of a general common market and for specific action in the fields of energy and transport. The basic idea behind the Benelux approach was that political unity was likely to prove difficult to achieve. It was the ultimate objective but it was one which could only be realized in the longer run. In the short and medium term the objective should be overall economic integration. Experience gained in working closely together would then pave the way for the achievement of the political goal. The memorandum called for the creation of institutions which would enable a European Economic Community to be established. These ideas were considered at the meeting of the foreign ministers of the Six at Messina in June 1955. They met with a favourable response. The six governments resolved that work should begin with a view to establishing a general common market and an atomic energy pool. Moreover, a committee should be formed which would not merely study the problems involved but should also prepare the texts of the treaties necessary in order to carry out the agreed objectives. An inter-governmental committee, presided over by Paul-Henri Spaak, was therefore created. The Messina resolution recorded that since the UK was a member of WEU and was associated with the ECSC,[1] it should be invited to participate in the work of the committee. The position of other OEEC countries was not so clear – the question of whether they should be allowed to participate was in fact left for later decision by the foreign ministers.

The Spaak committee held its first meeting in July 1955. British representatives were present and subsequently played an active part in the deliberations. However, as the committee's probing progressed, differences between the Six and the UK became evident. The latter was in favour of a free trade area arrangement, whilst the Six were agreed upon the formation of a customs union – the Messina resolution had explicitly called for this kind of arrangement. Then again the UK felt that little extra machinery was needed to put the new arrangement into effect. The OEEC, perhaps somewhat strengthened, would suffice. This view was

1. The UK signed an 'Agreement of Association' with the ECSC in 1954.

bound to antagonize the federalists who laid stress on the creation of supra-national institutions which would help to achieve more than mere economic integration. These differences culminated in the withdrawal of the UK representatives from the discussions in November 1955. Meanwhile, the Spaak committee forged ahead, although not without internal differences. The French, for example, were anxious about the transition period allowed for tariff disarmament, about escape clauses, about harmonization of social charges and they desired a high tariff round the union whilst the Benelux states were in favour of a low one. In April 1956 the committee reported and its conclusions were considered by the foreign ministers of the Six at Venice in May of that year. Attitudes among the six governments were not uniform. The French liked the idea of an atomic energy community, but were cooler on the idea of a general common market. The other governments held reverse views. However, despite all this, the governments agreed that the drafting of two Treaties, one to create the general common market and one to create an atomic energy community, should begin. Intensive negotiations followed and the two Treaties were subsequently signed in Rome on 25 March 1957. These were duly ratified by the national parliaments. The EEC (and Euratom) came into being on 1 January 1958.

The development of the EEC

1958–69

In practice by far the most important of these two Treaties was that which called for the creation of the EEC. This committed the Six to a far-reaching exercise in economic integration which was to be accomplished within a transition period of twelve years. Economic integration can take various forms and these can be ranged in a spectrum in which the degree of involvement of the participating economies, one with another, becomes greater and greater. The *free trade area* is the least onerous in terms of involvement. It consists of an arrangement between states in which they agree to remove all customs duties and quotas on trade passing between them. Each party is free, however, to determine unilaterally the level of customs duties on imports coming from outside the area. The next stage is the *customs union*. Here tariffs and quotas on trade between the members are also removed but in addition the members agree to apply a common level of duty on goods entering the union from without. The latter is called the common customs, or common external, tariff. Next comes the *common market* and this technical term implies that to the free movement of *goods* within the customs union is added the free movement of the *factors of production* – labour, capital and enterprise. Finally there is the *economic union*. This is a common market in which there is also a complete unification of monetary and fiscal policy. The latter would be controlled by a central authority and in effect the member states would become regions within the union.

The Rome Treaty quite clearly provided for the creation of a common market. This is apparent from the contents of Article 3 which lays down the key objectives of the EEC. Article 3(a) calls for the elimination of internal trade barriers, Article 3(b) provides for the creation of the common external tariff whilst Article 3(c) requires the member states to abolish obstacles to the free movement of factors. In order to facilitate this free movement of goods, services and factors of production, Article 3(h) provides for any necessary harmonization of member state laws and Article 3(f) supplies yet further underpinning by calling for the institution of a system which will ensure that competition in the common market is not distorted. The latter Article is of great significance because it clearly indicates that the integration of national markets is to be accomplished not by planning but through the agency of free and competitive trade interpenetration. The Treaty, however, went beyond a commitment merely to create a common market. Common policies were to be established in agriculture and transport – this was provided for under Articles 3(d) and 3(e) respectively. The Treaty also envisaged the establishment of institutions designed to improve the standard of living of workers and the development of the less developed regions of the Community. Hence the European Social Fund (ESF) and the European Investment Bank (EIB), to which Articles 3(i) and 3(j) respectively refer. The Community was also required to develop a common commercial policy *vis-à-vis* the rest of the world (Article 3(b)), and in particular to make special trade and development arrangements for the colonial and ex-colonial dependencies of the member states (Article 3(k)). Without those special arrangements the dependencies would have suffered from the automatic discrimination inherent in the common external tariff. The Treaty also recognized that the greater the degree of economic integration the greater would be the impact of national macro-economic policies on the other member states. This would be particularly the case when a member state took action to rectify a balance of payments deficit. Article 3(g) addresses this problem but does so in terms of cooperation and coordination rather than the unification and centralization which would be required in an economic union.

Between 1958 and 1969 (when the transition period came to an end) the Six proceeded to construct the kind of economic community envisaged in the Rome Treaty. We shall not attempt to describe all the various measures – they are discussed in detail in the subsequent chapters. Suffice it to say that the basic ingredients of the customs union – internal tariff and quota disarmament and the erection of the common external tariff – were established ahead of schedule. Initial steps were taken and measures proposed to deal with the many non-tariff barriers to the free movement of goods and services. Steps were also taken and measures proposed in respect of the free movement of factors of production so that by 1969 a recognizably common market could be said to exist. In the sphere of common policies variable progress was evident. Thanks in particular to French insistence and indeed threats, the Common Agricultural Policy (CAP) was virtually fully operational by 1969 – the common transport policy was, however, slow to evolve. The ESF and the EIB were duly established and were fully operational at an early stage. Steps were taken on the road to the creation of a common commercial policy, and the Six devised appropriate trade and aid arrangements in respect of their colonial and increasingly ex-colonial dependencies. A rudimentary system of macro-economic coordination was also devised. Although during this period progress was evident and optimism about the success of the European venture was very much in the ascendant, there were disappointments. Perhaps the greatest was the French refusal to accept the supra-national element in the Rome Treaty decision-making system. More will be said about that later and in Chapter 2.

1969 to the present

When in 1969 the transition period came to an end it would have been possible for the Six to have called a halt. Having said that, it is important to emphasize that a total cessation of activity at the Community level would not have been possible or appropriate. Firstly, having established policies in areas such as agriculture and competition, it would have been necessary to have continued to operate them. Thus decisions about agricultural prices have to be taken season by season and markets have to be continuously manipulated in order that those prices are obtained by farmers. Then again, the activities of businessmen and governments have to be continuously monitored in order that factors which would otherwise prevent, restrict or distort competitive trade are rooted out. Secondly, although substantial progress had been made in achieving the objectives listed in Article 3, when the transition period drew to a close it had to be admitted that substantial policy gaps still remained to be filled before it could be said that a truly common market existed.

Nevertheless it would have been possible for the member states to conclude that, subject to the need to operate existing policies and to fill obvious policy gaps, no further economic integration or institutional development should be attempted. In fact the Community decided quite the contrary.

Firstly, new areas of economic policy were opened up and old ones substantially recast. In 1969 the Heads of State and of Government of the Six held a summit meeting at The Hague. On that occasion they decided that the EEC should progressively transform itself into an Economic and Monetary Union (EMU). Although important measures were subsequently introduced in order to achieve that end, the enterprise ultimately failed. Nevertheless the idea did not go away, and in the late seventies a more modest scheme in the shape of the European Monetary System (EMS) was successfully introduced. The EMU proposal was only one of a succession of new policy initiatives during the period 1969 to 1972. Indeed this period can be described as a second *relance*. In 1970 the Six achieved a common position on the development of a fisheries policy although total agreement was not to be achieved until 1983. At the Paris Summit of 1972 agreement was reached on the development of new policies in relation to both industry and science and research. The summit also envisaged a more active role for the Community in the sphere of regional policy. A European Regional Development Fund (ERDF) was to be established to channel Community resources into the development of backwards regions. The summit also called for a new initiative in the field of social policy. Later in the seventies the relationship between the Community and its ex-colonial dependencies was significantly reshaped in the form of the Lomé Conventions.

Secondly, there was a series of institutional developments. We have already noted the role of summit meetings. These were not new, but in the period from 1969 they became much more obviously the vehicle for the identification of new areas of Community activity, and the meetings of the Heads of State and of Government were later formalized and given the title of the European Council. It is evident from what has gone before that the Community needs financial resources not only to pay for the day-to-day running of the Community but also to feed the various funds. We have already referred to the ESF and the ERDF and later, in Chapter 8, we shall be discussing the most important one of all, the European Agricultural Guidance and Guarantee Fund (EAGGF). In 1970 the Community took an important step forward by agreeing to introduce a system which would provide the Community, and specifically the Community budget, with its own source of income. These are referred to as own resources. Another step of great importance was the decision that the European Parliament should be elected by the people and not by the national parliaments. In addition the Community decided to grant the Parliament significant powers over the Community budget - this was to prove to be a very significant development! Finally, but by no means least, was the development of the political cooperation mechanism. Although this book is concerned with matters economic it is important not to forget that ardent Europeans had always hoped that the habit of cooperation in the economic sphere would spill over into the political arena – that is to say into foreign policy matters. That has indeed happened. The political cooperation mechanism as we know it today can be said to date from the Hague Summit of 1969 and was formally inaugurated in 1970. More will be said about political cooperation in Chapter 2.

Whilst there was abundant evidence of institutional change during the post-1969 period, it has to be acknowledged that by then the relationship between member states within the Community had undergone a significant change. In signing and ratifying the Rome Treaty the member states had opted for a system of decision-making which centred on the Community's own Council of Ministers which could take decisions on the basis of a supra-national majority voting system. That, as we noted earlier, was knocked on the head by the French at a fairly early stage and instead the Six regressed to a system in which any member state could insist that nothing should happen unless it agreed that it should happen. In addition, and most notably after 1969, the centre of gravity in decision-making within the Community began to shift in favour of the European Council. The latter was a body which was not envisaged in the Rome Treaty and whose method of operation was cast in the traditional inter-governmental mould. The development of what we may term inter-governmentalism might have been expected to slow down the pace of development within the Community. In other words, the unanimity principle would always force the Community to adopt the lowest common denominator and that might mean little or even zero change. But certainly that was not the case in the early seventies. As we have seen, a host of new initiatives was launched and in the main those initiatives were designed to further the process of integration. Inter-governmentalism still held sway in the eighties but the performance of the inter-governmental Community of the eighties was markedly less dynamic than that of the early seventies. There was a notable absence of new policy initiatives at a time when big problems called for imaginative and collective solutions. A good deal of activity within the Community centred on wrangles over such matters as the reform of the CAP, the reform of the Community budget and, as we shall see below, over the vexed question of the UK[1] contribution to the budget.

There are two other interesting and related institutional developments which we must note. The ebullient Paris Summit of 1972 also envisaged the establishment by the end of the decade of a European Union. The exact nature of the arrangement was not indicated. In due course Leo Tindemans, then Prime Minister of Belgium, was charged with the task of producing a report on this development, and in 1975 he duly presented his ideas (EC Commission, 1976a). We shall not attempt to summarize that report. One topic was, however, of considerable interest. The report laid emphasis on the need to relaunch EMU which by that time had run into the ground. Tindemans also entertained the interesting possibility of a two-tier Community. Those who had the will and ability to forge ahead with such a union should do so – the others could lag behind but would not be released from the need to achieve the ultimate goal. Interpreted pessimistically, the fact that such an idea was entertained suggested that cohesion was becoming more difficult to achieve. The idea could, however, also be viewed optimistically, since it meant that even in the absence of majority voting some could progress even if all did not wish to do so. In fact, the EMS was launched on such a basis since the UK refused to participate in the exchange rate aspect of the scheme.

Altogether more important was the decision of the first directly elected European Parliament to take up the European Union issue again and indeed to produce a *draft* treaty establishing the European Union (EUT). This was adopted by the European Parliament in 1984. More or less simultaneously the European Council had been exploring similar territory. In 1981 the German and Italian Governments had submitted to the member states a draft European Act designed to further European integration. This was remitted to the foreign ministers and the results of their labours were presented at the Stuttgart Summit in 1983. The Heads of State and of Government were aware that the Community had been increasingly paralysed by internal disputes and that a new initiative was needed which might help to relaunch the Community. Whilst those disputes were not yet resolved, a better atmosphere was desirable, and it was against this background that they received the report of the foreign ministers and adopted what was called the Solemn Declaration of Euro-

1. The UK had joined in 1973 – see below.

pean Union. They returned to the subject at the Fontainebleau Summit in 1984 and set up two committees. The Adonnino Committee was to examine ways of making the European Community more of a reality to its citizens (a People's Europe), while the Dooge Committee, the more important in practice, was to investigate institutional reform and related matters. Dooge reported at the Brussels Summit in 1985 and also recommended in favour of an inter-governmental conference (IGC) to negotiate a European Union treaty. This was agreed at the Milan Summit later in the year.

Before we proceed any further, it is important to recognize that the European Parliament and the European Council initiatives were not by any means identical. The Parliament's EUT, if agreed, would have radically altered the Community's decision-making structure. This the Parliament felt was essential, since, as we noted above, the Community was failing to make essential decisions particularly in the light of the need to respond imaginatively to problems such as the recession and competition from countries such as the US and Japan. This failure was at least in part due to the kind of institutional blockages to which we referred earlier.[1] The EUT would have (a) brought both economic and foreign policy matters within the ambit of the Union decision-making machinery, (b) strengthened the position of the Commission, (c) progressively phased out national vetoes, and (d) given the European Parliament an enhanced legislative (as opposed to a largely consultative) role similar to that which exists in national political systems. By contrast, the Solemn Declaration was to a large extent a set of laudable aspirations concerning the need for closer unity which even the most cautious member state could adopt without actually committing itself to any immediate change. This difference was also reflected in the Dooge report which opted for streamlining the institutional system rather than radical change. It also called for a number of policy changes. In fairness these were important – particularly the need to create a true internal market.

The IGC was duly convened, and the Commission and Parliament were also represented. The report of the IGC was submitted to the Luxembourg Summit in December 1985, which adopted several of its proposals. These were embodied in what came to be known as the Single European Act (SEA), which was signed by all member states in February 1986. In the case of Denmark[2] the SEA was subsequently approved by a referendum.

1. These blockages had been identified by the 'Three Wise Men' – a committee set up by the European Council in 1978.
2. Denmark had joined the Community in 1973 – see below.

Whilst the SEA disappointed the Parliament, and it certainly did not achieve a European Union, it did constitute a highly significant act of consolidation, contained commitments to carry integration forward and provided for improvements in the way the Community was to be run. The full import of these observations will become clearer in later chapters.

We now come to the third important development of the post-transition period. The creation of the common market in the period up to 1969 was the work of the Six alone. But at quite an early stage other states began to knock on the door and ask for admission. One of the significant achievements of the post-1969 period was that the Community was able to take new members into its midst and still survive. The first enlargement occurred in 1973 when the UK, Ireland and Denmark joined the Community. This was followed in 1981 by the adherence of Greece, and in 1986 by the accession of Spain and Portugal. The approach to the first enlargement was a long, drawn-out affair, and in order to understand fully how it came about we have to go back in time to 1955 when the Six were engaged in the discussions which led to the formation of the EEC and Euratom.

The Enlargement issue

The UK and the free trade area proposal

As we saw earlier (see pp. 10–11), at the end of 1955 Britain's attitude towards the Six cooled to such an extent that she withdrew from the Spaak committee. However, as the Six pressed ahead, the UK began to realize that it had severely underestimated the determination which lay behind the *relance*. As a result, a reappraisal of policy took place. In July 1956 the OEEC, under British stimulus, embarked on a study of the proposal that the OEEC states should create a free trade area which would embrace the customs union of the Six. The British hoped that the negotiations for the free trade area, and those relating to the common market, could take place simultaneously, but the Six refused. The OEEC report was completed in December 1956 and published in January 1957. Its conclusions were that a free trade area with the common market as an element was feasible. The UK took this as a signal to take the initiative and proposed that discussions should begin in earnest with a view to creating a European Industrial Free Trade Area. Detailed negotiations on the terms of a Treaty began in March 1957 and continued from October 1957 in an inter-government committee under the chairmanship of Reginald Maudling. These negotiations dragged on until the end of 1958 when they finally broke down.

The negotiations were extremely complex, and the reasons for their failure are equally complicated. However, basically the problems were as follows. On the political side, the 'Europeans' were suspicious of the UK's intentions. They suspected that the UK, after it had realized that it had underestimated the impetus behind the *relance*, had decided to take the offensive by proposing a free trade area as a means of wrecking the common market. Furthermore, it was recognized that whilst the path to the achievement of a common market (and what lay beyond) was bound to be hard, a free trade area would confer somewhat similar benefits and yet would involve a relatively less onerous régime. Because of this, some members of the Six might lose heart and decide to follow the easier course.

From the economic standpoint, the major difficulty was the UK's insistence on a free trade arrangement for industrial goods. Under such a system she would remain autonomous in respect of tariffs on goods emanating from outside the free trade area. This would enable her to go on enjoying her tariff preferences on exports of industrial goods to Commonwealth markets. Agriculture would also be excluded – this was certainly the basis of the earliest British proposals. This left the UK open to the criticism that she wanted the advantage of free access to West European industrial markets without giving a reciprocal concession to Continental food producers. The Commonwealth Preference system also meant that the UK would be guaranteed a continuing supply of food at low world prices. If, on the other hand, agriculture was brought within the free trade area framework, this low-priced supply of food could be in jeopardy. Indeed, if the agricultural protection systems of the Six were adopted, cheap Commonwealth food would be excluded. The UK would have to buy food at price levels approximating to those paid to farmers in the Six, and the traditional British deficiency payments system would have to be abandoned. It did not escape the attention of the Six that cheap food could have an effect on industrial wages such as to confer an artificial advantage on British industries when competing in the industrial markets of the free trade area.

Another source of difficulty was the degree to which harmonization of such things as social security charges was necessary. The French, particularly, tended to play this up, much as they did in the common market negotiations.

Undoubtedly one of the greatest bones of contention was the problem of the origin of imports and the possibility of deflections of trade. In a customs union, since there is a common tariff level on the imports, of, for example, raw materials coming from outside, competitive strength tends to depend on the ability of member states to transform such inputs into industrial (and agricultural) outputs. In a free trade area, however, member states are free to decide the tariffs on such imports. These tariffs can therefore differ from state to state, and imports of raw materials are therefore likely to be deflected through the low tariff countries. Methods of dealing with this problem gave rise to much technical discussion, but a unanimously acceptable solution was never achieved.

The failure of the negotiations was also in considerable degree due to diplomatic postures, particularly those of the British and the French. The latter left an impression of a certain deviousness. It was difficult to know whether, when they took a stand on a point of principle, it was because they really believed what they said, or whether it was because they found it useful as a means of opposing progress along a particular path. For its part, the UK exhibited some diplomatic weakness. The British undoubtedly underestimated the enthusiasm of the Six for their kind of arrangement. There was a failure to appreciate what the 'Europeans' hoped to achieve in the political sphere. Also there was a tendency to frame our proposals in too stark and provocative a fashion, as, for example, when the UK declared that agriculture should be totally excluded from the free trade arrangement.

The inter-governmental discussion at least served to create an identity of interest between the 'Other Six' – the UK, Norway, Sweden, Denmark, Austria and Switzerland. It was therefore decided early in 1959 that they should press ahead with a free trade area, and in this they were encouraged by their industrial federations. Portugal joined the discussions in February 1959 and on 4 January 1960 the Stockholm Convention establishing EFTA was signed.[1] Western Europe was now divided into two trade blocs.

The EFTA

The EFTA arrangement was one which admirably suited British interests. The institutional machinery was minimal. There was nothing to match the majority voting in the EEC Council of Ministers or the ECSC High Authority's[2] powers of independent action. There were absolutely no signs that EFTA was a stepping-stone to political unity –

1. Finland signed an association agreement with the EFTA in 1961.
2. In 1967 the Commissions of the EEC and Euratom and the High Authority were merged into one Commission located in Brussels – see Chapter 2.

basically it was a commercial arrangement. The emphasis was on free trade in industrial goods; in a limited number of cases agricultural goods were treated as industrial goods and therefore tariff reductions were applied to them. In the main, agriculture was left out of the arrangement, each member being free to decide its own method and degree of support. There was absolutely no question of the agricultural systems of the member states being organized within the framework of a common agricultural policy. Members were free to determine the level of protection applied to goods coming from outside. This enabled the UK to maintain Commonwealth Preference not only on industrial but also on agricultural commodities. The latter implied the continuance of a supply of cheap food and the deficiency payments system of agricultural support.

Two features of the EFTA arrangement deserve special mention. One is that because of differences in national tariffs on goods coming from without, it was necessary to elaborate origin rules and a customs procedure so as to determine whether goods could be accorded the full benefit of the EFTA tariff reductions. The other was that the EFTA Convention made few demands on members in the field of harmonization of taxation, social security charges and the like.

UK reappraisal and entry bids

The ink of the Stockholm Convention had not long been dry before the UK began a major reappraisal of policy. Until quite late in the 1950s various British Ministers went on record as saying that the UK could never become a full member of the Community. A number of factors were adduced in support of this view. The first was the effect upon the Commonwealth. Commonwealth Preference would have to give way to the Community common tariff on imports (the common external tariff). This would harm Commonwealth members at a time when the idea of a multi-lingual, multi-racial Commonwealth was still on the lips of most politicians and was still regarded as an important vehicle of British influence. Also, the elimination of Commonwealth countries' preferences in the British market was almost certainly likely to lead to a loss of British preferences in Commonwealth markets. There were also some specific problems. One was that New Zealand relied heavily on the UK as an outlet for her butter production. The other was the British import of sugar from low-income Commonwealth countries under the Commonwealth Sugar Agreement. Secondly, there was the British agricultural system. It was supported in a radically different way from that adopted on the Continent. The level of farm incomes and the participation of farmers in price determination were at stake. Also the adoption of a Community system was bound to raise prices and the food import bill. Thirdly, the formation of EFTA raised the problem that British membership of the Community would require that adequate arrangements be made for the EFTA partners. Then finally there was the critical point of supra-nationalism. The need to give up sovereignty was not welcomed then and it has remained a subject about which British politicians still tend to be wary.

However, it was apparent by 1960 that the Conservative Government was beginning to change its tune, and in the House of Commons on 31 July 1961 Mr Harold Macmillan,[1] the Prime Minister, formally announced that the UK had decided to apply for full membership. A letter to this effect was sent on 9 August 1961. The Irish Republic despatched its request before the UK – on the day of the House of Commons announcement. Denmark's application was despatched the day after the UK's. Norway, however, waited until 1962 before applying. Subsequently Austria, Sweden and Switzerland made separate applications for association. Portugal also applied, though no clear indication was given of the arrangement sought. The Council of Ministers decided to accept the British application on 26 September 1961 and on 10 October of the same year the UK, through Mr Edward Heath, made a comprehensive statement of its position at a Ministerial Conference in Paris. The negotiations which subsequently followed dragged on until 14 January 1963 when General de Gaulle at a Paris press conference declared that Britain was not ripe for membership and it was left to M. Maurice Couve de Murville, the French Foreign Minister, to deliver a *coup de grâce* on 29 January at Brussels by securing the indefinite adjournment of negotiations.

The issues involved in the negotiations were extremely complex. Basically the origin of the problem was quite simple. Britain did not approach with a view to signing the Rome Treaty as it stood. Rather, because of her commitment to the Commonwealth and EFTA, as well as her different farming system, she sought modifications and accommodations on most fronts.

In the short space available the issues involved can be sketched only in outline. On the agricultural front Mr Heath admitted that the UK would have to move over to the EEC system. One of the main areas of conflict here was the speed of transition. The UK thought in terms of a

1. The late Earl of Stockton.

transition period of up to twelve to fifteen years, but the Six were adamant that the CAP would have to be applied in its entirety by the end of the Treaty transition period (December 1969). On the question of a need for an annual farm price review the UK obtained a tolerably satisfactory solution.

The major problems of the Commonwealth sprang from the protection which the Community was destined to place around itself when the common external tariff and the CAP were fully operational. The UK accepted that the common external tariff was a *fait accompli* but called for a 20 per cent cut. The UK also called for nil duties on twenty-six industrial products. Progress on this issue was slow. By the time of the suspension of negotiations only ten products had been dealt with, some on the basis of nil solutions but others by virtue of the UK withdrawing its request and accepting a form of transitional provision. On the subject of industrial goods produced by Canada, Australia and New Zealand, the UK recognized that the common external tariff would have to be applied and an agreement was reached on its application by stages and full operation by 1970. The Community did, however, declare its willingness in 1966 and 1969 to examine the possibility of developing trade with these countries. In the case of processed foodstuffs, Britain produced a list of eighty products which were regarded as being entitled to nil duty or preferential measures. In practice in the case of half it was decided to apply the common external tariff at the same rate as industrial goods, but in the case of the other half a more gradual alignment was agreed.

One of the most acute Commonwealth problems arose in connection with temperate foodstuffs. Britain proposed that once she was within the Community the latter should provide comparable outlets to those which temperate food producers had enjoyed previously. The Six, however, were adamant that they would offer no permanent or indeed long-term guarantee to Commonwealth producers. They were prepared to negotiate specific and limited agreements but permanent solutions would have to be sought in the framework of world-wide agreements. New Zealand was considered as meriting exceptional treatment as regards butter, but no solution in terms of guarantees was achieved.

In the case of India, Pakistan, Ceylon and Hong Kong the general solution was twofold. Firstly, there was to be a very gradual application of the common external tariff but with special treatment in certain cases. Thus, in the case of tea there was to be a nil duty and in other cases there was to be an indefinite suspension of duties. Secondly, the Community would negotiate comprehensive trade agreements with India and Pakistan in order to guarantee or indeed increase their foreign currency earnings. For cotton goods special agreements would be made to ensure that exports to the enlarged Community were not harmed.

In the case of other less developed countries in Africa and the West Indies, the UK hoped that they would be able to take advantage of the association provisions.[1] Nigeria, Ghana and Tanganyika, however, disliked the political overtones and declined this offer. The Commission countered by offering either participation in a new Yaoundé Convention[2] (an arrangement which acknowledged independence of what were formerly colonial dependencies) or specific trade agreements.

The solution to the EFTA problem lay in the participants becoming either full or associate members. Three took one course and three the other, whilst Portugal's intentions were unclear. At the time when the UK negotiations were suspended the negotiations with Norway and Denmark were advanced. Formal talks on the Irish application had hardly begun. In the case of the three applicants for association the first round of talks to ascertain the problems to be dealt with had taken place between the EEC Commission and a delegation from the country concerned, and on this basis the Commission had reported to the Council. But no formal negotiations had been opened.

As already indicated, negotiations were abruptly terminated by General de Gaulle. Britain was an independent maritime power not yet sufficiently European to be admitted. This was a half-truth. The fact that she had applied indicated a new European emphasis in foreign policy. The fact that she did not merely accept the Treaty but sought to negotiate so many modifications in the interests of the Commonwealth was a reflection of the fact that her imperial past, although no longer a dominating interest, still exercised a significant constraint on policy. There can be no doubt that the arduous negotiations arising out of the need to seek special treatment on products as divergent as kangaroo meat and cricket bats played into the hands of the French. But the real root of French opposition was undoubtedly political. Firstly, Britain would be an American 'trojan horse'. Secondly, in a Community of ten, French influence would be watered down.

Having laid the blame largely at the door of the French, it is fair to ask whether the negotiations could have succeeded. The general impression of the delegations, except the French, was that there was a good chance of reaching a successful conclusion if the negotiations had continued. Professor Hallstein, President of the Commission at the time,

1. See Chapter 11 below.
2. ibid.

was more guarded. Speaking before the European Parliament in 1963 he observed

it is not possible to say of the negotiations at the moment when they were interrupted that they had in practice failed, or to say that it had been proved that they could succeed. (Quoted in Palmer *et al.*, 1968, p. 243)

The change of government in the UK did not, however, change the course of British policy, since the Labour Party itself became convinced of the need for the UK to join the Community. On 10 November 1966 the Prime Minister, Harold Wilson, announced to the House of Commons plans for a high-level approach to the Six with the intention of becoming a full member of the Community. This was followed between January and March 1967 by visits to the capitals of the Six. Having judged the prospects to be satisfactory, the Prime Minister announced to the House of Commons on 2 May that the UK would submit its second application. This was made on 11 May and was followed by applications from Ireland, Denmark and Norway.

The British approach on this occasion was radically different from that of the 1961–3 period. No attempt was going to be made to secure a multitude of accommodations and concessions. The areas for negotiation were reduced to these: the CAP was bound to have a substantial repercussion on the balance of payments and cost of living; the basis of the policy was accepted but an adequate transition period was required; also a more equitable sharing of the financial burdens of the policy would be necessary; a comprehensive annual review of the agricultural industry should be held, broadly similar to that introduced within the Community but with agricultural producers' organizations formally participating in the review procedure. There were some Commonwealth interests which needed safeguarding and in particular New Zealand and the sugar producers. The problem of capital movements would also require attention. The UK stance also differed in that on this occasion it claimed that it would bring with it a dowry in the form of its considerable achievements and potential in the field of science and technology. The latter led to suggestions about a new Community – the European Technological Community. The British bid was also sweetened, although somewhat weakly, by references to Britain's awareness of the possibility of progress towards political unity.

The application for membership was examined by the Council of Ministers on 10 July 1967 and the Council decided to obtain the opinion of the Commission. The Commission presented its conclusions in September. It noted that views differed as to the priorities that were given to solving the Community's own internal problems as opposed to solving the problems inherent in an extension of the Community. It recommended that an attempt be made to deal with both simultaneously and the negotiations should be opened. The Commission did, however, note the urgent need to solve the British balance-of-payments problem and to adjust the role of sterling so that it could be fitted into a Community monetary system. The reference to the problem caused by sterling was an entirely new and indeed ominous feature of the UK–EEC dialogue. As one observer has remarked of the previous negotiations

In those long weeks . . . in Brussels in 1962, everything else was gone into – every detail of Commonwealth trade from carpets to kangaroo tails – but never a word about sterling. (Strange, 1967, p. 5)

In October and November the question of negotiations was discussed by the Council of Ministers without result. In November the Prime Minister re-emphasized the UK's technical dowry, proposing a seven-point plan for European technology. These covered bilateral projects with other European partners, multilateral discussions on improving Europe's technological capability, the establishment of a European Technological Institute as well as offers to cooperate in the field of European business mergers, company law and patents. However, later that month General de Gaulle delivered another of his famous press conferences which effectively closed the door to entry. The General took the view that full membership for Britain would lead to the destruction of the Community. Some form of association would, however, be acceptable. Great play was made of the British balance-of-payments deficit which was said to indicate a permanent state of disequilibrium. The restrictions on the export of capital by the UK were contrasted with free movement within the Six. Then there was the sterling system with its large and vulnerable liabilities. At the Ministerial meeting on 19 December 1967, the Five expressed themselves in favour of commencing negotiations, but France took the view that enlargement would profoundly modify the nature and ways of administering the Community. In addition, the UK economy had to be restored to health before its application could be considered. No vote was taken. The Community once more agreed to disagree and the application remained on the agenda.

Subsequently, various member states put forward proposals to bring the UK closer to the Community and prepare her for membership. The Commission lent a hand by proposing a preferential trade arrangement with the states seeking membership, together with closer consultation and collaboration on scientific and technological matters. No progress was made. However, the events of May 1968 and the resignation of General de Gaulle in 1969 brought the subject of British membership back into the foreground. This was followed by the accession to power of President Pompidou, and at the Hague Summit of December 1969 the Six agreed to open negotiations with the applicant countries 'in the most positive spirit'. The Six were therefore agreeing to take up the British application which had lain on the table since the Labour Government's previous bid. Britain was accompanied by three other applicants – the Irish Republic, Denmark and Norway.

UK negotiations and terms

In June 1970 Anthony Barber was charged with the conduct of the British negotiations, but following the tragic death of Iain Macleod and the translation of Mr Barber to the role of Chancellor of the Exchequer the negotiating role was passed to Geoffrey Rippon. The negotiations were conducted relatively expeditiously as compared with 1961–3. Mr Barber made his opening statement at a meeting between the Six and the UK at Luxembourg on 30 June 1970 and the Six replied. A series of ministerial meetings then took place at roughly six-weekly intervals in the second half of 1970 and the first half of 1971. (There were of course more frequent meetings between the Permanent Representatives of the six states and a British team led by Sir Con O'Neill, and there was continuous study of the problems arising by all the parties involved, including the Commission.) Although considerable progress was made, it became apparent by the beginning of 1971 that some political impetus was needed if certain particularly knotty problems were to be solved, and that in practice it was necessary that Britain and France should come to a clear understanding. The Heath–Pompidou meeting of 20 and 21 May 1971 served this purpose. The discussions were centred on the difficult problems of EEC membership which still remained to be solved, in particular those concerning New Zealand, sugar, the role of sterling and the UK contribution to the Community budget (for an explanation of the latter see below). The available evidence suggests that the two leaders achieved at least a close identity of view, and political commentators noted the relatively rapid pace of the negotiations after the summit. The final ministerial round was completed in Luxembourg on 23 June – the entry talks had been completed successfully. The terms were embodied in a White Paper, *The United Kingdom and the European Communities* (HMSO, 1971), which was presented to Parliament in July

1971. Parliament had a 'take note' debate in July during which the terms were considered. Then in October both Houses debated the issue again with the intention that a final vote for or against entry should be taken. This vote occurred on 28 October. The House of Commons voted 356 to 244 in favour. The House of Lords majority was even greater – 451 to 58. The problem of getting the subsequent enabling legislation through both Houses still remained but was eventually surmounted.

With respect to the actual conduct of the negotiations, the British attitude was again to reduce the number of issues to manageable proportions. Membership of Euratom and the ECSC would not pose major problems and the UK would seek only a short transitional period. The EEC would, however, throw up more difficult problems. These related to agricultural policy, the UK contribution to the Community budget, Commonwealth sugar exports, New Zealand dairy exports, and certain other Commonwealth issues. There was also a new problem – fisheries policy. Undoubtedly, of all these the major obstacles were bound to be encountered in negotiating an acceptable UK contribution to the budget. The length of the transitional period before the barriers to free movement of industrial and agricultural goods were removed was also capable of causing some difficulty, as was the role of sterling.

It is not intended in this account to list in detail all the terms of the final settlement. The reader can find these laid out in the 1971 White Paper. This account will only be concerned with major issues.

One of the early matters to be settled was the length of the transitional period. The UK originally asked for three years for industry and six for agriculture. A solution was finally hammered out. The UK and the Six compromised on a transition period of five years' duration for both agricultural and industrial goods. On the assumption that the UK joined on 1 January 1973 (which she did) industrial tariffs on trade between the Six and Britain would be removed in five stages, consisting of five cuts of 20 per cent, one in each of the five years 1973 to 1977. The UK would also adopt the common external tariff in four movements, one in each of the four years 1974 to 1977. In the case of agriculture the UK would in the first year of membership introduce the Community system of support. Prices for agricultural products would be set which at first would be lower than those in the Community, but they would be gradually increased to Community levels in six steps over the five-year period. From a negotiating point of view as long a transition period as possible was desirable in the case of agriculture, since this would put back the day when the full weight of the Community agricultural policy would be felt. Weight in this sense relates not only to the effect on the price of food but also to the contribution which the UK would have to make to the Community budget.

At this point we must remind ourselves of the role of the Community budget. Its function is to finance not only the administration of the Community but also the various funds concerned with particular aspects of Community policy. In practice the biggest drain on the budget has been the cost of financing the CAP (financing the sale of surpluses at a loss, etc.). The longer the transition period the longer the UK could delay paying a full contribution to the financing of the expensive farm policy.

At the time the UK was negotiating its way into the Community, the Six were on their way to fully implementing a new system for financing the budget. In its final form this would involve the member states paying 90 per cent of the proceeds of the common external tariff (10 per cent being allowed for collection expenses), 90 per cent of the proceeds of levies on agricultural imports (the UK is a big importer of food), and if necessary the proceeds of up to a 1 per cent VAT rate on a common assessment base. All these would constitute the Community's own resources to which we referred earlier.

The UK proposal on the budget was that its initial contribution to it should be 3 per cent, rising to 15 per cent by the end of the transition period. This was a highly provocative proposal since the Commission envisaged two possibilities which both involved a much more onerous régime. One envisaged an initial contribution level of 21·5 per cent and the second involved a progressive rise in contributions from between 10 and 15 per cent in the first year to 20 to 25 per cent in the final year of the transition period. There was then the question of what would happen thereafter – as we have seen the Community had agreed on a final solution to the financing of the budget.

In the event the negotiated settlement involved the UK in paying the following percentage costs of the budget – 1973 8·64, 1974 10·85, 1975 13·34, 1976 16·03, 1977 18·92. From the UK point of view this was certainly better than the Commission had originally proposed, but worse than it had initially hoped for. In 1978 and 1979 the UK would normally have been subject to the Community budgetary system. It was, however, agreed that in 1978 the UK contribution should not increase above the 1977 level by more than two fifths of the difference between the 1977 level and what the level should be under the new system. Likewise in 1979 the increased contribution over the 1978 level would be similarly determined. Then there was the question of what would happen in 1980 and beyond – in other words what would the permanent as opposed to the transitional system be? The answer was that the UK would be subject to the Community budgetary finance system and 90 per cent of levies and customs duties would be paid into the Community budget, together with the proceeds of up to a 1 per cent rate of the value added tax. In other words, the UK accepted the Community system as it stood. The 1971 White Paper pointed out that the size of the commitments so arising was not susceptible to valid estimation nor was the size of any possible benefits. Because of this the White Paper went on to point out that the Community had declared in the course of the negotiations that if unacceptable situations should arise 'the very survival of the Community would demand that the institutions find equitable solutions'.

New Zealand was a particularly difficult problem. Butter and cheese represented about 15 per cent of her exports, and 85 per cent of her dairy export receipts came from sale to the UK. The problem was therefore one of attempting to guarantee New Zealand access to the UK market after membership. The solutions devised were as follows. In the case of butter the guaranteed quantity would be reduced over the first five years by 4 per cent per annum. Thus in the fifth year she would still be able to sell at least 80 per cent of her 1971 entitlement in the UK. She would also enjoy a guaranteed price at a level equal to the average of prices in the UK in the four years 1969 to 1972. In the third year after the UK accession the Community would look again at the position and would decide 'on suitable measures for ensuring beyond 1977 the continuation of special arrangements for New Zealand butter' (1971 White Paper). For cheese, access would be reduced so that in the fifth year she would be able to market 20 per cent of her 1971 level of sales. No guarantee was held out after 1977 in the case of cheese, but substantial sales were expected to continue because New Zealand cheese did not compete directly with Community production. According to the 1971 White Paper, New Zealand described the agreement as highly satisfactory. In the case of lamb no common organization existed within the Six. A common external tariff of 20 per cent was therefore agreed. The White Paper stated that the UK and New Zealand believed that an acceptable level of trade in lamb would continue to flow over such a tariff.

In the case of sugar, Mr Rippon sought what he termed 'bankable assurances'. The UK's contractual obligations under the Commonwealth Sugar Agreement, which required it to buy agreed quantities until the end of 1974, would be fulfilled. Thereafter it was agreed that the arrangements for sugar imports from developing Commonwealth sugar producers would be made within the framework of an association or trading agreement with the enlarged Community. It was further agreed 'that the enlarged Community will have as its firm purpose the safeguarding of the interests of the developing countries concerned whose economies depend to a considerable extent on the export of primary products and in particular of sugar' (1971 White Paper). The countries concerned expressed the view that this solution was satisfactory.

One of the important issues which seems to have concerned France in particular was the role of sterling and indeed the whole question of how in monetary terms the UK could be fitted into the Community. In the weeks before the Heath–Pompidou meeting the French built the subject up into a major negotiating issue. But more or less immediately after the meeting the French did a *volte-face* by agreeing without demur to the British proposals to discuss sterling's role after her entry. However, the UK agreed to stabilize the size of the sterling balances and in the longer term to run them down. But no agreement was reached about just how they would be run down or how long the process would take.

The UK also had to deal with the market-access problems of developing countries in the Commonwealth. The details of the position of various countries will not be discussed here. Basically the solution was that a variety of arrangements would be brought to bear. Independent Commonwealth countries in Africa, the Caribbean, the Indian Ocean and the Pacific could choose between the renewed Yaoundé Convention, some other form of association, or a commercial agreement. All British dependent territories (except Gibraltar and Hong Kong) would be offered association under Part Four of the Rome Treaty. Hong Kong would be included within the scope of the Community's Generalized Preference Scheme (see Chapter 11 below). In the case of India, Pakistan, Ceylon, Malaysia and Singapore the Community was willing to examine with them trade problems which might arise, taking account of the Generalized Preference Scheme which would benefit them considerably. One specific problem which the Community expressed its willingness to discuss was India's sugar exports to the enlarged Community. The continued suspension of the tariff on tea would help India and Ceylon. Malta, as we shall see, concluded a trade agreement. Arrangements would be made for Cyprus and Gibraltar.

On the matter of fisheries policy the UK indicated that the existing policy was not satisfactory. The Community agreed that the arrangements would have to be reconsidered in the light of enlargement.

The successful conclusion of negotiations for UK entry was also accompanied by successful conclusions in respect of the Irish Republic, Denmark[1] and Norway. However, the latter did not ultimately join – a national referendum did not produce the necessary votes for membership. The Irish and Danish negotiations were not as complicated as those relating to the UK. Their terms were similar to those obtained by the British but a number of special accommodations were provided and are detailed in the Community's *Fifth General Report* (EC Commission, 1972b, pp. 49–57). A link with those EFTA states who had not become full members was provided by means of industrial free trade arrangements. Countries benefiting from these agreements were Austria, Finland, Iceland, Portugal, Sweden, Switzerland and Norway. (Austria, with the agreement of EFTA, had been seeking association with the Community for a number of years. Under the State Treaty of 1955 Article 4 precluded any form of economic union with West Germany and the best that Austria could hope for was some form of association.)

UK renegotiation

The entry terms were those obtained by the then Conservative Government. The opposition Labour Party expressed itself willing to enter the EEC if the terms were right but concluded that the settlement actually obtained was unacceptable – in the words of Harold Wilson it involved 'an intolerable and disproportionate burden on every family in the land and, equally, on Britain's balance of payments'. In the subsequent election the Labour Party committed itself to a renegotiation of the terms of entry. The Labour Party was indeed returned to power in February 1974 and very quickly set in hand a process of renegotiation, indicating that if the settlement obtained was acceptable it would put it to the people for approval, either by referendum or general election.[2]

The then Foreign Secretary, Mr James Callaghan, followed this up in April with a statement to the Council of Ministers at Luxembourg, setting out the British Government's position. This was reproduced as a White Paper (HMSO, 1974).[3] The Foreign Secretary made it clear that the UK would negotiate in good faith with a view to obtaining an early and successful result. However if the renegotiation did not succeed the UK would not regard the Treaty obligations as binding on it and would

1. Greenland gained home rule from Denmark in 1979. By a referendum in 1982 it decided to leave the Community. This took effect in 1984.
2. Whether the Government would commend the terms to the people was at that stage not made clear.
3. Mr Callaghan also made an amplifying statement to the Council of Ministers at Luxembourg in June 1974 which was somewhat more conciliatory – largely it seems because the Labour Government had already discovered that some of its fears were groundless.

consult the British people on the advisability of negotiating a withdrawal.

The main points of the Foreign Secretary's April statement were as follows.

(a) EMU by 1980 was dangerously over-ambitious. It should be remembered that under the Rome Treaty there was no commitment to such a union. As we noted earlier the Rome Treaty merely provided for a coordination of national monetary policies. However, at the Hague Summit in 1969 the Heads of State and Heads of Government had decided not only to open the Community to new members but also to launch the Six on the path of EMU – the target date subsequently adopted being 1980. The full details of what was implied by such a union will be discussed in Chapter 7 below. From the UK point of view the main concern was the effect on exchange rates. Under the Bretton Woods system, which governed postwar international monetary arrangements, each country was required to maintain fixed exchange rates, but devaluations, etc., were allowed in certain defined circumstances. Small margins of fluctuation were also allowed around the central parity. EMU involved irrevocably fixing the rates of exchange between member state currencies and progressively eliminating even the small margins of fluctuation. This could be the precursor to a common currency. The British Government saw this as removing from its grasp an important policy weapon and threatening heavy unemployment. For example, if inflation in the UK proceeded at a faster rate than in the rest of the Community, British exports would become uncompetitive and would fall (imports would increase) and unemployment would rise. The appropriate Bretton Woods response would be a devaluation but EMU would preclude it. It might be possible to prevent disparate national rates of inflation but only at the expense of centralized control over items such as the money supply – here the problem was one of diminished sovereignty.

(b) The method of financing the Community budget was unfair – for example, the UK percentage contribution was likely in due course to be significantly greater than the ratio of its GNP to the Community GNP. The ways in which budget funds were spent (i.e. mainly on agriculture) did not fairly take account of UK interests.

(c) The CAP was in need of major change. It represented a threat to world trade and kept low-cost producers out of the UK market. It had been unsatisfactory in a number of ways – for example, it had given rise to costly surpluses (cheap butter for the Russians).

Emphasis should be placed on greater financial control and on the interests of consumers.

(d) There should be no harmonization of VAT which involved the taxation of necessities.

(e) The British Parliament should retain powers needed to pursue effective regional, industrial and fiscal policies.

(f) The economic interests of the Commonwealth and developing countries needed to be better safeguarded. This involved continued access to the UK market, and intensified Community trade and aid policies.

(g) The UK Government should be able to control capital movements in order to protect the balance of payments and full employment.

The negotiations which then ensued were finally brought to an end at the Dublin Summit in March 1975. It finally resolved some major outstanding issues. The British Government then pronounced itself satisfied with the new terms[1] and it declared that it would commend them to the electorate in a referendum which would be the final determining factor. On 5 June 1975 the first nationwide referendum in British history took place. The electorate was asked 'Do you think that the United Kingdom should stay in the European Community (the Common Market)?' Seventeen million voted 'Yes' and eight million voted 'No'.

The reader will obviously wish to know what exactly were the terms which the UK Government secured and which it successfully commended to the UK electorate. It should be said that they consisted partly of accommodations made by the Community and partly of a realization by the UK Government that on some issues its fears were groundless.

The concern over EMU proved to be a damp squib. Quite simply Foreign Secretary Callaghan found out from his opposite numbers that such a union by 1980 was not on the cards. Indeed, as we noted earlier, the scheme had run out of steam – more will be said on this issue in Chapter 7 below.[2]

On the issue of the Community budget the UK did make what it thought was progress. The Dublin Summit of 1975 endorsed a correction

1. The statement of Prime Minister Harold Wilson commending the new terms is to be found in *Membership of the European Community*, Cmnd 5999 (HMSO, 1975a), and a report of the negotiated terms is to be found in *Membership of the European Community: Report on Renegotiation*, Cmnd 6003 (HMSO, 1975b).

2. In fairness it should be pointed out that the original UK position on monetary union was quite judicious. It did not oppose such a union but emphasized the danger of fixing parities before there was a convergence of price movements, etc.

mechanism which enabled not just the UK but any member who was unfairly treated to secure a refund – the mechanism is described in the Appendix to this chapter.

On the question of the CAP the British were able to claim that they had helped to institute a full-scale reappraisal of the policy – this was referred to as a stocktaking. In addition it was claimed that farm prices had been held down, that the British had managed to persuade the Community to adopt more flexible arrangements (i.e. surplus beef had been dealt with by subsidies designed to cheapen it and extend demand) and financial control had been tightened up (this included the taking of steps to prevent fraudulent use of agricultural support funds).

The concern over VAT also proved to be a damp squib. By the time the renegotiation was in process the Community was considering proposals as to the nature of the common base for VAT and these provided for zero rating.

The UK concern about the possibly adverse impact of membership on regional policy was wholly misconceived. In the first place one of the results of the 1972 Paris Summit was the decision to create the ERDF. This was a wholly new departure. Prior to that, Community policy was largely devoted to seeing that regional aids did not distort competition in the Common Market. The new Fund now meant that the Community would be actively engaged in giving aid. It should be added that the UK was undoubtedly interested in this Fund because she saw herself as a major beneficiary from it – this was one way of securing a *juste retour* – a flow of receipts to balance her payments into the Community budget! There was some concern over the fact that the European Communities Commission (ECC) was responsible for vetting aids but this was clearly likely to assist countries such as the UK since it was intended to be operated in a way which prevented extravagant and unnecessary aid-giving in the central regions of the Community. The UK had everything to gain by such control, and if the Community had broken up Britain would have been hard pressed to compete with the more prosperous economies of West Germany and France in attracting foot-loose investment. In 1975 the Commission issued a Communication relating to regional policy which indicated that the control of aid-giving would leave British policy intact.

On the question of protecting the interests of Commonwealth countries progress was made. In the case of New Zealand the original terms did not contain satisfactory provisions for a continuing relationship between New Zealand and the Community after 1977. The Dublin Summit in fact provided for imports of New Zealand butter in 1978–80 to remain close to deliveries in 1974–5. It was also accepted that there was a need for a periodic review and, as necessary, an adjustment of the prices paid to New Zealand. The Dublin Summit invited the Commission to produce as soon as practicable special import arrangements for butter after 1977. It was also agreed that the position in respect of imports of New Zealand cheese after 1977 should be urgently considered. In respect of Commonwealth sugar the Community offered access for up to 1·4 million tons of sugar per annum from the Commonwealth developing countries for an indefinite period – prices would be negotiated annually and would be related to prices paid to Community producers. As for trade and aid generally in respect of developing countries, the British position was overtaken by events. For example, the new Lomé Convention, discussed below in Chapter 11, was greeted with little short of ecstasy by the then Minister of Overseas Development, who was not known for her enthusiasm for the European cause.

The capital movements issue was yet another damp squib. Quite simply the British Government discovered that without special agreement governments could act to control capital movements when it was necessary to do so.

Although in 1975 the British people had fairly decisively decided to remain within the Community, the relationship continued to be an uneasy one. Opposition to UK membership continued to smoulder, particularly in the Left Wing of the Labour Party, and a commitment to pull the UK out became part of the Labour Party programme in 1982. Within the public at large, a positive enthusiasm for the European cause was markedly absent, although this opposition was not based on any really thorough understanding of the Community and its workings. Thus in 1981 *Which?* carried out an attitude survey among a sample of 1000 citizens. Only 24 per cent felt the EEC was a good thing – 59 per cent were opposed. Only 31 per cent wished to stay in – 58 per cent wanted to pull out. These views, however, were based on a profound ignorance of the facts. For example, only 8 per cent of the survey could identify the other members of the Community. Equally revealing was the fact that just over half the survey believed that the UK's net contribution to the Community budget was greater than UK social security spending. In fact the net contribution for 1980 was expected to be of the order of £1·2 billion whereas social security spending was of the order of £18·5 billion!

Whilst this lack of enthusiasm for the Community was in the main founded in ignorance, there was one topic on which the UK had legitimate grounds for complaint – that was its position in relation to the

Community budget. Despite the renegotiation and the prospect held out by the correction mechanism, it became increasingly obvious that by 1980 the UK would be required to make an unacceptably high net contribution. This gave rise to a long, drawn-out wrangle, and we shall return to this topic in Chapter 3 below.

Greek, Portuguese and Spanish membership

The relationship between Greece and the Community goes back to the early sixties. A Treaty of Association came into operation in 1962 and provided for the eventual formation of a customs union between Greece and the Six. However, following the *coup d'état* in 1967, the Greek association agreement was frozen but was reactivated in 1974 as a result of the restoration of democracy.

As we saw earlier, Portugal was a member of EFTA from its foundation in 1960. We also saw that when the UK eventually joined the Community a free trade area agreement was entered into between the enlarged Community and the remaining members of EFTA. The agreement with Portugal was signed in 1972. It provided for the elimination of all tariff barriers on exports from Portugal to the Community. In the case of certain sensitive products (textiles, clothing and cork manufactures) quantitative restrictions were, however, to apply until 1983. In respect of imports from the Community, products were divided into three categories and trade liberalization was to be achieved respectively in 1977, 1980 and 1985. The free access to the Community market was of course limited to industrial goods, although some concessions were made in respect of specific Portuguese agricultural commodities.

Spain did not become part of EFTA – its preference lay with the EEC. Three factors disposed the Spanish Government to seek a closer relationship with the EEC. The first was a sympathy on the part of some members of the Franco Government with the longer-term political objectives of the Community. The second was the decision of the UK in 1961 to seek full Community membership. Given the dependence of Spain on the UK market, it was important that negotiations should be opened with the Community with a view to securing a trade agreement which would at the same time maintain the UK connection. The application was made in 1962 but evinced no immediate response. In 1964 the Community did agree to open exploratory talks, but negotiations did not start until 1967 and an agreement was not signed until 1970. Basically it provided for a free trade area between Spain and the Community. Detailed provisions were only entered into in respect of the first six-year stage. The second stage was left for subsequent negotiation. On the industrial front the arrangement was supposed to embody the principle of reciprocity, but Spain in fact gave up less than the Community. The Community offered for most products a tariff reduction of 60 per cent by 1973, although exceptions were made in respect of certain sensitive products (for example textiles, footwear and clothing). According to Loukas Tsoukalis (1981, p. 78) Spain in return granted tariff reductions in the region of 25–60 per cent with most falling in the 25 per cent category. Some limited concessions were made by the Community in respect of imports of Spanish agricultural produce.

The factor which transformed the relationship between these three Mediterranean countries and the Community was the disappearance of dictatorships. Whilst ever they existed, full membership was not feasible. In June 1975 the Karamanlis Government of Greece submitted an application for full membership. In March 1977 the Soares Government of Portugal, against a background of substantial national indifference, did likewise. In July 1977 the Suárez Government of Spain, with substantial national enthusiasm and in the light of a long-term commitment, followed suit. Although the Community recognized that membership was a way of keeping these countries in the Western camp, of maintaining their political stability and protecting newly emerged democracies, their accession was regarded as posing substantial problems and challenges.

If all three became full members they would increase the Community population base by a fifth and its collective GDP by a tenth. More to the point they would add a new dimension to Community economic problems since, unlike the new members of 1973, they were at a distinctly lower level of development than the countries they proposed to join. This was particularly true in the case of Portugal.

Adding to the number of member states would also create difficulties for the decision-making machinery. Achieving agreement among the Nine was difficult – it would be even more difficult between Twelve. This would apply to political as well as economic matters. The EC Commission did not, however, see the decision-making issue as posing an insuperable problem. On the Rome Treaty front it recommended a mixture of devolution of executive power to the Commission, more majority voting in the Council of Ministers in areas which allowed for it, and the extension of majority voting to areas which otherwise required unanimity.

But there were other problems, and it is important to recognize that the membership negotiations of Spain and Portugal were dragged out because they coincided with a growing appreciation within the existing Community of these problems. One was budgetary. Whilst the Mediterranean countries would add resources it was also recognized that they would make demands upon them – indeed there was likely to be a net transfer to the Mediterranean members. Whilst the Portuguese and Spanish applications were still lying on the table it was becoming increasingly apparent that the budget's own resources were nearing their ceiling, and the admission of these two countries would pose a considerable problem whilst the budget problem remained unresolved – see Chapter 3. If additional own resouces were not found, or were found in inadequate amounts, the only way to accommodate the Iberian claim would be to cut down on certain forms of spending. Countries which gained from the CAP would not warm to that idea! It was also easy to see how countries such as the UK could lose by enlargement. As things stood they had first priority claim on the budget's Regional Fund and Social Fund spending. But after enlargement they would be further down the list.

Major obstacles were also to be found in the agricultural, industrial and fishing sectors – notably in the case of Spain. In the field of agriculture it was the existing Mediterranean producers within the Community who were most at risk – i.e. producers of olive oil, fruit, vegetables and wine. Greek membership would help to increase the degree of self-sufficiency, and adding Iberian produce would greatly exacerbate the problem. Surpluses would lead to pressure on prices, and if that was to be prevented more support buying would be necessary. This would add to the burden of the CAP at a time when proposals were being made to cut CAP spending! Reducing food imports from other Mediterranean countries would be one possible if only partial solution, but it would upset the whole concept of an overall Mediterranean policy. In the industrial field, notable problems arose in steel and textiles. The problems were threefold: (a) the lower wage levels of Iberian producers would pose a threat – this seemed a real possibility in the case of Portuguese textiles; (b) steel and textiles in the Community were already faced with over-capacity problems, and increased penetration by Iberian producers would make the problem even worse; (c) in the longer term some of the industries upon which the Iberian countries had based their industrialization programmes were ones which the Community would be progressively abandoning – the latter under pressure from developing countries who expected it to adopt a strategy which involved a shift up market to higher technologies. The large Spanish fishing fleet was also seen as posing a substantial problem. Its tonnage was 70 per cent of the fleet of the Nine. This threatened to create a substantial disturbance of any balance of catches which might eventually arise when the details of the Common Fisheries Policy, then not agreed, were finalized.

Despite these problems the Greek negotiations were carried to a successful conclusion, and Greece became a full member on 1 January 1981. The relatively early success of the Greek application was due to a combination of factors. Firstly, her application preceded those of the Iberian countries by about two years. Secondly, her application enjoyed consistent French support – unlike the Iberian bids. Thirdly, as we have already pointed out, problems such as those concerning the budget and agriculture had not become sufficiently serious to justify calling a halt to enlargement. Under the accession agreement, Greece accepted the *acquis communautaire* – i.e. the various treaties and the secondary legislation. In effect she had accepted the Community's achievements up to the date of her entry. In respect of industrial products a five-year transition period was allowed for the progressive elimination of residual customs duties on goods imported into Greece which originated in the Community. A similar period was allowed for the progressive alignment of the Greek tariff on the common external tariff. Quantitative restrictions between Greece and the Community had to be eliminated on accession, with the exception of fourteen products. In the latter cases a progressive enlargement of quotas was required over the five-year period, after which they had to be totally eliminated. A general transition period of five years was allowed for agriculture, although for a few products the period was extended to seven. The Community agricultural system was to be progressively phased in. Producers of cotton, dried figs and raisins would benefit from new production-aid systems. Although certain subsidies had to be eliminated the need to avoid abrupt changes was accepted. These aids would therefore be progressively phased out during the transition phase.

Freedom of movement of workers was to be established over a seven-year period. The drachma would be included in the ECU basket of currencies by the end of the transitional period.[1] Capital movements had to be liberalized from the date of accession, but in respect of certain types of transaction the adjustment could be delayed until the end of 1985. Although Greece had to apply the Community's own resources system from accession, arrangements were made to prevent her from becoming a net contributor during the first five years. Greece also

1. It was actually included from 17 September 1984.

became a full member of all the institutions, and in all cases appropriate adjustments were made.[1]

By contrast the Spanish and Portuguese applications became bogged down as the Community struggled with its own mounting internal problems – budgetary, agricultural, fishing, etc. The agricultural impact of Iberian membership was a source of growing concern as existing Mediterranean producers within the Community considered the effect of adding two more Mediterranean competitors. This gave rise to strong reservations, notably on the part of the French. It should be added that the newest member, Greece, was also opposed to further enlargement until adequate measures had been agreed which would help to insulate the Mediterranean region from its impact. It was only after (a) the Common Fisheries Policy had been agreed in 1983, (b) the Fontainebleau Summit of 1984 had settled the budget issues and had made a start on cutting CAP spending, and (c) integrated Mediterranean spending programmes had been agreed at the Brussels Summit of 1985, that the way was cleared for Iberian membership.

Both countries became full members on 1 January 1986. Both accepted the *acquis communautaire*. A seven-year timetable was agreed for the reciprocal dismantling of tariffs by stages. At the same time the new members agreed to progressively align their customs duties in respect of non-members on the common external tariff. In the case of agriculture differing arrangements were made. For Portugal a programme of two five-year periods was agreed. The first stage would be devoted to preparing for the introduction of the CAP system of market organization. The second stage would see the introduction of those systems. Special

1. Turkey, like Greece, entered into an association agreement with the Community at quite an early stage. It came into operation on 1 December 1964. It involved a preparatory period and was followed by a transition period during which a customs union was to be established between the original Six and Turkey. Subsequently the association agreement was increasingly criticized by the Turks, and in 1978 the Turkish Government decided to freeze the arrangement. Thereafter relations improved, and in 1980 the Community and Turkey revised the old agreement and the Nine agreed that Turkey would at an unspecified future date be able to apply for full membership. The military coup of 1980 put an end to that possibility, but the subsequent restoration of civilian government once more made it feasible. In April 1987 the Turkish Government applied for full membership. Commentators were of the opinion that the Community would not refuse to accept an application. However, they pointed out that there was likely to be considerable hostility in some quarters (notably Greece) and that full membership was not likely before the year 2000. In June 1987 the European Parliament greatly angered the Turkish Government when it passed a resolution calling on Turkey to acknowledge that 'genocide' had been committed against the Armenians during the First World War and listing a series of insurmountable obstacles to the consideration of Turkey's application.

aid would be advanced to facilitate the structural improvement of Portuguese agriculture over a ten-year period. In the case of Spanish agriculture a transition period of seven years was agreed, although for vegetable oils and fats and fresh fruit and vegetables a ten-year period was prescribed. A transition period of seven to ten years was decided upon in the case of fisheries – this covered trade in fish and access to waters and fish stocks. Spain undertook to introduce VAT from the date of her accession, but Portugal was allowed a three-year deferment. Transitional arrangements were also provided in relation to payments to the Community budget – both would receive reducing refunds on their VAT-related contributions. Portugal was exempted from paying into the Community budget customs duties and agricultural levies on imports covered by the two-stage arrangement. It was also to receive 1000 million ECUs of aid in respect of its balance of payments in the form of loans over a six-year period. Both countries became full members of all Community institutions and appropriate adjustments to numbers were accordingly made.

Conclusion

Thus by 1986 the Community had expanded to Twelve. It was a Community of 321 million people (1984) – a population greater than that of the USSR. Its collective Gross Domestic Product was greater than that of the USA. Its Gross Domestic Product per head was 270 per cent of the world average (1982). Its exports (including intra-Community exports) were 33 per cent of world exports (1984) – even if intra-Community exports were not included it still outstripped the USA or Japan in trade terms. These facts, conjoined with the cohesion which sprang from the Community relationships, were bound to confer upon the Twelve considerable leverage in world economic affairs. It should be added that the process of integration had spilled over into the foreign-policy field, so that here too the Community could increasingly speak as one in the international political arena. All this was a far cry from the devastation and division which existed in Europe in the early postwar period.

APPENDIX
The Community budget correction mechanism

The arrangement agreed at the Dublin Summit concerning contributions to the Community budget was as follows. The system was concerned with rectifying a situation where a country was paying a disproportionate contribution to the budget. The general idea was that a refund would be payable if the contribution went significantly beyond what was fair in relation to a country's proportionate share of the Community GNP. To qualify for a refund a country (a) would have to have a GNP *per capita* which was less than 85 per cent of the Community average; (b) would have to have a real rate of growth of less than 120 per cent of the Community average; (c) would have to be contributing own resources (levies, duties, VAT, etc.) which were greater than 110 per cent of a member state's share of Community GNP; (d) would have to have a 'net potential foreign exchange liability' (in other words an excess of contributions to the budget over receipts from it) as a result of the operation of the budget. Criteria (a) and (b) would be calculated on the basis of a three-year moving average.

If a country met these requirements the reimbursement would be calculated according to a sliding scale. There would be no reimbursement in respect of an excess contribution between 100 and 105 per cent of a member state's GNP share, but thereafter an increasing proportion would be refunded which would rise to 100 per cent for an excess contribution over 130 per cent of GNP share. The arrangement did however provide for a ceiling to be set on such refunds. The amount reimbursed would not be higher than the lowest of the following three ceilings: (a) 250 million units of account (which at the time was equivalent to about £125 million); (b) the 'net potential foreign exchange liability' referred to above; (c) the member state's VAT contribution (or GNP-related contribution in the absence of a VAT contribution). Ceiling (a) would be raised if the total budget rose above 8000 million units of account and would instead be set at 3 per cent of total budget expenditure. There was a proviso that if (on a three-year moving average basis) the balance of payments on current account of the member state was in surplus, the correction would be based on different criteria.

There were two provisions for review. If a state received a refund for three successive years the Community would consider what more needed to be done. The system was designed to run for a seven-year trial period after which its workings would be assessed.

2 The Community Decision-Making Institutions

Since what we are primarily concerned with in this book is the economic policy of the EEC, it is clearly important that we should appreciate how that policy is formulated. It was of course the hope of those who set up the Community that economic unity would give rise to political unity, and that has happened to a significant degree in the shape of European Political Cooperation. In the first part of this chapter we shall be concerned with how decisions are made in the EEC (there is considerable institutional overlap with the ECSC and Euratom but we will focus upon the EEC) and in the second part we will take a look at European Political Cooperation.

In Figure 1 we present a picture of the constitutional position as it exists following the Single European Act. The overarching body in the search for European unity is the European Council. Its evolution and functions in relation to the institutions which lie within its constituency are discussed below. Its constituency is in fact twofold. On the one hand there are the European Communities (i.e. the EEC, the ECSC and Euratom) and on the other there is European Political Cooperation.

As we saw in Chapter 1, one of the institutions which has been notably active in identifying new areas of Community activity, in setting up new Community institutions and in resolving Community deadlocks has been the summit meeting. The Hague Summit of 1969, the Paris Summit of 1972 and the Fontainebleau Summit of 1984 are outstanding instances. At the 1974 Paris Summit it was resolved that these meetings should henceforth be dignified with the title of the European Council. It was decided that the Heads of State and of Government, together with their foreign ministers, would meet three times a year (and, where necessary, in the Council of Ministers of the European Communities and in the context of European Political Cooperation). The President of the European Communities Commission also attended these meetings. It should be noted that the Paris Summit communiqué was careful to emphasize that the European Council procedure in no way affected the rules and procedures of the European Community Treaties and of European Political Cooperation. All this was very much the brainchild of the then French President Valéry Giscard d'Estaing. In practice the Heads of State and of Government, when meeting in the European Council, have not sought to assume the formal law-making role of the EEC Council of Ministers which, as we shall see below, is the properly constituted EEC law-making body. Rather the European Council has tended to produce communiqués. These have for the most part provided a basis for proposals which could then be inserted into the normal EEC decision-making machinery – for which see below. Occasionally the European Council has concluded agreements which did not give rise to an amendment to the Rome Treaty or to an act by virtue of it. Thus the detailed arrangements concerning the European Monetary System (EMS) were not inserted as amendments to the Rome Treaty – the EMS stood alone as an inter-governmental agreement but confined to Community member states.

Part of the importance of the Single European Act is that it quite explicitly and formally recognizes the supreme positions of the European Council. Article 2 declares that the European Council will bring together the Heads of State and of Government and will be accompanied by the President of the European Communities Commission. They are to be assisted by the ministers of foreign affairs and by a further member of the Commission. The Council is required to meet at least twice a year. Article 3 reiterates the safeguarding of the powers and jurisdictions of the three European Communities and of European Political Cooperation.

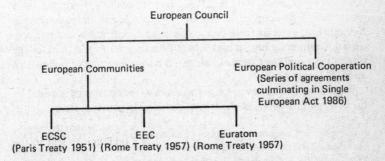

Figure 1. Institutions of European Unity under the Single European Act, 1986

The European Economic Community

The five main bodies which have an influence on policy-making under the Rome Treaty are the Commission, the Council of Ministers, the Court of Justice, the European Parliament and the Economic and Social Committee. The above order of listing does not reflect an order of influence on policy formation – there can, however, be no doubt that the Commission and the Council of Ministers are the most important bodies.

In addition there are said to be upwards of 2000 committees, subcommittees and working parties assisting the Community institutions in the formulation of policy and the prosecution of business. We should also not neglect the various interest groups which the Commission consults – for example COPA (the grouping of agricultural organizations) and UNICE (the industrial association). In this account we shall confine our discussion to the five main bodies – the role of other bodies will be made apparent in later chapters.

Before we proceed to discuss the role of the five main bodies, there are a number of preliminary issues which need to be dealt with. In the first place in this book we are dealing with economic policies which are founded on treaties. The Rome Treaty places a constraint upon the policies which the Community institutions can adopt, and it is always open to the Court of Justice to declare that this or that action or decision is not in accordance with the treaty. It must be admitted that this constraining factor has been variable in its impact. In some instances, such as EEC Transport Policy, the treaty said little more than there should be a common policy. As a result it was left to the Commission, working through the other Community organs, to make the policy. On the other hand, there are branches of EEC policy where the Rome Treaty is quite explicit. For example, Articles 85 and 86 enunciate the basic approach which has to be adopted in dealing with cartels and dominant firms. Nevertheless, even in these cases, this clear specification has not precluded Community institutions – here primarily we would think of the Commission and the Court of Justice – from putting a lot of policy flesh on basic treaty bones.

We should not, however, make too much of the constraint imposed by the original provisions of the treaty. Article 235 provides that:

If action by the Community should prove necessary to attain, in the course of the operation of the common market, one of the objectives of the Community and this Treaty has not provided the necessary powers, the Council shall, acting unanimously on a proposal from the Commission and after consulting the Assembly, take the appropriate measures.

Additionally Article 236 declares that:

The Government of any member state or the Commission may submit to the Council proposals for the amendment of this Treaty.

If the Council, after consulting the Assembly and, where appropriate, the Commission, delivers an opinion in favour of calling a conference of representatives of the Governments of the member states, the conference shall be convened by the President of the Council for the purpose of determining by common accord the amendments to be made to this Treaty.

Between them these two provisions enable existing powers to be altered and new powers to be taken. They therefore provide for the possibility of considerable expansion and change in the economic policies falling within the Community ambit.

The Commission

The Commission is in effect the civil service of the Community. Originally there were three civil services – one for each Community. In the case of the ECSC it was the High Authority, whilst the EEC and Euratom each had a Commission. However, by virtue of a treaty signed in Brussels on 8 April 1965 it was agreed that these three executives should be merged, or fused, as from 1 July 1967. It is perhaps worth mentioning that the three treaties remained separate (whether they will in due course be fused only the future will tell). The fused Commission was therefore left with the task of administering the provisions of three separate founding treaties.

Originally there were nine EEC Commissioners. This number was raised to fourteen in 1967 on the occasion of the fusion of the executives but in 1970 was slimmed back down to nine. As a result of the accession of six states the number of Commissioners has been raised, and currently there are seventeen. The United Kingdom, West Germany, France, Italy and Spain nominate two Commissioners whilst the other countries nominate one each.

All the Commissioners are appointed by the member governments for four-year renewable terms. The President and the six Vice-Presidents are chosen from among the seventeen and hold these offices for two-year renewable terms. Each Commissioner is responsible for a portfolio which is sometimes purely concerned with policy areas (for example, one commissioner is currently responsible for agriculture and forestry) and is sometimes a mixture of policy and administration (for example, one commissioner is currently responsible for competition matters but also for relations with the European Parliament). The President is currently responsible for one policy area (monetary affairs) and a host of administrative matters (legal service, spokesman's service, interpreting and conference service and the security office).

Each Commissioner has a private office or *cabinet*, the appointments to which are his private prerogative. Usually, but not invariably, the members of the *cabinet* are of the same nationality as the Commissioner. If the Commissioner is away the *chef de cabinet* will act in his stead at the weekly meeting of the Commission which is usually held on a Wednesday. Beneath each Commissioner there is usually at least one Director General in charge of a Directorate General, i.e. a broad *policy* area. A Directorate General (of which there are currently twenty) will in turn be split into areas relating to various aspects of the broad policy problem. They are presided over by Directors and below them are Heads of Division.

It is most important to note that Article 157 of the Rome Treaty requires that Commissioners 'shall neither seek nor take instruction from any Government or from any other body'. In other words Commissioners are *supposed* to act with complete independence.

The role of the Commission

To the EEC Commission fell the task of taking steps to see that the Community, as envisaged by the Rome Treaty, was established. In short, action was needed if the aspirations of Article 3 – that there should be common policies in agriculture and transport, that competition should not be distorted, that a customs union should be established and so forth – were to be turned into concrete realities. To this end the Rome Treaty conferred upon the Commission an important power – the right of initiative. It is the task of the Commission to draft proposals (for regulations, etc.) which the Council of Ministers (representing the member state governments) has to consider. The Council of Ministers has to decide whether to accept the draft or not. In some cases there must be unanimity (for example on the subject of new members) whilst in others a qualified majority vote is sufficient (but see below). If the Council accepts the draft proposal it is promulgated in the Official Journal and becomes law. If the Council does not accept it, it can only alter the draft by a unanimous vote. Generally we may assume that the various ministers will not be in a position to agree on the alterations which will be necessary to secure the degree of unanimity required. In this case the proposal has to go back to the Commission for it to come up with some alternative which will command the necessary support. This brings us to the second role of the Commission – it acts as a mediator, trying by means of negotiations with the member states to find an acceptable compromise which at the same time, hopefully, does not mean that the overall Community interest has been obscured by the horse-trading which may have taken place.

In approaching the Council of Ministers, the Commission feeds it with draft proposals which in due course emerge as Directives, Decisions, Regulations and Recommendations.[1] Only the first three have the force of law. Directives do not apply directly to individuals and companies. They are aimed at the member states and require them to modify national laws. For example, it may be that national laws concerning the design and composition of goods vary from state to state, and as a result trade cannot flow across frontiers. One solution has been to harmonize such laws. The Directive will require member states to amend their national laws and then individuals and companies have to obey the appropriately modified (harmonized) national law. Decisions and Regulations are directly binding on individuals, companies or governments. A Decision will name a person, company or state to which it specifically applies. A Regulation will be general in its application – for example, all companies rather than just one will be bound by it. It is essential to remember that when Community and national law conflict, the requirements of Community law must be regarded as paramount.

The Commission, having secured the Council's agreement to a particular line of policy, has to see that it is carried out. Here there is an administrative task. For example, the Council of Ministers, on a proposal of the Commission, fixes the prices of farm products for the coming agricultural year. These prices have to be achieved by various devices such as protection at the common frontier and support buying. This is a task which involves the Commission but it is not one that it discharges alone. In practice a large proportion of the staff of national ministries of agriculture have become effectively the agents of the Community, operating the CAP in cooperation with intervention agencies set up in each country. However, the Commission is involved in that the functioning of the CAP is supervised by Management Committees staffed by both national and Commission officials. Since the Commission staff totals only about 10 500,[2] whilst a larger ministry in the UK may employ upwards of 20 000, it is not difficult to see that the Commission could

1. This terminology refers to the Rome Treaty.
2. Many of whom are translators and interpreters. In addition about 2900 are employed in the separate scientific and technological Joint Research Centre and 330 are to be found at the Office for Official Publications.

not hope to be solely responsible for the administration of all the policies which it helps to initiate.

Finally the Commission discharges a very important policing task. It has to see that individuals, companies and member states do not act in ways which clearly run counter to the Treaty or to specific policies laid down by the Council. For example, groups of firms may enter into agreements which restrict competition and are clearly contrary to Article 3(f) (which calls for the achievement of conditions of undistorted competition) and Article 85 which prohibits agreements (subject to exceptions in clearly defined circumstances). The Commission may begin by seeking a voluntary termination of such an agreement, but if necessary it has the power to issue a formal Decision prohibiting the agreement. By a Decision it can also inflict fines on parties to an agreement. Equally the Commission can take member states to task. In the case of state aids, for example, it will usually ask a state to voluntarily terminate an infringement, but if the state refuses the Commission can take the matter to the Court of Justice for a final determination.

The Council

The Council is a body which represents the member state governments. It is clearly the ultimate controlling authority since draft regulations and draft directives (perhaps stemming from European Council communiqués) only become the law of the Community if the Council agrees.

The Council is not a fixed group of individuals in the way that the Commission is. Where matters of agriculture are under discussion it will be the ministers of agriculture of the member states who will meet as the Council, and when transport is under discussion it will be the ministers of transport and so on. The ministers of foreign affairs, of agriculture and those concerned with budgetary matters meet frequently – the former both within the ambit of the economic communities and political cooperation (for the latter see below). Typically the ministers of transport, science, social affairs, etc., tend to meet less regularly, although the frequency of their meetings will of course depend upon whether at a particular point in time the Community has decided to place emphasis on the need for policy developments in their area of responsibility. The ministers of foreign affairs and of agriculture are in effect the senior body, and the former (usually referred to as the General Council) tend to be called in when colleagues in specialist fields are locked in disagreement. The chairmanship or presidency of the Council also rotates –

each member state holds it in turn for a period of six months. The chair is in fact passed on in alphabetical order.

The EEC Treaty laid down important rules concerning voting procedure within the Council. Generally in the early stages (the transition period was divided into three four-year stages) decisions required a unanimous vote. However, in certain areas, such as agriculture, it was provided that subsequently a qualified majority of the votes in Council was adequate for a measure to be adopted. For this purpose France, West Germany and Italy had four votes each, Netherlands and Belgium two votes and Luxembourg one. Twelve votes were necessary for a measure to be passed. It was this which constituted much of the supranational element of the EEC Treaty. Unlike the normal system of international organizations where unanimity is necessary, it was possible to evolve policies if only a qualified majority of the votes had been cast in its favour. This was a protection for the Commission since in its task of setting up the various Community policies it did not indefinitely face the prospect of having to achieve a unanimity among the member states.[1]

Three observations are now necessary. Firstly, not all subjects were ones in which qualified majority voting was in due course envisaged. The admission of new members was one exception – hence the possibility that the French could, had they chosen, have blocked the admission of the UK indefinitely. Secondly, where the Council was acting on a proposal not initiated by the Commission, in addition to the twelve-vote requirement four states also had to agree to the measure. This was a protection against the smaller Benelux states being overridden by the three bigger ones. Thirdly, in practice qualified majority voting has since 1966 ceased to have the significance which had been envisaged earlier. The issue arose in 1965 in connection with the Commission's proposals to tie into one package three elements: the completion of the farm finance regulations (desired by France), the independent financing of the Community out of its own resources (strongly desired by the Commission), and the granting of greater budgetary powers to the Parliament (desired by both the European Parliament and the Netherlands). France strongly disliked parts of this package and virtually absented itself from the Council for seven months. Much of the wrath of the French was directed against the Commission, which in their eyes was getting ideas above its station, and against qualified majority, due to apply amongst other things to agriculture in 1966, which France apparently feared might be used against it. The upshot was the famous Luxembourg

1. Purists may wish to know that there are six issues upon which a simple majority will suffice.

compromise of January 1966. There was also an agreement to modify the status of the Commission, although the changes were not really of great significance. In respect of Council voting the Six agreed as follows:

I Where, in the case of decisions which may be taken by majority vote on a proposal of the Commission, very important interests of one or more partners are at stake, the members of the Council will endeavour, within a reasonable time, to reach solutions which can be adopted by all the members of the Council while respecting their mutual interests and those of the Community, in accordance with Article 2 of the Treaty.

II With regard to the preceding paragraph, the French delegation considers that where very important interests are at stake the discussion must be continued until unanimous agreement is reached.

The effect of this was that by tacit agreement Council hardly ever took decisions by majority vote despite the fact that the Rome Treaty provided for such a procedure on a wide range of issues.

In the light of this significant change in procedure it is interesting to note that at the Paris Summit of 1974 the Heads of State and of Government stated in their communiqué:

In order to improve the functioning of the Council of the Community they consider that it is necessary to renounce the practice which consists of making agreement on all questions conditional on the unanimous consent of the member states whatever their respective positions may be regarding the conclusions reached at Luxembourg on 28 January 1966.

It is not too clear what this entailed in practice. The Heads did not formally renounce the Luxembourg agreement. Rather the communiqué seemed to be more a statement of what was desirable. Nevertheless it seemed to have the effect of relaxing the post-Luxembourg system. Thus the Commission's *Ninth General Report* (EC Commission, 1975a, p. 20), *Tenth General Report* (1976, p. 34) and *Eleventh General Report* (1977a, p. 23) noted a tendency for decisions to be taken by majority rule. Nevertheless some members, notably the UK, have continued to insist on the right to veto acts which they deem affect vital national interests. Such was the case in 1982 when the UK withheld its support for farm price increases because of the lack of progress on its budget problem. In the end the Council decided that the vital matter of increasing the price of farm products could no longer be held up and took a decision on a majority basis – much to the disgust of the UK! The Commission noted this development with approval. However, in observing: 'There is, of course, not likely to be any sudden change from former practice' (*Six-*

teenth General Report, 1982, p. 299) it clearly indicated that the spirit of Luxembourg 1966 was by no means dead.

The gravely unsatisfactory nature of this reluctance to employ the majority voting possibility was frequently criticized. As we noted in Chapter 1, the European Council set up a committee (the Three Wise Men) in 1978 to consider what adjustments in machinery and procedures would make the Community more effective. Most of the criticism of the Three was in fact directed at the Council of Ministers, which was seen as being too inter-governmental in character – the supranational element had been lost sight of and much more use needed to be made of majority votes. We have in Chapter 1 also seen that the European Parliament, in drafting its European Union Treaty, was conscious of this deficiency and of the increased paralysis which was likely to ensue if the enlarged and more diverse Community of Twelve continued to require unanimity before anything could be agreed. The heightened consciousness of this deficiency was instrumental in influencing the content of the Single European Act of 1986. Significantly, it has led to revisions of certain articles relating to the completion of the internal common market by requiring qualified majority voting to be substituted for unanimity. The articles in questions are 28, 57(2), 59, 70(1), 84(2) and 100.[1] Modified Article 100 is particularly significant since it relates to the power to harmonize national laws which by virtue of their diversity impede the creation of a true internal common market. It should, however, be noted that not all harmonization activity will be shifted to a majority voting basis.

Following the admission of new members in 1973, 1981 and 1986 the voting formula had to be changed. Currently West Germany, France, Italy and the UK have ten votes each, Spain has eight votes, Belgium, Greece, the Netherlands and Portugal have five votes each, Denmark and Ireland have three votes each and Luxembourg has two. This gives a total of seventy-six votes and fifty-four represent a qualified majority. When the Council acts on a proposal that does not emanate from the Commission, fifty-four votes and the support of eight states are both necessary.

Thus far we have presented the legislative process as one in which the Commission proposes and the Council of Ministers disposes. However, it is important to recognize that two other bodies have in particular to be consulted – the European Parliament and the Economic and Social Committee (see below for both). The Rome Treaty indicates the issues

1. A voting modification has also been made in respect of science and technology spending – see Chapter 10 below.

upon which the opinion of these two bodies has to be obtained. If, for example, the Rome Treaty says that on a particular kind of proposal the Parliament must be consulted, but the legislators had failed to consult, then the proposal adopted by the Council would be invalid. It is crucial to recognize that whilst the views of the Economic and Social Committee and Parliament must be sought, the Commission and Council are not in general required to agree to what they say. Here we see a crucial difference between national parliaments and the European Parliament. Generally speaking, the Council of Ministers can make laws even if the European Parliament disagrees with them, whereas under national systems ministers can only usually make laws if they command a majority vote in parliament. Having said that, we have to note a couple of qualifications. Firstly, the Parliament possesses certain powers in relation to the Community budget – see Chapter 3. Secondly, the Single European Act has introduced a cooperation system, in other words a system of legislative cooperation between the Council and Parliament. This new procedure obliges the Council and Commission to take Parliament's amendments to proposals into consideration, although a unanimous vote by Council remains the last word.

When approaching the Council with draft proposals, the Commission proceeds by way of a number of committees [1] of which one of the more important is the Committee of Permanent Representatives – known as Coreper, which is an abbreviation of its French title. Coreper has been divided into two. Coreper 1 is made up of deputy heads of member state delegations to the Community and Coreper 2 consists of the heads of delegations. Coreper is located in Brussels. Proposals are discussed in Coreper and its sub-committees before they arrive on the Council table. If Coreper reaches full agreement the matter can pass through the Council without debate. In other cases it may be possible for the permanent representatives to agree on large sections of a draft proposal, but areas of disagreement (either as between states or between states and the Commission) are placed in square brackets and left to be settled around the Council table. In some cases little headway may be made by Coreper and the matter is then left to the ministers themselves to thrash out.

1. There is, for example, a separate committee for agricultural matters which is called the Special Committee for Agriculture, a Budget Committee and a Monetary Committee.

The Court of Justice

Whereas the Commission is located in Brussels, in and around the Berlaymont building, and the Council meets (and its 1900 or so staff operate) in the Charlemagne building close by, the Court of Justice has its seat in Luxembourg in a five-storey building on the Kirchberg. It has a staff of about 480.

The Court of Justice originally came into being in connection with the ECSC, but it now dispenses a legal function for each of the three communities. There are currently thirteen judges, each appointed for a six-year term. Like the members of the Commission they are not representatives of national interests but are required to act as independent judicial officers. They are protected from pressure from member state governments by two procedural arrangements. Firstly, although hearings are in public the deliberations of the judges are in secret. Secondly, a judge can only be removed from office by a unanimous vote of his colleagues to the effect that he is no longer capable of carrying out his functions. In order to speed up its process, the Court is divided into five chambers. The decisions which the Court reaches are read out in the presence of the parties, usually some two to three months after the hearing. The Court produces its own reports containing the basic facts, the summing-up by the Advocate General and the judgement. This official (there are six of them) is a stranger to English legal procedure. After the main hearing his tasks are to summarize the issues for, and to recommend a decision to, the Court. The Court is not bound by his views but great attention is paid to his arguments. The fact that the Court may not follow the Advocate General was well illustrated in 1973 in the *Continental Can* case when the Court took a fundamentally different line from that suggested by the Advocate General.

We have already given some indication of the kind of situations in which the Court is called upon to act. The Commission may call upon a member state to desist from some line of conduct which is contrary to the treaty, as for example the giving of state aid. If the member state does not desist the Commission can take the state to the Court. In the field of competition policy the Commission may by Decision forbid some action or impose fines. The enterprises concerned can appeal to the Court of Justice. Thus in one case several aniline dye producers appealed to the Court against the fines imposed upon them for an alleged concerted practice in relation to dye prices, and in another, Continental Can appealed to the Court against the Decision of the Commission forbidding its take-over of a Dutch can producer. The Parliament can take the

Council of Ministers to the Court, as it did in 1983 in connection with the alleged failure of the Council to implement the Common Transport Policy. Equally the Council can take Parliament to the Court as it did in 1986 in connection with an alleged procedural breach in connection with the adoption of the Community budget. Individuals can of course sue their governments for breaches of treaty rules in matters such as equal rights.

In addition to all these combinations of protagonists, mention should be made of the function of the Court in giving preliminary rulings for the benefit of national courts. Inevitably at national level issues arise which call for an interpretation of Community law, and this is a major task discharged by the Court. These preliminary rulings can be very important. We shall see later, when discussing State Monopolies, that such rulings, although relating to situations in one member state, have established precedents which have endowed the Commission with the authority to outlaw *generally* certain activities which have precluded the free flow of trade.

In conclusion we should note that the Single European Act provides for the Court of Justice to have attached to it another court which would have a right of appeal to it. The new lower court would be empowered to deal with certain kinds of cases brought by 'natural or legal persons'. It would not, however, be empowered to hear cases brought by Community institutions or member states, or cases referred for preliminary rulings.

The European Parliament

The location of its activities is complex. Until 1981 one third of the Parliamentary plenary sessions were held in Luxembourg – the remaining two thirds were held at Strasbourg in France in a building which belongs to the Council of Europe. In July 1981 Parliament decided not to hold any more of its plenary sessions in Luxembourg. This provoked the Government of Luxembourg to complain to the Court of Justice but in 1983 the Court rejected the Luxembourg plea. Over three quarters of Parliament's secretariat, which in total numbers about 2800,[1] is based in Luxembourg. As a result there has been a good deal of expensive transportation of eurocrats, machinery and documentation between Luxembourg and Strasbourg. This by no means exhausts the locational complications. In April 1983 Parliament held a plenary session for the first time in Brussels in the Palais de Congrès. Parliamentary committee

---

1. Many of these are translators.

meetings are held in Brussels and in the capital of the country holding the Presidency of the Council of Ministers. Parliamentary group meetings are held in Strasbourg and in Brussels. It seems possible that in the longer term most of the plenary sessions will be held in Brussels and that most of the secretariat will move in the same direction. This would certainly make good sense.

The Parliament is primarily consultative rather than legislative. A glance at the main policy areas of the EEC Treaty indicates that the Council has to consult the Parliament before deciding on a Commission proposal. In order to discharge its role the Parliament has a number of specialist committees (which representatives of the Commission may attend), and their reports are submitted to the House for debate and decision by vote in plenary session. Members can ask questions in the House and written questions can be addressed to the Commission. Representatives of the Council and the Commission attend the meetings and so it is possible to clarify matters on the spot.

A major power of the Parliament is that it can dismiss the Commission. For this to happen a motion of censure must be passed by a two-thirds majority of the votes cast, representing a majority of the members of the Assembly. This has never actually occurred but it was threatened at the end of 1972. The motion, which took the Commission to task for failing to introduce new proposals designed to increase Parliament's powers of control over the Community budget, was withdrawn before it was put to the vote. The very size of the implications of a motion of censure may make it of limited practical significance. In any case there are other limitations. The Parliament may dismiss the Commission but it has no control over the selection of the new Commissioners who would replace the old ones. Also the villain of the piece may not be the Commission but the intransigence of the Council. As we shall see in Chapter 3, Parliament also enjoys certain very significant powers in relation to the budget. It can propose modifications to certain kinds of expenditure, it can within limits amend certain other forms of expenditure and it has the power to adopt or reject the budget.

Originally, European parliamentarians were nominated by national parliaments by a process called indirect election. Each state adopted its own procedure of selection. But the Rome Treaty envisaged the possibility that in due course the members of the European Parliament would not be nominated by the national parliaments but would be elected by universal suffrage, a process referred to as direct election. For a considerable period no progress was made on this issue, but in 1974 there were signs that movement was possible. The European Parliament decided to press the matter of direct elections, and the Paris Summit communiqué of December 1974 indicated that the Heads of State and of Government awaited with interest these Parliamentary deliberations and envisaged the possibility that direct elections could take place in or after 1978. The UK, whilst not opposing the idea of direct elections, reserved its position on the ground that renegotiation was not complete. The Danish Government also chose to reserve its position. In January 1975 a new draft convention on direct elections was adopted by an overwhelming majority in the European Parliament, and at the European Council at Rome in December 1975 it was formally agreed that direct elections should be held in May or June 1978. During 1976 a good deal of effort was devoted to hammering out the direct election details. The Council of Ministers finally approved and signed the Decision and Act relating thereto in September 1976.

The first direct elections to the European Parliament were not held until June 1979. The second were held in June 1984. Currently the European Parliament has 518 members: 81 each from West Germany, France, Italy and the UK; 60 from Spain; 25 from the Netherlands; 24 each from Belgium, Greece and Portugal, 16 from Denmark, 15 from Ireland and 6 from Luxembourg. The Iberian members are, as a transitional arrangement, not directly elected. The Members of the European Parliament form political rather than national groups. As of 2 May 1986 they were divided as follows:

Socialists	172
Christian Democrats in the European Peoples Party	119
European Democrats	63
Communists and Allies	46
Liberal and Democratic Reformist Group	41
European Renewal and Democratic Alliance	34
Rainbow Group	20
European Right	16
Non-affiliated	7

The Economic and Social Committee

This body,[1] which operates in respect of EEC and Euratom matters,

1. It has a secretariat of about 440.

and its ECSC counterpart, is purely consultative. The total membership of Ecosoc is 189 and is made up as follows:

France	24
West Germany	24
Italy	24
UK	24
Spain	21
Belgium	12
Netherlands	12
Greece	12
Portugal	12
Denmark	9
Ireland	9
Luxembourg	6

The membership is representative of the various categories of economic and social life and in particular includes representatives of producers, workers, farmers, merchants, the liberal professions, transport operators and the general interest. The members are selected by the Council from lists submitted by member states. A glance at the EEC Treaty indicates that on a range of issues, before action is taken by the Council, Ecosoc must be consulted. Commentators do not, however, assign any great weight to its advisory role. The truth is that, as indicated earlier, the main power in the Community lies with the Council and the Commission.

European Political Cooperation

Whilst this book is primarily concerned with economic matters, we did note in Chapter 1 that the ultimate hope was that the process of integration would spill over from the economic to the political sphere. Given then that the fruits of integration were not conceived of as being purely economic, it is appropriate that we should give some consideration to the political impact of the European Community. Quite simply, a spillover has occurred – to an important degree.

Attempts at political integration are long-standing – as we have seen within the Six they go back to the EDC and EPC era. Subsequently, a number of political initiatives were launched. For example, in 1960 the French President, General de Gaulle, following bilateral talks with the other Five, proposed the setting up of a supreme authority to formulate common foreign and defence policies. A summit of the Six was held in Paris in February 1961. This in turn led to the establishment of a committee to examine the problem of political cooperation, initially under the chairmanship of Christian Fouchet (of France). A second summit was held at Bad Godesberg near Bonn in July 1961. The Bonn Declaration issued at the end of the meeting contained three decisions. Political cooperation between the Six should be adopted on a regular basis leading in due course to a joint policy. Heads of State and of Government should meet regularly to concert policies. The summit members also instructed the Fouchet Committee to submit proposals 'on means and ways which would make it possible to give a statutory character to the unification of their peoples as soon as possible'. Later in 1961 the French Government put a 'Draft Treaty establishing a Union of States' to the Committee. The institutions proposed were as follows: (a) a Council of Heads of State and of Government and of foreign ministers whose unanimous decisions would be binding on members; (b) a European Parliament with power of interrogation and deliberation but having no decision-making role; (c) a European Political Commission, in Paris, to be staffed by senior officials of the foreign ministries of each participating state. The aim of this was to achieve common foreign and defence policies. There was to be a general review after three years which it seemed could lead to steps being taken to bring the European Communities within the union.

Disagreements between France and the Five soon became evident, although the Dutch had been distinctly nervous about the implications from the outset. The other Five were concerned because they saw the defence arrangements as being outside NATO and the ambit of the Atlantic Alliance. They also saw a threat to the existing communities – the supra-national elements of the Paris and Rome Treaties could be lost if they were subsumed within the new union which was clearly based on the unanimity principle. Although a later draft of the Fouchet plan went quite a way to allay fears, a third draft, drawn up by de Gaulle himself, went back on these accommodations and a reference to economic matters being within the competence of the union opened up all the old fears about a watering down of supra-nationality. The plan ultimately foundered on UK participation. Originally the Dutch and Belgians had indicated that their participation was contingent upon the British being involved in the discussions – it should be remembered that the UK was then negotiating for membership of the EEC and its sister bodies. This the French refused to accept but a compromise was reached in December 1961. The UK was to be kept informed and membership of the union would be automatic for new members of the economic communities. However, ultimately the problem was raised again in April 1962 when the UK pressed its desire to take part in the discussions. This in turn precipitated a split within the Six. France, Germany, Italy and Luxembourg were willing to continue discussing the text of the treaty, to agree it, to communicate it to the UK and, if the latter did not have a major objection, to put it into effect. But Belgium and the Netherlands agreed only to examine the project and communicate it to the UK – they would not sign it until the UK had become a member of the economic communities. This was sufficient to provoke a termination of the formal negotiations.

Thereafter, despite other developments such as the de Gaulle–Adenauer[1] Franco-German treaty of friendship and cooperation, there was a distinct cooling on the political front. After the 1963 French rebuff to the British bid for membership of the three communities the other members showed their strong disapproval of de Gaulle's actions, temporarily bringing the Brussels machinery to a halt. By mid 1963 a formula for achieving progress on the economic plane was found and the EEC began to gain ground. The disappearance of Adenauer from the stage and his replacement by Erhard was a blow to further progress on the Franco-German front. The supra-nationality crisis by 1965–6 did nothing to cement trust between the Six. The accession to the French Presidency of Georges Pompidou in 1969 did, however, open up a more cooperative era. The participants at the Hague Summit agreed to instruct their foreign ministers to study the best way to achieve progress in respect of political unification – a report was expected by July 1970. The foreign ministers duly reported in July 1970, and their 'Luxembourg Report', *The Problem of Political Unification* (EC, Council of Ministers, 1970), inaugurated the Davignon (named after the Belgian diplomat) or political cooperation procedure.

The political cooperation procedure has been separate from the institutions of the European Community. Its membership has, however, been identical with that of the Community. It has not compelled the member states to agree on any issue. There has been no majority voting. It has been essentially an exercise in inter-governmental cooperation in which the member states have endeavoured to iron out common posi-

1. Konrad Adenauer was the West German Chancellor. He and de Gaulle had close personal links and successfully strove to establish good relations between their two countries.

tions and to agree on common actions in foreign-policy matters. In the words of the Luxembourg Report:

The objectives of this cooperation are as follows:
- to ensure, through regular exchanges of information and consultations, a better mutual understanding on the great international problems;
- to strengthen their solidarity by promoting the harmonization of their views, the coordination of their positions, and, where it seems possible and desirable, common actions.

Not all foreign-affairs matters have come within the purview of this system. Defence was excluded – for the most part that has been a NATO function. However, since 1980 significant moves have taken place, encouraged by the UK, France and West Germany, to introduce discussion of security matters regardless of the sensitivities of some smaller states. Disarmament, on the other hand, has been frequently discussed. The main focus has been on foreign policy towards non-member countries, and so issues which have divided members, such as Northern Ireland, have been taboo. There have been a number of other topics which have been out of bounds, of which West Berlin is just one instance.

At the top of the political pyramid has been the European Council. Under that title it did not exist when the mechanism of political cooperation first began to operate. As we saw earlier the Heads of State and of Government have met three times a year, and foreign-policy matters as well as European Communities matters have come within the ambit of their consideration. It will be recalled that the Paris Summit communiqué of 1974 also provided for them to meet as often as necessary in the context of political cooperation. In practice, the major burden of cooperation has fallen on the foreign ministers, and it should be noted that they were the original focus of activity when the system first began to operate in 1970. The Presidency of these foreign ministerial meetings has rotated alphabetically and has run for a term of six months, in parallel with the Presidency of the Council of Ministers. Theoretically such meetings were supposed to take place twice in each six-month Presidency, but in fact they have occurred more often, frequently being held at the same time as the Council of Ministers' meetings in Brussels or Luxembourg.

The system has worked with the minimum of bureaucracy. There was until recently no permanent secretariat. Meetings of ministers and officials have been organized by the foreign ministry of the country which was providing the Presidency. In order to pave the way for such ministerial meetings, a steering body, called the Political Committee,[1] was

1. The Political Committee was part of the original machinery established in 1970.

established. It has consisted of the senior foreign-policy civil servants of the Community countries. These political directors, as they have been called, have met once a month. In addition to preparing for the meetings of the foreign ministers, the Committee has acted in a similar way for other meetings including the European Council and the UN General Assembly. There has indeed been something of a parallel between the roles of Coreper and the Political Committee. A series of expert working groups were established to cover geographical areas and particular issues. These groups were made up of national civil servants and operated under the jurisdiction of the Political Committee and reported to it.

The hammering out of common positions has been very much in the hands of the foreign ministers and their senior civil servants in the Political Committee. The instruments of cooperation have, however, been diverse. The cooperating partners have kept in touch with each other via a special coded telex network known as COREU (after the French *correspondance européenne*). Although there have been no common embassies abroad,[1] member state ambassadors of the foreign capitals have often worked together. For example, during the siege of the American Embassy in Tehran, the ambassadors protested in unison to the Ayotollahs. At the United Nations in New York the ambassadors of the member states have endeavoured to ensure that they all voted the same way.

Originally there was a lot of opposition to the involvement of the EC Commission in the political cooperation mechanism. However, it came to be realized that Community policy and political cooperation were capable of being at cross purposes, and so a liaison system came to be established. Apparently, since 1974, the position of the EC Commission has been satisfactory – the President and members of the Commission have been able to attend meetings of the foreign ministers without restriction.

The Single European Act 1986 has been of considerable significance for political cooperation. In the first place the Act formally recognizes European Political Cooperation, alongside the European Communities, as one of the twin pillars of European unity. In most significant fashion it declares that the High Contracting Parties will endeavour to jointly formulate and implement 'a European foreign policy'.[2] They have undertaken to inform and consult each other on foreign-policy matters

---

1. The EC Commission has a number of offices abroad.
2. Security matters are also referred to although the emphasis is on economic aspects. There is also a provision which guarantees that cooperation in NATO and WEU will not be undermined.

so that their combined influence is exercised as effectively as possible through the convergence of their positions and the implementation of joint action. The European Parliament is to be kept informed and its views taken into account. It is once more recognized that the external policy of the European Communities and European Political Cooperation must be consistent, and to this end the EC Commission will be 'fully associated' with the proceedings of political cooperation. A secretariat in Brussels has now been created to assist the Presidency in preparing and implementing the activities of political cooperation.

The obvious question is, how successful has political cooperation been? This is not an easy question to answer since much of its work is of a diplomatic kind which by its nature is veiled in secrecy. The impression which emerges is that it has been quite successful in bringing positions closer together and in enabling members to act in concert. Ardent admirers will point to the fact that the Nine were able to speak with one voice at the Helsinki Conference on European security and were a powerful force in determining the western stance in the follow-up meetings. They will also point to the Community's common approach to the Middle East as exemplified by the Venice Declaration of 1980. The Community was also able to agree on the imposition of economic sanctions on Rhodesia after 1975 (in concert with the UN), on Iran after the taking of hostages in 1980, on the Soviet Union and Poland after the imposition of martial law in 1981, with some wavering on Argentina in 1982 after the invasion of the Falklands and on Israel after the invasion of Lebanon in 1982.

A limited common response was also forthcoming in 1986 in the face of alleged Syrian involvement in international terrorism. During the same year the Twelve, although divided, managed to devise a formula to which all could subscribe in connection with South African sanctions. In so doing they were able to go some way to satisfy international opinion. There have, however, been failures. The inability to agree on the Cyprus question, the inordinate delay in responding to the Russian invasion of Afghanistan and the lack of a powerful response by the Community in 1983 to the Russian shooting down of a South Korean airliner are three instances. Nevertheless there is no doubt that the political cooperation mechanism is highly valued by the Twelve, and it is highly valued because, taking a broad view, it works. It has gone some way to confound those who in earlier days tended to see the Community as an 'economic giant and a political dwarf'.

3   The Community Budget and Borrowing Powers

The primary focus of this chapter is the Community budget. This relates to the taxing and spending of the Community. At the end of the chapter we shall consider the ability of the Community to borrow money.

If the EEC had been merely a common market the financial transactions under the Community budget would have been small. The member states would have had merely to make provision for the raising of money to pay for an administrative and judicial machine designed to set and keep in motion the free flow of goods, services and factors of production. However, the Rome Treaty was less modest in its aims since it envisaged policies and institutions which involved spending on a scale which went well beyond the employment of eurocrats and judges. In the first instance these policies and institutions included the CAP and the EAGGF, social policy and the ESF and overseas trade and aid policy and the European Development Fund (EDF). The EDF was the aid part of the trade and aid policy which the Six devised for their colonial and ex-colonial dependencies. Later the above three were joined by, amongst others, regional policy and the ERDF.

How the budget is financed

In the early days the Community budget was financed by direct contributions from member states, and percentage contributions were stipulated for each country. This arrangement was provided for under Article 200 of the Rome Treaty. The largest countries – France, West Germany and Italy – paid the biggest percentage contributions, Belgium and the Netherlands paid a good deal less, and not surprisingly Luxembourg paid very little indeed. The reader should, however, note that there were separate percentage contribution systems for different categories of spending such as the operational side of the budget, the EAGGF, the ESF and the EDF. The variation of particular member state contributions between the different types of spending was a reflection of two main factors – differences of ability to pay and differences of obligation and interest. Thus whilst Italy paid the same percentage contribution as West Germany and France in respect of the operational part of the budget, her weaker economic position was reflected in the fact that she paid proportionately less than the other two in connection with all other categories of spending. Differences of historical responsibility and of economic interest explain why the percentage contributions of France and West Germany to the EDF were comparatively high. In the case of France it was a reflection of economic obligations to her extensive overseas territories. In the case of West Germany it was recognized that since she would now enjoy trade access to these territories she should by way of *quid pro quo* bear a fair share of the associated aid burden.

Article 201 of the Rome Treaty envisaged that ultimately these national contributions might be replaced by a system of financing based on what were called the Community's *own resources*. In particular, Article 201 identified the proceeds of the common external tariff as one such resource. The idea of shifting to a more *communautaire* system in which the budget revenue was based on own resources was approved by the Heads of State and of Government at the Hague Summit of 1969. The member states formally agreed when in 1970 they took the enabling Decision. The Six in fact decided that own resources should include not only the proceeds of the common external tariff but also the income stemming from agricultural import levies together with a VAT component. All this requires further elaboration.

Prior to the introduction of the own resources system, the proceeds of both the common external tariff and agricultural import levies accrued to the national exchequers – the place to which they had gone in the days before the formation of the EEC. These proceeds were in truth the Community's own resources and thus the member states were merely custodians pending the development of the own resources system. Under this new system the duties derived from applying the common external tariff were to be paid over to Brussels – member states were allowed to retain 10 per cent to cover their collection costs. The new system also required member states to pay over to Brussels the proceeds of levies imposed on agricultural imports coming into the Community from without. These were an integral part of the CAP and were designed to raise the price of imports and prevent the latter from undermining agricultural product prices within the Community. Again 10 per cent could be retained by the member states to cover collection costs. There was in fact another source of agricultural income, namely sugar storage levies. The

VAT component is somewhat more complex, and it should be added that in budget theology it is not strictly a true own resource. In Chapter 5 we shall see that the community decided to adopt the VAT as the common form of turnover tax. Under the 1977 Sixth VAT Directive the Six agreed on a common assessment base – a common collection of goods and services upon which VAT would be levied. The original own resources system required the member states to pay to Brussels the proceeds of up to a 1 percentage point VAT upon that common assessment base. This requirement was the subject of much misunderstanding. Some commentators appeared to believe that member states were required to pay 1 per cent of their national VAT revenue to Brussels. Were that to have been the case then member states could have reduced their contribution to the budget by lowering their national VAT rates – the latter are still determined by the member states since a harmonized rate level has not yet been agreed. It should be added that although the new own resources system was agreed in 1970 it did not become fully operational until 1980.

The relative importance of the various components of own resources is shown in Table 1. Quite clearly VAT provided more than half the own resources revenue. It should also be mentioned that member states were originally only obliged to make *up to* a 1 percentage point VAT contribution. Any movement beyond the 1 per cent level would have had to be agreed by the member states and would have been likely to give rise

Table 1. Community budget revenue 1985 (million ECU[1])

		% of total own resources
1 Customs duties	8 310·1	32·0
2 Agricultural levies	1 121·7	4·3
3 Sugar levies	1 057·4	4·0
4 VAT (and VAT-related) revenue	15 219·1	58·7
5 Financial contributions (GNP)	260·9	1·0
6 Total own resources	25 969·2	100·0
7 Non-repayable advances	1 981·6	
8 Miscellaneous revenue and other items	466·4	
Total	28 417·2	

Note: 1. In 1985 1 ECU = £0·57 (approx.).
Source: EC Commission, *Nineteenth General Report on the Activities of the European Communities*, OOPEC, 1986, p. 66.

Table 2. Community budget expenditure by sector 1985 (million ECU)[1]

	Appropriations for Commitment	%	Appropriations for Payments	%
1 EAGGF Guarantees	19 955	65·18	19 955	70·18
2 Structural Policies				
EAGGF Guidance	655	2·14	632	2·22
Specific agricultural measures	56	0·19	55	0·19
Fisheries	154	0·51	111	0·39
European Regional Development Fund	2 289	7·48	1 610	5·66
Mediterranean programmes	140	0·46	10	0·04
Miscellaneous regional	67	0·22	42	0·15
Transport	91	0·30	35	0·13
European Social Fund	2 010	6·57	1 410	4·96
Miscellaneous social	182	0·60	180	0·64
Education and culture	20	0·07	20	0·07
Environment and consumers	18	0·06	15	0·05
3 Research, Energy and Industry				
Energy policy	144	0·47	86	0·31
Research and investment	841	2·75	561	1·98
Information and innovation	21	0·07	13	0·05
Industry and internal market	38	0·13	44	0·16

4 Repayments and Reserves				
Repayments to member states	1 070	3·50	1 070	3·76
Other payments	23	0·08	23	0·08
Miscellaneous guarantees	172	0·56	172	0·61
Reserves	5	0·02	5	0·02
5 Development Cooperation and Non-Member Countries				
European Development Fund	—	—	—	—
Food Aid	635	2·08	507	1·79
Cooperation with Latin America and Asian developing countries	285	0·93	142	0·50
Specific and exceptional measures	101	0·33	81	0·29
Cooperation with Mediterranean countries	236	0·77	248	0·87
Miscellaneous	63	0·21	63	0·22
6 Staff and Administration	1 332	4·35	1 332	4·69
7 Total	30 616	100·00	28 433	100·00

Note: 1. Figures do not always add up exactly, due to rounding.
Source: EC Commission, *Nineteenth General Report on the Activities of the European Communities*, OOPEC, 1985, Table 1, p. 55.

to a renegotiation of the whole package. In the first half of the 1980s, budget expenditure rose faster than own resource revenue from customs duties and import levies, and as a result the VAT rate had to be raised to compensate. In 1980 it was 0·73, in 1982 it was raised to 0·92 and in 1984 it hit the ceiling of 1 per cent. Clearly if this trend had continued and member states had refused to make any accommodation the budget would have run out of resources. We shall return to this topic later.

How budget monies are spent

Table 2 shows the breakdown of the budget for 1985 under the main expenditure heads. The distinction between appropriations for commitment and appropriations for payment needs to be explained. The Community sometimes approves programmes of expenditure which extend over several years – only a part of such a programme falls in the budget year in question. Appropriations for commitment cover such future as well as present spending. Appropriations for payment refer to the spending of the current year and must of course be matched by current income. From Table 2 we can see that appropriations for payment in 1985 were 28 433 million ECU which was almost exactly equal to the 28 417 million ECU budget revenue shown in Table 1.

It is overwhelmingly apparent from even a cursory glance at Table 2 that budget spending in 1985 was dominated by agriculture. This is a persistent feature. CAP spending represented 72 per cent of the total. Under the CAP heading 70 per cent of spending was devoted to guarantee purposes – i.e. spending involved in buying up and storing surplus produce and expenditure necessary to finance the loss when surplus produce is bought up at relatively high Community prices and sold in the world market at relatively low prices. By contrast CAP guidance spending – i.e. expenditure to improve farm structures and efficiency – absorbed only 2 per cent of the total budget appropriations. The ERDF and ESF between them claimed only 11 per cent of the available funds, which is small beer – as indeed is everything else.[1]

The ECSC and Euratom

Up to this point the discussion has focused on taxing and spending in relation to activities in the EEC. We must now say a few words about the budgetary arrangements of the ECSC and Euratom. Originally each

1. This refers to appropriations for payment.

of the three communities – ECSC, Euratom and EEC – had its own separate budgetary arrangement. There were in fact five budgets – the EEC budget, the ECSC administrative budget, the ECSC operational budget, the Euratom operational budget and the Euratom research and investment budget. However, as time has passed these have become increasingly intertwined. The reader will recall from Chapter 2 that under the 1965 Brussels Treaty the executives of the three communities were to be fused. As a result of that Merger Treaty, from the end of 1968 the administrative budget of the ECSC and the operating budget of Euratom were combined with the EEC budget, in what we now call the Community budget. The practical effect of this is that the Community budget now includes appropriations to cover the cost of administering the ECSC and Euratom as well as the EEC. This combined administrative cost is shown as item 6 in Table 2. It should also be noted that the ECSC has a power to raise income by imposing a levy of up to 1 per cent of the value of coal and steel output. Since, following the fusion of the executives, the cost of administering the ECSC is now borne by the Community budget, the ECSC is by way of compensation required to pass over some of its levy income to the Community budget. This is included in item 8 (Miscellaneous revenue) in Table 1. During recent years the financial position of the ECSC has been difficult, notably because of the crisis in the steel industry. Falling prices and output have undermined the levy income and the Council of Ministers has been unwilling to agree to any great increase in the levy for fear of making the position of producers even worse. At the same time the ECSC has been under pressure to spend more to help its troubled industries. In order to supplement the inadequate levy income the Council of Ministers has made two special arrangements. Firstly, it has relieved the ECSC by reducing the amount of levy income which has to be transferred to the Community. Secondly, member states have made *ad hoc* contributions to the ECSC – under Article 49 of the Paris Treaty the coal and steel Community is allowed to receive gifts. These independent incomes form part of the still separate ECSC operational budget. For completeness it should be added that Euratom spending is now totally under the Community budget. This follows from the fact that under the 1970 Treaty of Luxembourg the research and investment spending of Euratom was brought under the central budgetary system – it is included in item 3 of Table 2.

The adoption of the budget

We have now explained what the Community budget consists of. We have not yet explained how the budget comes into existence. This is the topic to which we now turn. The initiating role is as usual vested in the EC Commission. It collates estimates of the various kinds of spending and embodies them in a *preliminary draft budget* which it submits to the Council of Ministers. The latter subjects the preliminary draft to a 'first reading'. Acting on a qualified majority voting basis the Council adopts[1] what is called the *draft budget*. Needless to say the budget which emerges from the Council of Ministers does not have to be the same as the one presented to it by the Commission. In practice it usually gets cut down in size. The draft budget is then dispatched to the European Parliament. There then occurs what euphemistically may be called a dialogue between the Parliament and the Council in which both sides can propose changes. At the end of the day the hope is that the European Parliament will be disposed to adopt the budget, thus bringing the process to a close. For the record it should be mentioned that the present budgetary powers of the Parliament derive from the Luxembourg Treaty of 1970 and the Brussels Treaty of 1975.

In order to understand the relationship which exists between the institutions in respect of the budget we have to look a little more closely at the powers which have been conferred upon them. To this end we must first recognize that budget expenditure is divided into two broad categories – compulsory (sometimes called obligatory) and non-compulsory (non-obligatory). Compulsory is defined as expenditure resulting from the Treaty or acts in accordance therewith. The reader may find this definition confusing rather than enlightening. He may wonder how budget expenditure can result from anything other than the Treaty and acts in accordance therewith. The reader is, however, advised that no benefit would be derived from delving into the logic of this nomenclature. It is more fruitful to note that in practice compulsory expenditure has included EAGGF guarantee spending (e.g. buying surpluses), some EAGGF guidance spending (e.g. grants to improve farm structures and efficiency), interest rate rebates on loans granted in connection with the EMS, some food aid given to developing countries, and financial assistance to African, Caribbean and Pacific states and to non-member Mediterranean countries. Clearly this expenditure is dominated by

1. The Rome Treaty actually speaks of the Council *establishing* the draft budget.

EAGGF guarantee spending which of course also dominates the budget. The non-compulsory section has included the balance of EAGGF guidance spending, some food aid, the expenditures of the ESF and ERDF, spending on energy, research, information, industry and transport and the salaries and pensions of members of the staff of the Community institutions, together with administrative costs. The exact division between these two categories has been a matter of dispute between Council and Parliament. In rough terms compulsory expenditure absorbs about three quarters of the budget appropriations – the remaining quarter is consumed by the non-compulsory section. Although there is a dialogue about both categories of expenditure, at the end of the day by virtue of Article 203 Council has the last word on compulsory spending and the Parliament has the last word on the non-compulsory category. The reader will quickly realize that Council has the final say over the great bulk of the budget.

In respect of the non-compulsory section, Parliament's final word means that it can increase or decrease the total of such spending and of course it can transfer expenditure between Heads. It must, however, be added that Parliament's power to increase such spending is not unconstrained. This arises from the fact that, whilst there is no limit to the degree to which compulsory expenditure can be increased (provided the Council and Parliament are so minded), the Commission is required to calculate and thus determine the maximum amount by which non-compulsory spending may be increased. This is called the maximum rate. The maximum rate is governed by three factors – the trends in the previous year in member states' (a) real Gross Domestic Product, (b) public spending and (c) cost of living. In, for example, the case of the 1985 budget those three factors produced an indicated maximum rate of increase of 8 per cent.

However, things in this area of policy are rarely as simple as they seem – the reader is warned that the maximum rate of increase may not prove to be the maximum! This arises from the fact that the European Parliament enjoys a margin for manoeuvre equal to half the maximum rate. The relevant Treaty provision declares that if in the draft budget the actual increase proposed by the Council of Ministers is *more* than half the permitted maximum rate, then Parliament can itself add to that proposed increase a further increase equal to half the maximum rate. It follows that if the Council was in generous mood (a possible but improbable circumstance) and itself proposed an increase equal to the maximum rate, Parliament could add an extra half so that the actual increase would be one and a half times the maximum rate. Having said that, it is still true to say that normally[1] there is a definite upper limit to the increase in non-compulsory spending whereas, in principle, compulsory spending has no limit. This discrimination whereby, for example, spending on unwanted agricultural surpluses has no upper limit, whilst spending to train workers and to create new jobs (ESF and ERDF) is limited, seems difficult to justify.

We noted earlier that it is the function and prerogative of the European Parliament finally to adopt the budget. This also carries with it the possibility that the Parliament may find the products of the dialogue unsatisfactory. If indeed the Parliament believes that there are 'important reasons' why the budget should not be adopted then it can reject it and ask for a new draft budget to be submitted to it. For this to happen the motion to reject must be supported by two thirds of the votes cast and those votes must represent a majority of the members of the Parliament.

Such a rejection has occurred. In Chapter 2 we discussed the first direct election of the European Parliament. That Parliament had not long been elected before it began to flex its muscles and the budget became the main source of contention. The contest originally centred on votes for additional spending in 1979 but finally focused on the Community budget for 1980.

The lines of battle became clear in November 1979. Parliament refused to make time available for consideration of a special vote to release extra funds to buy surplus farm products. Tension was heightened when later in the month the Council rejected a Parliamentary move designed to cut the amount of money available for buying up surplus dairy products. In December attention centred on the £10·8 billion Community budget for 1980. Parliament wanted a larger overall appropriation and a switch in emphasis away from agriculture to areas such as the ERDF. The Council of Budget Ministers considered Parliament's demands but replied with promises of possible agricultural curbs in the following spring and a number of small concessions. This did not satisfy the Parliament, and on 13 December it voted by 288 to 64, with 1 abstention, to throw out the budget. The Community remained without a budget until July 1980 – by that time the Commission had produced its preliminary draft budget for 1981! The reader will obviously wonder how the Community can carry on its activities if it has no budget. The answer is

1. We use the word 'normally' because there is a provision whereby, if Council and Parliament agree, a rate greater than the maximum rate can apply. This of course requires a formal act of approval on the part of both those parties, whereas overshooting of the maximum rate of the kind referred to above is a built-in possibility which does not require a specific formal act of approval.

that if the budget remains unadopted it can spend per month one twelfth of what was spent in the previous year. Parliament has flexed its rejecting muscles more than once! In 1984 it did it again when, because the Community was running out of budget resources, the Council sent to Parliament a draft budget which did not cover the whole year in respect of certain items. Parliament rejected this as an unacceptable practice, and for several months the Community was once more back on the twelfths system. This latter experience was repeated for a short period in 1987.

A brief mention must be made of the auditing of the Community budget. In earlier days external auditing was carried out by the Audit Board and the ECSC Auditor. As a result of the 1975 Treaty, which conferred the previously discussed budget adoption power upon the Parliament, a European Court of Auditors was created. It began work in 1977.

Budget problems and reform

It will be apparent from what has gone before and from Chapter 1 that the budget has been a controversial issue. Some of this controversy has been concerned with the division of powers between the Parliament and the Council of Ministers and with the details of the budget-making process. We shall not concern ourselves further with such issues. Our task will be to examine the economic aspects and impact of the budget. This will require us to consider matters such as the equity, expenditure structure and distributional role of the budget as well as the need for additional resources. It should be added that these topics are highly interconnected.

The need for equity

Criticism has been directed at the budget for its lack of equity. That in turn raises the question of what we mean by equity. In public finance theory a distinction is made between horizontal and vertical equity. Horizontal equity requires that equally situated individuals should be taxed equally. Thus in the context of personal income taxation, horizontal equity requires that two families with the same income should pay the same amount of tax. The phrase 'equally situated' would require that families of *equal size* and so forth should pay the same tax. The concept of vertical equity flows naturally from the horizontal concept. If equals are to be taxed equally then unequals should be taxed unequally. Usually vertical equity has been translated into the ability-to-pay principle, according to which those most able to pay should pay the highest taxes. Very often therefore the notion of vertical equity is taken to be synonymous with progressivity.

If we look at Community budget revenue-raising it is difficult to see how its basic principles can satisfy either of these two equity criteria. Quite simply equals do not inevitably pay the same tax. Thus two countries may have the same GNP and the same GNP *per capita* but if one country imports more food from third countries than the other then it will correspondingly pay more levies into the budget. Equally the common external tariff component could lead to one country paying in more than the other. This would arise if one country's foreign trade was more oriented towards third countries than the other. Indeed, it has been pointed out that part of the UK's budget problem arose from its greater orientation towards the outside world. It should, however, be said that, notably in respect of non-agricultural products, this problem has declined more recently as trade with the Community has become proportionately more important. It is difficult to see how these two revenue sources accord with the vertical equity principle. There is certainly no reason to expect that richer countries will pay proportionately more levies and duties into the budget. It has also been maintained that the VAT element is unsatisfactory. Daniel Strasser (Director of Budgets in the Commission) has indeed pointed out that the VAT component has actually been regressive. There are a number of reasons for this including the fact that consumption in poorer countries is a higher proportion of GNP and it attracts VAT whereas other components, such as investment, do not.

The UK budget problem

There is, of course, another concept of equity, namely the benefit principle. It emphasizes the obvious point that the impact of a budget on an individual arises from what he gets out of it as well as what he pays into it. The benefit principle of taxation stresses the idea that those who reap the benefits of government expenditure should pay the taxes. This is a suitable concept with which to introduce the UK budget problem, the essence of which was that whilst the UK made a fair, indeed more than fair, contribution, her benefits were limited. We have already seen that the budget is dominated by CAP spending. Much of the money is devoted to buying up surpluses (i.e. guarantee spending). Since the UK is a relatively small producer (farming in the UK in 1981 represented just over 2 per cent of Gross Domestic Product whereas, for example, the figure for Ireland was close to 18 per cent) she got little back in the way of CAP guarantee spending. On the other hand, she was in a good position to benefit from the ERDF and the ESF, but since they commanded so little of the budget these return flows could not compensate for the smallness of her CAP benefits. This imbalance was expected to lead to the UK making a net contribution to the budget of £1·2 billion by 1980. The unfairness of this is heightened when it is recognized that whilst she would be a net contributor, and the biggest net contributor at that, she was in *per capita* terms one of the poorer countries in the Community – see Table 3.

Table 3. Estimated net budget receipts 1980 and per capita national income in 1979

	Estimated net budget receipts for 1980 (£m)	Per capita GDP 1979 relative to average	
		(a)	(b)
Belgium	} + 557	124	108
Luxembourg		125	111
Denmark	+ 188	138	116
France	− 48	116	112
Germany	− 724	135	118
Ireland	+ 289	49	61
Italy	+ 491	62	77
Netherlands	+ 193	117	105
UK	−1 203	76	91
Community		100	100

Note: GDP (a) is based on a straight exchange rate conversion; GDP (b) is based on 1979 purchasing power parities.
Source: Budget: W. Godley, 'The United Kingdom and the Community Budget' in W. Wallace (ed.), *Britain in Europe*, Heinemann, 1980, p. 73.
Per capita GDP (b): ibid.
Per capita GDP (a): D. Strasser, *The Finances of Europe*, OOPEC, 1980, p. 346.

The reader will recollect from Chapter 1 that one of the items included in the 1974–5 renegotiation was the subject of the UK contribution to the Community budget. It will also be recollected that at the Dublin Summit in 1975 a Correction Mechanism was agreed which was designed to limit the UK contribution to the budget. Unfortunately, the provisions of the Correction Mechanism were such that it was never triggered into operation, and it was thought to be unlikely that it would be triggered in 1980. It will also be recalled that the Correction Mechanism applied to gross contributions whereas, as we have recognized, the inequality in UK eyes was the net impact. Equally it should be noted that there was a limit to the refund allowed. Even if triggered, the maximum refund was quite incapable of achieving the broad balance between payments and receipts which the Conservative Government aimed for. The British Prime Minister, Margaret Thatcher, therefore demanded a cut of £1 billion in the UK contribution, and this was discussed at the Dublin Summit which opened in November 1979. However, the Community was not prepared to make such a concession – the maximum reduction offered was £350 million. The UK was not willing to accept this proposal but signified its willingness to compromise, and the matter was put off until a later summit. The EC Commission was asked to prepare more detailed proposals for extra spending to help the UK. The French for their part intimated that progress on the budget issue depended on the UK being willing to be more accommodating on other issues such as the fisheries policy and access to North Sea oil.

The budget debate was renewed at the European Council in Luxembourg in April 1980. Matters were complicated by the fact that the rest of the Community continued to couple agreement on the budget with other issues. Apart from the two previously mentioned, the UK was under pressure to accept an average 5 per cent farm price increase, although she wished to freeze the prices of products in surplus and to allow an increase of only 2·4 per cent on other products. The French also pressed for a Community-financed régime for sheep-meat. It will be recollected that France had defied the Court of Justice ruling that she should allow UK sheep-meat into the French market. The UK for her part resisted the coupling of all these issues with that of the budget and took the view that these other topics should be dealt with separately on their merits. In the upshot the summit failed to resolve the budget issue. The rest of the Community advanced their Dublin offer – the UK net contribution was to be set at £325 million. The size of the reduction still did not meet Mrs Thatcher's target but an equally important factor was that of duration. The offer was only guaranteed for 1980 whereas the UK was looking to an agreed reduction which would apply for several years. The summit broke up in some disarray with the UK indicating that it would veto the farm price increase until a better budget settlement was offered.

However, subsequent discussions within the Council of Foreign

Ministers in May 1980, under the distinguished presidency of Emilio Colombo, solved the immediate budget problem. The UK net contribution in 1980 was reduced to £370 million and in 1981 it was to be £430 million. There would also be a concession in 1982 if the Community had, by that date, failed to agree on a restructuring of Community finances. The UK for its part agreed to an average 5 per cent increase in farm prices. A community régime for sheep-meat was agreed. The agreement on fisheries was, however, relatively loosely worded and the details were left for subsequent hard bargaining. As things transpired, a restructuring had not been agreed by 1982, and therefore further *ad hoc* annual rebates were agreed in respect of the UK for the years 1982, 1983 and 1984, whilst from 1985 onwards a new system was agreed which will be discussed below.[1]

Closing the gap – the MacDougall Report

We must now move away from the problem of the UK although we shall return to the subject later. However, before we shift the focus of attention it is important to note that although the UK's adoption of the benefit principle was one which also brought her benefits, that approach has one severe drawback – it does not change the distribution of income. Under such a system each individual gets what he pays for. There is no question of poorer individuals getting more than they pay for in tax at the expense of richer individuals who therefore get fewer benefits than they pay for in tax. It is however possible to envisage a Community budget which could redistribute in this way.

Before we turn to consider that possibility it is important to establish where the Community budget stands in relation to such a notion. We could, for example, point to the preamble to the Rome Treaty which refers to the desirability of 'reducing the differences existing between the various regions and the backwardness of the less favoured regions'.[2] That is indeed what the contracting parties declared, but it would be wrong to conclude that as a consequence such an evening out (or con-

1. These rebates were not always immediately forthcoming. In December 1982 Parliament blocked the 1982 rebate, not because it was opposed to it but partly because of accounting technicalities in connection with the rebate and partly because of its frustration at the delay in achieving a reform of the Community's financial system which would provide a long-term solution to the UK problem. However, Parliament lifted its veto in the following February, having been satisfied that measures of reform were shortly to be proposed. The rebate for 1983 was not agreed until the middle of 1984 when the budget system was finally reformed – see below.
2. We can interpret differences between regions to include differences between states.

vergence of standards of living) has been one of the functions of the Community budget. It has had no such objective – its role has been to finance whatever policies the Community decided to establish and finance. In any case, even if such a redistribution was an objective of the budget, its effectiveness would be severely limited by its size – in 1984 it represented only 0·9 per cent of Community GNP and only 2·7 per cent of national public spending. To be able to exercise a significant evening-out role the budget would have to be much bigger. The reader will, however, be aware that although the budget was not designed to even out, it does redistribute! The problem is that its redistributive effect can be haphazard. It can take from the relatively poor and give to, amongst others, the relatively rich – as the UK case illustrated.

Some consideration has been given to the question of whether a larger budget with an evening-out role would be desirable. In 1974 the Commission invited a group of experts to examine the role of public finance in European integration. The resulting MacDougall Report (EC Commission 1977b) was published in 1977.

The group noted that whereas public expenditure by the member states within the Community was about 45 per cent of the gross product of the area as a whole, expenditure by the Community institutions was less than 1 per cent. They also noted that in federal systems such as those in West Germany and the USA quite a high proportion of public spending was federal, as opposed to constituent state, spending. Indeed, federal spending tended to be in the region of 20–25 per cent of gross product. The group was particularly struck by the extent to which federal spending took the form of transfers from richer to poorer states within a union.

The group contemplated the possibility of increasing Community budget spending to federal levels. It was possible to conceive at a distant date of a European Federation, when the federal spending level of 20–25 per cent might be attained, An earlier stage of federation might involve a figure of 5–7 per cent, or 7·5–10 per cent if defence was included. However, they concentrated most attention on a much more modest pre-federal stage where the level might be 2–2·5 per cent.

Consideration was given to the reasons why such an increase might be desirable – in so doing the group focused on economic considerations rather than merely on the point that such increased spending would be symbolic of European unity. There might, for example, be economies of scale in concentrating expenditure at the Community level – perhaps this might be accompanied by a compensating reduction at national level. However, the main motive for envisaging an increase was concerned with redistribution, since they placed emphasis on the growth of Community-financed structural, cyclical, unemployment and regional policies. The purpose of such measures would be to reduce inter-regional differences in capital endowment and productivity. In other words, the budget would seek to facilitate convergence. The group also noted that political cohesion was likely to be fostered if the less prosperous regions were able to share in the general advance of living standards. A larger reformed budget could also act as a built-in stabilizer.

Such a development would require greater Community revenue, and the group opted for a further tranche of VAT resources. Although the expenditure would itself be redistributive, they also recommended the injection of an element of progressivity into budget income.

Reform at last

The reader will already sense that as the 1980s progressed the budgetary system was coming under increasing strain. A major problem arose from the limitation on the own resources available for the budget. As we saw earlier, expenditure was rising faster than own resources from customs duties and levies, and therefore the VAT rate had to be progressively increased until, as we noted above, in 1984 it reached the 1 per cent ceiling. Quite simply the Community was in danger of running out of own resources. Indeed it did so in 1984. Whilst in respect of their own domestic budgets member state governments have a more or less automatic right to cover any excess of expenditure by borrowing, the Community has no such automatic right. In principle the budget must balance. However, what the Community did in 1984 was to adopt a wholly *ad hoc* arrangement whereby member states were asked to make repayable advances in order to cover the budgetary shortfall. The same happened in 1985 except that on that occasion the advances were not repayable. Clearly the Community needed additional resources and the obvious answer was to raise the VAT rate above 1 per cent. Indeed the Commission produced a Green Paper in February 1983 – *The Future Financing of the Community* – in which it envisaged such a solution. It also gave considerations to injecting an element of progressivity into the contribution so that those countries which were most able to pay on the basis of *per capita* income would be hit hardest. The Commission also considered the 1979 (Lange) Resolution of the European Parliament, which called for a system of equalization transfers between the member states. The Commission, however, pointed out that the smallness of the budget precluded any possibility of significant egalitarian effects. But it did accept that a limited programme of transfers to the least prosperous states would be a possibility.

Additional income for the budget was also necessary if the deadlock over Iberian membership was to be broken, since their entrance was almost certainly going to add more to expenditure than to income.

There was also a further problem, namely the excessive slice of the budget which was devoted to agriculture – i.e. to the storage and sale at a loss of surpluses. Steps needed to be taken to grapple with the surplus problem. At the same time as the Community devised its temporary settlement of the UK budget problem, the Commission was charged with the task of carrying out a review of the operation and funding of Community policies. This was called the Mandate. The Commission duly reported in 1981 – *Report from the Commission of the European Communities to the Council pursuant to the mandate of 30 May 1980* (EC Commission, 1981a). In the event, the report did not produce the basis for a quick solution to the budget problem – hence the behaviour of Parliament in December 1982.[1] The message the Commission appears to have wanted to get across was this. The budget should not continue to be dominated by the CAP. In the depressed industrial circumstances of the times there was a need to shift the emphasis of budget spending towards the ERDF and ESF. If CAP spending was to be reduced then the gap between Community and world agricultural product prices would have to be narrowed. This appeared to mean that CAP prices would have to fall so as to discourage surpluses, although the Commission also seemed to be interested in the idea that world prices ought to be increased. Obviously, even if only the latter occurred, such a change would reduce the size of the export subsidy burden which fell upon the EAGGF when surplus Community produce was got rid of on the world market. It should, however, be recognized that an improvement in world prices would not be likely to occur unless the Community itself ceased to dump surpluses on the world market. A radical reduction in the farm price level within the Community or some other equally effective remedy therefore seemed inescapable. The Commission was also critical of other aspects of the CAP, including the degree to which the protection of farm incomes dominated price policy, and the open-ended nature of the guarantees accorded to products in structural surplus. More will be said on this subject in Chapter 8.

Finally there was the problem of the UK budgetary contribution, which needed to be settled on a permanent basis as opposed to a series of

1. See footnote 1 on p. 79 above.

ad hoc annual settlements – the European Parliament held this view very strongly. (It should be added that the UK was not the only country which made a disproportionate contribution – West Germany could also legitimately claim some relief.) It is also important to note that the UK was determined not to support any move to increase own resources unless (a) its long-standing complaint about its excessive contribution was dealt with and (b) farm spending was brought under control. Whilst the UK was committed to securing a rectification of its budgetary contribution it did ultimately accept that it should remain a net contributor.

The atmosphere began to improve in 1983 when the Stuttgart Summit adopted its Solemn Declaration on European Union and also agreed that there would have to be not only adequate budgetary resources but also budgetary fairness and budgetary discipline. The next step occurred in January 1984 when the Presidency of the Council of Ministers and the European Council passed into the skilled hands of France. The Council of Ministers made a breakthrough when it agreed (subject to an Irish reservation) to radically control milk production by means of quotas and agreed to other significant agricultural measures. At the Fontainebleau Summit in June 1984 the agricultural settlement was followed by an agreement to reform the budget. It was accepted that from 1986 the ceiling on VAT contributions would be raised by 1·4 per cent (the Commission had hoped for 2 per cent). The possibility of raising the ceiling to 1·6 per cent in 1988 was recognized, but this would require unanimity. The UK problem was dealt with by agreeing that from 1985 it would receive a rebate equal to 66 per cent of the difference between its share of VAT payments and its share of expenditure. The Summit also cleared the way for repayments to be made to the UK and West Germany in respect of 1983. It also re-affirmed the March 1984 Summit agreement on budgetary and financial discipline. This, amongst other things, required that net expenditure on agricultural markets should grow at a lower rate than the own resource base. In other words the CAP should progressively attract a smaller proportion of budget resources.

Whilst these reforms were a considerable step forward, it soon became clear that they did not deal with the problem of own resource inadequacy. By 1986 the Community appeared to be heading for another budgetary crisis since agricultural spending was still excessive – thanks to the continued accumulation of surpluses. It is true that at the end of 1986 the Council of Agricultural Ministers did take some tough decisions, particularly in the milk sector – we will consider these further in Chapter 8. However, these measures were only likely to help in the medium term, and by 1987 a budgetary shortfall of about 6 billion ECUs was being forecast. Early in 1987 the President of the EC Commission, Jacques Delors, put forward a new plan for the financing of the Community budget. It suggested an own resource ceiling up to 1992 of 1·4 per cent of Community GNP. The funds raised within this limit would be derived from four sources. The first would be agricultural levies but with no deduction for collection costs. The second would be the proceeds of a common external tariff – again with no deduction for the costs of collection. The third would be the proceeds of a 1 per cent levy on the VAT base – including goods which were zero-rated. The fourth would be a levy on what was to be called the additional base, i.e. the difference between the collection of goods which make up the VAT base and the GNP. The additional base levy would, for example, apply to items such as investment which are not included in the VAT base. The total GNP of each member state would therefore serve as a basis for financing the budget although the rates of the VAT base and the additional base would differ.

The Delors Plan was considered by the Heads of State and of Government at the Brussels Summit in July 1987. Unfortunately no agreement was forthcoming on the provision of additional long-term financing for the budget. Despite reference to the need for control of expenditure, as well as the need for greater revenues, the UK Prime Minister, Margaret Thatcher, rejected the package on the grounds that the provisions on controlling spending, particularly on agriculture, were inadequate. Work continued on the package, and it was hoped that sufficient progress would be made for agreement to be reached at the Copenhagen Summit in December 1987, but this did not happen. The immediate problem of the budgetary shortfall in 1987 was dealt with by switching to paying farmers in arrears rather than in advance and by other savings. The highly controversial oil seeds and fats tax (much opposed by the US) was rejected. It was designed to raise revenue and, by making products like margarine dearer, it would switch consumption to butter. As a result less would be spent on buying up surplus butter. The ultimate agreement may also go some way to meeting the demand of the southern members of the Community that the structural funds (social and regional) should be allocated a bigger proportion of the budget's resources. See Epilogue.

Borrowing powers

So far the emphasis in revenue raising has been on taxing. Governments can of course raise revenue by borrowing. Can the Community do likewise? The answer is that it can. A power to borrow has been enjoyed by the ECSC since its inception. Under Article 54 of the Paris Treaty the old High Authority and now the Commission can borrow on the international capital market with a view to lending to coal and steel enterprises in connection with expansion and modernization programmes. Under Article 56 it can also lend to create new employment opportunities, in or outside the coal and steel industries, for redundant coal and steel workers. Although the Commission can make grants under the Paris Treaty, borrowed funds must not be used for that purpose (Article 51). Originally the EEC Commission did not enjoy such a borrowing power. Nor, as we have seen, was there any question of automatically allowing budget expenditure to exceed tax revenue and financing the deficit by borrowing. The budget must balance. The EIB does of course enjoy substantial borrowing powers, and more will be said on that topic in Chapter 9. Subsequently, however, the EEC acquired its own (non-budget) borrowing powers. The first power was taken in 1975 and was designed to raise money on the international capital market in order to lend on to member states in balance of payments difficulties. Loans to Italy and Ireland were authorized in 1976. More recently, loans were made to France (1983), Greece (1985) and Portugal (1986–91 – see Chapter 1 on Portuguese accession). The other EEC power, which goes under the title of the New Community Instrument (the so-called Ortoli Facility), came into existence in 1978. On the basis of it the EEC raises long-term loans on the international capital market and then passes the money over to the EIB which uses it to make loans for investment projects. Loans have been primarily provided for infrastructure investments connected with regional development; energy projects which have helped the Community to attain greater independence, security and diversification in its energy supplies; promotion of innovation and new technologies (particularly in small and medium-sized firms) and reconstruction after earthquake disasters (Italy).

4 Tariff Barriers and the Customs Union

The immediate aim of the Rome Treaty was to promote the process of economic integration. Economic integration involves the removal of barriers to the free movement of goods, services, factors of production and possibly money and the creation of a situation in which the national economies are increasingly interconnected and enmeshed. Such a state of integration could be achieved by a planning mechanism. Let us think purely of the trade in goods. Country 1 could be instructed to produce good A and country 2 could be commanded to produce good B and so forth. They could also be commanded to exchange their surpluses of A and B and a price could be prescribed – i.e. so much A for so much B. However, the predominant economic mode of operation in Western Europe did not admit of such an arrangement. The integration of economies had to arise through competitive trade interpenetration. In simplistic terms, if country 1 was indeed more efficient at producing good A, then removal of trade barriers would enable it to expand its sales of A to country 2 whose industry would contract. If country 2 was more efficient at producing good B, its B industry would expand if the barriers to trade were removed. It would sell B to country 1 whose industry would consequently contract. The two countries would become enmeshed in beneficial trade exchanges (we are assuming that in each country unemployed factors could shift from declining to expanding industries). Such free competition is indeed at the very heart of the Rome Treaty, and to that end Article 3(f) calls for the creation of conditions of undistorted competition.

The reader will recollect that the Rome Treaty envisages the creation of a common market. That is to say the participating parties agree to remove tariffs, quotas, etc., on trade flowing between them and also agree to apply a common level of tariff on goods entering the EEC from without. The Rome Treaty refers to the latter as the common customs tariff but we will call it the common external tariff. In addition, the common market arrangement also envisages the free movement of factors of production such as labour, capital and enterprise. It is, however, important to note that some integration theorists have argued that even limited exercises in economic integration are capable of giving rise to spillover effects which may indeed lead to the process of economic integration proceeding further than was originally envisaged. The following is an example of a possible spillover effect. Assume that a group of countries have indeed embarked on a limited economic integration exercise which involves the free movement of goods, services and factors but excludes monetary matters. Because of the latter, exchange rates are free to rise and fall as market forces dictate. Subsequent experience may suggest that flexible exchange rates inhibit the flow of goods, services and factors. This arises from the uncertainties which are associated with exchange-rate volatility. It may therefore be argued that flexible exchange rates should be replaced by fixed rates. But exchange rates cannot remain fixed unless the monetary conditions in the member states are harmonized so as to give rise to uniform rates of inflation (or deflation). Such harmonization would require that national sovereignty over monetary matters would have to be given up in favour of a Community monetary coordination or even one Community currency controlled by a Community authority. This is what is meant by a spillover effect. It implies that although the member states may embark on a limited integration exercise they may be remorselessly driven down the path to greater and greater economic integration. That at least was the expectation entertained by some theorists. Subsequent chapters will reveal to what extent that expectation has been fulfilled.

Having contemplated this longer-term possibility, we now return to the point that at least as far as the trade in goods was concerned the Rome Treaty's immediate requirement was for the creation of a customs union – i.e. internal free trade and a common external tariff. We shall begin by considering each of these two elements.

The removal of internal protection

It will be recalled that Article 3 of the Treaty sets down the basic objectives of the EEC. Article 3(a) calls upon the member states to eliminate customs duties and quantitative restrictions (quotas, etc.) on the import and export of goods in intra-Community trade, and it also requires the members to abolish all other charges and measures having the equivalent effect of customs duties and quantitative restrictions. Article 9 reiterates this specific requirement and Articles 10 to 17 and 30 to 37 contain associated implementing powers, provisions and exclusions. The exclusions of Article 36 are particularly important and we shall come back to them later.

The member states therefore imposed upon themselves four obligations. They agreed to remove (a) import (and export) duties; (b) charges having the equivalent effect of import (and export) duties; (c) quantitative restrictions; (d) measures having the equivalent effect of quantitative restrictions.

The reader will recall from Chapter 1 that at the time of the negotiation of the Rome Treaty the French, particularly, were anxious about the transition period to be allowed for tariff removal. In the event it was decided that the period should be one of twelve years so that all tariffs would have to be eliminated by 31 December 1969. Table 4 shows the progress in tariff reduction on industrial goods and indicates that the original Six accomplished their tariff disarmament ahead of schedule. When the UK, Ireland and Denmark joined the Community on 1 January 1973 they were allowed a five-year period within which to dismantle their various forms of protection. Greece, which became a full member on 1 January 1981, was given a similar period within which to adapt, whilst Spain and Portugal, which became full members on 1 January 1986, were given seven years.[1]

We noted above that member states accepted an obligation to eliminate charges which have the equivalent effect of import (and export) duties. The Italian Government, for example, was in the habit of applying what it called a statistical levy to imports and exports. The Commission pointed out that this was the equivalent of a customs duty and should be eliminated. When the Italian Government refused to comply, the matter was referred to the Court of Justice which upheld the Commission's action.

In addition, member states were required to remove quantitative restrictions on intra-Community trade. Clearly high on the list were quotas. Article 30 calls for the abolition of import quotas – they were to be eliminated by the original Six by the end of the transition period. Article 34 also required the abolition of the export variety – a shorter timespan was envisaged for their removal. In practice, quota disarmament gave rise to no great difficulty since by the time the Rome Treaty was signed such quantitative restrictions were no longer the hindrance to trade that they had been in the period immediately following the Second World War. The fact that quotas had ceased to be a major problem was due to

1. During these transition periods all forms of protection – i.e. tariffs, quotas and equivalent charges and measures – had to be removed.

Table 4. Internal tariff reductions of the EEC (per cent)

	1.1.59	1.7.60	Acceleration of 1.1.61	1.1.62	Acceleration of 1.7.62	1.7.63	1.1.65	1.1.66	1.7.67	1.7.68
Individual reductions made on 1 January 1957 level	10	10	10	10	10	10	10	10	5	15
Cumulative reduction	10	20	30	40	50	60	70	80	85	100

Source: EEC Commission, *Tenth General Report on the Activities of the Community*, OOPEC, 1967, p. 66.

measures of liberalization evolved within the framework of the IMF, the GATT and, above all, the OEEC.

Not only were quantitative restrictions to be eliminated but also measures having an equivalent effect were to be removed. What, it may be asked, are these equivalent measures? The answer is that there are many types and we shall content ourselves with two examples which will serve to indicate the general nature of the problem. A particularly good instance was provided by the *Cassis de Dijon* case which we shall return to in Chapter 5. Cassis de Dijon is a French liqueur manufactured from blackcurrants. The German company Rewe-Zentral AG sought to import the French liqueur and requested an authorization from the West German Federal Monopoly Administration for Spirits. The latter informed Rewe that West German law forbade the sale of liqueurs with less than 32 per cent alcohol content although for liqueurs of the Cassis type a minimum of 25 per cent was allowed. This was no help to the Cassis importer since Cassis had an alcoholic content of only 15 to 20 per cent and thus it was illegal to import it. Rewe contested the ban in the German courts and the matter was referred to the Court of Justice for a preliminary ruling. The Court declared that the German law in question was in these specific circumstances an equivalent measure of the kind prohibited under Article 30 of the Rome Treaty. The minimum alcoholic content rule had in this particular case the effect of a zero import quota.

A particularly dramatic example of a measure equivalent in effect to a quantitative restriction was provided by the UK car market. During 1981 a vigorous press campaign drew attention to the marked difference between the price of cars on the continent as compared with the UK. The UK consumer paid more for cars than any of his EEC counterparts. Basic prices in the rest of the Community, less tax, were in some cases as much as 50 per cent cheaper. Clearly, in a free market, such differences would lead to trade flows from low to high price markets which would tend to iron out the differences. The fact that the differences were not ironed out indicated that some form of barrier existed. Indeed, the problem centred on national type-approval regulations which detail the British safety and technical standards to which cars allowed on British roads must conform. Significantly, the UK Government delegated the issue of certificates of conformity to official car distributors. Not surprisingly individuals, and commercial importers outside the official dealer network, encountered great difficulty in getting certificates. Either they were refused or extremely high prices were asked for the service. The official dealers had a vested interest in preventing imports because it would undermine dealer profit margins, whilst the UK Government was clearly fearful that if car prices fell it would have to pay even bigger subsidies to the ailing sections of the UK motor industry. There was one loophole in the system. Individuals could import 'personal cars' provided they had used the car abroad. This provision had been introduced to assist businessmen, servicemen and diplomats returning from abroad. Such personal imports did not require a type-approval certificate. However, it was reported in 1981 that the Society of Motor Manufacturers and Traders had approached the Department of Trade about the growth of personal imports and were pressing the UK Government to tighten up the rules.

The press campaign and pressure from the EC Commission were ultimately effective. The UK Government decided that official distributors should give rival importers the necessary certificates automatically without charge or fuss. It was also decided that the rules on personal imports should not be tightened up. The EC Commission also attacked specific abuses. Thus in 1984 it fined British Leyland £210 000 for trying to prevent the reimportation of left-hand-drive Metros for conversion. In the same year the Commission was engaged in actions relating to the difficulties which British nationals were experiencing in obtaining supplies of right-hand-drive cars in Belgium and Luxembourg. The problem was in fact EEC-wide and did not just affect UK consumers. Thus in 1983 the Commission had to attack German car dealers who had advertised that they would not carry out guarantee work on cars reimported from other parts of the Community. In 1985 the Commission returned to the attack. It introduced a regulation which exempted car distribution arrangements from the Rome Treaty competition rules (Article 85) but required that consumers should be able to reimport and also have their repairs done under manufacturers' warranties anywhere in the Common Market. The Commission warned that if it encountered cases of unjustified price differentials it would suspend the exemption. Clearly the task of eliminating measures equivalent to quotas is an exceedingly onerous one.

From all that had gone before it would appear that member states are obliged to eliminate *all* forms of protection. The obvious question which arises is – is this obligation absolute? Are there any escape clauses? There are in fact two possible major loopholes.

The first is provided by Article 109. It is to be found in the section of the Rome Treaty devoted to macro-economic policy. Article 109 allows a member state to take protective measures when it experiences a sudden crisis in its balance of payments. No limit is placed on the protective measures which could be applied so that, in principle, tariffs, quotas, etc., could be reimposed. However, in practice this is not a realistic possibility for the following reasons. Article 109 requires that any protective measures must cause the least disturbance to the functioning of the Common Market and must not be wider in scope than is strictly necessary in order to remedy the sudden difficulty. Altogether more important is the point that a member state, having applied such protection, is not free to retain it. The Council of Ministers has the power, certain procedural requirements having been met, to amend or indeed to abolish protective measures. In practice, if a member state experienced balance-of-payments problems it would be expected to pursue courses other than protectionism and facilities exist to enable it to do so. In the first place credit arrangements exist within the Community under the EMS and the 1975 loan arrangement, as well as externally via the IMF, which would enable the member state to finance the deficit whilst other policy measures were being introduced which would eventually rectify the problem. The state could deflate demand, thus reducing imports and forcing goods into the export market, and in the longer term deflation might be expected to restore international price competitiveness. Even membership of the EMS super-snake has not in practice precluded devaluations of the exchange rate, and this would be another possible avenue to a restoration of competitiveness. Domestic interest rates could also be raised and this could encourage a helpful inflow of foreign currencies. If the balance of payments deficit was at least in part associated with capital movements, and if those capital movements disturbed the functioning of the capital market in the member state, then protective measures relating to capital movements could be introduced. This is provided for in Article 73. The upshot of all this is that whilst restoration of tariff and other protection is possible *de jure*, *de facto* it is not normally a serious option.

The other loophole is to be found in Article 36. It declares that member states may, under certain circumstances, continue to apply quantitative restrictions and measures having equivalent effect. It does not, however, allow member states to retain tariffs. Restrictions on imports or exports can be maintained when they are:

justified on grounds of public morality, public policy or public security; the protection of health and life of humans, animals or plants; the protection of national treasures possessing artistic, historic or archaeological value; or the protection of industrial or commercial property.

The concepts of public morality, policy and security are not easy to define and differences of national interpretation are likely; indeed the

Court of Justice is prepared to allow a margin for national discretion. The protection of public morality has been invoked as grounds for a ban on imports of pornographic material. The second clause obviously allows member states to prevent the importation of dangerous drugs, foodstuffs containing dangerous additives and animals and plants which may spread diseases and so forth. Bans may also be placed on the export of national treasures.[1] Finally it would appear that the protection of patents, trademarks and copyrights may also justify the application of protection.

Article 36 does, however, throw up some knotty problems. We know that member states do seek to protect their citizens by laying down standards in respect of drugs, foodstuffs, etc. Such standards may differ between states, and to that extent trade is prevented. On the face of it, Article 36 legitimizes the laying down of such protective standards. Were that the end of the matter then trade could be severely impeded. In order to circumvent that problem Article 100 provides for the possibility of standards being harmonized. Such standards can continue to protect citizens but by being uniform they allow goods to cross frontiers. We shall return to this point in Chapter 5. The provision relating to commercial and industrial property also poses a difficulty. On the one hand Article 36 seems to permit the restriction of imports on the grounds of the need to protect such property, but this conflicts with the concept of goods being free to move between markets, and the latter is central to the idea of a common market. Which principle, we may ask, should prevail? We shall return to this topic in Chapter 5.

Two final points remain to be made. We have seen that, subject to certain very limited exceptions, the free movement of goods is a cardinal principle of the Rome Treaty. The other cardinal principle of the treaty is that there must be no discrimination on grounds of nationality. This principle is set out in Article 7, and it provides a reinforcing general authority for the attack on a wide range of barriers to trade. The other point relates to dumping. The prevention of dumping normally provides grounds upon which a state may take protective action. Anti-dumping powers do not, however, exist in respect of intra-Community trade. It is of course possible that a cartel or a dominant firm might finance loss-making export sales out of monopoly profits made in the home market. If such was the case then the appropriate remedial action would have to be based on Articles 85 and 86. The nature of these anti-trust powers is discussed in Chapter 5. Alternatively, such loss-making sales might be

1. Provided they are outside the area of commercial exploitation.

financed by the state. In which case remedial action would have to be based on Articles 92 to 94 which relate to state aids. We also discuss these powers in Chapter 5.

The common external tariff and related issues

Article 3(b) requires the member states to establish a common external tariff. Article 9 reiterates this specific requirement and Articles 10 to 11 and 18 to 29 contain associated implementing powers and provisions. We should also note that Article 3(b) calls for the creation of a common commercial policy towards third countries.

In accordance with Article 18, the original common external tariff was calculated on the basis of an unweighted average of the import duties of the four customs territories (Germany, France, Italy and the Benelux Customs Union) on 1 January 1957. There were, however, a series of lists of commodities in respect of which rates of duty other than those based on the simple averaging rule were to apply. Taking the structure of imports into the Community in 1958 as a base, it appears that the unweighted average incidence of the original common external tariff was 7·6 per cent whilst the weighted average was 9·1 per cent. However, these figures conceal considerable variations. Whereas the average incidence for raw materials was 0·1 per cent, that for capital goods was 12·5 per cent and in the case of industrial products 17·3 per cent.

The Community subsequently took part in international tariff negotiations within the GATT which reduced the level of the external tariff. The Dillon Round (1960–61) led to a cut of 7 to 8 per cent whilst the Kennedy Round (1964–7) resulted in the further fall of 35 to 40 per cent. More recently the EEC was involved in the somewhat protracted Tokyo Round (1973–9). This was planned to lead to a reduction of about a third over an eight-year period which began in 1980.[1] The Community was satisfied that this cut would still preserve a reasonable degree of protection for its producers.

Although Article 23 merely envisaged that the Six would align their import tariffs on the common level by not later than the end of the transitional period, in fact the alignment was completed by 1 July 1968 – see Table 5. Under the terms of the accession treaties, new members were given five- or seven-year periods within which to bring their tariffs into line.

We turn now to the common commercial policy referred to in Article

1. In fact the Community decided to speed up the process. The final cut was brought forward from 1 January 1987 to 1 January 1986.

Table 5. The creation of the common external tariff (per cent)

	Acceler-ation of 1.1.61	1.1.62	Acceler-ation of 1.7.63	1.1.66	1.7.68
Industrial products adjustment	30		30		40
cumulative adjustment	30		60		100
Agricultural products adjustment		30		30	40
cumulative adjustment		30		60	100

Source: EEC Commission, *Tenth General Report on the Activities of the Community*, OOPEC, 1967, p. 66

3(b). The key provisions are to be found in Articles 110 to 116. Article 111 required that during the transition period the member states should coordinate their trade relations with third countries so as to pave the way for a common commercial policy. According to Article 113 such a policy would be based:

on uniform principles, particularly in regard to changes in tariff rates, the conclusion of tariff and trade agreements, the achievement of uniformity in measures of liberalization, export policy and measures to protect trade such as those to be taken in case of dumping or subsidies.

One of the most important aspects of the common commercial policy is that member states cease to be free to unilaterally determine the level of tariff and quota protection *vis-à-vis* third countries. Thus if changes in the level of the common external tariff are to be negotiated (as for example in the Tokyo Round) or if quotas are to be negotiated in respect of imports (as was the case in the Multi-Fibre Arrangements[1]) then Article 113 implies that the Council of Ministers will lay down the guidelines and the Commission will do the bargaining. When the negotiations are finalized they will be adopted by the Council of Ministers (according to the Treaty this will be done on a qualified majority basis) and are then binding on the individual member states.

Protective action against dumping *by third countries* is possible. But it is important to note that individual member states are not empowered to initiate protection. This (other than on an interim basis) is the prerogative of the Council of Ministers acting on a proposal of the Commission.

1. See Chapter 10.

Moreover, such a protective response is only permitted when the dumping threatens to cause, or actually causes, material injury to a *Community* industry. Normally, damage suffered by a national segment of a Community industry will not provide sufficient grounds to launch an action.

However, we should not conclude that injury suffered by a national industry, as a result of imports from third countries, can never justify protective action. Regulations have been introduced which enable *quotas* to be applied to imports from third countries or state trading nations where the increase of such imports threatens a national industry. A member state may take such protective action on an emergency basis but that action can be revoked by the Commission. In the absence of a revocation other member states can appeal to the Council of Ministers to terminate the protection. Once again we see that member states are not normally [1] free to impose unilaterally permanent protection.

In 1984 a new development occurred when the Community adopted what has come to be called the New Commercial Policy Instrument. Unlike the above two measures, it can be invoked against illicit practices which affect Community exports to the rest of the world as well as Community imports. When such illicit practices are proved to exist, various retaliatory actions can be introduced by the Council of Ministers, including increasing the level of import duties and the application of quotas.

The growth of trade interdependence

It would hardly be surprising if the removal of internal protection and its retention *vis-à-vis* the rest of the world led to the Community becoming more interdependent in terms of trade. This has indeed happened. Intra-Community exports as a proportion of total exports and as a proportion of Gross Domestic Product have increased quite markedly – see Table 6.

The basic theory of a customs union

We have now seen how the Treaty has required the member states to construct a customs union, and we have seen something of its effects. It is now appropriate to consider what economic theory has to say about

---

1. We use the word 'normally' because there is one exception which needs to be noted. Some EEC members have concluded various forms of voluntary export restraint (VER) with foreign exporters. The most notable examples have been agreements by Japan to restrict its exports of cars. Some restrictions have been a good deal less voluntary, since they have taken the form of quotas negotiated prior to the formation of the Community. More will be said about this in Chapter 11.

Table 6. Intra-Community exports

	% of Total Exports		% of GDP		
	1958	1980	1958	1973	1980
Benelux	35	71	15·0	35	38
Denmark	58	50	14·0	10	13
Germany	35	48	5·4	9	11
France	28	51	2·5	8	9
Ireland	83	74	19·0	25	36
Italy	32	48	2·7	7	9
Netherlands	57	73	19·0	29	34
United Kingdom	20	42	2·8	6	9
The Nine	34	53	4·9	10	13

Source: EC Commission: *The Economy of the European Community*, OOPEC 1982, p. 24.

customs unions. Present understanding of the theoretical implications of such arrangements is based on the pioneer study of the subject by Professor Jacob Viner. The issues involved were subsequently developed by Professor James Meade and others. What follows is an elementary analysis based on Meade's basic theoretical formulation. This is designed for readers who do not have any knowledge, or only a limited knowledge, of economic analysis. Those who have some knowledge may prefer the partial equilibrium approach which follows the elementary analysis and should regard the exposition immediately below merely as an introduction to the problem.

Elementary analysis

An important point which emerges is that the advantages of trade liberalization within the framework of such a union need to be kept in perspective. Customs unions *per se* are not so unambiguously beneficial as is universal free trade. Classical economists, such as David Ricardo, were able to demonstrate theoretically that the universal elimination of protection, particularly if it was at a high level, would lead to a great increase in world welfare.[1] Each country would specialize in the production of those goods for which it was best fitted – in economists' language,

1. We ignore special arguments for protection, for example that relating to infant industries.

countries would specialize in producing those goods in respect of which they had a comparative advantage. Taking the world as a whole, greater production would result than if countries insisted on protecting their industries and producing all or most of the goods which they needed. The division of the increase of production would, of course, depend on the terms of trade – i.e. the rate at which one country's specialism(s) exchange for other countries' specialisms. But we cannot conclude that because a customs union involves an element of freeing of trade it likewise is unambiguously beneficial. Quite evidently a customs union is not a case of universal free trade – it represents free trade within a bloc and discrimination against the rest of the world. Thus in appraising the results of a customs union, two effects have to be distinguished. One is trade creation, which represents an improvement in resource utilization, and the other is trade diversion, which narrowly defined [1] represents a deterioration. These two effects are illustrated in Table 7. We assume the following:

1. The world consists of two countries, I and II, who wish to form a customs union, and a third outside country which we term country III.
2. Only three commodities are produced – A, B and C.
3. Prior to the customs union, country I applied a 50 per cent *ad valorem* tariff to all imports, but after the formation of the union the tariff only applies to imports from country III.
4. Transport costs can be ignored.

Taking good A first, the lowest-cost producer is country III, which lies outside the proposed union. Before the union, good A produced by country III (with duty applied) undersells A produced by country I, or A produced by country II (with duty applied). But after the union is created, A produced in country II no longer has duty applied to it and as a result undersells A produced in country III (bearing duty) and A produced in country I. This is called trade diversion. In the case of good B the lowest-cost producer is country II. But even prior to the union B produced in country II does not enter country I. This arises because the customs duty renders B produced in country II uncompetitive with B produced in country I. But after the union is created B produced in country II no longer has a customs duty applied and it enters country I and undersells B produced in country I. Here we have trade creation. In the case of good C, the lowest-cost producer is country I. It produces the good before and after the union. As a result neither trade diversion nor trade creation occurs.

---

1. The meaning of the phrase 'narrowly defined' will become apparent later in this chapter.

Table 7. Trade creation and trade diversion (£)

Good	Cost or cost plus duty per unit	Country III exporting to country I	Flow of trade	Goods produced by country I	Flow of trade	Country II exporting to country I	Results
A	Cost	12		20		14	Trade diversion
	Cost plus duty prior to customs union	18	↑	20	No trade	21	
	Cost plus duty after customs union	18	No trade	20	↓	14	
B	Cost	14		17		12	Trade creation
	Cost plus duty prior to customs union	21	No trade: country I produces B	17	No trade: country I produces B	18	
	Cost plus duty after customs union	21	No trade	17	↓	12	
C	Cost	16		10		12	Neither trade creation nor trade diversion. Country I is the lowest-cost producer and provides C before and after the union
	Cost plus duty prior to customs union	24	No trade	10	No trade	18	
	Cost plus duty after customs union	24	No trade	10	No trade	12	

It follows that in assessing the effects of a customs union we have to take into account that it can shift production away from the lowest-cost producer to a higher-cost member of the union. Such trade diversion is a departure from a previously more rational pattern of resource allocation. On the other hand, the creation of the union can shift production away from a less efficient to a more efficient member of the union and such trade creation represents a shift towards a more efficient pattern of resource allocation. As a first approximation, therefore, we can conclude that whether or not a customs union is beneficial depends on the balance of these two effects.

How can the balancing be carried out? In the case of good A in Table 7, suppose that country I imports one million units first from country III and then from country II. The original cost was therefore £12 million but is now £14 million.[1] The cost of trade diversion – the extra cost incurred by virtue of obtaining supplies from the higher-cost source – is therefore £2 million. In the case of good B, suppose country I consumes half a million units; then the saving of trade creation is £2·5 million. On balance therefore, taking account of production effects only, the customs union is beneficial.[2]

This analysis, like all simplifying devices, has its strengths and its weaknesses. Its strength is that it does enable us to see how the customs union can lead to both improvements and deteriorations in resource allocation. It does so via the production effects – a shift to a more efficient source of supply (as in good B) leads to a production gain whilst a shift to a less efficient source of supply (as in good A) leads to a production loss. Its main weakness is that it is based on a number of simplifying assumptions. Not the least of these is the point that demand for the goods in question is totally price inelastic. That is to say when price falls, because of the change in the tariff level, the quantity consumed does not change. This assumption rules out consumption effects. We shall be able to take consumption effects into account when we adopt the partial equilibrium approach to which we now turn.

The partial equilibrium approach

Before we endeavour to apply partial equilibrium analysis to a customs

---

1. This cost is calculated exclusive of tariff, the point being that although consumers in country I pay the tariff, the proceeds of the tariff accrue to the government of country I which we will assume provides its consumers with an equivalent and thus compensating quantity of free goods. The cost to consumers of the tariff is therefore not material to the argument. The material point is the cost *net of tariff* of obtaining supplies of good A (and good B) from alternative sources.
2. We can ignore good C since there was no change from pre- to post-union.

union we need to acquaint ourselves with the welfare effects of tariffs. It will perhaps be helpful if we begin by considering the situation where a country which has applied a tariff then decides to remove it. This will throw up some of the relevant effects which also arise when a country decides to participate in a customs union and is therefore required to lower some of its tariffs. When we have acquainted ourselves with the relevant effects of removing a tariff we can move on to apply these ideas to customs union situations.

In Figure 2 we show country I's domestic demand curve dd, and country I's domestic supply curve ss, for good A. The supply curve ss has the normal positive slope – it indicates that the industry within country I supplying good A will be disposed to supply more per unit of time the higher the price of the good. The dd demand curve has the

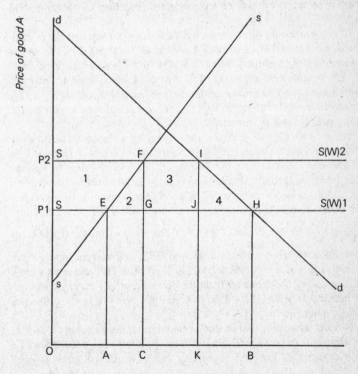

Figure 2. Welfare effects of a tariff

normal negative slope – it indicates that consumers in country I will be disposed to demand more per unit of time the lower the price of the good.

Since we are dealing with tariffs and trade we now have to recognize that there is a competing source of supply of good A in the form of imports from the rest of the world. This is represented by the supply curve SS(W)1. This is drawn as a perfectly elastic supply curve. The assumption here is that the imports of country I represent only a very small part of the demand for the good in question in the world market. Country I is therefore a price taker – it must take the price of imports of Good A as being determined in the world market by world supply and demand. Whether it imports a little or a lot of A it will not drive the price down or up by so doing. We are in fact assuming that there is no terms of trade effect arising from country I importing good A.[1]

If we assume that there are no tariffs then we can say that the price in the domestic market of country I will be OP1. This follows from the intersection of the supply curve sES(W)1 with the demand curve dd at H. The equilibrium price is OP1 (the price at which imports enter the domestic market). Domestic demand is OB, and domestic supply is OA (read off from the domestic supply curve ss), and imports will be the difference, i.e. AB in quantity.

Let us first assume that country I decides unilaterally to adopt a protective stance by applying an import tariff. Whether the tariff be *ad valorem* (i.e. a certain percentage on the import price) or specific (i.e. a certain absolute sum imposed on the import price) the effect on the supply curve of imports SS(W)1 will be to cause it to shift up – for example, to SS(W)2. (The *ad valorem* tariff is the percentage rate $\frac{P1P2}{OP1} \cdot \frac{100}{1}$; the specific tariff if P1P2.) The effect of the tariff will be to raise the price in the domestic market to OP2. The relevant supply curve is now sFS(W)2 and it intersects dd at I. At price OP2 domestic supply will expand to OC (read off from the domestic supply curve ss), domestic demand at price OP2 will be OK, and imports will be the difference CK in quantity.

Now let us assume that in similar unilateral fashion country I decides to remove its import tariff. What will be the effect of so doing? First we should note that imports, now being free of tariff, will enter at price

---

1. We shall assume throughout the chapter that the supply curves of countries other than country I are perfectly elastic.

OP1. It follows that the effective supply schedule will be sES(W)1 and it will intersect the demand curve dd at H. The equilibrium price will fall back down to OP1 and the equilibrium quantity will rise to OB. Domestic output will contract from OC and imports will rise from CK to AB. The *welfare* effect of the change will be favourable in two ways. How, it may be asked, do we arrive at such a conclusion?

Consider first area 1. When the tariff was in operation it raised price from OP1 to OP2. This gave rise to a producer rent or surplus equal to the area sP2F – i.e. the cost of production was only OsFC (the area under the supply curve) but producers actually received OP2FC. When the tariff was removed and the price fell, producer rent declined by the amount of area 1. Taking country I as a whole no gain or loss arises. Producers lose area 1 but consumers enjoy a counterbalancing benefit in that they pay that much less. There is a straight transfer of benefit, and if we attach no welfare significance to the redistribution then we can say that area 1 is neutral in its effect on welfare.

Consider now area 2 – this does represent a positive welfare gain. More precisely we can say that a production effect arises which takes the form of a production gain. When country I originally applied the import tariff the effect was to cause its output of A to rise from OA to OC. As a result it sustained a production loss since quantity AC was originally imported at cost AEGC whereas the cost of producing AC domestically is AEFC – a production loss of EFG therefore arose. However, when country I reduces its tariff domestic output falls from OC to OA – i.e. by AC. This generates a production gain since by reversing the previous logic we know that AC obtained by importation costs only AEGC whereas AC when domestically produced costs AEFC. It is important to note that this net gain does presume that the resources previously used to produce AC can be transferred to alternative uses. Indeed their value in alternative uses will be AEFC so there is no doubt that country I has gained by being able to import AC at a lower cost than that which it would incur if it produced it itself.

Now let us focus on area 3. When the tariff was operating, this area represented the tariff revenue which accrued to the government. Let us assume that as a result the government supplied its citizens with free goods such as schools and parks. When the tariff was removed the government would no longer have the revenue to supply these free goods but, on the other hand, consumers would be paying a reduced amount for imports and that reduction would be equal to area 3. The fact that consumers pay less for good A offsets the fact that they no

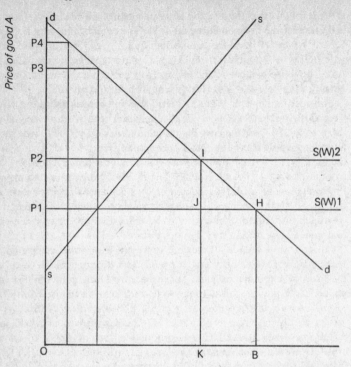

Figure 3. Consumer surplus and consumer gain

longer receive free goods. Again we shall attach no welfare significance to any redistribution of income which might result.[1]

Finally there is area 4 – here too there is a positive welfare gain. More precisely we can say that there is a consumption effect which takes the form of a consumption gain. This is new to our analysis – it arises because the abolition of the tariff causes price to fall and demand or consumption to extend. Our earlier elementary analysis of customs unions precluded this possibility because we assumed that demand was totally price inelastic.

1. Quite clearly redistribution can occur. If good A was luxury yachts then rich citizens would gain by lower prices and this would then help to offset their loss of free goods. On the other hand poor citizens, who presumably do not purchase luxury yachts, would have nothing to offset their loss of free goods.

The origin of this consumer gain is connected with the concept of consumer surplus which is illustrated in Figure 3. When the import tariff is not operating, the price of good A will be OP1. Consumers will purchase OB and pay OP1 per unit, so their total expenditure will be OP1 HB. However, the welfare they derive from consuming OB is greater than this. For example, there are some consumers who value the good so highly that they will be prepared to pay as much as price OP4 and there are others who will be prepared to pay somewhat less, i.e. OP3, and so on. We shall assume that the price they are willing to pay is a measure of the utility or welfare they derive, or expect to derive, from consuming the good. In practice they all pay OP1, but if we take the price consumers are *willing* to pay as an indicator of the welfare they derive, then in total the latter is equal to the area under the demand curve, i.e. OdH B. The excess of the area under the demand curve over the amount they actually pay – P1dH – is called consumer surplus. The application of the tariff reduces consumption from OB to OK, i.e. by KB. The welfare loss in respect of good A is therefore the area under the demand curve, i.e. KIHB. However, expenditure equal to KJHB can be transferred to other goods and, following the equi-marginal principle, the utility or welfare per unit of expenditure on the other goods will not be greater than that which is enjoyed on the OBth unit of good A. Therefore when the expenditure is transferred to those other goods the welfare they produce will not be greater than KJHB. Therefore there is a net loss of welfare – a consumption loss – equal to JIH. It also follows that if the tariff is removed consumption of good A will increase by KB. Consumption spending will be transferred from those other goods to good A. The welfare lost on the other goods will be KJHB but the welfare derived from the extra KB of good A will be KIHB and so there will be a net gain of welfare – equal to JIH.

By way of recapitulation we can say that of the four areas only areas 2 and 4 constitute welfare changes. Indeed these areas, often called Marshallian triangles, respectively represent the production and consumption gains which country I derives from unilaterally abolishing its tariff.[1]

We can now proceed to apply this type of analysis to a customs union. We shall identify two cases. The first gives rise to trade creation, the second to trade diversion together with an element of trade creation.

In Figure 4 we show the usual domestic demand and supply curves dd

1. The welfare benefit is easily measured. We know the former tariff was P1 P2 and that the increase in imports was AB minus CK. The product of these multiplied by one half approximates areas 2 + 4.

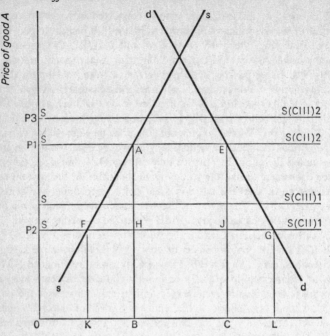

Quantity supplied and demanded of good A

Figure 4. Pure trade creation

and ss for country I. We now have to introduce supply curves of imports from country II, who will be the customs union partner, and country III, who will remain outside the union. The relative position of the supply curves of these two latter countries is important. In other words it is important whether the more efficient of the two is inside or outside the union.

In Figure 4, SS(CII)1 is the supply curve of country II and SS(CIII)1, the supply curve of country III, in both cases before tariff. Prior to the union, country I applies a non-discriminatory tariff – that is to say it applies the same tariff to imports irrespective of where they come from. The tariff of course raises the supply curve of both outside countries but because country II is the more efficient, its supply curve with tariff – SS (CII)2 – lies below the supply curve with tariff of country III, i.e. SS (CIII)2. It follows that the effective supply curve prior to the union is sA S(CII)2 and it intersects dd at E. It follows that the equilibrium price prior to the union is OP1. Domestic production is OB, domestic consumption is OC and imports are BC. Note that since country II is the lowest cost and therefore most competitive outside supplier it is the source of the imports BC.

Now let us assume that a customs union is formed between countries I and II whilst country III is discriminated against by having to face the old tariff. (We are in fact assuming in this case and the next one that the common external tariff which countries I and II agree to apply is country I's old non-discriminatory tariff.) Country II can now supply at price OP2 since its supply no longer bears the tariff, whilst country III will only be able to supply at price OP3. The effective supply curve is therefore sFC(II)1. Equilibrium is now at point G where sFC(II)1 and dd intersect. The price falls from OP1 to OP2. Domestic output contracts from OB to OK. Domestic demand expands from OC to OL and imports rise from BC to KL.

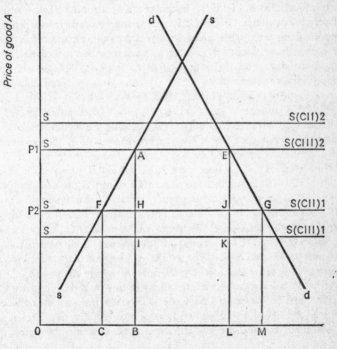

Quantity supplied and demanded of good A

Figure 5. Trade diversion and trade creation

In this case we have trade creation. Additional trade is created equal to K B plus C L. This increased trade is also directed towards a more efficient source, i.e. country II. The fall in price causes a shift in production – country I produces less and extra imports K B come from more efficient country II. This gives rise to a production gain F A H. But the fall in price also causes an extension of demand and this is also met by extra imports C L which also come from country II. This gives rise to a consumption gain J E G. Incidentally, we can ignore the areas represented by reduced producer surplus and lost tariff revenue for reasons which were explained in connection with the analysis of the welfare effects of a tariff.[1] One thing is clear – the customs union gives rise to welfare gains and no losses. This result stems from the fact that the most efficient of the two previously outside suppliers is now within the union.

Now we come to our second case, and here we shall observe the existence of a welfare loss of the kind identified by Viner. This second case is illustrated in Figure 5. On this occasion the most efficient source of supply is country III. S S(CIII)1 is the supply curve before tariff of imports from country III, and S S(CII)1 is the supply curve before tariff of imports from country II. Once again we start with a situation where a non-discriminatory tariff is applied to all imports. This causes both supply curves to shift up, but because country III is the more efficient its supply curve with tariff, i.e. S S(CIII)2, lies below that of country II, i.e. S S C(II)2. The effective supply curve is s A S(CIII)2. Equilibrium will be at E, the equilibrium price will be O P1, domestic production will be O B, domestic consumption will be O L and imports will be B L. Since country III is the most competitive outside supplier it supplies the imports B L.

Now let us assume that once more countries I and II form a union, whilst country III is left facing the external tariff. Country II can now supply at price O P2 but country III, although more efficient, can only supply at price O P1 because it has to continue to bear the tariff. The effective supply curve is now s F S(CII)1. Equilibrium point will be at G. The price will fall from O P1 to O P2. Domestic output falls to O C, domestic demand expands to O M and imports rise to C M. *Most significantly those imports, which used to come from country III, now come from country II.*[2]

How do we assess the welfare effects in this case? Firstly there is a welfare loss in the sense that trade is diverted from a more efficient source (country III) to a less efficient source (country II). This as we know arises because the less efficient source is within the union but

---

1. In the second case discussed below the tariff revenue element is however relevant.
2. Country III will, however, be no worse off, because the resources originally used to produce good A supplied to country I will now be transferred to other uses where their value productivity will be just as high.

escapes the tariff, whereas the more efficient source is outside the union and therefore has to go on bearing the tariff. This trade diversion is represented by the rectangle IHJK. This requires a little more explanation. The pre-union level of imports BL used to come from country III and cost BIKL exclusive of tariff. Those imports now come from country II and cost BHJL (they bear no tariff). The extra cost (ignoring tariff) is therefore IHJK. Another way of looking at this development is as follows. Prior to the union country I collected revenue equal to IAEK. The amount consumers paid for imports was consequently inflated by exactly that amount. By way of compensation the revenue was used to provide free goods. After the union there is no tariff revenue and therefore the supply of free goods declines by IAEK but, on the other hand, the amount which consumers pay for imports only declines by the smaller amount HAEJ and the difference – IHJK – is a pure social loss.

However, the new situation is not purely one of welfare loss. The price of good A has fallen, and because of that country I experiences a decline of production and an increase in consumption, and respectively they give rise to a production gain FAH and a consumption gain JEG.

The reader will note the contrast between the two cases. In the first case there is an increase in the original level of trade – which gives rise to welfare gains. In the second case there is a diversion of the original level of trade – which gives rise to a welfare loss – but there is also an increase in the original level of trade which gives rise to welfare gains. The situation is a little less clear cut than our elementary analysis would suggest – it envisaged nothing but gain in the trade creation situation and nothing but loss in the trade diversion situation.

We can now appreciate the full import of the observation by Viner that customs unions are not unambiguously beneficial. They can give rise to welfare gains but they can also give rise to welfare losses. Thus, in the second case if the Marshallian triangles of production and consumption gain are greater than the rectangle of trade diversion then the customs union leads on balance to a better allocation of resources and greater welfare than the previous protected situation. But if the rectangle is greater than the sum of the triangles then the customs union leads to an inferior allocation of resources and a lower level of welfare than previously.

Economists have also pondered as to why groups of countries decide to involve themselves in customs union arrangements. The dilemma has centred on the point that even if in respect of all goods the customs union gave rise to benefits similar to our first case, it would not be superior to a policy of unilateral tariff reduction of the kind which we considered when analysing the welfare effects of a tariff. One solution, which has much to commend it, is that there are other benefits which arise from clubbing together which would not be available if countries merely adopted an independent policy of unilateral tariff reduction. One obvious benefit is the political cohesion which is expected to spill over from economic integration. This manifests itself in terms of greater harmony between the member states, but in addition it also promises to provide them with greater political influence on the world stage than they could hope to enjoy in isolation. On the economic plane the participating states can also enjoy the fruits arising from collective bargaining in the context of international trade and monetary negotiations.

General conclusions

One thing is clear: the static analysis of customs unions does not of itself provide a basis for categorically commending or rejecting them. Whether they are good or bad depends upon the particular circumstances. However, some generalizations do emerge, although it must be admitted that there is no substitute for measurement in deciding the actual results of a union. Firstly, a customs union is more likely to be advantageous on balance if the economies of the partners are actually very competitive but are potentially complementary. If they produce similar products but efficiencies differ, they will each contract their relatively inefficient industries and expand their efficient ones. There will be a beneficial increase in mutual trade without much diversion of imports or exports from other markets. If, on the other hand, their economies are already complementary, the prospects of gains on the production side would be correspondingly small. Secondly, a customs union is more likely to increase economic welfare the higher the initial duties on imports from partners. High duties imply high levels of inefficiency which are being protected. Thus the higher the inefficiencies the greater the gains from trade after such protection is removed. Thirdly, the production effects of a customs union will be the more advantageous the lower its tariff against the outside world. Fourthly, a union is more likely to raise welfare the greater the proportion of world production, consumption, and trade covered by it. The larger the union becomes, the greater the probability that trade creation will outweigh trade diversion, until, in the case of a union embracing the world, trade diversion ceases to exist.

Empirical findings on static effects

There is now an extensive literature on the static effects of customs unions. These studies have attempted to estimate to what extent trade flows have been created and diverted as a result of the EEC customs union. Michael Davenport has recently surveyed the various findings.

The studies have usually produced a number of alternative estimates, and Table 8 presents the results preferred by those carrying out the studies, or the ones which Davenport felt were based on the most defensible assumptions. There is a fair degree of consensus that trade creating flows have outweighed trade diverting flows. The majority cluster in the range from $7½ billion to $11½ billion for the former and $½ billion to $1 billion for the latter. Davenport points out that if we take trade created as $10 billion and trade diverted as $1 billion then the net 'gain' would be some 10 per cent of the combined imports of goods of the EEC at the time or nearly 2 per cent of Community GDP. This is non-negligible. However, these estimates relate to changes in trade *flows*, which is not the same thing as the welfare effects with which the Marshallian triangles are concerned. Estimates of such static gains suggest that they were less than 1 per cent of the members' combined GNP.

Why is the beneficial effect so limited? One answer is that a rather small part of total production is traded internationally. Thus services, building and much of the purchases of the public sector do not enter into international trade and the net gain from customs unions can only arise in connection with that part of production which is traded. Secondly, as has been pointed out by Nils Lundgren (1969, p. 52), if the removal of protection is to be significant it must have been costly to maintain. However, examples of really costly protection are rare since there is no great political support for such protection. For example, raw materials are normally duty free, largely because the production of them at home would involve astronomic costs. Much the same is true of more specialized commodities such as ships and aircraft. It is important to stress that we are not implying that the gains from international trade are small. On the contrary, because of the uneven geographical distribution of natural resources and so forth, they are enormous. But the fact is that these gains are already being substantially reaped since no one can afford not to reap them, and the existence of a substantial volume of international trade is a proof of this fact. As a consequence further gains from customs unions are bound to be limited.

Dynamic analysis

We may therefore legitimately ask why so much emphasis is placed on the creation of customs unions. The answer is, as we noted earlier, partly political, in that the process of economic integration prepares the ground for political unification. But the other reason is that the trade creation/trade diversion analysis of customs unions ignores many of the other advantages which can accrue to the participants. Firstly, a larger

Table 8. Estimates of trade creating and trade diverting flows in the EEC[1]

Study	Date	Coverage	Trade Creation ($ billion)	Trade Diversion ($ billion)
Truman	1968	Manufactures	9·2	1·0
Balassa	1970	Manufactures	11·4	0·1
Balassa	1970	All goods	11·3	0·3
Verdoorn and Schwartz	1969	Manufactures	11·1	1·1
Aitken	1967	All goods	9·2	0·6[2]
Kreinin	1969–70	Manufactures	7·3	2·4
Truman	1968	Manufactures and raw materials	1·8	3·0

Notes: 1. Original Six only; 2. Diversion from EFTA only
Source: M. Davenport, 'The Economic Impact of the EEC' in A. Boltho (ed.), *The European Economy Growth and Crisis*, Oxford University Press, 1982, Table 8.1, p. 227.

market gives rise to opportunities for the fuller exploitation of economies of large-scale production. National markets may not be big enough to enable firms to expand sufficiently to achieve the minimum optimal scale, and such a scale of plant or firm may require the sales area of the much larger Community market. (However, whether this is strictly a dynamic effect as opposed to the once-for-all nature of the trade creation/trade diversion static analysis is doubtful. It can be argued that once the economies of scale have been reaped the effect is exhausted and thus it is really static in character.) The much bigger Community market may also enable firms to expand and thus mount the research and development efforts which are necessary if European firms are to compete successfully with their American and Japanese rivals. Secondly, there are some reasons for believing that the intensity of competition may increase as a result of the formation of a union. For example, industrial structures undergo a change. National monopolies become Community oligopolies and the situation in established oligopolies becomes more fluid, with a reduction of oligopolistic collusion and mutual awareness. Then again there is a possibility of a psychological change. Thus it has been argued that prior to the formation of the EEC, relations between competitors in the relatively small national market were personal and friendly. Competition manifests itself in the attempts of producers to expand at each other's expense. This was unlikely to happen under such circumstances. However, when trade liberalization occurred firms in one national market could seek to grow not at each other's expense but at the expense of producers in other national markets with whom relations are impersonal. Not only that but producers in those other markets would tend to behave likewise. As a result, every firm would become aware of the fact that its own national market share could no longer be regarded as secure. Because of this they would tend to look less favourably on the preservation of less efficient compatriots. (The competition effect can only be said to be dynamic if it leads to a *sustained* higher rate of investment and/or technological improvement.) Of course, the much more aggressive business behaviour which now exists in the Community is due not only to the opening up of markets, but also to the infiltration of US and Japanese investment which has brought with it more aggressive business strategies and better management techniques. But this infiltration was undoubtedly to a considerable degree the result of the bigger market, or the prospect thereof, which the Rome Treaty opened up, and is in effect another advantage of the customs union from the point of view of the members. The point about the foreign influence also emphasizes the fact that access to the enlarged market may not only stimulate a greater level of investment by Community firms but may also attract direct investment from outside Europe.

5 Non-Tariff Barriers in the Customs Union

Although the EEC was able to complete its internal tariff disarmament by the middle of 1968, the task of creating a truly unified market in which goods could move freely was not thereby achieved. There still remained other significant non-tariff barriers which could continue to prevent totally, or in some degree to restrict, or in some way to distort, the flow of intra-Community trade. Some of these factors pose considerably greater difficulties than mere tariffs. We shall discuss the nature of these non-tariff barriers (NTBs), what the Rome Treaty says about them, and what specific actions have been taken by the Commission, Council of Ministers and Court of Justice. It is perhaps worth adding that in dealing with NTBs the focus will be on industrial goods – agricultural goods are of course subject to a separate régime.

Before we turn to a discussion of the various NTBs, it is necessary to point out that by the beginning of the 1980s it was becoming increasingly obvious that although the Community had been in existence for more than twenty years, the creation of a true internal market for goods (and services) had not been achieved. This was of great concern to the EC Commission, which noted that in the recession which afflicted the Community from the middle of the 1970s onwards, member states had become more protectionist – barriers tended to rise rather than fall. Subsequently the mood changed, and in a series of summits (Copenhagen 1982, Fontainebleau and Dublin 1984, Brussels 1985) the European Council called for the completion of the internal market. However, the creation of an internal market depends upon deeds and not just words. In 1985 the Commission said just that in a White Paper entitled *Completing the Internal Market* (EC Commission, 1985a) presented to the Milan Summit. This aspiration was incorporated in the discussions of the IGC held later that year. As a result, the Single European Act 1986 amended the Rome Treaty so as to require the progressive establishment of the internal market by the end of 1992. It also made procedural alterations designed to help the achievement of that aim – see below and Chapter 2. The year 1986 also saw an encouraging increase in the pace of Community legislative activity. During that year no less than sixty-eight measures designed to encourage free trade were introduced. Many of these occurred during the U K Presidency of the Council of Ministers, but great credit must also be given to the previous Dutch Presidency.

Cartels and concentrations

These were an obvious device which could frustrate the process of integration through trade. There was plenty of evidence that prior to tariff and quota disarmament various forms of business arrangement, sometimes international in membership, existed which restricted trade flows and allocated and partitioned markets. It was recognized that where such devices did not exist initially, as the tariff barriers went down businessmen might resort to various practices in order to offset the effects of the removal of protection.

The anti-trust problem can be divided into two main compartments – (a) restrictive arrangements between otherwise independent firms, and (b) the practices of dominant (or even monopoly) firms coupled with phenomena such as mergers, which can create conditions of dominance or monopoly.

Instances of the former abound in Community case law. For example, there are price agreements whereby firms in one member state, when selling to another, agree on the prices which they will charge for exports. Sometimes indeed such firms may create a separate company which will conduct the export sales of all the participants – this is known as a common selling syndicate. These arrangements have been common in fertilizers: we can cite Cobelaz (Belgium – ammonium sulphate), CFA (France – ammonium nitrogenous fertilizers), Seifa (Italy – simple nitrogenous, phosphatic, potassic and compound fertilizers) and Supexie (France – phosphatic fertilizers) as instances of this practice. Parallel price behaviour may indeed be international in character. Thus in the *Aniline Dye* case the Commission and Court of Justice had to deal with a situation in which equal and simultaneous price movements were made by ten firms – six were from Common Market countries but three were Swiss and one was British. As a result of international agreements, each home market may be reserved for home producers. Quota agreements may be entered into whereby home and foreign firms agree not to overstock the home market. Firms supplying a home market may enter into reciprocal exclusive dealing arrangements whereby signatory suppliers will only supply signatory dealers, and signatory dealers will only buy from signatory suppliers. If most of the dealers in a member state are locked in the arrangement, non-signatory suppliers, perhaps located in another member state, may have difficulty in penetrating the market. Firms in a member state may operate an aggregated rebate system in which domestic purchasers enjoy a progressive scale of rebate dependent on the (usually annual) volume of purchases from the signatory firms as a totality. The effect of this is to induce domestic purchasers to buy from the domestic firms rather than to import.

In respect of the concentration problem, it is not difficult to see how a dominant firm would, for example, be in a powerful position to induce domestic dealers to deal exclusively with it, and as a result importation would be reduced or even eliminated. Mergers and takeovers can have similar effects on the flow of trade. Thus in the now famous *Continental Can* case the burden of the Commission's case was that Continental Can, already dominant in the German market, had taken over one of its few remaining competitors in the shape of Thomassen & Drijver-Verblifa of the Netherlands.

Cartels

The key provisions are to be found in Rome Treaty Articles 3(f) and 85. Article 3 lays down the prime objectives of the EEC, and amongst these is a call for 'the institution of a system ensuring that competition in the Common Market is not distorted'. It is, however, in Article 85 that we find the substantive law. This is best viewed in three parts. Article 85 (1) prohibits a range of practices – agreements, decisions of associations of enterprises and concerted practices in the supply of services as well as goods. The first would include not only enforceable agreements (i.e. those that have some documentary base) but also gentlemen's agreements that are not intended to be enforced in the courts. Decisions of associations of enterprises covers the possibility that a firm being part of an association might conveniently claim that it did not agree with this or that association policy. Being a member of the association it will be assumed to be bound by the decisions thereof. Decisions of associations of enterprises also covers the situation where a trade association makes a recommendation to its members even when there is no obligation to comply. A concerted practice is more difficult to define. It may be invoked where there is a parallelism of action but where straightforward collusion may not be admitted nor indeed exist. Mere parallelism of action would not, however, be sufficient proof. This concept was first used in the *Aniline Dye* case where on three occasions the most important suppliers of dyes in the EEC introduced equiproportionate price increases within a few days of each other. Although agreement was not admitted by the parties, the Commission did point to circumstantial evidence of collusion and the firms were found guilty of being involved in a concerted practice and were fined. In the appeal case before the Court of Justice the Commission pressed the matter further when it observed that:

In order that there should be a concerting, it is not necessary that the parties should draw up a plan in common with a view to adopting a certain behaviour. It suffices that they should mutually inform each other in advance of the attitudes they intend to adopt, in such a way that each can regulate its action in reliance on its competitors behaving in a parallel manner.

The Court of Justice upheld the Commission's Decision observing that a concerted practice was:

. . . a form of coordination between undertakings which, without going so far as to amount to an agreement properly so called, knowingly substitutes a practical cooperation between them for the risks of competition.

It added that parallelism of action was not to be identified with a concerted practice although it constituted a strong indication of such a practice, particularly when it led to prices above the equilibrium level expected from competition. The concept of a concerted practice also arose in the *Sugar* cases. On that occasion the Court amplified the concept saying:

Although it is correct to say that this requirement of independence does not deprive economic operators of the right to adapt themselves intelligently to the existing and anticipated conduct of their competitors, it does, however, strictly preclude any direct or indirect contact between such operators. The object or effect thereof is either to influence the conduct on the market of an actual or potential competitor or to disclose to such a competitor the course of conduct which they themselves have decided to adopt or contemplate adopting.

In short the Court lays emphasis on conscious efforts to evoke matching responses from competitors – as we have just noted mere parallelism of prices is not sufficient to carry the day.

The second feature of Article 85(1) is that the object or effect of the forms of conduct discussed above must be to prevent, restrict or distort competition *in the Common Market*. This provision does not mean that Community law only applies to Community firms. Firms belonging to states outside the EEC can be subject to the anti-trust rules. Thus in the *Aniline Dye* case to which we have just referred British and Swiss firms were fined by the Commission for their involvement with Community firms in activities leading to parallel price movements within the Common Market, and this was prior to UK membership of the Community. In short the Commission and Court of Justice have claimed an extra-territorial jurisdiction in their application of Article 85. The Article provides some examples of preventions, restrictions and distortions such as direct or indirect fixing of selling or purchasing prices and terms, limits on production, market allocation, etc. These are not exhaustive but merely illustrative.

Thirdly, a prevention, restriction or distortion of competition in the EEC must be one which 'may affect trade between member states'. The word 'may' implies that this provision covers both agreements, etc., which actually do affect such trade and also those which have the potentiality to do so and may actually have that effect in the future even if not at present. The effect may be direct or it may be indirect. It would be direct if a group of firms in one member state agreed the prices which they charged for exports to other member states. It would be equally direct if various national groups decided to keep out of each other's national markets. It would be somewhat more indirect if producers and dealers in one member state agreed to deal exclusively with each other. Such an arrangement would not directly regulate inter-state trade but it would have the effect of inhibiting or even totally preventing the entry of third party supplies from without.

It would be easy to interpret the inter-state clause as meaning that the offence is to reduce the level of such trade below that which would obtain if the competitive restriction did not exist. However, this is not true. An effect upon trade between member states also arises when a restrictive arrangement artificially stimulates it. In the *Cimbel* case Belgian cement producers operated a price equalization scheme as between the home and other member state markets. The practical effect was to subsidize sales in the latter and thus to stimulate them. The Commission observed that the arrangement 'artificially distorts trade between the member states because exports which, if the agreement did not exist, would not take place or would be made to a country situated at a more favourable distance, are deflected from their natural channels'. In short, trade must not be distorted one way or the other.

Article 85(2) declares prohibited agreements to be automatically void. It is, however, in Article 85(3) that we encounter the exemption aspect. It holds out the possibility that the Article 85(1) prohibition may not apply if an agreement, etc., 'contributes to improving the production or distribution of goods or to promoting technical progress'. There are, however, a number of caveats. (a) Any agreement, etc., which contributes to such an improvement must allow consumers a fair share of the resulting benefit. (b) The agreement in achieving the improvement and the fair sharing must not impose restrictions which are not indispensable to the attainment of those objectives. In other words, if an agreement is to get through it must impose no more restrictions than are absolutely essential. (c) The agreement must not allow the parties to eliminate competition in respect of a substantial part of the products in question. All these conditions are cumulative.

It should be added that for Article 85(1) to apply there has to be an appreciable restraint of competition. In 1970 the Commission issued a Notice on agreements of minor importance[1] – thus establishing a *de minimis* rule. Currently, if the firms participating in an agreement have a market share of not more than 5 per cent in a substantial part of the Common Market and their aggregate turnover does not exceed 50 million ECU, then a significant restriction of competition does not exist.

The application of Article 85 lies primarily with the ECC although its formal Decisions to prohibit, etc., are subject to appeal to the Court of Justice. To aid it the Commission has established a system of notification. Notification is clearly of assistance to the Commission in locating violations. There is also a strong incentive for companies to notify since if they do not do so there can be no question of their agreement being exempted. For example in the *Quinine* case the parties were advised to notify but decided not to do so. Subsequently they were caught by the ECC and not having notified they were denied the possibility of an exemption hearing and were indeed heavily fined. If on the other hand the agreement is duly notified it enjoys a provisional or temporary validity, until the Commission renders a formal decision to the effect that it falls within Article 85(1).[2] But once the Commission issues a Decision to the effect that the agreement is prohibited (exemption not being possible) then it would be an offence to continue it, and financial sanctions could be applied. Apart from formal prohibitions and exemptions, mention should be made of the Negative Clearance. This is granted when the Commission finds that the contents of an agreement are not such as to render it subject to Article 85 – in short the Commission finds no reason to intervene. It should be emphasized that prior to the

1. However, a Notice is merely for information and ultimately has no legal status. The Commission earlier (1968) issued a Notice indicating the various kinds of cooperation which did not in its view violate Article 85 – they cover such things as joint market research, joint advertising, joint selling where the parties do not compete, joint collection of debts, etc. The Notice stated that the Commission welcomed cooperation among small and medium-sized enterprises where such cooperation enabled them to work more rationally and increase their productivity and competitiveness in the larger market. It went on to add that cooperation among large enterprises could also be economically desirable and might not raise difficulties from the competition standpoint.

2. When a group of companies introduces a new agreement, etc., they are well advised to notify immediately. If, for example, they introduce the agreement first and then notify it at a later date, the act of notifying does not put an end to a pre-existing state of infringement. That is to say if, when the Commission comes to investigate the agreement, it decides to prohibit it then fines can be imposed for the period between entry into operation and the date of notification – see *Pittsburgh – Corning* case.

granting of a Negative Clearance or an Exemption the parties may have had to modify the agreement, stripping it of offending matter. However, even with some stripping the agreement may not be capable of being made innocuous or acceptable, and a formal prohibition may be on the cards, in which case the parties may choose to abandon rather than press the matter to the stage where a formal prohibitory Decision has to be issued.

The Commission in locating violations does not rely solely on notifications. It also keeps its eyes and ears open, receives complaints from injured parties (for which there is a formal mechanism) and can carry out sectoral investigations where the flow of trade between states is suspiciously small or in some way distorted. The Commission is endowed with powers to obtain from governments, competent state authorities, trade associations and undertakings information necessary for the prosecution of a case. Associations and undertakings who fail or refuse to render information, or give false information, can be fined.

We turn now to the record of the EC Commission in applying Article 85 to horizontal cartels concerned with price fixing, output restriction, market sharing, etc. The record is extremely impressive – virtually no cartel with significant market power has been exempted.

Price agreements have been consistently attacked. We have already referred to the *Aniline Dye* case, where exemption was precluded by virtue of the fact that the concerted practice had not been notified. Heavy fines were ultimately imposed upon the participating firms. In the *Glass Container* case the major manufacturers of bottles, jars and flasks in five member states had entered into a fair trade practice rules agreement which was operated by the International Fair Trade Practice Rules Administration (IFTRA), registered in Liechtenstein. Ostensibly the agreement was designed to eliminate unfair practices. Parties were precluded from selling below cost in order to drive out competitors, it was unfair to discriminate and to operate tie-ins, etc. However, the true purpose of the agreement was to ensure that a manufacturer making deliveries outside his normal business territory did not undercut the prices of a party to the agreement who was the national (or local) price leader. In order to achieve this, price-lists and terms were circulated so that it was possible to check on quotations made by other suppliers. Equally crucial to the system was the obligation not to deviate secretly from the listed prices. In order to strengthen group solidarity, the IFTRA partners had devised a common method of calculating costs and had agreed to adopt a delivered price system. The Commission saw the fair trading rules and the system of aligning on a national price leader's offer as offending under Article 85(1) but not being capable of exemption, not least because it seemed to offer no benefit to consumers. Quite the contrary – the consumer lost the benefit which import competition would have provided had such alignment not been required. The other parts of the agreement (information, costing and delivered price arrangements) had not been notified and could not be exempted. The whole arrangement was formally prohibited.

Common sales syndicates are best treated as a form of price agreement and in so doing we should note that the Commission has taken a consistently hostile attitude where significant market power has been apparent. Syndicates of this kind have usually been encountered in markets where products are homogeneous and price-cutting activity could be intense – i.e. fertilizers, cement, sulphuric acid, etc. Several early cases concerned fertilizers. In, for example, the *CFA* and *Cobelaz* cases the arrangements covered both home and export sales. Modifications therefore had to be made so that sales to other EEC countries were carried out independently by individual manufacturers. This change having been carried out, the Commission was able to grant a Negative Clearance. Interestingly, three leading French producers of fertilizers, who were involved in the *CFA* arrangement, also set up an export sales syndicate during the year in which the *CFA* Decision was handed down. This was called Floral Gmbh. It handled their compound fertilizer sales in West Germany. In 1979 the Commission banned this arrangement. In doing so it pointed out that the legal position of common selling syndicates had been made abundantly clear to the firms in the 1968 *CFA* Decision. However, because Floral handled only a small proportion of their fertilizer sales the fine imposed was a modest one. Where a common selling syndicate controls only a small proportion of the relevant market and thus has no appreciable market power, the arrangement may be granted a Negative Clearance as it stands.

Competition may also be restricted by the application of quotas to output or sales. Again the Commission has consistently opposed such arrangements. For example, in the *Cementregeling voor Nederland* (*CRN*) case of 1972 the Commission attacked the remaining elements of a cement cartel which had been in existence for decades. Dutch, German and Belgian cement producers shared out the Dutch market in the proportion 69 per cent, 14 per cent and 17 per cent with a limited amount being left to free competition. This particular cartel was part of an older and more comprehensive arrangement which had prescribed not only quotas but also prices and had also prohibited the construction of new cement works. The Commission gradually forced the older cartel to dismantle its restrictions and the successful attack in the *C R N* case was in effect the *coup de grâce*.

Territorial market sharing is an obviously offensive practice and one which has been consistently opposed. In 1984 the Commission revealed that it had been investigating major EEC producers of hydrogen peroxide and its derivatives for a period of twenty years. These included Solvay, Laporte Industries, Air Liquide, Degussa and Produits Chimiques Ugine Kuhlmann. The firms had operated an arrangement whereby they restricted their sales to a certain national market or markets. In addition, a national market where more than one producer was selling was shared in agreed percentages. Because of the gravity of the offences fines totalling 9 million ECUs were imposed.

The Commission has also attacked exclusionary practices which have sealed off a part of the Common Market. This was so in its recommendation to the Belgian Pottery Convention, which was concerned with reciprocal exclusive dealing arrangements affecting the Belgian market, and in the *German Wall and Floor Tile* case, where a group of German producers had instituted an aggregated rebate arrangement. The rebate was payable only on purchases from German manufacturers which had obvious implications for inter-state trade. The Commission objected that rebates should relate to purchases from individual producers in which case they had the possibility of reflecting actual savings. Moreover if the aim of the arrangement was to favour tiles relative to substitute products, purchases of foreign tiles ought to be taken into account.

The Commission has also encountered a number of important cases of information exchange and has not hesitated to insist on the termination of offensive elements. It did so in 1977 in connection with an informational arrangement operated by enterprises in the UK, France and West Germany who were engaged in supplying metal and plastic paper machine wire. In its original form the agreement required the parties to supply to the Secretariat-General of the International Association of Paper Machine Wire Manufacturers (a) price-lists and terms within two to three weeks of their becoming effective and (b) copies of all invoices for deliveries (except to the US) within ten days – the invoice to specify the name of the customer, the type of wire, the price and any other relevant terms. The Secretariat-General was authorized upon request to communicate the price paid by any particular customer to any national association or member firm, the object being to prevent customers playing one supplier off against another. The Commission saw this interchange as being inconsistent with a competitive relationship. Following the Commission's intervention, the parties agreed to cease the exchange of price-lists, to supply copies of invoices without identifying the customer and to use the latter purely for the purpose of preparing statistics.

Quite early on, the Commission showed itself to be concerned with (vertical) sole or exclusive distribution agreements. The key case – the first occasion on which a prohibition was handed down – was *Grundig-Consten*. The West German firm Grundig had appointed the Paris firm Consten as sole dealer of its products at its particular stage of the distributive chain (i.e. importer/wholesaler). Grundig had banned its sole dealers in other states from delivering goods into the French distributive network and undermining Consten – this is known as territorial protection, whilst lawyers like to refer to it as the no-poaching rule. The position of Consten was reinforced by the assignment to it of the trade mark GINT (Grundig International). The Commission prohibited the agreement, but on appeal to the Court of Justice the sole distribution element was upheld, the offending element being the territorial protection. The latter buttresses the sole dealer's monopoly in the chain of distribution and by compartmentalizing the Common Market gives rise to differences in prices for the same goods in the different member states. Goods which have entered into trade must be allowed to move freely across frontiers in the hope that inter-state price differences will be ironed out. Sole dealers are allowed to poach. The sole dealing element does constitute a restrictive agreement within the meaning of Article 85(1), but because it gives rise to advantageous effects in aiding the penetration of markets it is capable of being exempted. A number of pure sole dealing agreements were subsequently exempted and this was followed by Regulation 19 of 1965, and Regulation 67 of 1967, under which bilateral sole dealing agreements (between enterprises in two states) unencumbered by devices such as territorial protection were accorded block exemption status. This concern with the need to allow parallel imports has with only minor exceptions characterized the Commission's general stance in approaching all forms of distribution agreement. Under Regulation 83 of 1983, Regulation 67 of 1967 was modified. The structure and essential contents of the earlier Regulation were retained, but changes were made in the interest of facilitating intra-Community trade.

Those firms that seek to prevent parallel imports within their European distribution systems run the risk of severe penalties. In 1979 in the *Pioneer* case, Pioneer Electronics Europe, a subsidiary of a Japanese multi-national ranking among the world's leading suppliers of hi-fi equipment, was, together with its sole distributors in France, Germany and the UK, fined 6 950 000 EUA for operating what were in effect export bans.

Restrictions of competition may arise in connection with industrial and commercial property – i.e. trademarks, patents and copyrights. Recognizing that these are supposed to confer a monopoly position on the owner (or licensee) of the propery right in question, it seems possible that, particularly in the light of Article 36 (see Chapter 4), they could legitimately be invoked to prevent imports, thus compartmentalizing the Common Market. However, this is not so, thanks to Article 85 which has been successfully applied in such situations. It should be added that Article 30 *et seq*, relating to the free circulation of goods, has also been applicable. This is a complex area of Community law and we shall not attempt to present an exhaustive account of relevant cases. Rather we shall confine ourselves to outlining a couple of instances in which the Rome Treaty Articles have been employed to prevent the partitioning of the Common Market.

A good example is provided by the *Sirena-Eda* case. It concerned trademarks. In this particular instance an American company, Mark Allen, had assigned its trademark Prep, registered in Italy, to an Italian company Sirena. Mark Allen had also allowed a German company to use the mark. There was no problem while the two companies confined their sales of Prep toiletries to their own national markets. However, an import–export company, Novimpex SRL, obtained supplies of the German product and sold them in Italy and this provoked Sirena to ask the appropriate Italian court to forbid these imports. They were under-mining Sirena's trademark monopoly. The matter was referred to the Court of Justice for a preliminary ruling. The case was considered under Article 85 because an agreement existed in connection with the assign-ment of the trademark. The Court decided:

Article 85 therefore applies where, by virtue of trademark rights, imports of products originating in other member states, bearing the same trademark because their owners have acquired the trademark itself or the right to use it through agreements with one other or with third parties, are prevented.

The Court was therefore prepared to allow goods bearing a particular trademark to flow across frontiers and offer competition to dom-estically produced supplies bearing that same trademark. In the *Centra-farm* v. *Sterling Drug* case the matter at issue was patents and patent licensing. Sterling Drug possessed parallel drug patents in several member states including the Netherlands, UK and West Germany. It licensed its subsidiaries in the various member states to produce and market the drug. The case arose because the Dutch firm Centrafarm obtained supplies of the drug in West Germany and shipped them into the Netherlands. This provoked an appeal by Sterling on the grounds that its Dutch patent was being infringed. This was referrred to the Court of Justice for a preliminary ruling. The Court did not consider the case under Article 85 because no agreement arises between a parent and a subsidiary. The Court instead based its judgement on Article 30 *et seq*. It maintained that an attempt by the owner of a patent to prevent the import of a product, protected by that patent, which had been marketed in another member state by the patent owner, was incompatible with the concept of the free movement of goods. The Sterling subsidiaries exhausted their rights in the first marketing of the goods. If a party who acquired them sought to sell them in another territory where a parallel patent existed, that was perfectly compatible with the idea of a common market.

Thus far the Commission has been cast in a prohibitory role. But not all agreements have fallen foul of Article 85. Following the 1968 Notice on Cooperation, the Commission has been anxious to encourage certain forms of cooperation where efficiency gains are in prospect. The 1968 Notice referred primarily to forms of cooperation which were not likely to give rise to restrictions of competition, but in the Notice the Commission indicated its intention to address itself to situations where there was some restrictive effect but where counterbalancing gains might none the less accrue. There followed a number of Decisions concerning specialization and joint research and development. The former can be fairly obvious candidates for exemption. The arrangement is restrictive in that it reduces the number of competitors, etc. On the other hand, the longer runs reduce costs. Provided the parties have only a small share of the market, competition will probably ensure that some of the efficiency gains are passed on to the consumer. The Commission will clearly require that the agreement contains no extraneous restrictions, and the small share of the market will ensure that the last element of Article 85(3) is satisfied. These conditions were amply fulfilled in the *Jaz-Peter* and *Clima Chappée-Buderus* cases, but in others such as *Fine Papers* structural conditions were different. *Fine Papers* involved the principal French producers of cigarette paper, who had a market share of 80 per cent in France and 70 per cent in Benelux. However, the Commission found effective competition from

West German and Italian producers, potential competition from third country producers, countervailing power in the shape of the French and Italian tobacco monopolies as well as other larger producers, and noted that the agreement was not irreversible.

The Decisions on cooperation cases paved the way for a block exemption regulation. Regulation 2821 of 1971 provided general enabling powers to block exempt standardization, joint research and development and specialization agreements. Regulation 2779 of 1972 provided a specific power in respect of specialization agreements. The limitation on size and market shares is contained in Article 3 – the products subject to specialization must represent in a substantial part of the Common Market not more than 20 per cent of the volume of business done in similar products, and the aggregated turnover of the participating producers must not exceed 500 million ECU. In 1984 the Commission complemented this by a Regulation applying block exemption to joint research and development agreements. Again, restrictive conditions were imposed concerning the share of the market enjoyed by collaborating firms who were previously competitors. If however the participating firms were not previously in competition with each other then no market restriction would apply.

Dominant firms and mergers

The Rome Treaty provisions concerned with concentration situations are to be found in Article 86, which provides that:

Any abuse by one or more undertakings of a dominant position within the Common Market or a substantial part of it shall be prohibited as being incompatible with the Common Market in so far as it may affect trade between member states.

There are three important elements. (a) There must be a dominant position. (b) But dominance is not the sin, it is the abuse thereof. (c) There must be the possibility of an effect on trade between the member states – this is typical of the Rome Treaty approach. The first two call for further comment.

The dominant position has a geographical element since it may relate to the whole of the Common Market or it may be in a substantial part thereof. The Treaty offers no definition of what substantial means, but the territory of one member state, West Germany, was deemed to be large enough in the *GEMA* and *Continental Can* cases, and that of Belgium when the Court of Justice dealt with a copyright dispute. In the

Sugar cases the Commission treated Holland on its own, and Belgium and Luxembourg combined, as substantial parts of the Common Market.

The concept of dominance also implies that the company (or companies) involved must enjoy some market power, and this requires that the relevant market and the degree of control thereof must be identified. The *Continental Can* case provides a particularly good example of the approach which is adopted. *Continental Can* concerned the activities of the Continental Can Company Inc., a large American multi-national manufacturing metal containers, other packaging materials and machines for the manufacture and use of containers. It acquired a majority shareholding in a large West German producer of light metal containers – Schmalbach-Lubeca-Werke A G of Brunswick. Continental Can then transferred its holdings in Schmalbach to a holding company, the Europemballage Corporation. It also agreed to make an offer for the shares of the large Dutch can producer Thomassen & Drijver-Verblifa N V of Deventer – actually the offer was made by Europemballage. This was accomplished and thus control of both Schmalbach and Thomassen came to be vested in the one holding company created by Continental. The ECC then intervened. It saw the acquisition of Schmalbach as being a violation of Article 86. This was a controversial interpretation of Article 86 since it was being applied to a merger. Essentially the Commission was arguing that Schmalbach had a dominant position in the West German market for light containers for preserved meat and fish and metal caps for preserve jars. (Proof of the existence of a dominant position is stage number one in the successful prosecution of a case under Article 86.) The Commission also argued that the extinguishing of Thomassen's competition, via the acquisition, was an abuse within the meaning of Article 86. An effect on inter-state trade was likely in that Thomassen would not now sell competitively in the West German market, and for that matter Schmalbach would not now do likewise in the Benelux market. The case is instructive because much turned on the question of whether Schmalbach really had a dominant position in West Germany. The Court in fact found against the Commission. In doing so it did not invoke any particular market share as being critical but pointed to the existence of other sources of ongoing or potential competition such as containers made of plastic or glass, suppliers of metal containers for other goods who could turn their attention to the meat and fish container market and the fact that food packers could manufacture their own containers. Although Schmalbach did not dominate the West German market it might appear that the merger did suppress one source of independent competition. However, it appeared that there had been little competition from Thomassen. Apparently the Commission had been investigating the possibility that there was an agreement at the time of the merger but had not completed its investigation. In the circumstances the Commission ultimately had to rely on the notion that the merger would suppress potential competition.

Whilst *Continental Can* was instructive in indicating the kind of considerations which are important in defining the relevant market, that case did not, as we have just seen, indicate what *proportion* of the market has to be controlled if a firm is to be declared dominant. A number of subsequent cases did throw light on this issue.

Obviously a 100 per cent share must be one of dominance – this was so in the *GEMA* case. In the *Sugar* cases, Raffinerie Tirlemontoise had an 85 per cent share of the Belgium–Luxembourg market and it too was declared to be dominating. However, the proportion can sink much lower. In the *Hoffman-La Roche* case 47 per cent of the market for vitamin A was deemed to be dominant. In that case however the fact that the two largest competitors only possessed 45 per cent of the market between them was important. In the *Chiquita* case, concerning the market in bananas (see below), United Brands possessed only a 40 per cent share. But there were good structural reasons for accepting such a low figure. Firstly, the competitors of United Brands were very small. Secondly, there were substantial barriers to new entrants. In the more recent *IBM* case, IBM had 40 per cent of the computer market (mainframe and mini) and only 39 per cent of the data processing market. But again, IBM was in sales terms seven times larger than its nearest rival.

The second aspect of Article 86 is the abuse of the dominant position by a firm or firms. A number of examples are given but these are merely illustrative. They are: directly or indirectly imposing unfair purchasing or selling prices or other unfair trading conditions; limiting production, markets or technical development to the prejudice of consumers; applying dissimilar conditions to equivalent transactions with other trading parties, thereby placing them at a competitive disadvantage – this obviously refers to price discrimination; making the conclusion of contracts subject to acceptance by other parties of supplementary obligations which, by their nature or according to commercial usage, have no connection with the subject of such contracts – clearly this refers to tie-ins.

In actual cases one of the main forms of abuse encountered has been the granting of fidelity rebates. In the *Sugar* cases two large West German sugar producers had in concert offered rebates which were conditional upon buyers taking all their supplies from them. In *Hoffmann-La Roche* the Commission dealt with a similar practice in respect of supplies of vitamins for bulk use in medicines, foods and feeding stuffs. The Commission observed 'Whether to compensate for the exclusivity or to encourage a preferential link, the contracts provided for fidelity rebates based not on differences in costs related to the quantities supplied by Roche but on the proportion of the customer's requirements covered.' Moreover, Roche was able to extend its power to products where it was not dominant, since the rebates were not calculated separately for each particular group of vitamins but were aggregated across all purchases. A fine was imposed.

The Commission has also attacked the practice of refusal to supply. This arose in the *Commercial Solvents* case. Commercial Solvents, a monopolist of raw material needed to produce a particular drug, decided (through its subsidiary) not to supply the raw material to an existing producer of the drug. The Court of Justice stated that an undertaking which is in a dominant position in the supply of a raw material, and is thus in a position to control the supply to producers of products manufactured from that material, cannot refuse to supply such a customer with the effect of eliminating all competition therefrom.

In the *GEMA* case the Commission objected to the activities of a performing rights society which in fact enjoyed a monopoly of the German market. GEMA was established to protect the rights of member composers, authors and publishers. Rights were assigned to it and it exploited them in return for royalties. GEMA had imposed unduly restrictive terms on its members – they had to assign to it all existing and future rights in all respects and in all countries, for a minimum period of six years. The Commission objected to the universality of the assignment required of members. It felt that they should be free to assign only a part of their rights and be able to retain the other part for individual exploitation. The Commission also singled out for criticism the exclusion of non-residents – a provision which was apparently designed to consolidate the market power of other national societies.

In the *Chiquita* case the Commission attacked the practice of charging different prices in different parts of the Common Market for the same product. On appeal the Court took the view that prices should be related to costs and should not be set at the various levels that the different national markets would bear.

In the *IBM* case the allegations, which led to a negotiated settlement, concerned matters such as the failure of IBM to produce advance technical information about its equipment, failure to offer equipment without items which other suppliers could offer to attach and failure to exclude software from the price of the hardware. The latter two are referred to as bundling – i.e. different pieces of equipment, or equipment and software, are bundled together in the total price. The effect of these devices was to delay competitors producing equipment which could be plugged into IBM products (i.e. equipment which was plug-compatible) and in the case of bundling to eliminate the possibility of other firms supplying hardware and software which could be used in conjunction with IBM hardware. In the more recent *AKZO* case another abuse has been identified, namely predatory pricing, whereby a firm sells below cost in order to drive out a competitor, thereafter being able to hoist prices to more profitable levels.

We have already touched upon EEC merger policy when discussing the *Continental Can* case. Our discussion in that instance was concerned with the light that *Continental Can* threw on the meaning of Article 86. In that case the ECC attempted to prohibit a merger but failed to provide the proof of dominance necessary to convince the Court of Justice that the ban on the takeover of Thomassen & Drijver-Verblifa ought to be upheld. But there was also the important question at stake as to whether Article 86 could actually be said to apply to mergers. There were some who said it did not. They argued that Article 86 does not proscribe a dominant position – it attacks the abuse thereof. Therefore if a dominant firm took over another and became more dominant no offence arose. An offence would only arise if the now more dominant firm misbehaved. However, the Commission, at least as far back as 1965, maintained that the Rome Treaty was seriously deficient without a power to control mergers. It considered a number of possible remedies, one of which was that Article 86 could be applied to acquisitions. In its memorandum on *Concentration by Firms in the Common Market* (EEC Commission, 1965) it declared that if a dominant firm took over another and so established a monopoly, that was an abuse within the meaning of Article 86.

The real importance of the *Continental Can* case was that it considered these opposing views and came out in favour of the Commission. The Court of Justice did so because it adopted a pragmatic approach. It noted that Article 3(f) of the Treaty called for the establishment of conditions of undistorted competition. It also saw that if firms were debarred from colluding by virtue of the effect of Article 85(1) they could still acquire their control of the market by merging. There was a serious loophole and this dictated that Article 86 be given the more generous interpretation. The Commission maintained that in *Continental Can* an undertaking in a dominant position had strengthened its position by means of a merger so that actual or potential competition in the Common Market (or a substantial part of it) was almost eliminated. The Court concurred that such an elimination, and it need not be total, was an abuse of Article 86. The important point to prove was that 'competition was so substantially impaired that the remaining competitors could not constitute an adequate counterweight'.

Unfortunately, Article 86 is not a perfect merger instrument. It requires a firm to be in a dominant position before it can be invoked. It may in fact be desirable to prevent that dominance arising in the first place – otherwise it is a case of locking the stable door after the horse has bolted. Therefore the Commission is seeking a new power to control mergers and a draft regulation has been produced which has, however, not yet received the assent of the Council of Ministers. In the interim the Commission has continued to investigate mergers which appear to come within the provisions of Article 86. However, in November 1987, the Court of Justice handed down a decision which is likely to be of considerable significance in this context. The case concerned a merger between cigarette manufacturers. In its judgement, the Court agreed with the Commission that Article 85 can be applied to mergers. In other words, a merger may in some circumstances be regarded as an agreement by means of which one firm acquires control over the actions of another.[1] Incidentally, this would dispose of the need to prove the existence of a dominant position. This was designed to provoke the Council of Ministers into approving the draft merger-control regulation, and late in 1987 the ministers indicated their intention to do so.

Fiscal factors

Our primary focus will be indirect taxes. Within that area two forms of tax fall due for consideration. One is the turnover tax. The other is the excise duty.

It is not immediately obvious why indirect taxes such as the turnover variety should give rise to an NTB problem. The full import of that remark must, however, wait upon a discussion of two other issues. The

---

1. Early in 1988 the Commission used its new found power to block a merger in the French can industry.

first is the nature of turnover taxes as they existed in the Community at the time when the Rome Treaty was being drafted. The second is the traditional treatment of indirect taxes on goods entering into international trade.

Within the general category of turnover tax the Community operated two main kinds – the cascade and the value added systems. (The latter was of course adopted by the UK in place of purchase tax and selective employment tax in anticipation of British membership of the Community.) The French had opted for the TVA (*Taxe sur valeur ajoutée*, i.e. VAT) but the rest of the Community applied cascade systems.

The cascade tax was a multi-stage tax in that it was levied at each stage of the productive process. In practice it covered a broad range of products. It was therefore unlike the British purchase tax, which was a single-stage tax levied at the wholesaler stage, covering a relatively narrow range of goods. Cascade taxes were levied on the gross value of output at each stage in the chain of production. The important point to note is the cumulative nature of the system: tax is applied at each stage upon the whole selling value including tax. If the product is used in further production, the selling price of the resulting product upon which tax is charged will be inflated by tax paid at the previous stage. Under the cascade system the cost of producing a given item excluding tax (that is, the value added) may be the same whether produced by a vertically integrated firm or by a vertical series of independent enterprises, but the tax paid on the product of the latter will be greater than that levied on the former.

The basic feature of VAT is that it is paid at each stage in the process of production upon the value added at each point in the productive chain. The final price of the product, in the absence of turnover tax, is equal to the sum of the values added at each point. Because of this fact it makes no difference whether the tax is collected at several points or as a single payment on the final product. The tax collected will be the same in either case – the tax is therefore neutral as between production which is carried out in a vertically integrated firm and production which is carried out by several separate firms with tax levied at the intermediate stages.

We turn now to the treatment of indirect taxes in international trade. (In practice we will assume that the trade takes place between members of a customs union.) Here we have to distinguish between the origin and destination principles. The origin principle can be explained as follows. Let us suppose that good X is manufactured in Country I and Country I applies a general turnover tax which amounts to 10 per cent on the cost of producing a good. If good X is exported to Country II it retains the 10 per cent and is thus delivered to consumers in Country II with the tax applied. Suppose that Country II applies a 20 per cent tax to good X which it produces itself then, other things being equal, good X coming from Country I has an artificial competitive advantage. Indeed if producers of X in Countries I and II are equally efficient then producers in Country II will find their sales falling as they are undersold by Country I producers.

In the case of the destination principle, however, good X produced in Country I will when exported have the 10 per cent tax remitted. It would thus be exported to Country II free of the tax and Country II would apply its own tax at the 20 per cent rate. In other words the exported good bears the tax of the country of destination and not of origin.

The importance of the remark made earlier is now clear. In the case of the destination principle, *and this is the principle normally applied in international trade,* good X produced in Country I and good X produced in Country II are treated equally, in terms of the tax levied on them, when sold in Country II. *Differences in tax rates do not therefore lead to distortions of competition between the two countries.* Then why be concerned with the need to harmonize the tax *systems* and *rates* of the countries in the customs union?

In a large measure the answer lies in a consideration of the problems encountered in remitting turnover taxes on exports when a cascade system is operating. Specifically the problem is that it is extremely difficult to know with any accuracy just how much tax is incorporated in the price of the good and therefore how much should be remitted. Too little could be remitted, in which case exports are artificially disadvantaged. But too much may deliberately be remitted in which case an artificial export aid, and probably a concealed one at that, will operate. In this case we have an NTB which *distorts* trade and production.

Politically such artificial aids are divisive. There are, however, a number of other points which have also compelled action. From what has gone before it is evident that the cascade system gives an artificial incentive to vertical integration. This has several disadvantageous effects. Firstly, it may be more efficient to specialize in one stage of a productive process, but the tax discourages this. There may, of course, be no advantage as between vertically integrated and non-vertically integrated firms from the point of view of productive efficiency. But the vertically integrated firm enjoys an artificial competitive advantage. Secondly, although from the view of maintaining competition it is usual to regard horizontal concentrations as a main problem, there are reasons for fearing the vertical variety. A firm which is integrated backwards can control supplies of raw material and semi-finished products to competitors and force them out of business or force them to conform to its wishes. However, this problem only arises if firms at an earlier stage in the production process are concentrated horizontally, and this is not inevitable since the tax does not bias industrial structures in this way. But it could be argued that by integrating vertically an enterprise could acquire financial resources which would enable it to concentrate horizontally. Such resources would enable it to endure the price wars which might be necessary to discipline non-vertically integrated firms. Thirdly, there are reasons for believing that vertical integration in industry tends to impede cross-frontier competition. This argument is based on the proposition that in the absence of such integration, firms at any stage of production have the alternative of buying the products of the previous stage either from domestic enterprises or from foreign firms. In effect an import gap exists. With vertical integration this possibility does not exist.

There were two other arguments favouring a change in the Community's tax structure. One was that in creating the Common Market the aim had been to produce within the enlarged market of the Six conditions which were analogous to those existing in a national market. But the destination principle meant that the administrative procedures for reimbursing indirect taxes and applying countervailing duties had to be maintained, and this constituted a fiscal frontier not normally present when goods flowed within national boundaries. The other argument related to the obvious fact that a common market could hardly be said to exist when consumers in the various member states paid different prices for the same goods because national tax rates differed.

The need for action in the field of taxation was recognized in the Rome Treaty – Articles 95 to 99 are the relevant ones. It should, however, be noted that although Article 99 refers to harmonization of taxation it is only in respect of indirect taxes that specific action is contemplated. Article 99 requires that the Commission

Shall consider how to further the interests of the common market by harmonizing the legislation of the various member states concerning turnover taxes, excise duties and other forms of indirect taxation . . . [and] shall submit proposals to the Council.

The actual process of harmonization is provided for in Article 100.

In practice the Community chose to approach the problems discussed above by harmonizing turnover taxes on the value added model. In 1967 two directives to this end were adopted by the Council. All the original members had to adopt the VAT by not later than 1 January 1970 (subsequently Italy and Belgium were granted time-limit extensions). New members were also required to adopt it – Greece however was not expected to introduce it until the end of 1986. Directives also laid down the base (i.e. collection of goods and services) upon which the tax was to be levied. These included the Sixth Directive of 1977 which also provided the uniform VAT assessment base which was necessary if the Community budget own resources system was to be fully operational. Having significantly harmonized the form and base, the Community was still left with the crucial problem of rates. As the reader can see in Table 9, these are as yet unharmonized.

We mentioned earlier that in the run-up to the Inter-governmental Conference of 1985 the Commission produced a document which called for the completion of the internal market, and indeed the Single European Act pledged the Community to achieve such a situation by the end of 1992 (although the shift of the Article 100 harmonization power from unanimity to majority voting will not apply to fiscal matters). As part of the plan to complete the single market the Commission has proposed three developments in the field of VAT. Firstly, the base needs to be fully harmonized – at present there are gaps and derogations which need to be dealt with. Secondly, the number of rates needs to be harmonized – some countries have only one rate (e.g. the UK), some have four (e.g. Italy). Thirdly, the actual rates need to be harmonized. The Commission has suggested that identical rates are not necessary. All that is needed is that they be brought close together so as to prevent any significant distortion of trade and competition. If rates were sufficiently harmonized it would then be possible to shift to the origin system. The problem of the fiscal frontier would disappear and a truly common market in terms of the level of tax would arise. In order to deal with the second and third problems, the Commission in July 1987 proposed a standard band of 14 to 20 per cent together with a lower band of 4 to 9 per cent. The Commission showed flexibility by being prepared to accept, at least temporarily, zero rating for some goods – a matter which concerns the UK and Ireland. The ending of zero rating would be likely to raise considerable opposition in the UK, which has continued to insist on applying it in respect of commodities such as food.

The Commission has also indicated its desire to harmonize excise duties. What, it may be asked, are the reasons which lie behind this proposal? We must begin by pointing out that the reasons are in the

Table 9. VAT rates in the EEC, 1 January 1986[1]

	Lower	Standard	Higher
Belgium	6 and 17	19	25 and 33
Denmark	—	22	—
Germany	7	14	—
Spain	6	12	33
France	·5·5 and 7	18·6	33·3
Ireland	0 and 10	23	—
Italy	2 and 9	18	38
Luxembourg	3 and 6	12	—
Netherlands	5	19	—
Portugal	8	16	30
United Kingdom	0	15	—

Note: 1 Greece had not then introduced VAT.
Source: EC Commission, *The Approximation of European Tax Systems*, OOPEC, European File 9/86, p. 8.

main different from those which apply in the case of turnover taxes. The problem is *not* one of distortions of competition arising from excessive remissions on export. The problems in fact spring from differences of excise rate for *particular* products as between *states* and differences of excise rate as between *different* products *in any particular member state*. Let us take them in that order.

In the case of mineral oils, the excise rates (and exemptions from excise duty) are different in the various member states. Excise duties constitute a part of the cost of producing goods and these differences therefore distort competition between the states. The industries in the countries with the highest excise duties on mineral oils are at an artificial competitive disadvantage. It would be phenomenally difficult to use the destination system to eliminate the disadvantage which the high-duty country faces when it exports its goods. The mind boggles at the size of the administrative task involved in calculating the size of the disadvantage encountered by a particular kind of good and devising a compensating mechanism. The obvious path is to harmonize rates and exemptions imposed as between the member states.

As we have indicated, the other problem arises from differences of excise rate as between different products in any particular state. Here we should note that Article 95 requires states not to impose internal taxation on the products of other member states which affords indirect protection to *other goods*. What, it may be asked, is that particular provision trying to prevent? The answer is that it refers to situations where two products may compete (i.e. are substitutes) and a member state applies a higher excise duty on one as compared with the other. The most obvious temptation is to apply a high excise duty on a mainly imported good and a lower one on the domestic substitute. For example, the UK was accused by the Commission of applying a higher excise burden on wine (largely imported) as compared with beer (largely home produced). That was the issue in a case before the Court of Justice – *Commission* v *UK* – and ultimately the UK lost. In a similar case – *Commission* v *Denmark* – the Danes were accused of applying a lower excise on schnapps (largely home produced) as compared with other spirits (largely imported). The Commission claimed that the behaviour of the Danish Government was an offence under Article 95 and the Court concurred.

Clearly, the kind of problems which have arisen with mineral oils and beverages would not exist if excises were harmonized as between products and as between states. For this to happen it will be necessary to agree on the products which are to be subject to excise duty – at present there are wide variations between states. The EC Commission would like to see the tax confined to tobacco, beer, alcohol, wine and mineral oils with an agreement that member states should not thereafter extend the coverage. It will also be necessary to agree on common structures – these too vary with some taxes taking a lump sum or specific form and others being based on an *ad valorem* or percentage system. The actual rates would have to be harmonized or brought nearer together. As early as 1972 a programme of harmonization was proposed by the Commission but little has been achieved. The only notable step has been a series of directives on tobacco products which envisaged the ultimate harmonization of rates. The concrete element of these directives has been concerned with the tax structure for cigarettes. The Community system will be part specific and part *ad valorem*. The Commission now plans (see July 1987 proposal) a comprehensive harmonization of excise duties by 1992 as part of the completion of the internal market.

State aids

It is not difficult to see that aids given to enterprises by states may distort competition between union members by giving some an artificial competitive advantage. Articles 92 to 94 of the Treaty are designed to deal with this problem.

Article 92(1) enunciates the basic principle. State aids which distort (or threaten to distort) competition by favouring certain enterprises, or the production of certain goods, are *in so far as trade between member states is affected* incompatible with the common market. Obviously aids with purely local effects are excluded – there is a parallel here with the law on cartels and dominant positions. With this as its general posture, the Treaty then explicitly recognizes two categories of exception. One consists of a series of aids which are *definitely* excepted from the general ban (Article 92(2)). The other consists of a series of examples of aids which *may* be excepted (Article 92(3)).

The definitely excepted category consists of aids of a social character granted to individuals. Aid granted to children in the form of free school milk would presumably fall into this class. The aid has, however, to be given without reference to where the goods come from. Discriminatory treatment whereby British milk was subsidized but other E E C milk was not would not normally be acceptable. Aids may also be given in connection with natural disasters and to areas in West Germany bordering on the German Democratic Republic which have been disadvantaged by that geographical division.

We come now to the second category. Clearly, although there was no separate title in the Treaty relating to regional policy, those who drafted it were aware of pronounced differences in standards of living within the E E C and of the existence of regional problems which could only be dealt with if policies of (possibly intensified) regional aid were pursued. There is in effect a recognition of all this in the Preamble and in Article 2 which calls for the promoting '. . . throughout the Community [of] an harmonious development of economic activities, a continuous and balanced expansion . . .' It was therefore inevitable that Article 92 would have to provide for the possibility of regional aids being deemed compatible with the Common Market. This is indeed the posture – they may be, but are not automatically, compatible. Clearly a blanket exception could not be given since regional aids might be excessive and thus become not a means of offsetting or overcoming certain locational disadvantages but a source of unfair competitive advantage. The theory that aids may be compatible applies not only to regional aids but also to assistance for the development of certain economic activities (i.e. industries). We have therefore the possibility of sectoral as well as regional aids. Aids may also be compatible if designed to promote an important project of common European importance or to remedy a serious disturbance in the economy of a member state.

Article 93 imposes on the Commission the task of keeping state aids under constant review. Member states are required to inform the

Commission of plans to grant aids or to alter them. Member states must also abide by the Commission's recommendations in connection therewith. If the Commission finds that an aid is not compatible with the Treaty it can issue a Decision requiring the aid to be terminated or modified. If member states do not comply, the Commission can initiate an enforcement action under Article 169. This carries with it the ultimate possibility that failure to comply could involve the Commission in taking the offending state to the Court of Justice for a final determination.

Before we turn to a discussion of the approach of the Commission to the different forms of state aid, it is important to note a trend. State aids have always posed a problem for the Commission, but since the middle of the 1970s, and particularly in the early 1980s, states have increasingly sought to give aids in order to cope with the generally depressed conditions and the problems encountered by specific industries. The Commission for its part has been involved in an increasing number of actions which have informally or formally led to modifications or abandonments of aid-giving plans.

Regional aid schemes have indeed posed a very considerable control problem for the Commission. The basic difficulty was that the various regions of the Community began to compete with each other to attract footloose investment capital. Regional aid schemes became more costly as a result of competitive outbidding and this process of bidding up did not appreciably increase the flow of investment. Rather it tended to give rise to reciprocal neutralization with unjustified profits for the beneficiary enterprise. Also aids tended no longer to correspond to the relative seriousness of the situation and in some cases the aid schemes were such that it was difficult to estimate just how generous they were. In 1971 the Commission decided to take action to control this process of aid escalation. Proposals were elaborated governing the scale of aid-giving in different regions. This was further developed in 1975 and 1979. These proposals were transmitted to and accepted by the Council of Ministers. The basic idea is that there should be differentiated aid limits. In the central regions of the Community, regional aid levels should be low since they are relatively prosperous and unemployment tends to be relatively low. As the regional problem becomes more severe the aid limit should be higher, with the highest limits being found at the extremities of the Community, where the most severe problems are usually to be found. These aid limits, which take the form of grant ceilings, are expressed either in relation to the initial investment or jobs created. For example, in the central regions the basic rule is that the aid ceiling is 20 per cent of the initial investment, or 3500 ECUs per job created; in the regional development areas of France, Italy (other than the Mezzogiorno) and the UK (other than Northern Ireland) the figures are 30 per cent and 5500 ECUs, whilst in Ireland, Northern Ireland and the Mezzogiorno the ceilings are 75 per cent and 13 500 ECUs.

It is important to emphasize that these are aid *ceilings*. It does not follow that, for example, a member state can automatically make a grant of 20 per cent in a particular part of a 'central' region. Rather, the EC Commission will exercise supervision and will ultimately be able to decide whether that particular area can be scheduled as one entitled to receive regional aid. Equally, the Commission will appraise the socio-economic conditions in the area and determine what degree of aid (up to 20 per cent) is acceptable.

Before we leave the subject of regional aids, it needs to be recognized that the Commission has sought to regulate not only the level of aid given, but also the kinds of aid instrument employed. The UK has been particularly influenced here, since the regional employment premium – a continuing labour subsidy – was not acceptable to the Commission. It was never banned and eventually the UK abandoned its use except in Northern Ireland. The UK regional development grant has also been attacked. The Commission favours once-for-all aid that should render a project sufficiently profitable for the enterprise to replace the capital in due course. In the case of the UK regional development grant, aid was not only granted initially but also made available when the capital was depreciated and was being renewed. Moreover, the second dose of aid was also granted even though no new employment was being created. The Commission has forced the UK Government to modify the grant system accordingly.

Another main area of the Commission's supervisory activity is sectoral aid. As already indicated, aids to specific industries can be compatible with the Common Market, but the Commission has laid down certain criteria which must be respected. These (as spelled out in its *First Report on Competition Policy*, EC Commission, 1972a, p. 130) are as follows:
(a) Aids must be selective and must only be granted to enterprises the development or reorganization of which justify the presumption that they will be competitive in the long run having regard to the expected developments in the industrial sector concerned.
(b) Arising out of (a) is the condition that aids must be degressive. Aid must eventually be phased out and the enterprises must then be able to manage without further assistance. Aids must therefore not allow in-definitely a continuance of a situation of less than optimum allocation of resources. Aids may, however, be envisaged as going on indefinitely if

at the Community level it is decided to continue them in order to compensate for competitive distortions emanating from outside the Community.

(c) Aids must be as transparent as possible so that they can be evaluated by, amongst others, Community institutions.

(d) Aids must obviously be well adapted to the objectives in view and if there is a choice of method, then the method adopted should be that which has the least effect on intra-Community competition and the common interest. ·

Subsequently, the economic position within the Community changed. From the end of 1974 onwards the Community economy was depressed, and added to that was the problem of intense competition from Japan and the Newly Industrializing Countries (NICs). State aids had a role to play here in keeping firms afloat whilst they introduced rationalization programmes. These take time to implement, and given the rising unemployment it was increasingly difficult for displaced workers to find new jobs elsewhere. The problems of industries in distress had been highlighted at the Copenhagen Summit of 1978 and this was followed by a dialogue between the Council of Ministers and the Commission, after which the latter issued new aid guidelines. Whilst these reiterate some of the ideas of 1972 there is a noticeable softening of tone, particularly in respect of the need for a breathing space which would allow longer term restructuring solutions to be worked out. Aids could be used as an interim measure to avoid sudden and severe social and economic shocks. The new guidelines also explicitly recognized the valuable role that state aids could play in (a) speeding up the response of the private enterprise system to new investment and technological opportunities and (b) the adaptation of industries which need to contract and redeploy resources.

The Commission has not defined its attitude to aid in every specific industrial sector. Only in the case of industries which have been encountering structural problems across the Community has the Commission felt the need to take a specific stance. This has been the case in textiles, clothing, man-made fibres and shipbuilding. We shall not discuss these approaches at this point but reserve discussion until Chapter 10 when we consider Community Industrial Policy and notably its policy stance towards problem industries.

Three further developments are of particular note. First, following the post-Copenhagen guidelines, the Commission became more sympathetic towards aids designed to stimulate research and development (R & D). This was undoubtedly a reflection of the growing appreciation of the need for the Community to match the technological might of the US and Japan. However, because assistance was increasingly taking the form of aid to R & D, the Commission decided in 1985 to lay down a Community framework. The basic rules are as follows: (a) such aids must be notified like any others; (b) the level of aid for *basic* research should not exceed 50 per cent of the research programme or project, and the nearer the research is to the market place (i.e. applied as opposed to basic) the lower the aid level must be; (c) the possibility that such aid will distort competition and affect inter-state trade has to be taken into account.

The second point is that there has been a growing tendency for sectoral aid to take the form of state participation in the capital of *private* undertakings. The Commission maintains, and has been supported by the Court of Justice, that this constitutes an aid if the capital is injected at less than commercial terms. The Court made this clear in the 1984 *Intermills* case when it said that loans advanced on more favourable terms than are available in the market and equity capital advanced when private investors would not do so are just as much aids as is a straight capital grant.

The third point is an extension of the second. The Rome Treaty does not preclude nationalization. However, Article 90, subject to one qualification,[1] does declare that the rules on competition (Articles 85 and 86 *et seq.*) and on state aids (Article 92 *et seq.*) do apply to such enterprises. In respect of state aids, the Commission has been concerned about the financial relationship between governments and their public corporations. Obviously the concern of the Commission is that capital could be provided at favourable rates and that this would give the corporations an artificial competitive edge when competing with firms in the same industry in other member states who operate on a private basis. In order to more effectively regulate the activities of member states in relation to their public enterprises, the Commission in 1980 took the controversial step of adopting a directive requiring states to provide data on the financial relationships between themselves and their public corporations. This provoked strong opposition from some member state governments. They challenged the Commission's action in the Court of Justice – in the event the Court supported the Commission.

There is also a third category of aid, which in recent years has caused the Commission some trouble. This is the general aid which, as its title suggests, has no designated specific objective and can be applied on an

1. Article 90 declares that although public utilities and state monopolies of a commercial character (see below) are subject to the competition rules, the application of those rules must not obstruct the performance of tasks assigned to such enterprises.

individual, sectoral or regional basis as the national need arise. The attitude of the Commission has been that, as they stand, such aids are incompatible with the Rome Treaty and ought to be made specific – i.e. they ought to be transformed into sectoral or regional aids which address themselves to particular kinds of problem. The Commission also indicated that it should be kept informed about such general aids. (Its attitude was well summarized in *Second Report on Competition Policy* (EC Commission, 1973, pp. 101–6).) However, as we noted earlier, the economic situation subsequently worsened. During the second half of 1974 the Community economy began to enter its worst postwar recession. Unemployment began to rise and the economic downturn began to aggravate the situation in industries which had structural problems dating from the energy crisis and earlier. Even in sectors not suffering from such problems, some enterprises found themselves in financial difficulties. The upshot of all this was an intensification of general aid schemes and the implementation of various general recovery measures. Although the Commission could have raised objections, it seems to have recognized that the exceptional economic and social situation confronting the member states justified the adoption of these exceptional measures. In so doing it drew attention, prudently perhaps, to Article 92 (3)(b) which allows aids to be granted which are designed 'to remedy a serious disturbance in the economy of a member state'. The Commission has, however, required that the established practice whereby it is notified about general aid schemes should also apply in the case of recovery measures, and it has continued to discharge a policing role.

Before we leave the subject of general aids, a little more needs to be said about the notification system. The Commission seems to have become reconciled to the idea that member state governments find it beneficial to have general aid powers at their disposal. The Commission does not therefore tend to intervene at the point in time when the governments pass such laws. The Commission has, however, made it clear that the fact that it does not intervene at that stage does not mean that the member states have a *carte blanche* to apply their general aid powers. Rather, the Commission waits until the state uses its general aid power in some particular way. The Commission will then consider whether the particular application is justified by any of the escape clauses provided in Article 92. If not, the Commission will forbid the aid. The reader who wishes to see this process at work is referred to the very instructive 1979 *Philip Morris* case.

Finally, we must note the other important form of state assistance – the export aid. The Commission has taken a very categorical stance on this topic. Such aid cannot benefit from any exception whatsoever and the Commission has constantly been on the attack. For example, in 1976 it took the Italian Government to task because the Istituto Nazionale per il Commercio Estero (ICE) was making grants to cover approximately two thirds of the promotional cost of toy sales in the French market. Subsequently, it was discovered that ICE was also making grants in respect of the sales promotion of footwear, textiles and clothing in other member state markets. The Commission therefore initiated a procedure which finally led to the issuing of a Decision formally instructing the Italian Government to desist.

Official and technical standards

Member state governments interfere on a very considerable scale in establishing official and technical standards. These are laid down for a variety of reasons but mainly to protect the public against physical harm and deception. As an example of the first we can cite the case of drugs and proprietary medicines. The need for government surveillance and control is all too obvious – experience with thalidomide leaves no doubt on that score. Then in the case of foods, standards have to be established in respect of flavouring, colouring and other additives; we can cite the ban on cyclamates as a case in point. But there are many others – electrical equipment and the emission of pollutants by road vehicles are two examples taken at random. Where the consumer is not likely to be harmed he may be deceived. For this reason there are rules on labelling designed to indicate to the consumer what certain designations, for example of textiles, really mean.

The desirability of such standards is not in question, but to the extent that they differ significantly between states they do undoubtedly constitute a form of NTB. Either they mean that goods cannot be exported, with a consequent loss of competition across frontiers, or if they are exported they have to be adapted to the rules of each national market. Either way the economies of large-scale production, in the form of long runs of a standardized product, are in some degree sacrificed. The obvious answer is to harmonize standards, and the EC Commission has pointed out that such harmonization can raise the quality of life in matters such as safety and the environment, since the Community standard can be based on the best national practice available. Consumer choice is also increased. The notion that harmonization leads to less variety is erroneous. Rather, the existence of non-tariff barriers reduces national choice. Although products may be standardized in certain essential respects, they can still exhibit wide variations of styling and performance. Thus the car in the EEC has been subject to considerable harmonization but the range of choice is still vast.

The need to harmonize standards was recognized by those who drafted the Rome Treaty, the relevant provisions being Articles 100 to 102 on the approximation of laws. Article 100 provides for the Council, on a proposal by the Commission, to issue unifying directives when laws, regulations or administrative actions of member states directly affect the setting up or operation of the common market.

Harmonization measures have fallen into either the 'total' or 'optional' category. Total harmonization required that all products covered by a directive had to conform to the standards set out in the directive. In such a case national standards had to be abolished and the Community standard substituted. Such total harmonization was usually adopted when consumer safety was involved (e.g. cosmetics), although this approach was also adopted in the case of textile labelling which was purely informational. Optional harmonization permitted the parallel existence of Community and national rules. Manufacturers who produced in accordance with the Community standard acquired access to all national markets, whilst those who continued to apply only national standards had access to only their home market.

Up to 1985 the Council of Ministers had adopted approximately 180 directives relating to industrial products and approximately sixty concerned with foodstuffs. The industrial products include motor vehicles, metrology (i.e. measuring instruments), cosmetics, solvents (and other dangerous substances) and electrical equipment. In the case of foodstuffs, directives govern their labelling (durability, additives used, etc.), packaging (restriction on the use of PVC), presentation, advertising and composition. Additives have been subject to provisions specifying maximum levels. Much has therefore been achieved but there is still a long way to go, since the Commission estimates that in the industrial field alone 300 directives will be necessary. Moreover, the harmonization process is very time consuming. Not only that, but technological progress renders existing standards obsolescent, and therefore effort has to be diverted into bringing them up to date. The Community has in fact been forced to adopt a speedier process in respect of amendment to standards.

In Chapter 4 we said we would return to the *Cassis de Dijon* case. We do so because it and related cases have implications for harmonization. It will be remembered that that case involved the application of a standard which in practice precluded the importation of the liqueur in question. The standard therefore had the effect of a zero import quota and was an offence under Articles 30 *et seq*. In the process of delivering its judgement the Court of Justice also made the point that any product legally made and sold in one member state must in principle be admitted to the markets of the others. National rules and standards can only create barriers where they are necessary to satisfy 'mandatory' requirements such as public health, consumer protection, etc. Moreover, and this is the key point, any rule must be the 'essential guarantee' of the interest, the protection of which is regarded as being justified. It will be remembered that in the *Cassis* case the German Government defended its minimum alcoholic content rule on grounds of consumer protection. But the Court noted that that objective could have been achieved by merely requiring the label to show the actual alcoholic content. The rule was not essential to guarantee the protection of the consumer. It did not follow that in the light of *Cassis* the need to harmonize no longer existed. There would be some situations where the need to have rules was inescapable, and goods not conforming to them would be excluded. In such cases the only way forward was to harmonize. But there would be many cases where the differences of standards as between states were really relatively trivial and were not essential to protect the public. In such cases harmonization would no longer be required.

Despite the progress made in harmonization and the promise held out by *Cassis* and other cases, by 1985 the Commission had come to the conclusion that a change of approach was needed. Mindful of the point made earlier about the time-consuming nature of the process and the fact that there is a long way still to go, the Commission decided to adopt a different method. This was outlined in the 1985 document on completing the internal market. The essential features seem to be as follows. (a) In the light of *Cassis*, etc., where there are no threats to safety, health and so forth (of the kind which under Article 36 allow imports to be forbidden), free importation should be allowed. The fact that goods are designed or composed differently is no reason for preventing their free circulation. Harmonization is therefore not needed in such a case. (b) Where there are threats to safety, health, etc., harmonization will be needed. But two changes will be made. Firstly, thanks to the Single European Act, such harmonization activity will only require a qualified majority vote. Secondly, Council harmonization activity will concentrate on identifying those factors which are essential for safety, health and so forth. In respect of other peripheral matters goods may differ, and henceforth time will be saved, since no attempt will be made to iron them out. Provided national standards conform in respect of these essentials, goods manufactured under such standards will be free to circulate. The Commission will arrange for a mutual recognition of standards as between member states. Apparently, as a provisional arrangement, goods produced in accordance with a national (as opposed to a harmonized) standard will be free to circulate, but the burden of proof that the good in question satisfies the essential requirements will then lie with the manufacturer.

Legal obligations

Since at least 1972 the EEC has been developing a policy on consumer protection. Apart from the harmonization, to which we have just referred, the EC Commission has tabled draft directives on matters such as unit pricing, doorstep selling and product liability. Except for the latter, these are not matters of central concern in this chapter.

Product liability refers to the liability of a producer towards a consumer who is injured or killed when using, or in some way consuming, his product. National laws on this matter vary. Some, as for example those of the UK, required the injured party to prove negligence on the part of the manufacturer. On the other hand, some laws adopt a 'strict liability' approach, whereby a producer is automatically liable for goods which lead to death or material injury. No proof of fault or negligence is necessary. These laws may also make manufacturers bear the development risk. In other words the producer is still liable even if at the time the good was produced it was from a scientific point of view regarded as harmless – i.e. the subsequent harm was unknowable. Thus if a strict liability approach, with the development risk falling on the producer, had been operative in the UK when the thalidomide tragedy occurred, there would have been an automatic case for compensation even though at the time when it was marketed the drug was, in the light of the existing scientific knowledge, thought to be harmless.

Manufacturers can insure against claims, but obviously the cost of the insurance will vary according to the posture of the law. Laws such as those of the UK made it difficult to establish a claim, because proving negligence was extremely difficult. Insurance costs in such circumstances will be modest, whereas they will be heavier when strict liability prevails. The EC Commission, noting that the laws of the member states varied, drew the conclusion that insurance costs would also vary and that this distorted competition. It also argued that the decision whether or not to sell in a market might be influenced by the kind of claims which might arise there. The Commission therefore proposed that national laws be harmonized. It also sought to kill two birds with one stone by espousing a measure which would improve the position of many consumers. To these ends it proposed in 1976 that national laws should be modified so as to provide for strict liability with the development risk falling on producers. In 1985 the Council of Ministers adopted a directive which required member states to introduce the strict liability principle into their national laws. During the first seven years a requirement that manufacturers bear the development risk is optional. At the end of seven years the Council will decide whether or not to make the latter mandatory. The UK has opted to avoid imposing development risk on manufacturers.

Public purchasing

The public sector – that is to say central and local government and nationalized bodies – is a major spender in the economic systems of western economies. Such public spending does not always take place in a non-discriminatory way. Rather than accepting the cheapest and/or best offers, the institutions of the public sector often adopt 'buy national' attitudes. The motives are various, but include balance of payments considerations, the desire to build up particular industries (for example computers), prevention of unemployment and sheer prestige.

This kind of discriminatory and restrictive behaviour is contrary to the Rome Treaty – specifically Articles 7, 30 and 34. It should also be said that the Council of Ministers adopted a directive in 1970 to give effect to the ban on discriminatory practices. That directive prohibits measures, imposed by law, regulation or administrative practice, which prevent the supply of imported goods from other member states, which grant domestic products a preference or which make the supply of imported goods more difficult or costly than domestic products.

The EC Commission seems to have recognized that a general directive would not suffice and that there was a need to produce specific directives relating to particular kinds of public purchasing. The initial focus was public works contracting. In 1971 Council adopted three directives. The first swept away all obstacles to the freedom to supply services, the second drew up common rules for the awarding of contracts and the third established an advisory committee on the subject of public works contracting. The second directive relates to contracts of one million ECUs and more but leaves those relating to energy and water for separate treatment. As a result of this directive, contractors throughout the Community are guaranteed free and effective competition on all major public works contracts offered by member states. Contractors are informed of pending contracts through the Community's Official Journal. Competent authorities are obliged to accept tenders from all qualified contractors in the Community and are required to award contracts on purely economic and non-discriminatory grounds. All discrimination of a purely technical nature was to be eliminated. A complaints procedure was established. In 1976 the Council followed up with a directive on public procurement – it was officially described as a directive co-ordinating procedures for the award of public supply contracts. As a result, central, regional and local authorities seeking to award public supply contracts in excess of 144 000[1] ECUs must publish a notice in the Official Journal, giving potential tenderers all the information needed to make an offer. In considering tenders the contract-awarding authority must treat all offers equally – i.e. there must be no discrimination as between home and foreign bids.

The settlement of complaints is dealt with by the body which discharges that role in respect of public works contracts – it has been given the title of Advisory Committee for Public Contracts.

All this legislative activity has not proved sufficient to persuade member states to behave in a non-discriminatory way. There is ample evidence that the Community law is flouted. For example, in 1981 the Commission had to institute cases against France and Ireland. Both were accused of encouraging and promoting the purchase of domestic goods in preference to imported ones – a clear breach of Article 30 of the Rome Treaty and of the obligations set out in the 1970 directive. France was under attack again in 1984 when it was accused of impeding the import of postal franking machines to be used by the French postal authorities. These had to be approved before they could be marketed. Apparently, applications for approval were deliberately delayed, refusals were given without adequate explanatory details being provided concerning defects, and some grounds for refusal were in fact false. The public supply contract directive has in fact been found to have loopholes in it, and late in 1986 the Council of Ministers took steps to deal with this problem. Unfortunately, the purchases of transport, water, energy and telecommunications authorities are not covered by the public supply contract directive. The Commission intends to take steps to remedy this deficiency as part of the programme for completing the internal market.

---

1. This relates to central and federal authorities. The figure for regional and local authorities is 200 000 ECUs.

State monopolies

In a number of member states – France, Italy and Germany – the Commission has encountered problems raised by what the Rome Treaty calls State Monopolies of a Commercial Character – a phenomenon singled out for attention in Article 37. The reader should note that these are not what are usually thought of as nationalized industries or public utilities. Indeed case law has indicated that nationalized industries engaged in transport, gas, electricity, water and broadcasting are not relevant. Rather, these monopolies are concerned with products such as alcohol and manufactured tobacco. The main reason for such monopolies is fiscal – the monopoly revenues of the sales organizations accrue to the state as part of its fiscal revenues. Additional motives for the foundation of these monopolies have been the protection of national production and the assurance of supplies. From the point of view of the common market the main drawback of these organizations is that they have a discriminatory effect on the conditions of supply and marketing of goods emanating from other member states. These have consisted of the following: (a) refusal to import; (b) quantitative restrictions on imports; (c) the application of relatively more onerous marketing conditions on imported goods as compared with home-produced goods; (d) discriminations against the advertising of foreign goods. These monopolies have also enjoyed exclusive exporting rights and, amongst other things, this has led to discrimination in the terms offered between home and foreign buyers.

Article 37 did not require the abolition of these monopolies. Rather, it required that during the transition period they should be adjusted so as to eliminate discrimination regarding the conditions under which goods are procured and marketed between nationals of the member states. The Commission has waged a long war of attrition on them with a view to securing changes in their behaviour which would bring them into conformity with Article 37. Fortunately, the task of the Commission was considerably eased by virtue of the fact that some monopolies were abolished and others were reformed in various ways. However, a hard core of problems remained – alcohol, manufactured tobacco and petroleum in France, alcohol in West Germany and manufactured tobacco and matches in Italy.

It was extremely important to eliminate the monopoly control over imports – this would then open up the national markets to supplies from other states. In 1970 the Commission was able to secure the compliance of Italy and France in the removal by 1976 of such restrictions in respect of imports of manufactured tobacco. Then in 1975, in the *Pubblico Ministero* v. *Manghera* case, the Court of Justice declared against exclusive rights to import. As a result, the Commission was endowed with authority to attack such rights not only in the tobacco trade but also in other areas. Having secured what appeared to be a victory, the Commission then found that the state monopolies were indulging in other activities which were designed to prevent free importation. Taxes were being manipulated and subsidies employed to keep imports out. Thanks however to a series of preliminary rulings by the Court of Justice these various loopholes were plugged. Considerable progress has therefore been made in this area of policy. But the battle is not over. Indeed the battle never will be over, since state monopolies will from time to time attempt to behave in ways which are contrary to the Rome Treaty. In addition, the Commission is now having to wrestle with Greek state monopolies. There are also Iberian state monopolies, so the Commission will have further problems to contend with.

Administrative barriers

The movement of goods across frontiers is still burdened by various administrative procedures and requirements. These give rise to costs which in turn significantly inflate the prices paid by consumers in the Community. In what can only be described as an angry outburst, the EC Commission observed that twenty-three years after the formation of the EEC the fact that 'the elimination of frontier formalities is still lagging behind that achieved in the Nordic Union must raise doubts as to the success of the internal market' (EC Commission, 1981b, p. 2). The Commission returned to the subject in its 1985 document on the completion of the internal market. It proposes that frontier barriers and controls should be eliminated in their entirety by 1992.

6 Factor Movements and the Common Market

The free movement of labour

In keeping with the concept of a common market, as opposed to a customs union, the Rome Treaty provides for the free movement of labour.[1] (There is a provision that freedom of movement can be limited on grounds of public safety, public security and public health.) Article 48 required that free movement be achieved before the end of the transition period. In fact in this sphere of operations the Six registered a distinct success in that complete freedom of movement was achieved in July 1968, one-and-a-half years ahead of schedule. Article 48 complements the principle of free movement with a ban on discrimination based on nationality in regard to employment, remuneration and other conditions of work.

The Six approached the establishment of free movement of labour in stages. The first, which was provided for in Council Regulation 15 of 1961, operated between September 1961 and May 1964. During this period the movement of labour into another member state required the issue of a permit by the state of destination. Workers were permitted to renew the permit for the same occupation after one year of regular employment. After three years they were able to renew their permit for any other occupation for which they were qualified and after four years for any kind of paid work. In effect after four years discrimination ceased. During this first period a preference was given to national workers in that any vacancies in the national labour market were compulsorily notified for three weeks in the labour exchanges of the home country, but after this period offers of employment were transmitted to other member states. But if, for example, an employer asked for a worker by name, the temporary preference for home market supply could be waived. During this stage a Community preference also existed,

1. It should be noted that free movement does not apply to employment in public administration.

in that Community workers were to have priority over workers from third countries in filling job vacancies.

During the second stage, which extended from May 1964 to June 1968, progressive freedom under the permit system was speeded up, in that after two years of regular employment a migrant worker could move to any job on the same terms as nationals. The national preference was abolished, but a safeguard clause was inserted which enabled a member state to restore it for fifteen days when a surplus of manpower existed in certain areas or trades. If a member state operated the safeguard clause it had to be justified adequately. The priority of Community workers over non-Community workers was preserved.

In July 1968 complete freedom of movement became a reality. The principle of national priority was abandoned and so Community workers could then have the same access to jobs as nationals. Work permits were abolished, and as a result Common Market migrant workers could take up employment without having to comply with any formalities other than those for residence permits. The latter are issued for a period of five years and are renewable automatically. The priority of Community workers over non-Community workers was, however, retained. New members have had to conform to these requirements. Those who entered in the 1970s were given five-year transition periods within which to adjust. Greece (from 1981) and the two Iberian members (from 1986) were given a seven-year adjustment period.

It hardly needs saying that complete freedom of movement could not have become a reality unless a lot of other problems had been dealt with. To take just two examples, workers need to be informed of job opportunities in other member states and social security rights need to be transferable. In order to deal with the first, the Commission in 1972 adopted its *Système européen de diffusion des offres et demandes d'emploi et de compensation internationale* (SEDOC). This was conceived as a uniform system for codifying jobs and their remuneration so that data on job availability might be transmitted between member states. A European Coordination Office to facilitate this process was established, and the system began to operate in 1973.

A generous level of social security benefits would be a considerable deterrent to labour mobility if a migrant worker had to sacrifice them on moving to another member state. Having made contributions to the social security system in one member state, a worker is less likely to migrate if his rights are not transferable. At a relatively early date the Community therefore addressed itself to this problem. An ECSC Convention on Social Security for Migrant Workers had been signed in

1957, ensuring that all social security contributions, in whatever member state they were paid, counted for benefit eligibility. The EEC Treaty contained a similar requirement, and in 1959 the provisions of the ECSC Convention were extended to *all* workers. As a result the following principles apply. Migrant workers from all the member states are eligible for the same social security benefits as national workers. Periods of employment and insurance completed in several member states are aggregated for the purpose of calculating benefits. At any time a beneficiary may request the transfer of benefits from one member state to another. In 1970 the Council of Ministers extended these principles to self-employed insured persons.

The upshot of all this is that Community nationals now have equal rights in applying for vacant jobs in any member state. They have equal treatment as compared with the citizens of the state to which they have moved in respect of social security and taxation. They are eligible for election to trade unions and works councils. They are entitled to equal access to property ownership and housing. Migrant workers can bring their family and dependants with them; this has however required the availability of suitable accommodation. Rights of this kind were progressively improved as the regulation of 1961 gave place to the 1964 regulation, which in turn was supplanted by that of 1968. For example, eligibility to vote for candidates for works councils was followed by the right to be a candidate. Originally, on moving the worker could only bring his wife and minor children, but this was modified later – the definition of the family being expanded to include not only the wife and minors but all children, parents and grandparents dependent on the worker. Although some of these issues seem to be relatively innocuous they were in fact the subject of keen bargaining and debate between the member states (see Dahlberg, 1968). The 1968 regulation did not see the end of progressive improvement. For example, in 1975 the Council adopted a regulation extending equality of treatment in the exercise of trade union rights to cover admission to the leading positions in trade union organizations.

It could be argued that the free movement of labour would be distorted if levels of personal income varied from state to state. Labour would shift to low tax states. In practice this is not felt to be a problem. When the Neumark Committee (EEC Commission, 1963) reported on various aspects of tax harmonization, it pointed out that labour was less mobile than capital and therefore the problem of disparities in personal income tax did not pose a major problem. It has, however, been proposed that workers crossing frontiers daily should be taxed according to their country of residence and that a husband and wife should be taxed separately. In 1985 the Commission indicated that the former should have a high priority in the programme for completing the internal market by 1992.

The free movement of capital

There are two main strands in Community policy in respect of the capital market. Firstly, as in the case of labour, the Rome Treaty calls for mobility of capital between the member state economies. The Treaty explicitly provides for the abolition of controls on capital movements. Secondly, there are a whole series of other factors which affect the free flow of capital, including some which can quite obviously give rise to serious distortions in the allocation of capital between member states. It is therefore desirable that such factors should be eliminated or harmonized as appropriate.

The Rome Treaty rules on capital movements

The Rome Treaty provisions in respect of the capital market are found in Articles 67 to 73, 106 and 109. The basic provision is to be found in Article 67. It states that during the transition period, and to the extent necessary to ensure the proper functioning of the Common Market, member states will abolish all restrictions on the movement of capital belonging to persons resident in the Community. Also, discrimination based on nationality, on the place of residence of such persons or on the place where the capital is to be invested shall be abolished. Article 67 also requires that current payments connected with the movement of capital should be freed of all restrictions by the end of the first stage of the transition period, and Article 106 declares that member states must authorize payments, in connection with the sale of goods and services and movement of capital, in the currency of the member state in which the beneficiary or creditor resides.

According to Article 68, when the movement of capital is liberalized it is also necessary that any domestic rules governing the capital market and credit system should be applied in a non-discriminatory fashion.

Article 70 is concerned with exchange controls, and it calls for the highest degree of liberalization. Originally, the treaty required that directives concerning the abolition or reduction of exchange controls should be agreed on a unanimous basis. However, as a result of the Single European Act of 1986 this legislative activity has now been put on a majority voting basis, and it has also been decided that measures which represent a step backwards from liberalization must command unanimous support. These changes have taken the form of amendments to the Rome Treaty. Article 71 contains a standstill requirement. Member states shall endeavour to avoid introducing within the Community any new exchange restrictions on the movement of capital and current payments connected therewith, and shall endeavour not to render existing regulations more restrictive. Article 73 contains a safeguard clause. If the movement of capital disturbs the capital market of a member state, the Commission shall, after the Monetary Committttee has been consulted, authorize such a state to take protective measures in the field of capital movements. The Council may, however, revoke such a decision. A member state may also, on grounds of secrecy or urgency, take measures without prior approval. In such a case the Commission and other member states must be informed of the measures not later than the date when they come into effect. However, the Commission, after consulting the Monetary Committee, may amend or abolish such measures. Whilst dealing with emergency measures, we should also take note of Article 109 which, as we recollect from Chapter 4, relates to balance-of-payments policy. Briefly, that Article allows a member state in case of a sudden crisis to take necessary protective measures, which could include control of capital movements.

Factors inhibiting capital movements

With the formal rules behind us, the subject which now falls due for consideration is the degree to which the Community has dealt with those factors which hinder the free movement of capital. We begin with exchange controls. Member states have in the past controlled, and in some degree still do control, the conversion of their domestic currencies into foreign currencies (and *vice versa*) in connection with the carrying out of international capital transactions. For example, a national might be denied the foreign exchange necessary for the purchase of securities on a foreign stock exchange. Here the restriction affects an outward capital movement. But also a state might, for example, prevent foreigners purchasing securities in the domestic market. Here an offer of foreign exchange, as part of an inward flow of capital, is refused.

The reasons why states adopt these postures are various. Outward flows may be controlled because the state in question is concerned that its life-blood, capital, will ebb away if all controls are relinquished. Capital, instead of modernizing domestic industry, will be used to increase the efficiency of another state, possibly a competitor. Outflows may of course be controlled because they tend to cause the exchange rate to weaken, and this can lead to inflation via rising import prices. In some cases, such as West Germany, the problem has not been one of losing capital but of gaining it. As we shall see in the next chapter, the D-mark has been such a strong currency, likely to appreciate rather than depreciate, that foreign capital has flooded into West Germany. This was an embarrassment to the Germans since it either caused their exchange rate to appreciate, thus making exporting more difficult or, by adding to the supply of money, threatened inflation, again making exports less competitive. Thus although the Germans were inclined to favour the abolition of exchange controls, they had, as an emergency measure, to impose restrictions on foreigners acquiring short-term securities, bonds or shares. Free capital movements also undermine the ability of a member state to operate an independent monetary policy. If one member state endeavours to raise interest rates above those existing in the other member states, money is attracted in and undermines the policy. If a member state attempts to depress interest rates relative to the levels existing outside, money flows out and monetary conditions tighten. For all these reasons it is not surprising that all forms of control on the free movement of capital, and not just exchange controls, are a delicate subject. It would hardly be surprising if member states exhibited some reluctance to abdicate totally their control of capital movements.

Nevertheless, the Community has introduced measures to loosen up foreign exchange controls, member states have also acted unilaterally to that end and other changes have occurred. We shall consider developments in that order.

Before we do so we will take stock of the present state of affairs. Whilst the position on exchange controls tends to fluctuate from time to time, the position in early 1987 appears to be as follows. Seven of the member states have significantly or totally abolished controls. Three countries, Italy, Ireland and Greece, still retain a range of controls. Spain and Portugal have until 1990 and 1992 respectively to get rid of theirs.

The degree of liberalization which has occurred has been partly due to directives introduced by the Community. The first two of these were introduced by the Six in 1960 and 1962. They lasted until 1985. In 1985 and 1986 further liberalization measures were agreed. Table 10 indicates the position which existed from 1960 to 1985 and also provides a useful device for assessing what has happened since. It is first necessary to distinguish between exchange controls relating to current transactions and exchange controls relating to capital movements. Let us begin by looking at current transactions. As we have already seen, between them

Article 67 and Article 106 of the Rome Treaty declare that member states are required to supply foreign exchange in respect of current transactions. Let us take the case of the trade in goods. Suppose firm A in member state A imported goods from firm B in member state B. The government of member state A would have to make available to firm A the appropriate member state B currency, since firm B would demand payment in that form. Clearly, without that obligation the lowering of

Table 10. Exchange liberalization rules 1960–85

Current Transactions	Member states must supply foreign currency for such transactions (Articles 67 and 106)
Capital Movements	
List A	
Direct investments	Unconditional Liberalization
Investments in real estate	
Personal capital movements	
Short and medium term commercial credits	
Transfers relating to life and credit insurance	
Transfers related to supply of services	
List B	
Buying and selling of securities dealt with on stock exchanges (listed securities)	Unconditional Liberalization
List C	
Admission of securities on the capital market	Conditional Liberalization
Buying and selling of unit and investment trust securities	
Buying and selling of securities not dealt with on stock exchanges (unlisted securities)	
Long-term commercial credits	
Medium and long-term financial credits	
List D	
Monetary Transactions:	No Community obligation to liberalize
Acquisition of short-term securities	
Short-term financial credits	
Opening of deposit accounts	

Source: EC Commission, *Bulletin of the European Communities*, OOPEC, no. 5/86, p. 15.

tariffs would have been meaningless, since protection could have been continued by refusing to supply foreign exchange. The above is not too difficult to comprehend, but complications arise when we turn to capital transactions. It was these to which the 1960 and 1962 directives related Such transactions were divided into four lists – A, B, C and D. Transactions in Lists A and B were *unconditionally* freed. Broadly speaking, the implication was that member states were obliged to make foreign currency available to enable these transactions to take place. However, it is important to remember that member states can seek to resort to protective measures. Items under List C were only *conditionally* freed. In this case the implication was that the liberalization which had been achieved by 1960 (or, in the case of new members, that which had been achieved by the accession date) should not be reversed. Again, exceptional circumstances could lead to protective measures which could override the conditional requirement. In the case of List D there was no obligation to liberalize.

In 1985 and 1986 further liberalization measures were agreed. Broadly, the effect of these has been to shift items which were only conditionally freed to the unconditional category. Examples are the admission of securities to the capital market; the buying and selling of unit and investment trust securities [1] and securities not dealt with on the Stock Exchange (i.e. unlisted securities); and long-term commercial credits. The ultimate aim of the Commission, as spelled out in its 1985 document on the completion of the internal market, is that by 1992 all exchange controls shall be abolished.

These acts of liberalization have really been the minimum requirements. In addition, some member states have unilaterally liberalized exchange controls and have gone a good deal further than the directives require. The UK is an example, although until the Thatcher Conservative Government of 1979 progress was slow. The UK promised to liberalize direct investment both ways within two years of accession – i.e. by the end of 1974. In fact she agreed to start easing the rules immediately. She also undertook to liberalize capital movements of a personal nature by the same date. Clearly these both fell within List A. In respect of portfolio investments (List B) complete liberalization was promised by the end of the five-year transition period – i.e. by the end of 1977. In practice the UK dragged its feet and secured a series of postponements of its commitments to liberalize. In 1977 the Commission began to pile on the pressure to conform, and the UK was given until the end of 1978 to get rid of the offending exchange controls. The UK did in fact make some

1. A directive of 1985 unifying national rules concerning unit trusts and investment trusts paved the way for the liberalization of these two items.

concessions in 1977. Previously, UK citizens wishing to buy foreign shares had to pay a dollar premium in order to obtain funds from a limited pool of currency made available for such investments. Also, when selling the shares they had to surrender 25 per cent of the proceeds of such a sale at the official exchange rate. From the beginning of 1978 the UK agreed that the surrender rule should be abolished, although the premium currency system would be retained. The controls on direct investment were eased – the ceiling on the amount a British company could invest abroad was doubled. The rules concerning personal capital movements were also made more liberal. For example, families emigrating could take £80 000 instead of £40 000 with them.

When the new Conservative administration came into office it set in process the final abolition of exchange controls. In the June budget of 1979 the required pay-back period on outward foreign investment (the so-called 'super-criterion') was abolished in respect of outward investments of less than £5 million. It had in fact already been eased in the 1978 modifications. Then, in July 1979, currency was made available without limit at the official rate for all outward direct investment. The budget statement also included the abolition of the two-thirds rule, which restricted the reinvestment of profits earned overseas. It also liberated portfolio investment – UK residents were allowed to invest at the official rate of exchange in most securities denominated in EEC member currencies. Finally, in October 1979, the UK Government announced the end of all remaining exchange controls. Although the Chancellor of the Exchequer noted the obligation to liberalize which fell upon the UK under the Rome Treaty, the liberalization of 1979, unlike that of earlier years, was not primarily prompted by Community pressure. Of course, we cannot rule out the possibility that if there was a change of government in the UK, the new government might seek to roll back at least some of the Conservative party's liberalization.

There is one other factor which has helped to free capital movements, and it did not depend on Community measures or unilateral national acts of liberalization. P. Maillet (1982, p. 23) has pointed out that a certain institutional development was of particular importance in facilitating capital movements. The development in question was the emergence of the Eurocurrency market. Member state A might be unwilling to allow its nationals to use the domestic currency to purchase that of member state B in order to finance a transaction in member state B. Such an unwillingness would be grounded in a desire to prevent the exchange rate of member state A currency from weakening. However, it would have no objection to its nationals borrowing Eurodollars in order to finance the transaction in member state B – that would not weaken the exchange rate.

Another factor inhibiting capital movements has been the imposition of rules governing where financial institutions such as banks may invest their funds. In Germany they have been able to put money in equities, but in France and Belgium only certain banks have been able to do this, and in Italy banks have been precluded from equity participation. Savings banks in Germany and France have only been able to buy the public sector bonds of their own countries. This has been quite important, since a considerable proportion of the savings in both these economies has been gathered through the medium of such institutions. Life Assurance companies are another important source of funds and again the national laws have tended to differ. For example the rules have discriminated in favour of national, often government, issues. Thus in Luxembourg, Life Assurance companies have only been able to invest in Luxembourg government bonds. These are examples drawn from past experience, but there is no reason to believe that such practices have ceased to exist. Indeed recent experience in the UK points to their persistence. For example, at the beginning of 1987 a system based on the idea of the Personal Equity Plan was introduced. It is designed to encourage small investors to take a stake in equities. Those who participate are relieved of income tax on dividends and the tax on capital gains when they dispose of their portfolio. One of the rules of the scheme is that participants can only invest in UK shares.

When we come to examine Community progress in coping with this problem, we find that the cupboard is largely bare. As early as April 1964 the Commission attempted by means of a draft third directive on capital movements to deal with these legal, administrative and regulatory obstacles. As yet this has not found favour with the Council of Ministers. In the longer run it is possible that the current vogue for deregulation of financial markets, which is evident in many financial centres, may assist in removing such inhibiting factors.

It has also been argued that another source of inhibition is the fluctuation of the exchange rate and the possibility of loss. This argument was emphasized in the Segré Report (EEC Commission, 1966). Here there is no progress to report. Indeed, there are clear signs of retrogression, since when Segré reported the only fluctuations allowed were the very modest movements around the fixed parities allowed under the Bretton Woods system and the European Monetary Agreement. Now, although the EMS is in existence, the permitted fluctuations around the fixed central rates are greater.

Factors distorting capital movements

A major source of distortion arises in connection with the corporation tax applied in the various member states. These distortions arise not only from differences in national rates of tax but also from the detailed operation of the various national systems.

The Rome Treaty makes no explicit reference to the need for the harmonization of direct taxation. But Articles 100 to 102, dealing with the approximation of laws, provide the basis for a solution where discrepancies in the rate of tax, and its method of operation, produce distortions in the free movement of capital. Let us first consider differences in rates. Such discrepancies can give rise to problems. Suppose that member state A levies a tax of 50 per cent whilst member state B is content with 25 per cent. Other things being equal, capital will flow from A to B until the accumulation of capital in B leads to an equalization in the rates of return net of tax in both countries (in respect of investments of equal risk). But if the rates of return net of tax are equal then it follows that the returns *before tax* must be unequal. This in turn implies that the distribution of capital is distorted. Theoretically, it could be argued that there would, from a Community point of view, be a gain if capital was shifted from the member state where its return before tax was low to one where its return was high. (It should be emphasized that such an approach ignores a number of problems, and also assumes that businessmen seek to maximize returns net of tax.) A harmonization of rates would help to solve the problem. But, as we indicated above, further difficulties also arise as a result of the way in which national corporation tax systems operate. The problem is essentially concerned with the double taxation of dividends. The latter arises when distributed dividends have corporation tax deducted from them and then that taxed income is also liable for personal income tax. In the classic system a single rate of corporation tax is applied to both distributed and retained profits. This it is argued discriminates unfairly against the shareholder, who is subject to this double taxation. It is said that it also distorts the system towards ploughing back profits when it might be desirable to distribute them in order that they can be reinvested in other companies needing to grow. Some on the other hand argue in favour of the system in that it encourages retention and therefore investment, whereas dividends may be spent on consumer goods.

Some Community countries have attempted to compensate for this double taxation effect. This has taken the form of the tax credit or imputation system, which grants the shareholder a credit to set against his personal tax liability. But although the tax credit system has much to commend it, the Commission, in examining national systems, encountered some major drawbacks. For example, the Belgian and French systems allowed tax credits for residents only and only for companies registered in their own states. The latter restriction induced French or Belgian investors to invest in French or Belgian companies rather than companies elsewhere in the Community. The former meant that residents in other Community countries who invested in Belgian or French companies were discriminated against.

In respect of the harmonization of corporation tax rates and systems, we must also record that no directive has yet been adopted by Council. The Commission did in November 1975 submit to Council a draft directive designed to harmonize national systems of company taxation, and withholding taxes, on dividends. The Council had in a Resolution of March 1971 agreed that such harmonization was an essential ingredient in the creation of an Economic and Monetary Union. Quite clearly free and undistorted movement of capital is an essential feature of such an arrangement, and its attainment would require not only the sweeping away of the distorting and inhibiting factors we are now discussing but also the elimination of the remaining exchange controls to which we referred a little earlier. The Commission's 1975 proposal would require the member states to adopt a common imputation system of corporation tax and a common system of withholding tax on dividends. The proposal would also lead to similar but not necessarily identical rates of corporation tax and tax credit and to an identical rate of withholding tax. Member states would in fact have to apply the same rate of corporation tax to profits whether distributed or undistributed. The normal rate would not be higher than 55 per cent or lower than 45 per cent. Each state would also grant tax credits which would, to quote the draft directive, 'be neither lower than 45 per cent nor higher than 55 per cent of the amount of corporation tax at the normal rate of a sum representing the distributed dividend increased by such tax'. Such tax credits would accrue not only to nationals but to recipients of dividends who were resident in other member states.[1] This approximation of corporation and tax credit rates would clearly go a long way to eliminating the distorting effects referred to earlier, and of course an important aspect

1. In the case of the cross-border tax credit the state where the dividend receiver lives would pay out the tax credit, but the draft directive observes that in principle the budgetary cost of the tax credit should be borne in the state where the profits, from which the dividends have been derived, have been subjected to corporation tax. Nevertheless, the directive sees no objection to the states agreeing bilaterally to share the cost.

of this attack upon distortion would be the fact that tax credits would accrue to residents in other member states.

We have also referred to withholding taxes and we now need to explain their role. They are basically designed to prevent tax fraud – i.e. the concealment of dividend income from the tax authorities. They take the form of a percentage deduction from distributed dividends. In a sense a tax credit is an incentive to declaration of dividend income, since it can be set off against the shareholder's personal income tax liability. For shareholders with small incomes this may suffice, but for those with large incomes it may be beneficial for them to conceal their dividends rather than declare them with a view to claiming the tax credit. This is where the withholding tax comes in – it too can be reclaimed and would make declaration worthwhile whereas the tax credit alone might not. The draft directive provides that, where a withholding tax collected by one member state is set off or repaid in another member state, the state collecting the withholding tax would refund it to the other member state.

The right of establishment and the freedom to supply services

Articles 52 to 58 of the Rome Treaty require the removal of restrictions on the ability of self-employed individuals and enterprises established in one member state to set up permanent operations – factories, offices – in other member states. This is what is meant by the right of establishment. Equally, just as by virtue of tariff and quota disarmament the self-employed and enterprises in one state are free to supply goods in other member states, it was also recognized in Articles 59 to 66 that they should be free to supply services across frontiers. This is termed the freedom to supply services. In the case of insurance, for example, the right of establishment would be exemplified by a UK-based insurance company establishing a subsidiary in West Germany – the West German enterprise would insure West German risks. The freedom to supply services would arise if the UK parent itself insured a risk in West Germany. The reader may wonder why this latter freedom was not dealt with in Chapter 4. The answer is that although it parallels the freedom to supply goods across frontiers, it is often intimately involved with the right of establishment, and we shall treat the two together.

At the outset we must take account of two important cases which were heard before the Court of Justice in 1974 – the *Reyners* case and the *Van Binsbergen* case. The upshot of these cases was that from the end of the transition period, the right of establishment and the freedom to supply services could be invoked in the courts, and all discrimination *on grounds of nationality* was automatically prohibited. The implication of all this will perhaps be clearer when we note that as early as 1961 the Council of Ministers adopted two general programmes, one for the abolition of restrictions affecting the right of establishment, and one on the removal of restrictions on the freedom to supply services. In these it established priorities for action and thereafter patiently started to produce separate directives for many areas of trade and industry and for some professions. As a result, a significant amount of liberalizing legislation was enacted. However, it would appear that some of this activity was really redundant since in the light of *Reyners* and *Van Binsbergen* this basic right and this basic freedom are automatically enjoyed.

However, it would not be true to say that there has been no need for legislative activity of any kind on the part of the Community. Take, for example, the position of many of the professions in earlier years. Despite what the Rome Treaty might say and how the Court might interpret it, the right and the freedom would not have been sufficient to enable a professional person to travel to another state and supply a service or to set up in business in another state and proceed to practise his or her profession. The reason for this was that member states have laid down the qualifications which various professional persons must possess before they can practise. Unfortunately, the qualifications possessed by a professional person may not be recognized in another member state. Moreover, the cases which we have discussed recognized the right of states to enact such protective legislation – as we have already emphasized; what those cases outlawed was discrimination on grounds of nationality. In order for professional persons to be able to practise anywhere in the Community, legislative activity is needed which leads to a recognition by states of each other's professional qualifications, provides for training to be harmonized, etc. We shall not attempt to provide an overall survey of Community activity in this field. Rather we shall focus on two areas – non-life insurance and medicine.

In 1973 the Council adopted a directive on the right of establishment in non-life insurance. It required the abolition of restrictions which prevented companies from establishing themselves in a host country under the same conditions and with the same rights as those enjoyed by the nationals of that country. For example, Ireland had previously required that in the case of insurance companies two thirds of the shares had to be owned by Irish citizens, and that the majority of the directors (other than the full-time managing director) had to be of Irish nationality. In the light of *Reyners*, national discriminations of this kind would appear to be automatically contrary to the Treaty. Not surprisingly thereafter a number of draft directives which were addressed to this kind of problem in other areas were dropped.

Much more important was the directive on the coordination of laws relating to the taking up and pursuit of the business of non-life insurance. This was necessary because in order to protect their citizens the member states require insurance companies to be licensed, and a condition of holding a licence is that companies meet certain standards in terms of reserves, solvency margins and so forth. These differed between states and therefore the possibility existed that a company wishing to set up a branch in another member state could be debarred from doing so if the conditions demanded by the host government were more stringent than those demanded by the government of the country in which the company had its headquarters. The directive requires that the taking up of the business of non-life insurance should be subject to official authorization by each member state. This applies to an undertaking which has its head office in a member state and also to branches of enterprises which have head offices in other member states. Most important of all, uniform standards are specified in respect of reserves and margins of solvency.

Although the 1973 directives dealt satisfactorily with the right of establishment, they did not tackle the problem of freedom to supply services. In other words, obstacles still existed when, for example, an insurance company *located in the UK* wished to insure a risk in West Germany. The problem here is that member states with consumer protection in mind tend to intervene in the matter of the terms and conditions of insurance contracts. Clearly, were a UK company's branch in West Germany to insure the West German risk then the West German authorities would be able to exercise control, since West German law would apply. However, in a situation where the insurance was carried out by the UK company direct then it is possible to envisage that the contract might be governed by UK law, West German law or indeed the law of a third country. Such a choice was indeed suggested by the EC Commission in its original draft directive. This was criticized in the European Parliament and the draft was subsequently amended so as to require contracts to be governed by the law of the country in which the risk was situated. However, in respect of certain risks the amended draft allowed for an important exception whereby the parties could choose the law which should apply. The effect of this was that in the case of large commercial risks, where those insured could be expected to be able to take care of themselves, the choice of law principle was to operate. In respect of the insurance of those risks where the insured were likely to be less expert, the domestic law requirement was to operate.

Unfortunately this amended proposal did not find favour. Much of this was due to West German opposition. The West Germans subject insurance contracts to relatively close legal control and were aware that countries such as the UK leave these matters more to self-regulation by the insurance companies. The West Germans were opposed to allowing some insurance business to be conducted under what they would no doubt regard as laxer systems. The UK, on the other hand, took the position that the amended draft dealt adequately with the need for consumer protection. For example, airlines are quite capable in a choice of law situation of insisting that the necessary protective terms be included in contracts. Those who are more vulnerable would continue to be protected by domestic provisions.

The EC Commission indicated that a resolution of this problem was essential as part of the programme for completing the internal market. Support for the idea that the insurance of *large* risks should not require establishment and local authorization came from a Court of Justice judgement in 1986. This arose from a case in which the EC Commission attacked France, West Germany, Ireland and Denmark for refusing to properly implement an earlier directive on co-insurance. The latter refers to collaboration between insurance companies when insuring large risks. The Court attacked the practice of requiring establishment and local authorization in such instances. Happily, agreement to introduce freedom to supply services in non-life insurance was achieved late in 1987.

In the case of doctors the main problem was one which we have already identified, namely differing professional qualifications and training. Because of the poor progress in the medical field, Commissioner Ralf Dahrendorf, before he left Brussels, decided to hold a unique Common Market meeting. This occurred in 1973 when the Commission invited ninety-nine doctors to a public hearing to discuss the central problem of the mutual recognition of medical qualifications and the training which lies behind them. The doctors who attended were members of the Standing Committee of Doctors of the Common Market, and of Universities, and there were observers present from other professional bodies and from governments. Draft directives had been published in 1969 indicating the solution envisaged by the Commission but much criticism had been levelled at them. The public hearing was judged to have been a success and certainly substantial progress was subsequently made in 1975 when two directives and two Decisions were adopted by the Council. The object of the directives was to make the right of establishment and the freedom to provide services a reality in the case of doctors. One directive provided for the mutual recognition of diplomas, certificates and other evidence of formal qualifications in medicine. The specific diplomas, etc., were listed in the directive. Provisions were also laid down which are designed to meet the requirements of a host state when proof of good character or good repute is called for. Clearly, requirements such as compulsory registration with a professional organization (i.e. the General Medical Council in the U K) could be an obstacle to the freedom to supply services. The directive therefore exempts nationals from other member states from that requirement but subjects them to the domestic rules of professional conduct in the state where the service is being supplied. The second directive in effect recognized that some greater degree of harmonization in the length and content of medical training – in terms of what is a minimum acceptable standard – was desirable. It therefore laid down such requirements and provides for their subsequent introduction. One of the Decisions established an Advisory Committee on Medical Training to assist in the introduction of comparably demanding standards of medical training as between the member states. The other Decision set up a Committee of Senior Officials in Public Health whose job it is to assist in dealing with difficulties arising in the implemention of the two directives.

7 Monetary Integration

Introduction

It is clear from what has gone before that the Rome Treaty provided quite explicitly for the creation not merely of a customs union but indeed a common market. We can be equally categorical in saying that it did *not* call *explicitly* for the development of an economic union. Nevertheless, as we noted at the beginning of Chapter 4, we have to recognize the possibility that having embarked upon the process of economic integration, it might prove difficult to stop short of economic union. In other words, having developed the kind of Community envisaged by the Treaty, the member states might find themselves forced to proceed yet further in order to make secure, and to more fully benefit from, the free movement of goods, services and factors and from the various common policies such as the CAP. Economic union might therefore prove to be an inescapable ultimate destination.[1] Moreover, by virtue of its self-expanding property, the Rome Treaty would not stand in the way of such an evolution. However, if in 1969 the member states had concluded that for the foreseeable future the original Rome Treaty blueprint was viably the end of the line then this chapter would be largely a speculative exercise. In practice we know that the Community did decide to embark on an EMU – the nature of the motivations which lay behind that decision will be discussed in due course. Although the venture did ultimately run into the ground, there is no doubt that EMU has continued to be a long-term possibility, and in 1979 the member states, in launching the EMS, took a *limited* step[2] in that direction.

1. Not all economists would accept that economic union is inevitable. Some would argue that it is possible to halt at any point along the spectrum.
2. Although the EMS is much more limited in scope than the earlier EMU proposal, it has to be said that the fixed exchange rate aspect of EMU was not a radical departure, since it was an essential feature of the Bretton Woods system. By contrast, the fixed exchange rate aspect of the EMS was a significant change, since by then floating exchange rates were very much the order of the day.

Definition and motivations

Before we turn to the details, it is necessary to deal with one problem of terminology. We have been talking rather loosely about economic union and EMU. Are they the same?

We must begin by admitting that the literature on this subject exhibits a degree of imprecision and ambiguity. Economic union is an established term in economics and refers to the ultimate state of economic integration in which member states become merely regions of the union. The important word here is region. The trouble with this definition is that it tells us little about the process of attaining such a state or indeed about the nature of the state itself. The phrase economic and monetary union is in some ways more helpful, although it is not an established term in economic theory but is one which has gained currency by virtue of its use in connection with EEC aspirations. The economic component refers (though not exclusively) to the existence of free movement of goods, services and factors of production. Here we note an unfortunate ambiguity, since we would prefer to describe such a situation as a common market and would reserve the term economic union for the ultimate state. The monetary component draws attention to the fact that the participating states have proceeded beyond a common market and have injected an element of monetary unification. As in the case of goods and services and factors of production, the monetary element emphasizes the idea of free movement, only in this case the free movement relates to money. In order to facilitate the latter, member states take steps in relation to convertibility, exchange rates and may even introduce a single currency. Whether there were several currencies or only one, central control over the quantity of money would be an essential ingredient. We now return to the word economic. It relates not merely to the common market element but also to the fact that policy makers have tended to divide macro-economic policy into economic and monetary components. The former covers matters such as budgetary and prices and incomes policies. It would be assumed that in an EMU they would be subject to coordination and indeed central control.

It is not too difficult to see that under this definitional schema, economic union and EMU are really one and the same. Nevertheless, the term EMU is somewhat more helpful in describing the ultimate state of economic integration, and we shall deploy it with that point in mind.

We can now proceed to summarize what an EMU would consist of. It would have five main ingredients – four of which have already been briefly identified. (a) It would require free movement of goods and services – that would be the customs union element. Internal tariffs, quotas and charges and measures of equivalent effect would be swept away. There would of course be a common external tariff. (b) It would also require that free movement of goods and services should be accompanied by free movement of factors – i.e. that there should in fact be a common market. In particular there would have to be free movement of capital. The latter would require the elimination of all factors which inhibit or distort free movement across frontiers. A substantial element of harmonization would therefore be required, notably on the direct tax front – see previous chapter. (c) National currencies would have to be fully convertible.[1] The exchange rates between member state currencies would have to be fixed. Any margin of fluctuation around the fixed exchange rates would have to be eliminated and the rates would have to be immutable. If national currencies continued to exist, a high degree of centralized influence over their supply would be essential. All this represents a minimum monetary condition. It is, however, possible to envisage that the member state currencies might be swept away in favour of a union currency. The supply of that currency would be determined centrally and this centralized control would determine the one set of interest rates for the union as a whole. Whether there is one currency or many, EMU implies one set of exchange rates with third countries, and realistically there would have to be one set of exchange controls. A pooling of reserves would also be possible. There is some difference of opinion as to whether pooling is essential, but it is generally agreed that even if reserves were not pooled there would have to be some system which guaranteed that they were available to countries that needed them. (d) A coordination of national economic (as opposed to monetary) policies would be required. Here again national freedom of action would be greatly curtailed, although some commentators point out that within broad central guidelines member state governments might enjoy some freedom to determine the particular mix of fiscal, prices and incomes, etc., policies which were appropriate to a particular situation. (e) We now come to an element which is new to the discussion. Some mechanism for producing what in a full union context would really be inter-regional transfers is also often included. The logic of this element needs further consideration. Presumably member states would be prepared to join the union because of the prospect of some economic or political benefit. In other words, they would be prepared to give up sovereignty because they

---

1. A common market requires that exchange controls should be removed in respect of capital movements – see previous chapter.

expected to be economically or politically better off within the union than outside it. Let us concentrate on the economic aspect. In practice not all would necessarily gain. In such circumstances the continued membership of the losers, and thus the continued existence of the union, would require some transfer of resources so that, after compensation, the losers would be better off inside the union than outside it. The gainers, after making this concession, would of course also have to be better off inside than outside. It is possible that in practice all would gain but that the disproportion between the gains of the various states would give rise to tensions which would require a more egalitarian distribution of benefits. Either way it would be necessary to have a union budget which by virtue of its size and powers was able to effect the necessary transfers.

We come now to motivations. We have in earlier chapters discussed the motivations which lie behind the creation of customs unions and common markets. The motivations discussed here are those which relate to the decision to proceed *beyond* the common market stage. These motivations are of two kinds. On the one hand there are reasons for forming an EMU which can be relevant to any such union. On the other hand there are motivations which are peculiar to a particular exercise because they relate to special aspects of the relationship between the member states or refer to special circumstances existing at the time of the union's formation. The CAP is an example of the former. The lack of confidence in the dollar and its destabilizing effect on European currencies is an instance of the latter. We shall discuss the general reasons now. The special factors which motivated the EMU in 1969 and the EMS in 1978 will be reserved until we discuss these exercises.

We turn now to the general motivating advantages.

(a) Most commentators refer to the benefits of fixed exchange rates. Businessmen thereby enjoy a greater degree of certainty and it is said that this stimulates cross-frontier trade in goods and services. As a result, consumers benefit to an even greater extent from intensified competition, the possibility of greater economies of scale and so forth. In other words the benefits of a customs union are *more fully* enjoyed.

(b) It is also argued that there is a beneficial effect on the allocation of factors of production. Notably, the optimum allocation of capital, associated with the equalization of rates of return at the margin discussed in the previous chapter, is more likely to be achieved under a fixed exchange rate régime. In other words the benefits of the free movement of factors within the Common Market are *more fully* enjoyed.

(c) If EMU gives rise to one currency then there is also an economy of resources associated with the elimination of the transaction costs incurred when one participating currency is exchanged for another.

(d) If the union currency becomes an international reserve asset then the participating states enjoy further benefits. One is seigniorage. The states can allow imports to exceed exports, the balance being financed by the willingness of the rest of the world to hold the union currency. There is therefore a transfer of resources from the rest of the world to the union. The benefits of seigniorage should not be exaggerated. The rest of the world will presumably enjoy interest on its union currency balances which gives rise to a reverse flow. It is also important not to underestimate the risks and problems of running a reserve currency. It is significant that whilst some European circles pointed to the advantages arising from the international status of the US dollar in the Bretton Woods era, European countries, notably West Germany, have shown a marked reluctance to assume a reserve currency role. The advantage of reserve currency status can also be viewed in terms of the reduction in the external constraints on internal demand management. Internal imbalance leading to a trade deficit is compensated by the willingness of foreigners to accumulate the reserve currency.

(e) If there is a pooling of international reserves then there will also be a saving of them. That is to say, the reserves needed to be held by the union would be less than the sum of the reserves needed to be held if the states acted independently. This economy of scale in international reserves arises from the law of large numbers whereby external shocks tend to cancel each other out. The participants in the EMU could, as a result, enjoy a once-for-all real resource advantage by allowing imports (real resources acquired) to exceed exports (real resources sacrificed) and thus running the reserves down to the new economized level. Pooling would also enable participating states to run higher temporary trade deficits than would be the case if they were to remain independent. In other words, the correction of trade imbalances could be postponed for a longer period.

(f) It is also maintained that EMU could give rise to greater efficiency or effectiveness in the administration of aggregate demand management. The argument runs as follows. The creation of a common market gives rise to participating economies which are significantly more open. This means that they are much more dependent on the course of events in other participating economies. It also means that internal demand management is less effective, because the increased marginal propensity to import will lead to much of any internal demand stimulus being dissipated abroad. If, for example, the economies of all the participating states are depressed then there will tend to be a holding back, since any country which inflates demand may find itself acting in isolation and thus will benefit relatively little and will suffer an adverse effect on its balance of payments. No country will therefore stimulate its economy until it is assured that others will do likewise. It is argued that an EMU with centralized powers will be able to produce the necessary complementarity of action which will eliminate the tendency to hold back. This sounds attractive but there may be difficulties. Participating states may have different policy priorities as between, say, the need for low unemployment and low inflation. Centralized decision-making may therefore produce long, drawn-out wrangles about the appropriate policy response. Even if the participating states can agree quickly, we are assuming that they will make the right policy choice!

(g) It is also argued that the union budget could be developed in ways which contributed to a reduction of economic instability in conditions where EMU would reduce the capacity for national action in that regard. By, for example, relating contributions to the level of income, and using receipts to finance at least a part of unemployment benefit, a built-in stabilizer device would be created. Assuming differential fortunes as between participating states, those enjoying boom conditions would make a net contribution to the budget, whilst those in a state of depression would enjoy a net benefit. This would help to even out the fluctuations in national economic fortunes.[1]

There are, of course, costs or risks in participating in an EMU. One is that a participating economy may experience a rate of inflation which is faster than that of its competitors in the union. The most obvious means of dealing with that problem, namely devaluation, will no longer be available. It is therefore likely that there will be some at least temporary unemployment. Christie and Fratianni (1978, p. 11) explain the problem as follows:

Any discrepancy between a region's *ex ante* rate of inflation and the common rate of inflation will be accompanied by movements in real resources, since exchange rates will no longer be available as a means of making the necessary

1. Proposals on these lines were made by the MacDougall Report – see Chapter 3 for other details of that report.

adjustment. Thus the creation of a monetary union would introduce new risks of high unemployment in its more inflation-prone member states. The risk here derives from the possibility that workers would demand equality of nominal wage rates (or nominal wage increases) in a situation where labour productivity growth rates were unequal. Thus the workers whose productivity (or its rate of growth) was lowest would be in danger of pricing themselves out of the market. Eventually no doubt the force of this would come to be widely appreciated and reflected in wage settlements. But the lesson might not be learned at once and, if unemployment increased, the cause might not immediately be perceived to be an unrealistically high level of money wages.

They also refer to a second cost, namely the sacrificing of freedom to determine economic policy at the national level. However, as we have already pointed out, economic integration tends to reduce the ability of participating economies to control their own destiny, and to that extent the sacrifice is capable of exaggeration. Moreover, whilst sovereignty may be lost at the national level, it is regained at the centre. It is usually argued that small economies in particular have little to lose and much to gain by EMU.

The original Rome Treaty system

Whilst it is true that the Rome Treaty, in its original form, did not call for the creation of an EMU, it did nevertheless contain rules regarding the conduct of macro-economic policy. We now turn to a consideration of them. The rules are to be found in Articles 103 to 109. Article 103 relates to conjunctural policy which may be best defined as policy concerned with cyclical problems or short-term trends. The remaining Articles 104 to 109 are concerned with policy towards the balance of payments.

Article 103 declares that member states shall regard their conjunctural policies as a matter of common concern and shall consult each other and the Commission on measures to be taken. Article 104 places the onus on member states to pursue the economic policies needed to ensure equilibrium in their balance of payments whilst simultaneously maintaining confidence in their currencies and maintaining a high level of employment and stability of prices – all of which sounds very worthy though not without its difficulties. In order to facilitate the achievement of these objectives Article 105 calls for coordination of economic policies. As we noted in the previous chapter, Article 106 required the member states to remove exchange controls in connection with those transactions in goods, services and factors which are liberalized under the common market arrangement. Article 107 declares that each member state must treat its policy with regard to rates of exchange as a matter of common concern but the rest of the Article clearly recognizes that member states are free to alter their rates. Article 108 provides that when a member state is in balance of payments difficulties the Commission shall recommend appropriate remedial measures. If action taken by the state and measures proposed by the Commission do not prove sufficient to overcome the difficulties, the Council of Ministers may grant mutual assistance. If mutual assistance is not granted, or if measures taken and mutual assistance granted do not rectify the problem, then the Commission can authorize the member state to institute protection. Council can, however, overturn the latter. Article 109 allows member states to apply protection in the case of a sudden crisis but again Council can call for the suspension of such an action.

The conclusion we can draw is that the EEC did not envisage a centralized control over macro-economic management. In broad terms the conduct of such affairs was left in the hands of member states. They were also free to alter exchange rates. They could even apply protection, although this could be revoked by Council. However, it was clearly recognized that economic integration gave rise to increased economic interdependence, and to that end the Treaty emphasized the need for consultation and coordination.

In order to facilitate the latter, the Treaty called for the creation of a Monetary Committee[1] which was to have advisory status. The committee, which was set up in 1958, had a twofold task. It had to keep the national and Community monetary and financial situation under review. It could also render opinions *ex officio* or on request. Its opinion would be sought when a member state altered its exchange rate or was in need of mutual assistance. In 1960 it was also decided to create a Short-Term Economic Policy Committee. It was designed to monitor the demand management policies of the six member states – as the process of economic integration proceeded these were increasingly affecting other members. When in 1962 the Commission produced its Action Programme for the second stage of the transition period, it emphasized the need for a more thoroughgoing approach to coordination in the macro-economic policy field. In 1963 the Commission made specific proposals to fill the gap, by calling for coordination of national policies in four areas – domestic monetary policy, international monetary policy, ex-

1. This committee still exists. For example, it was involved in discussions early in 1987 concerning possible exchange rate realignments under the European Monetary System (for which see below).

change rate policy and budgetary policy. The Council was initially cool, but in 1964 it decided to accept the Commission's advice. As a result there came into existence a Committee of Governors of Central Banks, a Budgetary Policy Committee and a Medium-Term Policy Committee.[1] This latter body was designed to promote the coordination of medium-term policies and to this end devised five-year plans for the Community as a whole which incorporated a common set of goals or targets. However, despite the panoply of committees,[2] and undertakings such as that whereby member states agreed to consult their partners before modifying the parity of their currency, we should not exaggerate the degree of actual coordination achieved. It is true that Recommendations were addressed to member states. For example, in 1964, when the Community was facing a strong inflationary threat, proposals concerning national economic policy were submitted by the Commission to the Short-Term and Monetary Committee and were adopted by the Council. The Recommendation included a limit to the annual growth of public expenditure of 5 per cent, a requirement to finance any unavoidable spending above this ceiling by taxation, a call for the maintenance and tightening up of existing credit policies and the introduction of a productivity-based incomes policy. But it is important to note the status of this act: it was only a recommendation. Kruse (1980, p. 18) has also pointed out that whilst the new committees were set up in response to the need for coordination, in practice member states were reluctant to concede their right to determine their own affairs. In practice it was consultation rather than coordination which was to prove acceptable.

Economic and political commentators have drawn attention to the fact that the rather modest steps of 1964 marked a high point in monetary developments, and Bloomfield (1973, p. 6) characterizes the period 1964 to 1968 as years of indifference. Why, it has been asked, did the Community fail to make any further advance towards EMU? The answers are not difficult to find. Firstly, the Six were preoccupied with the problems of creating the kind of Community envisaged by the Rome Treaty, a preoccupation which was made no easier by internal dissension over matters such as majority voting and the continuing French rebuff to the UK's membership aspirations. By 1969, however, the basic structure of

1. In 1974 the functions of the Short-Term Economic Policy Committee, the Medium-Term Policy Committee and the Budgetary Policy Committee were all merged into the new Economic Policy Committee, which has continued to operate since that date.
2. The 1964 package of measures also included a broadening of the Monetary Committee's mandate to include discussions and, where possible, prior consultations on international monetary questions.

the common market had been created, and political change in France had removed a major impediment to progress – the Community could then afford to look expansively to the future. Bloomfield (1973, p. 7) ascribes the failure to make appreciable advances in the field of monetary integration to the continuing payments surpluses and mounting reserves of the member states. There is some truth in that observation but a key factor was undoubtedly what Tsoukalis has called the agricultural mythology (1977, pp. 59–60). Under the CAP, the price of agricultural products was fixed in terms of a unit of account, and those prices were then translated into national currency terms. If a member state devalued, the price of agricultural products in national currency terms was automatically raised. Farm incomes would rise and output also. If a state revalued its currency, a contrary course of events would ensue. Clearly changes in parities would lead to prices, incomes and outputs other than those which were intended when the unit of account farm prices were originally fixed. It was therefore regarded as essential for the proper working of the CAP that exchange rates should not be altered. It was indeed assumed that the successful operation of the CAP was so important to the member states that they would be forced to pursue the necessary monetary discipline which would enable exchange rates to stay put. This somewhat naïve view was to prove unfounded. In 1969, following the political events of 1968 and the inflationary impetus to which they gave rise, France devalued and shortly afterwards Germany revalued. 1969 was also the year in which the Heads of State and of Government decided at The Hague that the Community should work together to create an EMU. The two events were of course not unconnected.

The EMU experiment

Motivations

What motivations lay behind this bold decision? It is possible to identify three sets of reasons. Firstly, and notably in the mind of the Commission, was the desire to make secure the achievements of the EEC. Whilst pinning some faith on what we have called the agricultural mythology, the Commission could clearly see that as far as the CAP and the free movement of farm products were concerned, EMU would make exchange rate assurance doubly sure. As for the industrial common market, the Commission was all too well aware that if a member state got into balance-of-payments difficulties it might be forced to take protective measures, thus jeopardizing the free movement of goods, services and indeed factors such as capital. This was very much the thinking behind the first Barre Plan (EC Commission, 1969). Raymond Barre was the member of the Commission responsible for economic and financial affairs – we shall return to the first Barre Plan later.

Secondly, there were national interests which, whilst they varied from state to state, all had one thing in common – they were best served by EMU. France in particular had much to gain from the CAP, and therefore an EMU with its immutable exchange rates was an attractive prospect. The smaller states were interested in EMU because the openness of their economies rendered them extremely vulnerable to events occurring in other member states. EMU offered them an opportunity to exercise an influence on those events. Some member states also entertained the idea that EMU would enable the EEC to develop a distinct monetary personality – this would help to redress the balance *vis-à-vis* the US dollar, which was regarded by some as enjoying an unfairly privileged position in the Bretton Woods system. Undoubtedly a major motivating factor was the desire to avoid having to devalue and revalue currencies. It should be explained that the Bretton Woods system involved fixed exchange rates, and parity adjustments were infrequent and tended to be preceded by fairly lengthy periods of trauma during which member states vainly tried to resist the inevitable. The French and German adjustments of 1969 were no exception. Parity changes were unpleasant for various reasons. Devaluation tended to be regarded as indicating that a particular economic strategy had failed – political credibility was therefore undermined. Devaluations were also usually accompanied by painful deflationary medicine. Even revaluations had unpleasant consequences, notably for export industries. In saying that EMU was seen as a way of escaping these traumas, we are not implying that the member states were naïvely assuming that, Canute-like, it was only necessary to declare that exchange rates were immutable in order for the problem of parity changes to go away. Clearly the necessary monetary discipline would have to be applied. Whether the immutability would compel the application of discipline or whether a disciplined condition should be attained first was a matter yet to be decided.

The third motivating factor was undoubtedly political. EMU would be symbolic of the growing unity of the member states. Whilst it would not be a backstairs route to political unification it would be a step in the direction of the ultimate unity envisaged by the founding fathers.

The first development following the Hague Summit was the decision by the Council of Finance and Economics Ministers to establish a machinery for prior consultation on short-term policy measures. This had been called for in the first Barre Plan. M. Barre had called for a system of compulsory consultation before the taking of any national decision, relating to the trend of prices, incomes and employment, overall budgetary policy and tax policy, which affected the economies of the other member states. More forward-looking was the decision to authorize formally the Central Banks to establish a short-term monetary support scheme. This would provide automatic and unconditional short-term credits for three months, renewable for a further three months. It amounted to $1000 million made up of the following contributions – $300 million each from France and West Germany, $200 million from Italy, $100 million from Belgium–Luxembourg and $100 million from the Netherlands. In addition, a further $1000 million of conditional short-term aid could be made available. This aid was obviously designed to tide over member states in balance-of-payments difficulties, thus reducing the possibility of parity changes or the imposition of protection.

Economists versus monetarists

Meanwhile the 'great debate' on monetary integration and economic union had begun, and it soon became evident that pronounced differences of view existed. Two schools, curiously called the economists and monetarists,[1] emerged. Insofar as countries can be said to belong to schools of thought, it can be said that the Germans and Dutch were economists whilst the French, Luxembourgers, Belgians (and the Commission) were monetarists. These two schools differed not in terms of the ultimate objective to be achieved but over the path that should be followed in order to achieve the objective. Boiled down to its essence, the monetarist position emphasized early action on locking exchange rates, on the assumption that the requisite monetary discipline would therefore be imposed upon member states. By contrast, the economists saw the need for a convergence of economic performance on matters such as the price level before proceeding to immutable parities.

The champion of the economist school was Dr Schiller, the West German Economics and Finance Minister. His 1970 plan for Monetary, Economic and Financial Cooperation envisaged a progression through four stages. Stage one would be mainly concerned with setting up a firm base for coordination of economic policies. Counter-cyclical weapons of control should be developed in each member state as required. The second stage would be concerned with securing a more evenly balanced

1. They are not to be confused with those who hold similar views to Professor Milton Friedman.

economic development between the various states. This would be achieved by central recommendations on budgetary policy and more cooperation through the various monetary and banking committees. A system of medium-term monetary aid would be set up. The third stage would witness the introduction of a supra-national element with majority decisions at Community level on such matters as national budgets and so forth. A federal reserve system on the US model would be introduced. The margin of exchange-rate fluctuation around basic parities would be reduced. At this stage the basic parity could still be modified, but an intensified degree of Community control would be applied in this area. A European Reserve Fund would be set up and a part of national reserves would be transferred to it. In the fourth and final stage power over economic, financial and monetary matters would be centralized under a system of supra-national control. Exchange rates would be totally fixed and irrevocable. A single unit of European currency would make its entry. The existing Committee of Central Bank Governors would become a European Central Council of Banks.

Economists will recognize this as being a sensible way of proceeding to the goal of economic and monetary union. In particular, until a very effective mechanism for coordinating the macro-economic policies of member states is established, any move to adopt irrevocably fixed exchange rates is exceedingly dangerous. Different national macro-economic policies can lead to differential rates of inflation, and exchange rates may begin right but end up being wrong. If a country inflates faster than its competitors, but is precluded from devaluing, then it is likely to experience an adverse balance of payments, and the only (or most likely) way to deal with this would be to deflate. The possible early adoption of irrevocably fixed exchange rates was at one stage regarded by many UK economists as being one of the most serious arguments against joining the EEC. Such critics had in mind the propensity of the UK to inflate relatively rapidly.

The monetarist school was really personified by M. Barre, who produced what is now called the second Barre Plan. It would be tedious to list all the various aspects of this proposal. Like the Schiller Plan, it envisaged a phased progression towards the ultimate goal. But it contrasted with the Schiller Plan in two respects. The first related to the role of exchange rates. Peter Coffey and John Presley in their study of this topic put the matter thus:

... the idea of allowing fluctuating exchange rates is categorically rejected as a matter of principle ... Whilst changes in exchange rates might be considered in cases of exceptional necessity, it would be preferable to *irrevocably* fix the exchange rates as soon as possible. A satisfactory move would be the immediate reduction of the margin of parity between the national currencies from 1·5 per cent to 1·0 per cent. The demand for fixed exchange rates could hardly have been stated in a more emphatic fashion! (Coffey and Presley, 1970, p. 12)

Secondly, Barre also laid considerable stress on the role of the Community in the international monetary sphere.

The Werner Committee

The response of the Council of Ministers to this diversity of view was to set up a Committee to examine the problems involved. This Committee was led by Pierre Werner, the Prime Minister of Luxembourg. The Werner Committee presented an interim report in June 1970 and a second and final report in October of that year (EC Commission, 1970). The Committee proposed the achievement by 1980 of an EMU. In particular, the nature of the final union was delineated. Community currencies would be freely convertible against each other and their parities irrevocably fixed. It would be preferable if they could be replaced by a Community currency. Monetary and credit policy would be centralized. There would be a Community monetary policy *vis-à-vis* the rest of the world. Member states would unify their policies on capital markets. The main components of budget policy would be decided at Community level. The Committee also recognized that significant institutional changes would be needed. There would have to be a central decision-making body which would influence such matters as national budgets, and the parity of the single currency (or the interlocked Community currencies). There would also need to be a Community central banking system to determine monetary conditions over the Community as a whole.

In explaining how the Community would achieve the union, the Committee was only really specific about the first stage – 1971 to 1973 inclusive. Its proposals for this stage involved an element of compromise between the monetarist and economist schools. It proposed that action should be taken on both fronts – exchange rates and policy coordination. This has been called the strategy of parallelism. The Committee did not follow the monetarists who were anxious to lock the exchange rates at the outset. Rather (thanks to the Central Bank Governors) it proposed a scheme in the shape of a reduction of the margin of fluctuation around the central parities when one Community currency was exchanged for another. This band of fluctuation was to be narrower than that operating in respect of exchanges of Community currencies for the dollar. This was the famous snake in the tunnel mechanism. The snake was the narrower band of fluctuation allowed in respect of intra-Community exchanges whilst the tunnel was the wider band allowed in respect of exchanges against the dollar. Emphasis was also placed on the need to achieve greater harmonization of national economic policies – a central plank of the economist position.

The first stage – eventually

The Werner Committee having duly reported, the ball was now back in the political court. A vigorous debate ensued which revealed the existence of substantial differences of opinion and hesitations. Nevertheless, in March 1971, the broad substance of the Werner blueprint for the first stage was formally adopted by Council. From June, intra-Community exchange margins were to be narrowed – an initial reduction would be made from 0·75 per cent[1] on either side of parity to 0·60 per cent. Procedures were authorized for strengthening central bank cooperation and the coordination of economic policies. Indeed, the Council of Ministers was to meet three times a year to establish guidelines for the short-term economic policies to be followed by the member states. A medium-term (two to five years) financial assistance mechanism was to be added to the existing short-term scheme. It would be endowed with $2 billion. Assistance would be conditional on the recipient member state taking effective steps to tackle the causes of its payments deficit. No *rallonge*[2] would be allowed.

However, before the system could be introduced a series of international currency crises obtruded. It should be explained that during the 1960s the US balance of payments steadily deteriorated, notably as a result of the combination of the Vietnam War and large-scale investment by US companies abroad. In the second half of 1970 and in 1971 the US balance of payments recorded deficits of unprecedented size. Increasingly the view was taken that the dollar would have to be devalued. In May 1971 a large movement of hot money occurred as dollars sought refuge from devaluation, and currencies, including the dollar, sought the benefit of a possible upward revaluation of the D-mark and the Dutch guilder. The former, particularly, was thought ripe for revaluation. The Com-

1 Under the European Monetary Agreement contracting states were only allowed a 0·75 per cent fluctuation either side of parity whereas under the Bretton Woods system the margin was 1 per cent either side.
2. Extension beyond the permitted limit.

munity showed little capacity to formulate a common stance in the face of this onslaught. While the US sought to press the Six to contribute to the adjustment of the American balance of payments by revaluing their currencies, France in particular was opposed. It took the view that it was up to the US to correct its deficit by applying controls on capital movements and by devaluing the dollar. The Commission was against revaluation and proposed that the Six should take concerted action to curb inflows. This was supported by France but was opposed by West Germany which suggested a joint float with each member state currency remaining fixed against each other within narrow margins. No agreement could be reached, so member states acted independently – the D-mark and the Dutch guilder were floated and Belgium ceased to intervene in the section of the market concerned with capital movements. In late July and in August the speculative flight from the dollar resumed – this time the main target was France and Belgium, since Germany and the Netherlands were effectively protected from inflows by virtue of their floating rates. On this occasion the US itself took action – it applied a 10 per cent import surcharge and suspended the convertibility of the dollar into gold. Once again the Community was unable to agree on a common stance. West Germany once more advocated a joint float and once more France refused to accept the idea. The idea of floating did, however, collect more adherents in the shape of Italy and the Belgium–Luxembourg Customs Union. Later in the year the Community was able to hammer out a common position in preparation for an internationally negotiated solution to what was essentially a US balance-of-payments and dollar problem. The Six would press for an end to the surcharge and a restoration of convertibility. They would accept appreciation of their currencies against the dollar but would require a formal devaluation of the dollar against gold. Agreement was reached at the Smithsonian Institute in Washington in December 1971. The Smithsonian Accords involved a return to fixed exchange rates, although the margins of fluctuation around what were now called the central rates were increased to 2·25 per cent on either side. The dollar was devalued in terms of gold by 7·9 per cent, the Italian lira declined by 1·0 per cent, the French franc and the pound remained unchanged, whilst the Belgian franc, the D-mark and the Dutch guilder all appreciated. In terms of the dollar, all the European currencies appreciated. The United States abolished the import surcharge. It was hoped that convertibility would be restored in due course.[1]

The way was now clear to set in motion the EMU experiment. This

---

1. This did not transpire.

was agreed in March 1982. The snake and the tunnel were, however, wider than previously conceived. Following the Smithsonian Accords the margin of fluctuation on either side of the central rate in relation to the dollar was 2·25 per cent, giving a maximum band of 4·5 per cent. This was the tunnel. However, the Council decided that this condition could not apply to intra-Community currencies since if, simultaneously, one currency rose from the bottom to the top of the band whilst another fell from the top to the bottom, then their relative fluctuation would be 9 per cent. This would have an unacceptable effect on the CAP pricing system. The Council, therefore, decided to restrict the intra-EEC rate band – the snake – to 2·25 per cent. It was, of course, necessary to intervene in the foreign exchange market in order to keep currencies within the prescribed limits. For example, if a currency was weak, what was called a debtor intervention involved the intervening country borrowing from its partner the strong currency needed to purchase its own weak one. A very short-term credit facility had, therefore, to be created in order to make such interventions possible. In a creditor intervention, the intervening country would buy the weak currency with its own strong currency which of course it would itself be able to supply. At the end of the month a settlement was required. The creditor would wish to exchange the weak currencies which it accumulated for a more acceptable asset. Equally it would require repayment of the credits it had extended to the debtor country.[1] In anticipation of their accession to the Community, the UK, Ireland, Denmark and Norway also joined the scheme.

The snake in the tunnel scheme enjoyed only a very limited success, although, as we shall see, the snake did outlive the EMU exercise. Quite quickly it was placed under considerable strain when in June 1972 the pound encountered heavy speculative pressure, and the support burden was such that the UK authorities decided to allow the pound to float out of the snake and the tunnel. Ireland and Denmark followed suit. The UK and Ireland stayed out permanently but Denmark rejoined and stayed inside. In February 1973 Italy floated out and stayed out. France left in January 1974, rejoined in July 1975 and finally left in March 1976. Thus by the end of 1977, although the Community consisted of ten members, only half – West Germany, Belgium, the Netherlands, Luxembourg and Denmark – had stayed the course. The arrangement also lost its Community character as a result of the adherence of Norway, who had rejected EEC membership, and Sweden, who joined in March 1973 but left in August 1977.[2] The system also departed from the original

1. This account leans heavily on the excellent description provided by B. Tew, *The Evolution of the International Monetary System 1945–81*, Hutchinson, 1982, p. 158.
2. Switzerland and Austria were also associated with the snake.

plan when, in March 1973, Germany, France, Belgium, the Netherlands, Luxembourg and Denmark decided to float collectively whilst maintaining the reduced level of fluctuation amongst themselves. More important perhaps was the fact that the latter aspect proved impossible in practice, and individual members of the snake were from time to time forced to resort to central rate changes.

It will be recalled that the other major objective of the first stage was the coordination of national economic policies. How did the Community respond? Here we can quote from John Presley, who carried out a review of Community endeavours in this field.

The Council of Ministers does meet three times each year to examine the economic climate in the Community, and it does put forward very general policy objective guidelines; but there is no detailed attempt to formulate economic policy, as the Werner Report envisaged, to achieve these objectives. Coordination Committees have been set up, their main function being to monitor the national policies, and to examine them in relation to the common guidelines laid down by the Council. Even the European Commission, however, admits that little progress has been made in coordination: 'few concrete measures have been adopted beyond recommendations of a very general nature'. (Presley, 1974, p. 153)

Kruse puts the matter quite bluntly when he observes:

... the member states continued to make decisions principally on the basis of national interest rather than according to the dictates of economic and monetary unification. (Kruse, 1980, p. 193)

We have so far been concerned with the main tasks of the first stage – the setting up of the exchange rate scheme and the coordination of national policies. As the Community progressed through the first stage, consideration began to be given to the second. A number of conditions were laid down which had to be satisfied if that progression was to occur. One related to regional policy. The Werner Committee recognized that, in an EMU, regional policy would have an important role to play, but it did not develop the theme. In March 1971, when the original decision to enter upon stage one was made, the importance of regional measures was highlighted as a means of reducing tensions which would otherwise impede progress to EMU. Kruse (1980, p. 177) takes this to imply a transfer of resources. At the Paris Summit of 1972 consideration was given to a series of developments which were preparatory to stage two. Included in these was the creation of the ERDF. In practice, differences of opinion over the size of the fund delayed its creation until 1974, when the issue was settled at the Paris Summit in the December of that year. The Paris Summit also decided to set up a European Monetary Cooperation Fund – this was to be achieved by April 1973. It was also required that in 1973 reports should be submitted on the adjustment of the short-term monetary support scheme and on the progressive pooling of reserves. The latter was no new idea – it had been identified as a topic for study at The Hague in 1969. The European Monetary Cooperation Fund was duly created. It was responsible for the running of the snake and for the associated very short-term credit facility, and in addition it was in charge of the short-term monetary support scheme. During 1973 the pooling of reserves was considered but rejected – the funds available under the short-term monetary support scheme were substantially increased.

In due course a vigorous debate ensued over the question of formally proceeding to the second stage. In the light of what had not been achieved this was more than a little absurd. In the end it was agreed that the Community could, from the beginning of 1974, proceed to 'a' second stage of EMU. The word 'the' was deliberately omitted. By 1974 it was increasingly realized that EMU was not going to materialize. At the Paris Summit in December 1974 the EMU scheme was to all intents and purposes shelved. The Heads of State and of Government noted the difficulties which in 1973 and 1974 had prevented the hoped-for progress being made. They reaffirmed that their will to achieve the union was not weakened, but they attached no date to its achievement. The 1972 Paris Summit aspiration that the grand design would be achieved by not later than 1980 was not reasserted. The mini-snake continued to exist, but of course it was very different in character from the original conception.

Post-mortem

Why did EMU fail to materialize? Two main reasons can be adduced. Firstly, it was launched at an unfortunate time. As we have seen, the international monetary system was very unsettled and the oil crisis, which began in October 1973, only served to aggravate matters. Lack of confidence in the dollar threw great strain on the snake in the tunnel arrangement – the Smithsonian Accords did not bring that strain to an end and neither did the dollar devaluation of February 1973. The second factor has already been noted, namely the failure of the member states to take seriously the need to coordinate their policies. In the absence of a convergence of economic performance on matters such as the price level, exchange rates were bound to need adjustment. Indeed, as Dennis has shown (see Table 11), differential inflation was very much the order of the day.

It is of course tempting to ascribe some of the failure of the EMU

Table 11. Annual inflation rates in the EEC 1971–5

	Belgium	Denmark	France	Germany	Ireland	Italy	Netherlands	UK
1971	4·3	5·8	5·5	5·3	8·9	4·8	7·5	9·4
1972	5·4	6·6	5·8	5·5	8·7	5·7	7·8	7·1
1973	7·0	9·3	7·3	6·9	11·3	10·4	8·0	8·1
1974	12·6	15·0	13·6	6·9	16·9	19·4	9·5	16·0
1975	12·7	11·0	11·6	5·9	20·8	17·1	10·2	24·1
1971–1975	49·5	57·4	52·2	34·7	86·4	71·3	51·2	82·5

Source: G. E. J. Dennis, 'European Monetary Union: in the "Snake-Pit"', *The Banker*, October 1976, p. 1109.

to the oil crisis. However, it should be pointed out that the first oil price increase did not occur until October 1973 and took time to feed into the system. By then EMU was well on the way to failure. In any case all the member states were affected by the oil price rise although not to exactly the same degree. Kruse emphasizes that the oil crisis was not the main underlying factor. The main factor was the failure to coordinate, and that gave rise to divergent trends. As Kruse so penetratingly points out:

It must be stressed that these differences in national economic policies and trends antedated the events of October: the oil crisis did not produce them but merely intensified and highlighted them. (Kruse, 1980, p. 154)

Although EMU was to all intents and purposes dead for the time being, there were some who would not let it lie down. We have already noted the Tindemans Report in Chapter 1 with its suggestion for a two-tier Community. In 1975 a study group set up by the Commission under the chairmanship of Robert Marjolin also produced a report (EC Commission, 1975b). Its verdict on the initial attempts at EMU was quite pessimistic – if there had been any movement it was backwards! But it would not be fair to lump Marjolin with Tindemans. The Marjolin report did not advocate any grandiose plans. It did not regard EMU as feasible in the then near future and concentrated its attention on some concrete short-term measures rather than another long-term plan. Mention should also be made of the 1975 All Saints' Day Manifesto on EMU. This was a proposal by nine prominent economists and contained at least one very interesting idea. It suggested that instead of regarding the Europa as a reserve currency it should at least initially be used as a private asset. In a sense it could be created as a kind of parallel currency which pragmatically could be left to sink or swim. If it proved popular then national currencies could be gradually phased out.

The EMS

Jenkins and Schmidt

When in 1977 the then President of the EC Commission, Roy Jenkins, made a strong plea for the Community to take up the idea of monetary union again, many felt that the timing was particularly inopportune. His initial plan envisaged a big leap forward with a single European currency and monetary authority. However, the idea did not fall on stony ground. At the Copenhagen and Bremen Summits of 1978 Chancellor Schmidt took up the initiative. On this occasion the plan which emerged was much less ambitious than the former EMU. There was no question of immutable exchange rates or a common currency. The emphasis was more modestly placed on the need to create a zone of monetary stability in Europe. It came to be called the European Monetary System. We shall turn to the details later. The immediate question is: What were the motivations lying behind this new proposal?

Motivations

Jacques van Ypersele, who was intimately involved in the EMS negotiations, draws attention to three factors. Firstly, there was a general dissatisfaction with the floating exchange rate system which came to replace the fixed rates of the Bretton Woods system. Secondly, fixed rates had a beneficial effect upon business conducted across frontiers. In his words:

Greater monetary stability would encourage business confidence and investment. In talks with European business executives one often hears complaints that they are unable to give their companies a full European dimension because of the ever-present exchange risks and uncertainty about exchange rates. It has been difficult to forecast correctly the cost in national currency of inputs from abroad or the revenue in national currency from exports. These uncertainties contribute to the fact that businesses are not harvesting the potential benefits of a market as large as Europe. (van Ypersele, 1979, p. 7)

Thirdly, exchange rates had been subject to over-shooting. The latter requires a little more explanation.

There can be no doubt that the main reason for the creation of the EMS was the destabilizing effect of foreign currency movements, particularly those of the dollar. *The motivation behind the EMS was therefore significantly different from that which inspired the EMU.* When people moved out of, say, the dollar, because of a lack of confidence in it, they did not tend to move equally into all European currencies. Rather they tended to rush towards one currency – the D-mark. This distorted the relationship between European currencies (and with other currencies). It caused the D-mark to move up and, since the D-mark was scarce, other Community currencies would command fewer D-marks – in other words they depreciated relative to the D-mark. These movements of both the D-mark and other Community currencies, caused by what may be termed international portfolio adjustments, tended to overshoot the levels justified by the relative price levels of goods and services in their respective economies. Van Ypersele maintains that overshooting, both upwards and downwards, was perceived as having a depressing effect on national economies. Excessive appreciation tended to depress profits and activity in export industries. Excessive depreciation tended to lead to inflationary pressures and made governments reluctant to revive economies for fear of adding yet more fuel to inflation.

The lead given by the German Government can be explained in terms of a desire to take the pressure of speculative inflows off the D-mark. If a really effective fixed exchange rate system could be established as between the member states then the pressure would be shared. An ex-dollar holder would be as happy to hold the French franc as the D-mark, since the former could always be turned into the latter without loss.

The ECU and the exchange rate mechanism

One of the central features of the EMS is the European Currency Unit (ECU). When the Community was first set up it needed some denominator of value. Whilst one of the member state currencies could have served that purpose, there were reasons which militated against such a solution. Firstly, there was the possibility that that particular currency might prove to be unstable. Secondly, national rivalries and prestige precluded selecting any one country's currency as the Community currency. Instead, the Six initially adopted the Unit of Account (UA), which has a gold content equal to that of the US dollar. Later, on the recommendation of the Monetary Committee, this was followed by the European Unit of Account (EUA), which was a composite currency – see below for the meaning of that term. In terms of construction, the EUA was a direct precursor of what came next, namely the ECU. The latter was introduced in 1979 in connection with the EMS.

Currently the ECU plays three main roles – two are official and one is unofficial. (a) The ECU acts as the denominator of Community transactions. Thus the Community budget is specified in terms of ECUs. When firms are fined, the penalty is fixed in terms of ECUs and so on. (b) But the ECU is also the central feature of the EMS, and it is this aspect which concerns us at this point. Briefly, in the EMS the ECU is the denominator of the exchange rate mechanism; it provides a basis for the divergence indicator; it acts as a denominator for operations in the intervention and credit mechanisms; and it acts as a means of settlement between monetary authorities. We shall say more about these below. (c) Unofficially, the ECU is also being increasingly used in connection with *private* transactions, both within and indeed without the Community. We will come back to this point later.

We now turn to the exchange rate mechanism. At its centre is the ECU. This is a composite currency – we may in fact describe it as a currency cocktail. That is to say it is made up of specified amounts of all the member state currencies. A basic question which had to be resolved was: What weight should be attached to each of the currencies in the basket? The criteria which had been used in the EUA were threefold – a country's share of collective GNP, its share of collective trade (exports) and its size (the latter criterion was employed in the short-term monetary support scheme which gave countries quotas according to whether they were 'large', 'medium' or 'small'). These criteria were also adopted in respect of the ECU, and the currency weightings (these were recalculated in 1984) are as shown in Table 12. Currently (1987) Spain and Portugal are not included in the ECU.

Table 12. Currency weightings in EMS basket (17 September 1984)

	Number of units of national currencies	Percentage weighting
D-mark	0·719	32·0
French franc	1·310	19·0
UK pound	0·0878	15·0
Italian lira	140·000	10·2
Dutch guilder	0·256	10·1
Belgian franc	3·710	8·2
Luxembourg franc	0·140	0·3
Danish krone	0·219	2·7
Greek drachma	1·150	1·3
Irish punt	0·00871	1·2
		100·0

Source: J. van Ypersele and J.-C. Koeune, *The European Monetary System*, OOPEC, 1985, p. 58.

The next point to appreciate is that at any time each member state's currency has a specified value in relation to 1 ECU. Moreover, these values, once fixed collectively, have to persist until a decision is made by the participating states to alter them. In Figure 6 we provide a purely hypothetical three-country example. The relationships between each national currency and 1 ECU are labelled 1, 2 and 3. If each national currency has a definite relationship to 1 ECU it inevitably follows that we can derive the implied relationship (i.e. cross rate) between each national currency and all the other national currencies. Thus in Figure 6, 1 Dm must be worth 2·5Ff (see 4) and 1 Dm must be worth 50Il (see 5). Equally 1 Ff must be worth 0·4 Dm (4 in reverse) and 1 Ff must be worth 20 Il (see 6). These are the bilateral central rates. A key obligation of each of the countries participating in the exchange rate mechanism is that they must not allow the exchange rate of their currency against the other currencies to fluctuate by more than a given percentage above and below these central rates.

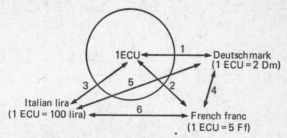

Figure 6. Hypothetical example of EMS bilateral grid (based on three states)

We now need to specify the exact conditions. Not all countries participate in the exchange rate mechanism. The UK is not a party, and currently (1987) neither is Greece, Portugal or Spain. The participating members are therefore West Germany, France, Belgium, Luxembourg, the Netherlands, Denmark, Ireland and Italy. The first seven have undertaken not to allow their currencies to fluctuate by more than 2·25 per cent above and below the central rate. Italy is allowed a margin of 6 per cent either way. When the EMS was set up, the UK and Ireland were also offered the wider band of fluctuation, but Ireland opted for 2·25 per cent and, as we have seen, the UK decided to stay outside the exchange rate scheme. (However, like Greece, the UK plays a part in the rest of the system – see below.)

In Table 13 we show the bilateral grid – i.e. the central rates and the permitted margins of fluctuation as they existed following the realignments of 11 January 1987.

Needless to say, the prescribing of such limits will not of itself keep actual exchange rates within those limits. For this to happen, interventions may be required. Once a currency reaches its bilateral limit

Table 13. EMS bilateral grid (11 January 1987)

		Netherlands	Bel/Lux	W. Germany	Denmark	Ireland	France	Italy
Dutch guilder 100	+2·25%		1 872·15	90·77	346·24	33·886 8	304·44	67 912
	central rate	100	1 830·54	88·752 6	338·537	33·129 3	297·661	63 963·1
	−2·25%		1 789·85	86·78	331·02	32·393 9	291·04	60 241
Bel/Lux franc 100	+2·25%	5·587		4·959	18·914 3	1·851	16·631	3 710·2
	central rate	5·462 86	100	4·848 37	18·493 8	1·809 81	16·260 8	3 492·21
	−2·25%	5·341 5		4·74	18·083 1	1·769 5	15·899	3 290·9
D-mark 100	+2·25%	115·235	2 109·5		390·16	38·182 5	343·05	76 540
	central rate	112·673	2 062·55	100	381·443	37·328 1	335·386	72 069
	−2·25%	110·167 5	2 016·55		373	36·496 4	327·92	67 865
Danish krone 100	+2·25%	30·21	553·0	26·81		10·008 7	89·925	20 062
	central rate	29·538 9	540·723	26·216 2	100	9·786 04	87·925 7	18 894
	−2·25%	28·882 5	528·7	25·63		9·568 3	85·97	17 794
Irish punt 1	+2·25%	3·087	56·511 5	2·740	10·451 1		9·189	2 050·03
	central rate	3·018 48	55·254 5	2·678 94	10·218 6	1	8·984 8	1 930·71
	−2·25%	2·951	54·025	2·619	9·991 3		8·785	1 818·34
French franc 100	+2·25%	34·36	628·97	30·495	116·32	11·383		22 817
	central rate	33·595 3	614·977	29·816 4	113·732	11·129 9	100	21 488·6
	−2·25%	32·847 5	601·295	29·15	111·2	10·882 5		20 238
Italian lira 1 000	+6%	1·66	30·387	1·473 5	5·62	0·549 952	4·941	
	central rate	1·563 4	28·618 7	1·387 54	5·292 68	0·517 943	4·653 62	1 000
	−6%	1·472 5	26·953	1·306 5	4·985	0·487 799	4·383	
ECU 1	central rate	2·319 43	42·458 2	2·058 53	7·852 12	0·768 411	6·904 03	1 483·58

Source: Financial Times, 13 January 1987.

against another currency, the two central banks concerned have to intervene in order to prevent yet further departure from the central rate. If, for example, the French franc falls to its 2·25 per cent floor against the D-mark the Bank of France has to sell D-marks whilst the West German Bundesbank has to buy French francs. If the Bank of France needs to borrow D-marks from the Bundesbank to finance its defensive intervention, its debt will be denominated in ECUs and will be repaid in them. Not all interventions are carried out in terms of Community currencies. In some instances the US dollar acts as the intervention currency. This appears to be the case when interventions take place at a time when a currency has not reached the fluctuation limit. Thus the French authorities could pull up the value of the French franc by purchasing the latter with US dollars.

The exchange rate mechanism also incorporates a divergence indicator. Once a country's currency has diverged by three quarters of its permissible margin above or below its central rate *against the ECU*, a divergence indicator warning light in effect begins to flash. There is then *a presumption* that a government will take remedial action. In the case of a weak currency, a rise in interest rates, a tightening of fiscal policy and support operations using a diversity of currencies would all be appropriate, and *vice versa* for a strong currency. Apparently there was some difference of opinion as to whether, when a currency had moved three quarters of the way to its permitted limit,[1] intervention was mandatory or whether all that was required was the initiation of consultations. The phrase 'a presumption' was a compromise.

There is one complication which we must address. As we have seen, the permitted fluctuation in the bilateral grid is ±2·25 per cent. It might also be assumed that the same fluctuation will be allowed against the ECU. But this alas is not so! Suppose that the D-mark appreciates equally against all the other currencies. It follows that they have all depreciated equally against the D-mark. It also follows that the D-mark has appreciated against the ECU and that the ECU has depreciated against the D-mark. Putting the latter another way we can say that the fixed quantities of the other currencies contained in the ECU will command fewer D-marks. If, therefore, the D-mark appreciates by 2·25 per cent against the ECU, it follows that it will have appreciated by *more than 2·25 per cent* against the other currencies, since the D-mark is itself part of the ECU and its value will not have been affected. It follows that the bigger the weight of a currency in the ECU basket the less can it be allowed to fluctuate *against the ECU* before the permitted

1. This point is called its divergence threshold.

2·25 per cent limit *against other currencies* is reached. For example, the Irish punt (because it has a small weighting in the ECU) can be allowed to move ±2·22 per cent against the ECU, whereas the D-mark (which has a relatively large weighting) is allowed only ±1·53 per cent. The threshold of three quarters relates to these smaller bands of fluctuation.

The exchange rate mechanism is a fairly flexible arrangement. Apart from the relatively wide margins allowed for Italy, the system quite explicitly incorporates the possibility that currencies may be devalued or revalued against the ECU or that countries may temporarily depart from the system. However, devaluations and revaluations are not unilateral acts but are subjects for negotiation among the exchange rate partners. Member states may not always secure the degree of adjustment they desire. For example, as David Llewellyn (1983, p. 254) has pointed out, in February 1982 Belgium wished to devalue by 12 per cent but had to settle for only 8·5 per cent. Adjustments may also involve an element of sharing. In March 1983 France was able to persuade countries with stronger currencies, e.g. West Germany, to revalue at the same time as she, and others, devalued. The fact that the system is so flexible means that it can exhibit significant fluctuation and change without being declared a failure – in practice the emphasis is on relative stability rather than immutability.

In establishing the system the member states were aware of the need for convergence of economic performance and recognized that this would be a particular burden on the less prosperous countries – Ireland, Italy and the UK being the economies in question. The EMS agreement therefore provided for a limited transfer of resources. Over five years the New Community Instrument (see Chapter 3), in collaboration with the EIB, would make available loans totalling 1000 million EUA per annum. Interest rate subsidies of 3 per cent would be available on these loans. This assistance would only be available to member states which fully participated in the exchange rate mechanism. Since the UK chose not to do so it did not benefit from that provision.

This conveniently brings us to the subject of the UK's relationship with the EMS. The original decision to stay outside represented a continuation of the Labour Party's attitude to European monetary experiments (see Chapter 1). Given the UK's inflationary proclivity, an inability to devalue would force the British Government to deflate, thus creating unemployment. When the Thatcher Government came to power the argument against membership was very different. When the pound was strong and rising it was argued that, were it a member, the UK would be required to adopt an expansionary monetary policy in order to prevent the pound from rising above its upper limit. Such an expansionary monetary policy would be at odds with the monetarist stance which had been adopted. The Medium-Term Financial Strategy was indeed incompatible with the EMS, since strict adherence to it implied no exchange rate target. David Llewellyn (1983, p. 265) has pointed out that subsequent UK monetary strategy switched from sole reliance on the money supply as the target and began to take account of interest rates and the exchange rate. This suggested that the stance of UK policy was becoming more compatible with EMS membership. Nevertheless, the latter was still regarded as posing problems, and the UK Government has merely indicated that it might join eventually. This hesitancy is probably a reflection of the views expressed in the 1985 report of the Treasury and Civil Service Select Committee of the House of Commons. It expressed reservations about membership of the exchange rate mechanism. It drew attention to the loss of autonomy – that is an old point. It expressed concern about the exchange rate relative to the D-mark. At that time Sterling was felt to be overvalued, and it was anticipated that there would be resistance to inserting it into the exchange rate mechanism at an appropriately adjusted rate. This may now be less of a problem, since subsequently Sterling fell relative to the D-mark. Another anxiety related to the point that Sterling was a petro-currency which would tend to rise when other EMS currencies tended to fall. In other words, high oil prices helped the UK but disadvantaged the rest and *vice versa*. Despite all this, sentiment towards the EMS became more favourable in 1986. It was, however, somewhat dampened by the currency upset in the EMS at the beginning of 1987. Critics pointed to the relative quiescence of Sterling and suggested that if Sterling had been in the EMS it too might have been drawn into the turmoil.

Financing the EMS

As we have seen, operations to support currencies require financing. The EMS incorporates and expands three previously existing EEC credit mechanisms – the very short-term financing and the short-term monetary support (STMS). Both of these are the responsibility of Central Banks. In addition there is the medium-term financial assistance (MTFA) which is granted by the Council of Ministers. It is ultimately envisaged that a European Monetary Fund (EMF) should be created. In the interim, the old European Monetary Cooperation Fund (EMCF) continues to exist as the precursor to the new institution. The EMCF is empowered to receive monetary reserves from the appropriate authorities of the member states and to issue ECUs in exchange. The latter can be used to settle debts between member states and in transactions with the EMCF. The ECU is thus an asset and not just a denominator for expressing debts and claims. Although the UK did not join the supersnake, it has participated in the work of the EMCF by depositing with it 20 per cent of its reserves of gold and foreign exchange in return for ECUs.

Convergence

When the member states agreed to set up the EMS, they recognized that it was important to coordinate their national macro-economic policies. In Community parlance this is referred to as policy convergence – the objective of which is to achieve a convergence of economic performance. In other words rates of inflation (or deflation), etc, should come into line. Without such a convergence, exchange rates cannot long remain unchanged. Thus those who inflate relatively rapidly will lose competitiveness and will be forced to devalue in order to restore it. It is of course possible for those who inflate too rapidly to seek to persuade their more successful partners to bear some of the adjustment burden by revaluing. This would make the latter less competitive and the excessive-inflation countries correspondingly more competitive. Convergence of policy sounds fine, but it does involve a giving up of national sovereignty – as we have seen, the UK is less than enthusiastic about the prospect. In the context of policy convergence, it is important to note the relevance of the Single European Act (SEA). The reader may have wondered why we referred earlier to the *original* Rome Treaty rules on macro-economic policy. The reason is that although the rules remain intact, the SEA has added Article 102A. It comes under a new section headed 'Cooperation in economic and monetary policy (Economic and Monetary Union)'. The new article goes on to call for measures to ensure the convergence of economic and monetary policy, and in that connection it requires the member states to take account of experience in the EMS and in developing the ECU. Thus whilst the SEA does not compel full membership of the EMS, the Rome Treaty now explicitly takes account of it.

Assessment

It is all too apparent that the EMS has not rendered currency realignments a thing of the past. Table 14 indicates that between the inception of the EMS in March 1979 and January 1987 there were eleven occasions when one or more of the participating currencies was realigned.

On the other hand there is evidence that as compared with currencies such as the Japanese yen and US dollar the scheme has had the effect of reducing day-to-day fluctuations between member state currencies.

Table 14. EMS exchange rate realignments 1979–87

23 September 1979	D-mark revalued by 2%, Danish krone devalued by 3 %, each against all other EMS currencies
19 November 1979	Danish krone devalued by 5%
22 March 1981	Italian lira devalued by 6%
4 October 1981	D-mark and Dutch guilder revalued by 5·5%, French franc and Italian lira devalued by 3%
21 February 1982	Belgian and Luxembourg franc devalued by 8·5% and Danish krone by 3%
12 June 1982	D-mark and Dutch guilder revalued by 4·25%, French france devalued by 5·75% and Italian lira devalued by 2·75%
21 March 1983	D-mark revalued by 5·5%, Dutch guilder revalued by 3.35%, Danish krone revalued by 2·5%, Belgian and Luxembourg franc revalued by 1·5%, Italian lira devalued by 2·5%, Irish pound revalued by 3·5%
20 July 1985	Italian lira devalued by 6%, all others revalued by 2%
6 April 1986	D-mark and Dutch guilder revalued by 3%, Belgian and Luxembourg franc and Danish krone revalued by 1%, French franc devalued by 3%
2 August 1986	Irish punt devalued by 8%
11 January 1987	D-mark and Dutch guilder revalued by 3%, Belgian and Luxembourg franc revalued by 2%

Source: EC Commission, *General Report* and *Bulletin*, various dates.

If we ask why realignments were necessary, the answer is partly provided by the data supplied in Table 15. Rates of inflation have varied as between member states. As we anticipated above, member states with unduly rapid rates of inflation have lost competitiveness and have been forced to devalue, whilst the successful ones have borne part of the adjustment burden and have had to revalue. This point is brought out in Table 16, from which it is apparent that, broadly speaking, in the period 1979–87 those with the lowest rates of inflation tended to revalue, whilst those with the highest rates tended to devalue.

Table 15. Consumption prices[1] in EMS 1979–87

	1979	1980	1981	1982	1983	1984	1985	1986[2]	1987[3]
D-mark	4·0	5·8	6·0	4·7	3·1	2·4	2·1	0·0	1·1
Dutch guilder	4·3	6·9	6·3	5·3	2·8	2·6	2·6	0·0	−1·0
Belgian franc	3·9	6·5	8·1	7·4	7·5	5·9	4·8	1·3	1·5
Luxembourg franc	5·2	7·7	8·6	10·6	8·0	6·4	4·0	0·5	1·3
Danish krone	10·4	10·7	12·0	10·2	7·2	6·5	5·0	3·3	2·8
French franc	10·4	13·2	12·8	11·2	9·5	7·3	5·5	2·5	2·3
Irish punt	14·9	18·6	21·2	16·0	8·2	8·5	4·2	3·7	3·2
Italian lira	15·1	20·2	19·2	17·0	15·1	11·1	9·4	6·2	4·0

Notes: 1. Percentage change per annum in consumption deflator. 2. Provisional. 3. Forecast.
Source: EC Commission, *European Economy*, No. 30, November 1986.

Table 16. Inflation 1979–86 and EMS realignments 1979–87

	Inflation league table[1]	Devaluations	Revaluations
D-mark	28·1	0	7
Dutch guilder	30·8	0	6
Belgian franc	45·4	1	4
Luxembourg franc	51·0	1	4
Danish krone	65·3	3	3
French franc	72·4	3	1
Irish punt	95·3	2	1
Italian lira	113·3	3	1

Note: 1. Price data is derived from Table 15 and covers the period 1979–86. It is based on a simple addition of the annual rates and does not take compounding into account.

Another factor which has affected the stability of the EMS has been external in origin – i.e. the state of the US dollar. When the US dollar has been quiescent there has been a better prospect of quiescence in the EMS. But when the US dollar has fallen, or has been expected to fall, there has been a flight out of it into safer havens. The safest haven in the EMS has been the strongest currency – i.e. the one most likely to appreciate rather than depreciate. That has tended to be the D-mark, since inflation in West Germany has been low and industrial performance has been impressive. There will always be strains within the EMS while ever there is a differential attractiveness as between national currencies, and of course such differentials reflect differences in economic performance. The realignment of early 1987 was, for example, partly due to a loss of confidence in the US dollar and a flight into the D-mark.[1] Clearly there is also a need to coordinate exchange rate policies *vis-à-vis* third countries, notably the US. This point has been neglected.

Yet another factor which may disturb currencies is internal unrest – particularly the industrial variety. The realignment early in 1987 was said to have been in part due to strikes in France.

We have identified three factors giving rise to realignments. The first two are related to differences in economic performance in matters such

1. The inflow into the D-mark was also partly the result of German interest rates. The Germans were reluctant to lower interest rates because of inflationary fears. A lowering of interest rates would have stemmed the inflow and therefore reduced the strains within the EMS.

as price movements. Ideally there is therefore, as we noted earlier, a need for a coordination of member state economic policy to parallel the agreement over exchange rates. *Formally* this does not seem to have happened to any significant extent. Kruse takes a very pessimistic view. He points out:

The member states were not prepared to cede their authority in 1971 or 1973, and they were not prepared to do so in 1980. (Kruse, 1980, p. 259)

Jacques van Ypersele, whilst not so categorical, does stress the need 'to work directly at improving . . . convergence of economic performances' – an objective which he declares is as yet imperfectly attained (Ypersele and Koeune, 1985, p. 114). Such convergence policy as exists seems to consist of the Council of Ministers from time to time examining the economic situation in the Community and producing general economic policy guidelines. This takes place on the basis of a Council of Ministers' Decision of 1974, the declared objective of which was the achievement of a high degree of economic convergence. Critics have pointed out that much more use needs to be made of the Commission's right to address recommendations to member states deviating from the guidelines. The reader will note the use of the words 'guidelines' and 'recommendations' which clearly reflect the reluctance formally to give up economic sovereignty.

Whilst divergence has been apparent in the past, some commentators observed signs of convergence as early as 1984. The EC Commission drew attention to it (EC Commission, 1984a, p. 71) and Dennis and Nellis (1984) and Zis (1984) did likewise. Dennis and Nellis were inclined to explain the phenomenon as a fortuitously identical response to a common threat – inflation following the 1979 oil price rise – rather than a deliberate decision to get together to coordinate policies. Nevertheless, there are now clear signs of convergence. This is shown in Table 17, where the national rates of monetary growth and inflation are seen to have become less disparate. An alternative explanation is that whilst member states formally continue to be reluctant to surrender their autonomy, they are equally aware that, having agreed the exchange rates, it is prudent for them to bring their policies into line with their competitors. This of course is the old EMU monetarist view. In practice, one of the most formidable competitors when it comes to keeping inflation at bay is West Germany. It follows that once a member state becomes part of the exchange rate mechanism, its main challenge is to keep its inflation rate down to the German level. It should be said that member states find this a useful discipline for keeping their domestic wage increases and price increases in check.

Table 17. Convergence of EMS inflation rates and monetary growth rates

	1979	1980	1981	1982	1983	1984	1985	1986[1]	1987[2]
Average EMS Inflation Rate	8·6	11·16	11·5	9·9	8·1	6·2	5·0	2·4	2·1
Mean deviation of national rates from the average	4·2	5·0	4·6	4·3	4·1	3·0	2·3	2·0	1·1
Mean deviation of national rates from the minimum	5·9	6·9	5·7	5·2	4·9	3·8	3·3	3·1	3·6
Weighted Average EMS Monetary Growth Rate	12·9	9·7	8·7	9·5	10·2	8·4	7·7	6·9	5·6
Dispersion of national rates in relation to average[3]	4·0	3·4	2·5	2·3	3·5	3·1	3·2	1·5	1·2
Dispersion of national rates in relation to lowest[3]	8·1	4·4	4·4	3·0	4·8	4·4	2·8	1·6	2·0

Notes: 1. Provisional. 2. Forecast. 3. The dispersion index is a weighted sum of absolute deviations from the respective reference value.

Source: EC Commission, *European Economy*, No. 30, 1986, pp. 29, 46.

If a member state fails to keep its price increases in check, it can of course deal with its exchange rate weakness by raising interest rates. This will attract an inflow of foreign capital and will also prevent domestic capital from flowing out – both of these help to prop up the exchange rate. However, high interest rates have a depressive effect, and therefore a failure to control inflation may be paid for by higher unemployment. But there is a possible way of escaping from this. The state with high inflation could apply exchange controls. This would halt the capital outflow. Without such a control, interest rates would have to be compensatingly higher. Here we see that inflation-prone states may regard membership of the EMS exchange rate mechanism as not being compatible with the abolition of exchange controls which we discussed in Chapter 6.

There is one other promising development which needs to be highlighted. We refer to the growth in the 'private' use of the ECU as opposed to its 'official' use between EMS central banks. The ECU is being increasingly used as a denominator of value in international bond issues by Community institutions, member state governments and companies. There has also been a growth of ECU bank deposits, and an inter-bank market with clearing facilities has also emerged. In some countries a substantial amount of international trade is invoiced and paid for in ECUs. The reason for all this is simple. Denominating securities and transactions in terms of a composite currency reduces risk as compared with the use of a single currency. Here we may be witnessing, in Darwinian terms, the emergence of a superior species!

8   Agriculture, Transport and Energy

The common agricultural policy

The logic of inclusion

First we must ask why such a policy was required at all. The Six could have adopted the approach of EFTA and left agriculture out of the arrangement. However, a programme of economic integration within the Six which excluded agriculture stood no chance of success. It is important to appreciate that the Rome Treaty was a delicate balance of the national interests of the contracting parties. Let us consider West Germany and France in terms of trade outlets. In the case of West Germany the prospect of free trade in industrial goods, and free access to the French market in particular, was extremely inviting. In the case of France, the relative efficiency of her agriculture (particularly her grain producers) as compared with West Germany held out the prospect that in a free Community agricultural market she would make substantial inroads into the West German market. This was obviously likely to result if the common price level of grain, for example, was set well below the West German level but at or above the French level. Agriculture had therefore to be included.

These factors do not, however, explain the emergence of a common policy. Agriculture could have been brought within the ambit of the Treaty without resort to common support systems and common price levels. Each member state could have operated its own agricultural support programme, with protection at the frontier and so forth in order to achieve predetermined price levels. Trade could have been fitted into such a system through the agency of bilateral agreements between members, whereby they could have agreed to absorb certain quantities of each other's agricultural output. In practice the Six chose to go further than this since they agreed to free inter-state agricultural trade of all obstacles. This in turn implied uniform prices over the whole Community market. It also gave rise to the establishment of a centralized system for deciding what the common price levels should be and Community machinery for manipulating markets in order to bring them about. A Community system for financing the support policy was also clearly called for. The decision to establish free movement of agricultural goods within the Community was probably the result of two factors. Firstly, anything less than free trade in agriculture would have struck the French as discriminatory when compared with the treatment proposed for industrial goods. Secondly, if trade was not free, and national price levels could differ, then countries with low price levels would enjoy a competitive advantage in so far as low food prices give rise to low industrial wages.

In explaining the inclusion of agriculture within the Rome Treaty, some account should also be taken of the sheer size of the agricultural sector in 1958. At that time farming occupied fifteen million persons – about 20 per cent of the working population of the Community. A process of economic unification, leading to eventual political integration, could hardly succeed if it failed to address itself to the problems faced by such an important section of the population. Within the Six, agriculture was an occupation in which the problem of relatively low incomes was particularly acute. In any case the agricultural vote was so important that agriculture could hardly be ignored. This kind of consideration was extremely important in the case of France. French farmers were highly dissatisfied with the kind of support provided by the French Government and looked to the EEC as a means of improving their lot. To them the exclusion of agriculture was unthinkable, and French politicians were fully aware of that point.

Policy objectives

The provisions relating to the CAP are found in Articles 38 to 47. The Rome Treaty did not specify the forms of price support which would be adopted for each product. Instead, Article 43 indicated that the Commission should convene a conference to thrash out the matter, after which it would make appropriate proposals for adoption by the Council of Ministers. The various methods of market organization which were finally adopted are discussed below. Whilst the Treaty did not commit itself on the form of market organization, it did specify the objectives of the CAP – these are to be found in Article 39. The policy should:

(a) increase agricultural productivity;

(b) ensure a fair standard of living for the agricultural community;
(c) stabilize markets;
(d) provide certainty of supplies;
(e) ensure supplies to consumers at reasonable prices.

We should also take cognizance of Article 110 relating to the creation of a common commercial policy. It indicates that the member states should aim to contribute to the harmonious development of world trade.

The reader will recognize that there is plenty of scope for conflict here. The improvement of farm incomes might require significant price increases, but this would conflict with the interests of consumers. It must be admitted that no indication is given as to what is a fair income level or what is a reasonable level of prices. Certainty of supplies could be taken to justify a greater degree of self-sufficiency, but that would reduce the access of third countries to the Community food market which in turn would jeopardize the achievement of the objective of Article 110.

The system of price support

Although the machinery differs from commodity to commodity, the basic features of the EEC support system for most farm products are as follows. The income support to producers is guaranteed by manipulating the market so as to bring about a high price – a price which in itself provides an adequate remuneration to farmers. The internal price level is partly maintained by a variety of protective devices at the common frontier. These prevent imports from the low-price world market from eroding the internal price level. But in addition, provision is made for official support buying within the Community so as to take off the market the excess of supply over demand at the predetermined support-price level. The commodities so purchased may be later unloaded on the Community market when demand exceeds supply at the support level. Alternatively, they can be conveyed to other uses. Then again, and this is particularly important, they can be unloaded on the world market, usually at a loss. In broad terms this policy was a direct descendant of the policies pursued at the national level prior to the signing of the Rome Treaty.

It will immediately be recognized that this approach is the opposite of that adopted in the UK. At the risk of some over-simplification, it can be said that the British approach was to import food at low world prices. (This followed a long tradition in British policy. In the nineteenth century the free-trade policy of the UK involved the exchange of British industrial goods for the primary commodities which the Empire could most efficiently produce. The import of food at low prices found a further expression in the reciprocal Commonwealth Preference system.) In so far as the UK farmer could not make an adequate living by selling at market prices arising under conditions of free importation, British policy consisted of granting deficiency payments (financed out of taxation) sufficient to build up the price received by the farmer to a level set out in the Annual Farm Price Review.

A better appreciation of how the Community market support policy works can be derived from considering particular commodities. In the case of soft wheat, barley and maize, the Community operates a system of target prices. During the transitional stage the national target prices could and did differ, because national markets were protected from each other. However, in 1967 all such protection was swept away and a common target price came into operation. In the case of soft wheat, the common target price was DM 425 per ton[1] in the area of greatest deficit in the Community. The latter is defined as the area with the least adequate supplies of soft wheat. The centre chosen was Duisburg in the Ruhr. It was therefore planned to manipulate the market so as to bring about a price of DM 425 at Duisburg. (Target prices in other main marketing centres were established which were essentially regional derivatives of the Duisburg price, but later this regionalization was abandoned.)

Intervention prices for the above-mentioned grains are currently (1986–87 agricultural season) set at 23 to 30 per cent below the target price. When the market price in the Community falls to the intervention price level, support purchases can begin. In this sense the intervention price represents the minimum support price for producers. This system prevents over-production within the Community from pushing the price level down.

In addition, the Community must protect the internal price level from imported supplies. This is done by applying a system of variable levies to supplies emanating from outside the Six. As part of this machinery, a threshold price level is determined. Imported supplies crossing the Community frontier at the threshold price level will, when they bear the further cost of transport, enter market centres at a price equal to the target price set for that centre. If imported supplies cross the frontier below the threshold price, a levy is applied equal to the difference between the price at the frontier and the threshold price. For example, suppose the target price of grain in the Belgian market centre of Brussels is $105.

1. This of course is not the current target price!

Suppose also that the cost of transport from Antwerp to Brussels is $5. Then the threshold price at Antwerp is $100. If supplies are imported at Antwerp at a price of $90 then a variable levy of $10 is applied.

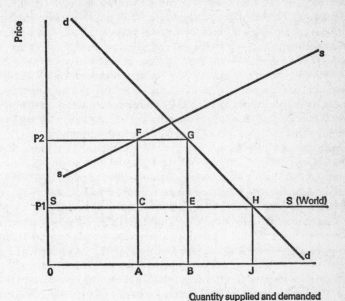

Figure 7. The UK Agricultural Support System

The reader may see the contrast between the UK and the EEC systems a little more clearly if we deploy some simple diagrams. In Figure 7 we show the UK system as it operated prior to entry into the EEC. The diagram does not represent the actual mechanism in respect of every product but encapsulates the general philosophy of the UK approach to the pricing of agricultural produce. dd represents the UK demand for agricultural produce. SS (World) represents the supply available by importation. We assume that the supply curve was infinitely elastic – whether the UK had imported a little or a lot, the world price would still have been OP1. Given the size of UK imports this is a little extreme, but for the sake of simplicity we will make this assumption. If the UK Government had pursued a policy of free importation, supplies would have flooded into the UK market at price OP1 – the world price.

The equilibrium point would have been at H – UK consumers would have consumed OJ, all of which would have been supplied by way of imports. This would have spelt disaster for UK farmers. We depict their supply curve as ss – it lies above SS (World), suggesting that the costs of production of UK farmers were above the world price level. (It should be remembered that if the world market was a dumping ground for national agricultural surpluses OP1 would be an artificially low figure.) In order to support the domestic farming industry, the UK Government carried out an Annual Farm Price Review. Guaranteed prices were set for various products (sometimes the National Farmers' Union and its sister organizations found themselves able voluntarily to agree with these prices, sometimes they did not). OP2 represents the guaranteed price. UK farmers would then supply quantity OA. Supplies were allowed to enter the UK market at price OP1 and this was the price which the UK farmer received from the market. However, in addition he was paid a deficiency payment equal to P1P2. The farmers' income thus had two components. OP1CA was the revenue from sales of the market. P1P2FC was the deficiency payment paid by the Exchequer and ultimately by the taxpayer. At price OP1, UK consumers would purchase OJ, of which OA was domestic output and AJ was imports. Price and income support were in a sense divorced. The price to the consumer was only OP1, but the price which determined farm incomes was OP2. The consumer paid a low price for his food (although he had to pay taxes to finance the deficiency payments), and the rest of the world enjoyed free access to the UK market. A profitable UK farming industry was kept in existence. Some import savings also resulted.

The Community system is depicted in Figure 8. Again we must emphasize that the régimes vary from product to product. The diagram therefore merely represents the general philosophy of the EEC approach. Again, SS (World) represents the price on the world market at which supplies could enter the Community market. Making it perfectly elastic in this case is even more dubious but does not invalidate the general argument. The supply curve of Community farmers is ss and we set it above SS (World) in order to suggest that Community farmers would not be able to stay in business at the world price level. It might in fact be the case that a small portion of the Community industry could survive even at a price below the world level – in which case a small portion of the ss curve should lie below SS (World). Clearly, in order to keep more or less the entire EEC industry in being, the undermining role of imports has to be dealt with. If we apply a variable level equal to P1P2 to imports, then a substantial domestic supply is guaranteed, whereas without (as the diagram is drawn) there would be none at all. Domestic supply with the levy would be P2A and imports would be AB. If the variable levy were even higher, i.e. P1P3, then domestic supply would be even greater, i.e. P3E, but domestic demand would only be P3C. There would be excess supply in the market equal to CE which would cause the price to weaken. If the authorities were aiming to achieve price OP3, then the excess supplies would have to be taken out of the market. This is where the second weapon, support buying, comes in. We can represent this as a shift of the demand curve from dd to d¹d¹. Consumer purchases P3C at price OP3 are supplemented by official purchases CE at price OP3 and price OP3 is maintained in the market. If the produce taken out of the market by support purchasing was sold outside the Community at a loss, i.e. P1P3 per unit, then an export refund would be payable. Clearly price and income support are one and the same thing in this system.

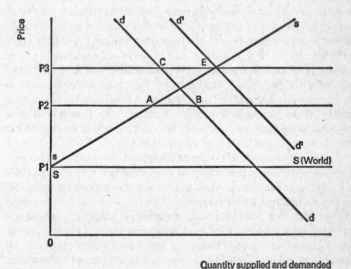

Figure 8. The EEC Agricultural Support System

There are a number of observations which need to be made in relation to the above account. Firstly, we must reiterate that the above description of the EEC mechanism merely describes the general thrust of support policy. Moreover, it relates not to the whole but to about 70 per cent of agricultural output. That statement of course implies that there is another 30 per cent or so which has been subjected to different régimes, and we will say more about those products in a moment.

Secondly, within the 70 per cent category there have been quite marked variations from product to product. The reader is invited to contrast the variable levy and automatic intervention buying at the target price minus 23 to 30 per cent for most cereals with the arrangement for fruit and vegetables. In the latter case the external protection has been limited to an *ad valorem* import duty or to a duty on top of a minimum import price. Internally, prices have been able to fall a long way before intervention buying has occurred. The internal régime has involved the calculation of basic prices – these have been derived by averaging EEC domestic prices over the previous three years. However, these basic prices have not been guaranteed. Indeed *national intervention agencies* were not allowed to step in until market prices had fallen to the buying-in level – i.e. 40 to 70 per cent (depending on the product) of the basic price level. In practice this device has been little used. Instead, a system of withdrawal prices has been determined, and when market prices have fallen to the withdrawal level *producer organizations* have been allowed to step in and buy up surplus produce. This produce has been used for animal feed, industrial purposes or has been destroyed. Such withdrawal operations have been financed by the Community. Withdrawal prices have been set at the buying-in level plus 10 per cent. The withdrawal price could therefore be as low as 50 per cent of the basic price (e.g. 40 per cent of the buying-in price plus 10 per cent).[1]

Thirdly, our general description of the régime in respect of 70 per cent of output is actually a description of a system which existed until 1984. In 1984 it began to change when quotas were introduced for milk – we will say more about this topic later.

Fourthly, as we indicated above, a significant minority of output has been subjected to different forms of assistance. *Broadly speaking*, in the case of about 25 per cent of output support has concentrated mainly on measures of external protection as opposed to a balanced combination of external protection and internal manipulation.

Finally, in a very small minority of cases the price of imports could not be raised because duties at nil or low levels had been agreed in various international accords. When the price of imports could not be

1. The pricing system is further complicated by factors which adjust for quality, size and variety.

raised to Community levels, Community prices have been brought down to match world levels by the granting of various forms of aid. Olive oil, oil seeds and tobacco appear to be cases in point.

The evolution of policy

Between the signing of the Rome Treaty and 1968, by which time the common price systems had come into operation, the Community achieved three things. Firstly, it dissolved national systems of support. Secondly, the latter were replaced by Community support systems. These were operated during the transitional phase in conjunction with protection between member states, and as a result differences in national price levels continued to exist. Thirdly, the protection between member states was swept away and thereafter the common support system was accompanied by common prices. The latter are of course agreed annually by the Council of Ministers in the light of proposals submitted by the Brussels Commission.

This evolution was not achieved without considerable difficulty. Indeed, the Community made progress through a series of minor crises. For longish periods the Six failed to resolve their problems. The solution of them was therefore left to marathon sessions of the Council of Ministers during which package deals were evolved. (It might be relevant to add that the ability of the Six eventually to agree was particularly due to the contribution of Sicco Mansholt, the Commissioner who between 1958 and 1972 was responsible for agricultural policy.) In December 1961 the Council embarked on a marathon which led to common policies in grains, pig meat, eggs, poultry meat, fruit and vegetables, and wine, and to the laying down of the broad principles to be adopted in financing the policy. In December 1963 another marathon dealt with regulations relating to milk and dairy produce, beef and veal, rice, and fats. In December 1964 the Council approached the extremely vexed question of the common target price for grain. It ought to be emphasized that progress up to this point had been concerned with support systems and not with the eventual common prices which those systems would produce. The common grain price was essentially the linchpin of the whole system. Once this price was adopted, all the others would tend to fall into place since they are all closely linked together. For example, grain is a major input cost in producing poultry, eggs and pig meat. But pig meat and beef prices are related by virtue of competitive substitution. In turn, beef prices must stand in a certain relationship to milk prices if the raising of beef and dairy cattle are to be kept in line with evolution of the demand for these two products. The common grain price issue was also important because it brought France and West Germany directly into conflict. Relatively speaking, the West Germans were inefficient producers of wheat when compared with the French. The West Germans were reluctant to agree to a common price which represented a significant fall below their national price level. However, a common price at the German level (it was the highest in the Six in the 1964–5 season) would have done nothing to restrict German output but would have led to a considerable expansion of the output of other producers such as France and the Netherlands. The Community would have had huge grain surpluses on its hands which would have been costly to dispose of on world markets. In addition, since grain is an important input in the agricultural sector, the prices of other agricultural products would have been pushed upwards. The French for their part recognized that a relatively low common grain price would tend to cause a contraction of German grain output and the resulting gap could be filled by French farmers. In the end, after dire threats from the French, the Germans agreed to a common price for soft wheat of DM 425 per ton. This was to be operational from 1 July 1967. This represented a significant cut, since the German farm lobby wanted DM 450. As a *quid pro quo*, Germany, together with Italy and Luxembourg, received temporary and degressive subsidies from the fund set up to finance the CAP. Agreement on common prices for other products followed. In the case of milk and dairy products, beef and veal, sugar, rice, oil seeds and olive oil, these were arrived at in another marathon session in July 1966 immediately following the end of the French boycott.[1]

If the common support systems were to produce the planned common prices, surplus produce would have to be bought up, and if agricultural efficiency was to be raised, improvement grants would be necessary. In other words a fund had to be created to finance the CAP. This was achieved in 1962 in the form of the European Agricultural Guidance and Guarantee Fund (EAGGF). The French abbreviation for the latter is FEOGA (Fonds Européen d'Orientation et Garantie Agricoles). The Guarantee section was to deal with the costs arising from support purchases and export refunds. The Guidance section was to finance structural improvements in farming.

At the outset the funds required by the EAGGF were provided directly by the member states – the proportionate contributions being

---

1. At this stage sheep meat fell outside the CAP. However, following the Lamb War between the UK and Ireland on the one hand and France on the other, sheep meat was brought within the ambit of the CAP. This occurred in 1980.

the same as those prescribed for the general budget in Article 200, although these national shares were subsequently modified. However, the system of national contributions was eventually swept away. The Community budget came to be financed from own resources (agricultural import levies, common external tariff duties and a VAT component). As the reader will recollect from Chapter 3, the EAGGF is the main beneficiary of budget allocations – in 1985 farm spending absorbed about 72 per cent of budget appropriations.

It is important to appreciate that only a part of the flow of funds received by farmers derives from the prices they receive for their produce. In the past, governments have given further assistance to farmers in the form of grants or aids. These may be capital or current. The former relate to assistance given to improve farm structures – the provision of water or electricity, the installation of machinery, etc.; the latter refers to subsidies to reduce the cost of farm inputs. In addition there is a tendency for some countries to undertax farmers.

Aid could quite easily undermine the CAP. Thus the Council of Ministers might decide to reduce the price of a product in order to curtail a surplus. But this would be frustrated if a member state decided to compensate its own producers of that product by making available, or increasing an existing, input subsidy. Not only would the beneficiaries not curtail output but the aid would confer an unfair competitive advantage. Quite early on, the Commission recognized that it would have to devise a system for controlling and harmonizing national aids. In 1966 it produced an inventory of aids which sought to distinguish between those which were acceptable and would not need to be notified and those which were capable of undermining the CAP and would have to be notified and controlled. We shall return to the subject of aids later.

A critique

How successful has the CAP been? In considering this question we shall not merely concern ourselves with the degree to which it has achieved the policy objectives discussed earlier, but will carry out a broad review of its impact and the problems which are associated with it. Not surprisingly our review will expose some major shortcomings. Nevertheless, it is important not to lose sight of the fact that the creation of the CAP was an outstanding political achievement, and without it the EEC would be a much less significant exercise. However unsuccessful its economic achievements may have been, its very existence has given substance to the EEC as a forum for collective international policy-making.

It was expected that the CAP would improve agricultural productivity, and the latter, measured in terms of crop and livestock yields, has indeed markedly increased. For example, the yield of wheat in kilogrammes per hectare rose by 68 per cent between 1960 and 1978. Over the same period the yield of milk in kilogrammes per cow increased by 29 per cent. In 1980 the Commission produced a document entitled *Reflections on the Common Agricultural Policy* (EC Commission, 1980). From Chapter 3 above, the reader will recollect that in 1980 the Commission was given what became known as the Mandate. This involved reviewing Community policies, not least because of their impact on the Community budget. The *Reflections* document involved an assessment of the achievements of the CAP as well as a consideration of future developments. In *Reflections* the Commission noted that agricultural output had risen at 2·5 per cent per annum and ascribed this favourable trend to the CAP. However, this was an unwarranted conclusion since increases in yields and output had occurred in most developed countries. Moreover it could be argued that the CAP acted as an umbrella under which the less efficient could shelter and that this might have had the effect of depressing the growth of output and productivity.

The CAP was also set the objective of ensuring a fair standard of living for the agricultural community, although, as we noted earlier, the word fair is not defined. In this context a generally accepted basis for assessing fairness is to consider agricultural in relation to non-agricultural incomes. According to *Reflections*, real income in agriculture since 1968 had increased by 2·8 per cent per annum. It also pointed out that between 1968 and 1976 the rate of increase in other branches of the economy had been the same. The Commission appeared to imply that the CAP had therefore performed well. Was this a legitimate judgement? We have to bear in mind that at the outset it was not disputed that, relatively speaking, agricultural incomes were low – indeed they were only about half the level of non-agricultural incomes. It was also accepted at the Stresa Conference of 1958 that capital and labour in agriculture should receive a remuneration comparable with that which they would receive in other sectors. Given that, agriculture in *relative* terms had only kept pace, according to *Reflections*, the Stresa objective had not been achieved, and it should be noted that the *absolute* gap had obviously increased.

Critics have also emphasized that the CAP gave rise to greater income disparities in two senses. Firstly, and even the Commission accepts this point, the CAP benefits the bigger and richer farmers most. Professor

John Marsh has pointed out that, since the CAP works primarily through raising prices, it follows that the more a farmer has to sell the more he benefits from the revenue-enhancing effect of the policy. Secondly, he also notes that the policy gives rise to greater regional disparities. Farm structures tend to vary from region to region. Some will be populated predominantly by small farms whilst others will in the main be made up of big producers. From the previous argument it can be seen that income levels in the latter type of region will rise absolutely more than in the former type. Marsh also draws attention to the fact that the support régimes for northern products (livestock and cereals) have been more generous than those of the south (fruit, vegetables and wine).

The CAP was also expected to stabilize markets. Here we have to record a distinct success. Thanks to the CAP intervention system farm prices in the EEC have been more stable than in the USA or on the world market. The raising and lowering of external levies, etc., insulates the EEC market from outside price fluctuations, whilst support purchasing, and if necessary the releasing of stocks, compensates for *internal* output (and demand) fluctuations.

The CAP was also supposed to provide certainty of supplies. If certainty is to be equated with the achievement of greater degrees of self-sufficiency then the policy has indeed met its objective! As can be seen from Table 18, out of the ten commodities shown the Six were originally self-sufficient in only four cases, whereas the Community of Ten was self-sufficient in eight. In addition, in respect of two of the four commodities where the Six were originally already self-sufficient the Ten were markedly more self-sufficient. The Commission in *Reflections* regarded greater self-sufficiency as being desirable and equated the desirability of not being over-dependent on imported food with the desirability of not being over-dependent on imported energy. We shall discuss the latter topic later in this chapter. At this point it seems reasonable to say that the comparison with energy was not legitimate. Over-dependence on imported energy – i.e. oil – has been undesirable because much of it has come from the Middle East which is politically unstable. It is much more difficult to imagine temperate food producers, such as the USA, Canada and Australasia, exhibiting similar instability. Oil was also vulnerable to the price-enhancing tactics of an international cartel, and this too is much more unlikely in the case of temperate food products.

When we refer to situations of more than self-sufficiency we are indeed talking about surpluses. These surpluses, notably of butter, wheat and

Table 18. Degrees of self-sufficiency

	Sugar	Butter	Wheat	Wine	Barley	Beef	Potatoes	Eggs	Pork	Maize
1956–60	104	101	90	89	84	92	101	90	100	64
1980	125	120	114	112	111	103	101	101	100	62
1983	123	147	117	101	108	105	99	103	102	82

Source: Statistical Office of the European Communities, *Yearbook of Agricultural Statistics* (various issues).

beef, have been a major point of criticism. Either they have had to be disposed of abroad at a loss – about which more in a moment – or they have had to be stored at considerable cost. The growth of intervention stocks of butter, wheat and beef in the 1980s is illustrated in Table 19. It was a most visible manifestation of the CAP's inadequacy [1] and helped to highlight the need for reform. We shall say more about the latter in due course. Incidentally, the most intractable surplus problem arose in connection with milk, and yet we have not mentioned that product in either Table 18 or Table 19. The reason is that it is not convenient to store milk. The price of milk has therefore been supported by making purchases of products made from milk – i.e. butter and skimmed milk powder. These have been put into stock or have been got rid of abroad.

The two key questions which now arise are these: Why have these surpluses arisen, and what costs and disadvantages arise from them? The problem ultimately stems from the high price policy adopted by the Community. Community farm prices are undoubtedly high by comparison with world market price levels, although it has to be admitted that the data on the latter often refers to thin markets. Table 20 shows that in the 1980–81 season wheat and barley prices were 30 to 40 per cent above world levels, beef was 90 per cent above and butter was more than 180 per cent above. These high prices tend to stimulate an extension of supply. Added to that is the point that the increased yields, which we discussed earlier, have tended to shift the supply curve to the right. Because the capacity of the human stomach is limited, the demand curve has not shifted to the right to a compensating extent. To put the latter point another way, the income elasticity of demand for food tends to be low. The normal consequence of this combination of supply outstripping demand is for prices to fall and for the latter to curtail surplus production. However, the intervention system has prevented this from happening. It has kept demand and prices up, and as a result surpluses have continued to arise. A further defect has been the open-ended nature of the guarantee system. That is to say the authorities had to buy up surpluses at the Community price – no limit was set to the amount the authorities were required to purchase at the favourable Community prices.

The deleterious effects of continuing surpluses have been several.

1. Stocks of beef were so embarrassingly high in 1986 that the Commission had to hire refrigerated ships lying in Rotterdam harbour in order to store the surplus. In January 1987, in order to get rid of surplus food, the Council of Ministers decided to give surpluses away free to old people and other victims of the cold weather. 50 million ECUs was voted for this purpose.

Consumers have had to pay high prices for the food they did consume – more about that in a moment. They have also had to pay for the storage, and the disposal at a loss, of food they did not want. Butter for Russians at knock-down prices has not inspired confidence within the public as paymaster.[1] Because the burden of storing and disposing of food has been so great, the Community budget, which we discussed earlier, has been dominated by EAGGF spending. (Most of this has been for guarantee purposes rather than structural reform.) As a result there was little left for other forms of spending, such as that arising from the European Regional Development Fund, the European Social Fund and the like.

Table 19. Growth of intervention stocks (000 tonnes)

	Butter[1]	Beef[2]	Cereals[2]
1980	399	268	2 710
1981	277	195	3 480
1982	371	176	2 740
1983	811	359	7 386
1984	1 247	548	4 510
1985	1 197	639	16 610
1986	1 542	547	15 730

Notes: 1. Public stocks – August.
      2. Public stocks – October.
Source: EC Commission, member state governments and Milk Marketing Board.

The CAP, it will be recollected, was supposed to provide consumers with food at reasonable prices. Given that CAP prices are well above world levels this objective does not seem to have been achieved. However, the analysis needs to be pressed a little further. What we are implying is that if the output of the CAP was drastically curtailed, European food consumers could turn to the world market and obtain supplies at significantly lower prices. But would not the consequent increase in demand on the world market drive up prices and eliminate the advantage? This is a serious point and it is one in respect of which it is difficult to make firm predictions. Some agricultural economists incline to the view that it is not a serious problem. They draw attention to the number of factors, including the point that major food producers, such as the US, have had

1. Butter was sold to the Soviet Union at 8p per pound in February 1987.

severely to cut back their output. If demand increased they could increase supply, and as a result a serious rise in price would not be likely.

Whilst dealing with the consumer interest, it is also worth noting that the CAP tends to be regressive in that it increases incomes, notably of large rich farmers, by raising the price of food, and the latter bulks relatively large in the expenditure pattern of the poorest members of society.

Table 20. Ratio of EEC prices to world prices

	1968–9	1970–71	1972–3	1976–7	1978–9	1980–81
Soft wheat	195	189	153	204	193	146
Rice	138	210	115	166	157	100
Maize	178	141	143	163	201	147
Barley	197	146	137	147	225	134
Sugar	355	203	127	176	276	85
Pig meat	134	134	147	125	155	135
Beef	169	140	112	192	199	190
Butter	504	481	249	401	403	286
Skimmed milk powder	365	218	145	571	458	204

Source: Statistical Office of European Communities, *Yearbook of Agricultural Statistics* (various issues).

According to Article 110, Community policy should contribute to the harmonious development of world trade. Quite clearly the CAP does not conform to this requirement. The growth of self-sufficiency has denied third-country food producers a market for their produce, and the dumping of European surpluses has undermined prices on the world market. The CAP has been a cause of considerable friction and has been at the centre of numerous trade disputes.

This by no means exhausts the criticisms which can be levelled at the CAP. Earlier we said that we would return to the subject of aids. The Commission has for many years indicated its desire to control and harmonize them. However, there is noticeable absence of progress on this front. If the level of aid was small the problem would not be serious. However, this is not the case. In recent years national aid expenditure has been roughly double that of the EAGGF. Moreover, member states have continued to give aids despite the fact that the Commission has declared them contrary to the Rome Treaty. This is a grossly unsatisfactory state of affairs.

The other major problem arises in connection with exchange rates. As originally conceived, the aim of the CAP was quite literally to provide for common prices. To this end prices were specified not in terms of national currencies but in terms of the Community's unit of account (UA), which had a gold content equal to that of the US dollar. In the pre-Smithsonian era, the US dollar was equal to 0·88867088 grammes of gold, and this was also the value of the UA. An assumption of the CAP, which early commentaries tended to overlook, was that the rates of exchange of individual Community currencies against the dollar and against each other would not be changed. If, however, a member state devalued this would have the effect of causing its farm prices in national currency terms to rise. The contrary would occur if it revalued.

In fact the common system of pricing had hardly begun to operate before it was subjected to the first of what was to prove to be a series of currency upsets. In August 1969 the French Government decided to devalue the franc by 11·11 per cent. This immediately created a minor crisis, since the common price arrangements were disturbed and there was a danger that French farmers would enjoy an increase in prices whilst farmers in other member states would not experience any improvement. More important, a rise in French prices would stimulate production and aggravate the already existing surplus problem. A Council meeting was therefore hastily summoned on 11 August. One possibility was that the UA could be devalued. However, although this could have offset the effect of devaluation on French producer prices and left them unchanged, it would have automatically worsened the prices received by producers in other member states. The policy was therefore rejected. Instead, a more complicated arrangement was adopted. During the marketing year 1969–70 the buying-in prices paid in respect of interventions in the French domestic market were to be reduced by 11·11 per cent, with the intention of preventing a rise in prices. The devaluation would also give French food exports a competitive edge, whilst imports into France would be disadvantaged. It was therefore decided that France should grant subsidies to imports from member states and levy compensatory duties on French exports in order not to distort the free movement of agricultural produce. In the 1970–71 period it was intended that intervention prices should be reduced by 5·5 per cent. Thereafter French agriculture was to be reintegrated into the CAP. In fact the reintegration took place in late 1972.

The decision to float the German mark, and then to revalue it at a new fixed rate which was 9·29 per cent above the old parity, also promised to upset the working of the common policy. The result, if not counter-balanced, would have immediately reduced the price paid to German farmers in terms of the domestic currency. This the German Government was not willing to accept. Instead, Germany was allowed to reduce her farm prices gradually, and in the meantime aid was given to German farmers on a diminishing scale – some of it being provided by the EAGGF. In the West German case the revaluation had the potential effect of cheapening imports and making exports dearer – the reverse of the French case. In order to offset this she was empowered to apply levies on imports and subsidies on exports – the reverse of the French case.

These levies and subsidies were in fact the precursors of the monetary compensating amounts (MCAs), which formally came into existence in May 1971. As events were to transpire they were not to be a transitory phenomenon. As a result of the Smithsonian Accord of 1971 and after, the currencies began to float or were adjusted from time to time, and the Community found itself with two exchange rates. One was the Green Rate, which was the rate employed to convert UA (and later ECU) farm prices into national prices, and the other was the actual market rate of exchange. MCAs, variable in amount, which might be positive or negative, were employed to bridge the gap. It also follows that prices in national currency terms can change for two reasons. Firstly, the ECU price might change. Secondly, the ECU price might not change but the Green Rate could change. The latter could be selectively applied to certain countries.[1] The important point about MCAs was and is that they have meant that common prices, a sup-posedly crucial feature of the CAP, ceased to exist. National prices for particular products have exhibited substantial variations. When the European Monetary System was introduced, an attempt was made to eliminate MCAs. This gave rise to a dispute which delayed the incep-tion of the system. In the end it was agreed to gradually dismantle existing MCAs within the context of annual price determinations and to eliminate within two years any new MCAs arising from subsequent currency adjustments. In practice, MCAs have continued to exist – however, in 1984 the Community made a determined start on their abolition.

. A country may have different Green Rates applied to different commodities.

Reform – farm structure

The CAP had scarcely got off the ground before the surplus problem began to loom large. A movement towards self-sufficiency or more than self-sufficiency leads on the one hand to a reduction of revenue from levies and to an increased expenditure on refunds on the other. A reform of what was proving to be an economically and financially burdensome system was therefore called for. It should, however, be emphasized that proposals for reform during the late sixties were centred on the farm structure rather than the pricing system.

In December 1968 Sicco Mansholt put forward a new ten-year plan – 'Agriculture 1980' (EC Commission, 1968b). It was obvious that the disparity between agricultural prices in the Six and the levels obtaining on world markets had to be narrowed. The cost of producing food in the Six had to be reduced. It also followed that if productivity per person or per acre was to increase, it would be necessary to have fewer people and fewer acres in production if output was to be prevented from outstripping internal needs. It was equally obvious that a policy of improving agricultural incomes by raising prices was likely to be extremely costly. A more acceptable way was to invest money in improving the farm structure. Bigger farms needed to be created which would eliminate the concealed unemployment that is characteristic of small farms. Strips needed to be consolidated so that time was not lost in proceeding from one plot to another. More mechanization would also help to increase labour productivity. In this way increased incomes could be paid to farmers without increasing the price of agricultural produce.

The Mansholt Plan therefore addressed itself to the task of increasing farm incomes and halting the spiralling cost of the CAP. To do this it aimed to shift the emphasis in the policy from market and price support to structural improvement.

The Commission proposed that farms of a more viable size should be created. The policy would be voluntary. Financial inducements and assistance would be used, but coercion was ruled out. Minimum-size units were conceived as being two to three hundred acres for wheat production, forty to sixty cows for milk, and a hundred and fifty to two hundred head of cattle for beef and veal production. This larger size of farm would lead to more efficient use of labour and capital. Given that output had to be kept under control, the increase in productivity had to be balanced by a reduction in the labour force on the land and by a reduction in the quantity of land devoted to agriculture. Labour was indeed leaving the land, but the Commission believed that if the standard of living of those remaining was to increase, the rate at which labour left agriculture would have to be increased. If its target were achieved, the actual farm population would fall to 6 per cent of the total working population by 1980; this compared with 20·7 per cent in 1960. As part of its plan of action the Commission called for a massive education and retraining programme. The Commission also envisaged that by 1980 the farming area in the Community would be reduced from 175 to 160 million acres. It was expected that if the whole programme could be carried through by 1980 then expenditure on supporting prices could fall from the existing level of about $2000 million to $750 million.

The Mansholt Plan came as a considerable shock. The CAP had barely been established when farmers were confronted with the unpalatable news that many of them were redundant! Not surprisingly Dr Mansholt was given the title of 'the peasant killer'. Clearly the Plan was a political hot potato – so much so that the Council of Ministers gave it the cold shoulder. The need for structural reform was, however, accepted, although change on the scale invisaged by Mansholt was not thought feasible. Instead, a series of limited measures were introduced in 1972. EAGGF finance was available to partially finance three schemes. One was designed to modernize farms. Another offered farmers lump sums or annuities in return for leaving the land. The land so released would first be offered to those farms which were being modernized as above. The third was designed to train and thus raise the income-earning potential of farmers. In 1975 another measure was introduced to assist farmers in mountainous and remote areas in order to prevent depopulation. In 1977 measures were introduced to facilitate structural improvements at the processing and marketing, as opposed to production, stages. Later on, and notably in the light of Greek membership, measures were introduced to facilitate structural improvements in the Mediterranean region.

In 1983 the Commission, noting that the 1972 socio-structural measures were due to expire, and that modifications were needed to the 1977 regulation, submitted new proposals. At the same time it also proposed that Integrated Mediterranean Programmes should be introduced for the benefit of Greece, Italy and France. We mentioned this point in Chapter 1 when we discussed the problems likely to stem from the accession of Spain and Portugal. The Mediterranean areas of the three former countries rely heavily on agriculture and suffer from relatively high unemployment and relatively low incomes. Assistance needed to be channelled in their direction because they would suffer from Iberian competition. We will reserve further discussion of this policy measure for Chapter 9 when we consider regional policy.

In 1983 a revised regulation concerning processing and marketing was agreed, and in 1984 a measure was approved in place of the 1972 socio-structural regulations. The 1984 regulation was introduced against a background of some disappointment with the 1972 socio-structural programme. The new structural policy has the following features. Assistance for structural improvement is to be aimed in particular at farmers in the lower income brackets. It will seek to improve incomes by cost reductions rather than output increases. Indeed, aid will not be given where output would be increased and the product is in surplus. Assistance will be given to enable younger farmers to establish themselves. It will also be designed to create alternative employment in tourism and craft activities and to turn land over to forestry. Payments will also be made in order to compensate farmers who adopt methods which are compatible with conservation.

Reform – price and income support

It is all too obvious from what has gone before that the Mansholt Plan did not represent a reform of the CAP as a system for supporting prices and incomes. It was concerned with structural improvements which were designed to increase efficiency and to deal with the problem of over-production. But the price and income support system was left intact. It is true that the individual market arrangements have shown some capacity for adaptation, but the basic system devised in the early days of the Community continued to endure despite all the strains which we detailed earlier. It is hardly surprising that in due course thoughts should begin to turn to the appropriateness of the price system itself. This became increasingly likely when the UK joined the EEC since, as we have seen, it had operated a basically different system and was expected to lose as a result of being integrated into the Community arrangements. Plans to reform the system sprang from many quarters and space does not permit us to review them all in detail. Rather we shall consider a few proposals and hope that these indicate the way in which thinking developed.

(a) Changing relative prices

One obvious measure, which did not involve a reform of the system but a more purposeful use of the original mechanism, was to change relative prices. Products in short supply should enjoy price increases, whilst those in surplus should either have prices cut or be held stable as general inflation proceeded. The Wageningen Memorandum of 1973 (produced by a group of distinguished agricultural economists who met at the Agricultural University of Wageningen in May 1973) suggested that the price of grains (particularly wheat) should be stabilized and that this should be coupled with policy measures designed to stimulate beef production. The report was obviously opposed to a policy of uniform across-the-board increases. At a time when the Community was less than self-sufficient in the majority of commodities such an approach had virtue. Resources should be channelled from surplus to deficit products. However, now that the Community is fairly generally more than self-sufficient this proposal no longer has great relevance.

(b) Reducing prices

A number of economists, including Josling and Marsh, have suggested various schemes for reducing prices in the hope that they would both benefit consumers and curtail production. Professor Josling (1973, pp. 95–8) proposed a reduction of import levies, thus bringing prices down nearer to world levels. However, such a policy would be likely to have severe political repercussions, since many farmers would be out of a job. He therefore proposed payments to the more efficient farmers to build their incomes up to reasonable levels. These payments would not, however, cover the cost of the higher-cost producers. In their case he suggested a supplementary payment which could be limited in duration – perhaps until the farmer retired or for a stipulated period of years. After that the farm would cease to operate and the land could be transferred to other non-agricultural uses. Clearly, a policy of inducements (including retraining facilities and new job creation) would ease the phasing out of income supplements. The Josling system also implies that price support and income support would no longer be indissolubly linked. The size of farm incomes and the incomes of certain groups would depend only partly on the supported price – the rest would derive from the Community budget and/or national exchequers. The reader will of course recognize that Josling was suggesting the implementation of the UK deficiency payments approach, although he did not propose its application in the case of all commodities but only to cereals and possibly dairy products.

Subsequently, Professor John Marsh (1977, p. 606) put forward a proposal which also involved a reduction in prices. He suggested that common prices should be replaced by common trading prices. Member states would be free to offer farmers whatever price they wished, but when goods were traded between member states the price charged would be the common trading price. If, for example, a country maintained an internal price above the common trading price (which it could do by taxing imports) but wished to sell to another member state, it would have to provide a subsidy which it would itself finance. The Community would, as presently, be responsible for the cost of dumping surpluses on the world market, but this would be less costly than at present since the common trading prices would be set nearer to world prices than is the case with prices at present. This scheme has much to commend it, since it makes those who generate surpluses more financially responsible for the cost of disposing of them. One of the weaknesses of the Community system has been that those who generated surpluses did not always pay the full cost of getting rid of them – hence the UK budget problem. The Marsh proposal was really an anticipation of an idea which has increasingly been discussed in recent years, namely that the CAP should be 'debudgetized' or re-nationalized. That is to say the financing of support operations should be wholly or partially financed by national exchequers. This idea has loomed large when the Community budget has been in danger of running out of own resources.

The Josling and Marsh proposals suggested radical changes in the CAP. The Commission too has looked to price reductions as a possible solution, but it has taken a softer line. It has pointed out that if the Council of Ministers could hold the line on price increases, then inflation would erode their real value and this would progressively cause production to be cut back.

(c) Co-responsibility levies

A co-responsibility levy was applied in the milk sector as early as 1977, and the Commission has advocated its use in the case of other products in surplus. The original idea was that a tax should be imposed on production and the revenue so raised should be used to promote the marketing of the product. To the extent that the effect of the tax was to reduce the price received by producers, it could be said to be a system whereby producers were made partly responsible for dealing with surpluses. Conceptually, such a tax can have the effect of simultaneously reducing supply and stimulating demand. Both effects help to cure an excess of supply over demand. However, in practice the levy was very modest (about 2·5 per cent) and as such could never have had more than a very marginal effect.

(d) A global standard quantity

Professor Marsh (1977, p. 609) also suggested the use of a global standard quantity system for products persistently in surplus, e.g. dairy produce. What Professor Marsh was really objecting to was the open-ended nature of the Community's original system. If supply exceeded demand at the support price, the excess was offered into intervention (i.e. for official support purchase for storage, etc.) or for export refund. In principle there was no limit to this commitment. Under the Marsh proposal, when the Community indicated a support price it would also indicate that there was a maximum quantity which it was prepared to underwrite through intervention support buying and export subsidy. When surplus produce was offered for intervention or subsidy, only a part of the payment, say 80 per cent, would be paid immediately. At the end of the year if the quantity produced did not go beyond the prescribed ceiling then the remaining 20 per cent would be payable. If, however, the ceiling had been exceeded then something less than 20 per cent would be paid. In short, overproduction would be penalized – the Community would only assume full responsibility for the standard quantity. This was in effect a quota system.

(e) Subsidies

In principle it might be possible to solve the surplus problem by using subsidies. In other words subsidies could be used to provide cheaper food for consumers and this would stimulate an extension of demand. There are two problems with such a policy. Firstly, given the present size of surpluses the subsidies would have to be very large. Commentators argue that the cost would indeed be prohibitive – much higher than that incurred under the traditional CAP system. Secondly, if agricultural yields continued to increase, output might rise to such an extent that no feasible price reduction via subsidy would clear the market.

(f) Diversion of resources

The Commission, in a document entitled *Perspectives for the Common Agricultural Policy* (EC Commission, 1985b), has given consideration to policies for paying farmers to leave land fallow – this is called 'set-aside'. It has also contemplated the possibility of using land to produce agricultural products for industrial use. For example, bio-ethanol is a source of energy which can be produced by fermenting beet or by indirectly fermenting crops containing starch (e.g. wheat, maize and potatoes). Forestry is of course another alternative use with industrial end-products in mind.

The reforms of 1984 and after

The above may appear to suggest that prior to 1984 nothing really happened on the reform front. This would not be a correct account of events. Since the Mansholt Plan of 1968 the Commission has from time to time gone on record saying that the CAP was in need of reform. In the 1980s its proposals became increasingly radical. Yet in retrospect the limited responses which emerged from the Council of Ministers have the appearance of what Benjamin Disraeli, in of course an earlier age, called a range of extinct volcanoes. This was not really the Commission's fault. The blame should largely be laid at the door of the Council of Ministers, which was quite simply unwilling to grasp the politically painful nettle. However, the prospect of bankruptcy, just as much as hanging, concentrates the mind wonderfully. Ultimately this is what happened. As the cost of the CAP grew, and the Community budget appeared to be in danger of running out of resources, it became increasingly obvious that drastic remedies were essential. As we noted in Chapter 3, the UK made it abundantly clear that it would not agree to more resources until the CAP was reformed (and its budget problem resolved). It should be added that the attitude of the Thatcher Government after the budget and agricultural reforms of 1984 continued to be that only tight control of the purse strings would force the Council of Ministers to take action to curb the surpluses.

The year 1984 marks the beginning of a serious reform process. It began in the milk sector where the surplus problem had proved to be particularly intractable and costly. The Community decided to impose quotas on Community milk output – these quotas would operate for five years. The Community total would be broken down among the member states and in turn the states would allocate quotas to their producers or purchasers. In order to discourage deliveries in excess of quota, a swingeing super-levy was to be imposed of 75 to 100 per cent of the target price for milk. In short, the Community was only prepared to pay the guaranteed price on the stipulated quantity – production in excess was to be penalized out of existence. The original total appears to have been designed to broadly stabilize deliveries. However, in April 1986 the Council of Ministers decided to introduce a 3 per cent cut – 2 per cent in 1987/88 and 1 per cent in 1988/89. Then in December 1986 it returned to the subject in a more decisive way – it agreed to bring about a 9·5 per cent cut by 1988/89. This was hailed as a major breakthrough.

It should be added that following the 1984 agreement member states introduced their own 'outgoers' schemes to ease farmers out of milk production. These compensation schemes were financed by member states. In the UK the quotas so released to the government were re-allocated to other producers to enable them to attain a more economic size. It should be added that the individual quotas have been attached to land. This raised some conflict between landowners and their milk-producing tenants, i.e. on cessation of production the compensation went to the former. Subsequently in 1986 the UK Government introduced legislation which granted tenants some compensation. Also in 1986, in consequence of the quota cuts, the Community introduced its own 'outgoers' scheme. The Community provided finance but also took over and destroyed the quotas so released.

The milk reforms were followed by a more determined attack in other sectors. Thus in 1985 the Council agreed on a general price package for 1985/86 which meant that agricultural prices in national currency terms increased by only 1·8 per cent as compared with 1984/85, whilst the rate of inflation in the Community in 1985 was running at 5·8 per cent. Real prices were therefore set to fall. In 1986 the prices package represented a 2·2 per cent increase in national currency terms (among the Ten) against an inflation rate of about 2·5 per cent. On this occasion the Community was just about holding the line in real terms. Significantly, it decided to apply a co-responsibility levy to cereals. Even more significantly, in December 1986 it decided to modify beef support arrangements. In the past the intervention price has acted as a floor. But on this occasion the Council decided that support buying would only occur when (a) the average market price in the Community was 90 per cent of the inter-vention price and (b) the price in the country where the intervention was to take place was 87 per cent of the intervention price. This implied a 13 per cent drop in price, although it was modified by some national Green Rate changes. The 1987 prices package was not agreed until July of that year. In general terms it provided for a price freeze together with cuts for cereals and vegetables. However, national Green Rate changes meant that some of the edge was taken off these measures. In the general context of reform, mention should also be made of the fact that in recent years the Commission has been increasingly introducing tougher quality controls – this meant that the policy became less open-ended. At the beginning of 1988 two radical policy changes were under discussion: agricultural stabilizers could be introduced whereby guaranteed prices for cereals and some other products would be reduced once specified output limits had been exceeded; set-aside measures could be applied whereby farmers would be compensated for taking land out of produc-tion. See Epilogue.

The common transport policy

There are a number of reasons why a common transport policy was called for under the arrangements envisaged by the Rome Treaty. The first is that transport costs are an important factor influencing trade. Since the Community was seeking to build up inter-state trade activity it was therefore desirable that there should be a cheap and well coordinated Community transport system. Another way of putting the above point would be to say that if the common transport policy led to more efficient methods of transporting goods between states, benefits would be derived which were similar to those derived from the trade creation arising from internal tariff cuts. Secondly, it is necessary to recognize that transport on the Continent was subjected to considerable state intervention. Since these interventions were not coordinated between states, considerable distortions could arise. But more important was the fact that transport had been manipulated so as artificially to aid exports and inhibit imports. Experience in the early days of the ECSC indicated that this would also be a problem in a general common market. But there was a third factor. As was indicated earlier in discussing agriculture, the Rome Treaty involved a delicate balance of national interests. In the case of the Netherlands it was clearly anticipated that since transport, particularly that along the Rhine, was a very important contributor to the Dutch GNP, a growth of intra-Community trade would be very advantageous to the Netherlands. It was therefore very obvious from the Dutch point of view that transport should be brought within the ambit of the Treaty and that, in so far as this could be accomplished, member states should be prevented from hiving off transport activity as a sphere where national interests would predominate. This desire to take advantage of the transport opportunities opened up by the Rome Treaty was reflected in Article 75. Whilst the treaty was remarkably silent on the detailed nature of the common transport policy, it did definitely require the Community to devise common rules applicable to international transport going from one member state to another or passing across the territory of a member state. It is also called for rules to be laid down whereby a non-resident carrier could operate transport services in another member state. In practice, the Council of Ministers neglected these requirements to such an extent that in 1983 the European Parliament took it to the Court of Justice because of failure to act. In its 1985 judgement the Court supported Parliament and instructed the Council to remedy the deficiency.

The Commission's original blueprint

The Rome Treaty itself is, as we have indicated, remarkably uninstructive on the nature of the common policy. It was left to the Brussels Commission to provide a basis for such a policy. In 1961 the Commission produced a memorandum which laid down what it thought should be the general principles of the common transport policy – this was known as the Schaus Memorandum (EEC Commission, 1961) after Lambert Schaus, who was the Commissioner responsible for transport affairs. Then in 1962 the Commission produced its Action Programme (EEC Commission, 1962) which reviewed the measures which the Commission proposed should be implemented. The memorandum outlined three main objectives which the transport policy should achieve. One was to remove obstacles which transport could put in the way of a general common market. Another was that the policy should not merely negatively aim to sweep away factors which delayed the creation of a common market, but should be a positive and powerful stimulant to the growth of trade and the opening up of national markets. Both these were generally acceptable. The third was much more controversial. The Commission suggested that the Community should 'endeavour to create healthy competition of the widest scope'. In the light of the highly regulated nature of transport within the Community this was bound to be a controversial proposition, all the more so as the Commission proposed that the common transport policy should apply to national as well as international transport activity. The Commission has continued to press for a policy which gives greater scope to undistorted competition and the forces of the market. As time has passed, this decision has been revealed to have been a wise one, since in various parts of the world, and notably in the US, opinion has moved in favour of deregulation. This has been particularly true in the case of road haulage (trucking) and air passenger transport.

Before we turn to discuss the Commission's approach, it is important to recognize that in the first instance the common transport policy only applied to three modes – road, rail and inland waterway. Air and maritime transport were excluded, although the Council of Ministers, on the basis of unanimity, could make provisions for these two latter modes. In fact the Council has in recent years been involved in policy making in these two areas, and later we will focus on one of them – air transport. It is also important to appreciate the relative contribution of the various modes. Table 21 clearly shows that the dominant mode for the transport of goods within the Community is road haulage.

Table 21. Domestic transport of goods – modal split within the Ten in 1981

	(%)
Road	85·1
Rail	7·5
Inland waterway	2·8
Shipping	2·3
Pipeline	2·3
Air	0·0

Source: EC Commission, *The European Community's Transport Policy*, OOPEC, 1984, p. 9.

In working towards a basically competitive solution, the Commission had to deal with the fact that national authorities in varying degrees exerted two general kinds of control over transport. One was a control over rates – in some cases transport rates were fixed by government agencies as opposed to being freely determined by competitive market forces. The Commission wished to see much more price flexibility. The other related to control over entry into the market. In the case of road haulage, which will dominate our discussion, control over entry was applied through the agency of licences and quotas. Licences may of course be qualitative – e.g. a haulier must be technically competent, financially sound and so forth. If these standards are relatively undemanding then such a system may not effectively restrict the number of enterprises in the market. Altogether more important is the quantitative variety – i.e. the actual quantity of licences may be deliberately restricted. In connection with quantitative licensing, the Commission identified two problems. Firstly, licensing by member states governing access to their own national markets had been too restrictive. The Commission did not propose to abolish national quantitative licensing but to (a) harmonize licensing practices and (b) to make the system more flexible. Secondly, the Commission saw the need for substantial changes in respect of international road transport. Here we have to make a distinction between own account operations, when producers carry their own goods, and hire and reward, when professional hauliers carry other people's goods. In respect of own account transport the Commission took the view that there should be complete liberalization. This would imply that producers could carry their own products in their own vehicles anywhere in the Community and that no member state should be able to set a limit to the number of such foreign vehicles that could be admitted to its territory. In respect of hire and reward vehicles, however, the Commission's original proposals were more complicated. This form of transport has been governed by agreements between the administrative authorities of member states. They were typically bilateral in character, in that each state laid down the number and load capacity of vehicles from the other state which it would allow on its territory at any one time. Broadly speaking, the Commission concluded that the quotas had not been expanded to the extent corresponding to the growth of trade between the member states concerned. The Commission therefore proposed, firstly, that bilateral quotas should be enlarged in conformity with the growth of inter-state trade. Secondly, it was proposed that the bilateral licences should be progressively phased out. As the bilateral licences disappeared, Community licences would come into existence at a rate sufficient (a) to compensate for the disappearance of the bilateral licences and (b) to cope with the growth of intra-Community trade. The new body of licences was to be termed the Community Quota.

In all this the Commission was being quite controversial. At that point in time there still existed a body of opinion which regarded transport, particularly road transport, as being inherently unstable. If unfettered competition was allowed to operate there would be bouts of intensive price cutting which would lead to a neglect of safety standards. Moreover, cut-throat competition would lead to firms being driven out of business and to the emergence of monopoly conditions. It should also be said that states were fearful of competition because it might lead to their railway systems being driven out of business by road hauliers.

A competitive solution also required a whole range of other changes. Inter-enterprise competition had to exist. Competition also had to be fair and undistorted as between enterprises in different states and as between different modes. Furthermore, transport rates should not be subject to discrimination; nor should they be manipulated so as to subsidize particular producers or industries. It was also desirable that the transport infrastructure of the various member states should be integrated, and that the Community should contribute financially and in other ways to the creation of a Community transport network.

Policy achievements

In respect of pricing, the Commission originally proposed what was in effect a compromise between the rigid fixed rate system which had been operated in West Germany and the relatively free rate system which was desired by the Dutch. This consisted of a rate bracket system which would apply to all transport modes – national and international. Under the system the relevant authorities would specify maximum and minimum rates for particular types of traffic on the various routes. Consignors and carriers would be able to negotiate rates within the spread. The apparent logic of this arrangement was that the upper limit was designed to prevent monopolistic exploitation, whilst the lower limit was intended to prevent the detrimental effects of excessive competition. In practice, the proposal was greatly whittled down. From 1968 tariff brackets only applied to international road transport. The authorities were to publish fixed upper and lower brackets with a maximum spread of 23 per cent below the ceiling level. Under certain circumstances tariffs could be agreed outside these levels. In 1977 the Community decided to provide a choice. A pair of states could continue with the obligatory bracket system or they could choose a reference rate system, in which the published price was purely a recommendation. In 1983 this was replaced by a system in which reference rates were to be the norm, but a pair of states could employ rate brackets. It seems not unreasonable to say that the Commission has achieved some loosening up in respect of pricing. Firstly, on many routes the system now in operation is based on the reference rate system. Secondly, the spread between brackets is about 45 per cent. The latter is so great that it seems reasonable to conclude that market forces rather than brackets are now determining the actual rates.

On the licensing and quota front, the picture is mixed. It is true that in 1974 the Community agreed to introduce qualitative criteria in respect of national road-haulage licences. The relevant directive laid down uniform requirements in terms of the professional competence, good repute and financial capacity of prospective operators. There is of course nothing to prevent a member state from operating these standards in parallel with a quantitative licensing system. In other words a haulier might satisfy the qualitative conditions but not be able to get a licence if the quantitative ceiling has been reached. It should be emphasized that the Community has not agreed to harmonize and loosen up national quantity licensing systems. Nevertheless, some countries have abandoned quantitative limits – the UK did so prior to EEC membership.

On the international front, we have to note that after some delay the

Community did in 1968 agree to introduce a Community Quota. But the member states did not undertake to phase out the bilateral licences. Until recently, the actual number of licences under the Community Quota (they are shared out among the states) remained miserably small. About 95 per cent of traffic continued to be carried under bilateral agreements. However, the 1985 Court judgement has had a powerful effect. In the same year the Council of Ministers agreed, as an interim measure, to accelerate the growth of the Community Quota (whilst keeping but expanding the bilateral system). The Council has also undertaken, as a final solution, to abolish quantitative restrictions on international road transport by 1992. This still leaves two matters to be dealt with. Firstly, the Commission feels that the member states must lay down uniform qualitative conditions in respect of international road transport licences. Secondly, there is the question of the Article 75 requirement concerning freedom of non-resident transport operators to carry out transport operations in a member state. Here we need to make a distinction. A road haulier has a right to establish himself in another member state and supply road haulage services therein. The Community has agreed on a mutual recognition of qualifications in order to make this Right of Establishment a reality. The haulier still has to satisfy national (but harmonized) qualitative conditions and any national quantitative conditions. The alternative possibility is that the haulier does not establish himself but seeks to avail himself of the freedom to supply services. Thus he might make a journey from Paris to Rome and on the return journey might make a backhaul from Rome to Florence and another backhaul from Florence to Milan. The intra-Italy journeys are examples of cabotage. The 1985 judgement quite clearly required the Council of Ministers to address itself to this possibility, and the Commission has put forward proposals to make limited cabotage a reality.

We now come to the issue of competition, distortion and discrimination. The following are some of the more important measures which have been agreed. In order to maintain inter-enterprise competition, the Council agreed in 1968 that, with modifications, transport should be subject to the Articles 85 and 86 competition rules. With regard to inter-country competition within modes, the Council has agreed the following measures which are designed to achieve equal conditions of competition. In 1968 it provided for social harmonization in the road haulage industry. This relates to uniform driving hours and rest periods – the most recent rules were decided in 1985. It also agreed in 1970 to the use of the tachograph (the so-called 'spy in the cab') to police these rules. In 1984 the Council also agreed on uniform weights and dimensions for lorries –

the UK and Ireland were granted some temporary exemptions. The Commission is aware that differences in national excise rates on fuel and in national vehicle taxes also distort competition. It proposes to harmonize both. In practice the latter have a bigger impact on the cost of operation. In order to create fairer conditions of competition between modes, the Commission a long time ago recognized that it was important to ascertain the costs of infrastructure – i.e. track costs – and to allocate them among beneficiaries. For example, it would be inequitable and uneconomic if railways had to pay for their rail-bed, etc., whilst road hauliers did not make their due contribution to the cost of building and repairing the road system. As yet no final agreement has been reached on this issue. The Community has also introduced measures which grant the railways greater commercial freedom and require them to be compensated when they are obliged to discharge social or historical obligations. Article 7 of the Rome Treaty requires that there should be no discrimination on grounds of nationality. Article 79 reiterates this in the case of transport. Article 80 concerns the activity of using transport rates to help certain firms or industries. Such rates are referred to as support rates and are banned.

There are two final points we need to note. One is that as far back as 1966 the Community agreed to coordinate national transport infrastructure investments. In 1978 a more comprehensive system was agreed, and in 1982 the Council declared that Community budget monies could be used to aid priority projects which would help to build up the Community network. The Commission has suggested that a growing annual sum should be devoted to this objective during the second half of the 1980s. The other point relates to border formalities. These are a major problem for international transport and give rise to considerable costs. The Commission has set itself the task of achieving a radical simplification.

Air transport

As we observed earlier, this form of transport does not automatically fall within the common transport policy. Nevertheless, the Council of Ministers can introduce appropriate measures. Until recently, little progress had been made. More recently a breakthrough occurred – see below. What have been the problems?

The fundamental problem was that air passenger transport has been subject to inter-government agreements and to international cartel price fixing. Access to routes between pairs of states has been governed by inter-government air services agreements. In Europe these bilaterals have tightly controlled entry – perhaps restricting entry to one designated airline from each state. Typically in Europe the revenue on any route has been pooled and the proceeds divided in proportion to the capacity supplied by each national airline. In the past, air fares have been agreed by airlines in the traffic conferences organized by the International Air Transport Association. Governments have subsequently approved these agreed rates. This has been the position in respect of scheduled services – charter operations have been relatively free of restraint.

The result has been that scheduled air fares in Europe have been high, and much play has been made of the lower fares in the US – distance for distance – under a deregulated, i.e. competitive, régime. The reader may therefore wonder why the Rome Treaty competition rules, and specifically Article 85, have not been invoked against this restrictive activity. The answer is twofold. In the first place it was not clear to what extent air transport was subject to the competition rules. However, in 1974 this point was resolved in the case of *EC Commission* v. *French Republic* before the Court of Justice. The competition rules do apply. However, a second problem then arose. Article 85 is only fully applicable if the Council of Ministers approves the necessary implementing regulation. In the first instance they neglected to do this. In the absence of such a regulation, the enforcement of Article 85 lay largely with the member states – the villains of the piece – although the Commission could play a limited role.

The position was not wholly without hope, since three avenues of attack were still available. Firstly, deregulation on a piecemeal basis was possible provided the parties to bilateral agreements were of a like mind. This happened notably in the case of the UK–Netherlands bilateral in 1984. Effectively, air traffic was deregulated, since the agreement provided for the free entry of new carriers, eliminated capacity controls and allowed the country from where the traffic originated to determine fares. Other agreements, although not as liberal, followed.

Secondly, the member states might be induced to accept at least a limited amount of liberalization. The EC Commission has been striving to achieve such an end since at least 1972, and memoranda on the subject were addressed to the Council of Ministers in 1979 and 1984. In 1986 a package of measures was under consideration by virtue of which the airlines would be exempted from attack under Article 85 provided agreement could be secured on some degree of liberalization. These measures involved reducing the share of traffic allocated to the designated national airlines, allowing more than one airline from a given country to fly the same route and permitting certain forms of price cutting. At the November 1986 meeting, when the UK was holding the presidency of the Council of Ministers, the Community failed to achieve agreement on what was regarded as a fairly weak package of such measures. Thus whereas the EC Commission would have liked to see each national airline's share being reduced from 50 per cent to 25 per cent, the UK opted to push a proposal which only required a reduction to 40 per cent over three years. Critics tended to see the UK position as reflecting anxiety about the effect which more radical measures would have on the privatization value of British Airways. In July 1987 the Council of Ministers returned to the reform proposals, but agreement was blocked as a result of a dispute between Spain and the UK over the status of Gibraltar airport.

The third approach was for individuals, companies or governments to seek to invoke Article 85 against airline agreements. Lord Bethell attempted to do this but failed. However, in 1986 a breakthrough occurred in the *Nouvelles Frontières* case. This concerned a French budget travel company which had sold air tickets at lower prices than those sanctioned by the French authorities. The case was first heard by a French court which decided to refer the matter to the European Court of Justice for a preliminary ruling. The important feature of the Court's verdict was the additional light it threw on the position which arises when an implementing regulation does not exist. This new light suggested that the EC Commission's hands were not entirely tied – there was a way forward. Thus the Commission could investigate the various agreements entered into in the airline industry and might then decide to prohibit them. In which case national courts would have to take cognizance of the fact that the agreements in question were null and void. This would then open the door to lawsuits against airlines. Such cases would of course require that those bringing the suits had the required legal standing and that the Commission had made the correct decision in the first place. Up to June 1986 the Commission held its hand, hoping that the Council of Ministers would agree to a liberalization package of the kind discussed above. When that failed to materialize the Commission decided to commence proceedings. These proceedings were obviously likely to provoke the ministers of transport into achieving an agreement, since it was always possible that the cases instigated by the Commission would outlaw the restrictions in their entirety, whereas the Council of Ministers was only willing to contemplate a limited degree of competition. This move seems to have done the trick since the ministers ultimately settled their differences, and this included the Anglo-Spanish dispute. An implementing regulation was agreed late in 1987 which introduced a limited degree of competition. The Commission then instructed the airlines as to the changes which they had to introduce in order to conform to the new and more competitive regime.

The common energy policy

We must begin by considering why a common energy policy has been thought to be necessary. At least two main kinds of justification can be advanced and they both spring from the effects of differential government intervention in the energy market.

Firstly, distortions of competition can arise from differing national energy policies. If, for example, third-country energy sources undercut domestic supplies, different national approaches may be devised. It would be possible to adopt a low price policy, allowing imports to enter without protection and subsidizing competing domestic supplies in order to enable them to survive. Alternatively, a member state could impose protection, by applying either import duties or indirect taxes, thus driving the price of imported energy up to equality with that of domestic sources. The problem which arises from such a difference of approach is that energy intensive industries under the latter policy would be at a marked competitive disadvantage as compared with their counterparts situated in states adopting a low price policy.

Secondly, left to themselves member states might adopt different approaches to the problem of dependency on third-country supplies of energy. Prudent countries would hold stocks in case of international crises affecting supplies and would seek to develop indigenous sources. All this would involve a substantial commitment of resources. Imprudent countries would allow themselves to become dangerously dependent and would avoid the resource cost of ensuring regular supplies. Whilst it is true that if an interruption of third-country supplies occurred the prudent would fare better than the imprudent, it is also true that the exports of the prudent to the imprudent would be depressed whilst the exports of the imprudent to the prudent would tend to hold up. In other words, and putting it metaphorically, since all the member states are in the same boat, it is important that they adopt similar policies towards dependency and bear an equitable share of the burden involved in reducing vulnerability.

Progress in the field of energy policy has been limited. There are four reasons for this. Firstly, the responsibility for energy matters has been a divided one. The Paris Treaty placed responsibility for coal fairly and squarely on the shoulders of the ECSC. The Rome Treaty established that oil, natural gas, hydro-power and electric current were the province of the EEC. The task of dealing with nuclear power was assigned to Euratom. Secondly, none of the three Treaties contains a word about a common energy policy or even lays down a timetable for its elaboration. In some degree this fact is a reflection of the circumstances of the time when the Treaties were drafted. They all belong to the period when coal was the major source of energy in the Six. (In 1950 it met almost 75 per cent of the primary energy needs of the Community.) The main problem then was guaranteeing that the supply of coal was available, firstly on non-discriminatory terms to all Community purchasers, and secondly at reasonable prices. The latter meant the Six had to address themselves to the problems of the coal cartels, in particular the Ruhr cartels of which Georg was the most notorious. The decline of coal, the emergence of associated regional difficulties, together with the growing dependence on imported sources of energy, were problems of the future and were not then foreseen. The third reason for lack of progress was the involved nature of the problem. Governments, even in liberal economies, tend to get caught up in regulating the energy market. The Six were no exception – the regional problem, state monopolies, nationalized undertakings and fiscal policy are just a few of the complicating elements. The fourth reason has also been connected with governments. Their pursuit of national self-interest has made it difficult to achieve a common policy. This concern to defend national interests has been evident from the beginning, but it became even more marked in the oil crisis of 1973 and after, which we shall turn to later.

Before we discuss the specific factors which have given rise to the need for a common policy, it is important to note that the motivating factors have varied over time. In the period 1956–73 the problem was that imported oil fell in price, as did imported coal. As a result the Community became increasingly dependent on imported energy – the Commission was of the view that the Community was *dangerously* dependent. As we shall see, not a great deal was achieved by way of response. Politicians tend to be concerned with pressing problems and there were no overwhelmingly pressing problems during this period. Indeed, energy was becoming cheaper by the day and interruptions of supply were purely speculative. The compulsion to act was lacking. After 1973 the problem was quite different. Imported energy rapidly became expensive. It was also uncertain in supply because most oil came from the Middle East, and the latter was much more obviously politically unstable.

The need for a common policy – 1956–73

As has already been indicated, during this period the main factor dictating the need for a common policy was the increased competition which coal encountered, particularly from oil. This threw up a series of issues including unemployment and regional decline, the problem of the security and stability of energy supplies as the Community became steadily more dependent on imported sources, and the likely long-term evolution of the price of imported energy sources.

An appreciation of this set of interrelated issues requires that we go back in time to the first half of the 1950s. In this period there was a coal shortage, which in turn prompted users to do two things. They sought to economize in the use of coal; for example, the steel industry succeeded in developing techniques which curtailed heat losses. They also began to turn to substitutes – in practice this usually meant oil. However, this tendency to take decisions against coal was masked by the rapid economic growth of the period. Indeed, when in 1956 the OEEC produced the Hartley Report (OEEC, 1956), the essential message was that there was a danger of a possible shortage of energy in Europe. Stress was also laid on the balance-of-payments problems inherent in dependence on imported energy. The Suez crisis appeared to vindicate this view since the immediate effect was rising prices stemming from high ocean freight rates for imported oil and coal. But the picture soon changed. The major oil companies, in order to cope with the growing demand, embarked on a programme of expanded production. They also began to diversify the areas in which they were prospecting and in so doing discovered substantial new reserves. In addition, the majors were joined by new companies who sought to carve out a place for themselves in the world market by offering low prices. The US Government also played a part. In order to protect the home market it applied import quotas and as a result the bulk of the increased supplies flowed to markets such as Western Europe. Moreover, the Soviet Government decided during this period to resume selling Russian oil on the world market. Then again, imported oil gained the advantage of lower freight rates arising from major economies in transportation as a result of the use of bigger and faster ships.

The result of all this was that coal's competitive position deteriorated drastically. After 1956 the price of oil fell and thereafter stayed low, whereas the price of domestically produced coal (despite a great increase in mechanization and in output per manshift) climbed steadily upwards. The position in 1956 and 1965 is shown in Table 22.

The effect of oil (and natural gas) on coal's position was dramatic. As

Table 22. Comparative price movements of imported coal and oil and community coal ($ per ton)

	Community coal[1]	Imported US coal[2]	Imported crude oil[3]
1956	12·53	21·60	20·30
1965	16·68	14·20	16·40

Notes: 1. Ruhr bituminous (schedule ex-mine).
     2. American coking fines c.i.f. Amsterdam/Rotterdam/Antwerp.
     3. Kuwait crude c.i.f. Naples.
Source: ECSC High Authority, *Fifteenth General Report*, Luxembourg, 1967, pp. 27–8.

we have indicated, coal was responsible for almost three quarters of the Community's primary energy supplies in 1950, and petroleum contributed 10 per cent. By 1966 coal had fallen to 38 per cent and petroleum had risen to 45 per cent. The rapid rise in the energy requirements of the Community was met by oil, whereas between 1957 and 1966 coal production fell by 12 per cent, the mining labour force below ground fell by 24 per cent and the number of pits in operation by 42 per cent.

This evolution presented the Community with three main problems. Firstly, there was the resulting unemployment. The problem would not have been so difficult if the employment in coal mining had been evenly spread; unfortunately it was concentrated in pockets, and this gave rise to the threat of a severe regional problem. The unemployment problem would of course have been more tractable if the rate of decline of coal had even been merely arrested. Secondly, there was the fact that unlike other major economic blocs (the USSR and USA), the Community was highly dependent on imported supplies of energy and was becoming more so. This raised the question of the stability and security of supplies. Had there been a major political upheaval in areas mainly responsible for the supply of energy to the Community, the consequences could have been disastrous. The need for security and stability of supplies provided an argument for supporting indigenous sources. There were, of course, other approaches to the problem, such as stockpiling oil and diversifying oil supplies. (The discovery of oil and gas in the North Sea did promise to help to alleviate this problem.) Thirdly, there was the question of the long-term evolution of the world energy market. In 1962 the West European coal producers and the National Coal Board produced a memorandum (*Meeting Europe's Energy Requirements*) which argued that by the mid 1970s there would be a world shortage of energy and that in this light the prices ruling in the early 1960s were only temporarily low. They argued that it would therefore be prudent to keep mines in production. Subsidies would be required in the short term but in the longer term the energy price level would rise and coal mining would become economic. There could be no question of closing the mines down in the short run and opening them up later, since mining communities would have dispersed and the source of labour would be lost for ever. Also the mines would flood and the cost of bringing them back into production would be extremely high. Sinking new pits would be extremely costly, and it has to be borne in mind that there could be a gap of ten to fifteen years between starting to sink a pit and reaching a high rate of production.

A common energy policy: the first steps

In 1964 the ECSC took the first step along the road to a common energy policy when the Council of Ministers formally adopted the Protocol of Agreement on energy policy. This laid down certain broad objectives – cheapness of supply, security of supply, fair conditions of competition among the different sources of energy, and freedom of choice for consumers. The Protocol did not generally lay down details of policy, but in the case of coal it did call for the speedy implementation of a coordinated system of state aids or subsidies. It is perhaps worth noting that in the case of coal the Community chose subsidies, whereas in agriculture the task of rendering Community production profitable was achieved by a different route. In other words, it was decided that coal would be rendered competitive not by raising the price of imported oil to meet the price of coal but by enabling Community producers to supply their output at a price less than would otherwise be the case. The Community indeed opted for a low-cost energy policy. There can be no doubt that this was the easiest path to pursue. Firstly, the Community was merely recognizing what was already happening, namely that as coal felt the impact of the competition from oil, member states were, in the interests of security and regional policy, granting their collieries half-concealed subsidies. The Protocol was therefore an open recognition of what had been happening anyway. Secondly, states such as Italy, which relied heavily on imported oil, would have strongly resisted any policy which raised their industrial costs.

It will, therefore, be appreciated that the Protocol envisaged a Community system of state aids or subsidies to the coal mines. This implied some coordination. Since subsidies were explicitly forbidden by the Paris Treaty, it also required the invoking of Article 95 which allowed the High Authority to take special decisions 'in all cases not expressly provided for in the Treaty' when this appeared 'necessary to fulfil one of the Objectives of the Community'. The basic principle of coordination was that measures of aid by member states should be scrutinized by the High Authority. The latter would have the power to authorize them on the basis of Community criteria. These criteria included assessment of the degree to which the aids enabled the mines to adjust to the new market situation, the degree to which they assisted in preventing unemployment and economic disturbance and the degree to which competitive behaviour between mines was distorted. In particular, the High Authority had to direct its scrutiny towards two kinds of aid. One was contributions towards the social security costs of mining firms. The change in the manpower situation had led to these becoming excessive, and the High Authority had to ensure that assistance did no more than defray the abnormal costs of social security and did not act as a positive subsidy which would put some mines at an advantage as compared with others. The other kind of aid was that made available for rationalization. The High Authority was given the power to authorize such subsidies in so far as they enabled mines to adjust to the new market conditions and did not distort competition between mines. Rationalization aid could take the form of assistance to enable mines to be closed, to improve the efficiency and productivity of mining enterprises and to help meet the cost of recruitment, training and retraining. The possibility was also envisaged that mining areas might be so badly affected by the competition from oil that serious disturbances were possible. In such cases extra aid was possible.

Two points are worthy of note. Firstly, although a Community aid system was envisaged, this did not extend to Community financing. The cost of subsidies was to be borne by national exchequers. It could be argued that Community finance was appropriate. For example, in so far as keeping coal mines in production is dictated by the security-of-supply argument, why should Italy be able to enjoy the advantage of cheap oil imports and be allowed to avoid the cost of coal subsidies and yet be able to turn back to coal on non-discriminatory terms if oil supplies became inadequate or oil prices rose steeply? The second point is that at no time did the Council of Ministers take a decision on the amount of coal which was to be kept in production. However, the High Authority did, in 1966, propose that the Community should guarantee outlets for 190 million tons of coal in 1970. By so doing, the Community would keep the proportion of energy requirements met from Community sources close to 50 per cent. One way of doing this was to place quantitative restrictions on coal imports. Another was to subsidize domestic coal used by the iron and steel industry.

In 1966, however, a Community element did creep into the subsidy system. This arose in connection with coking coal. The impetus for this move was the difficulties arising from the import of cheap American coal. Because there is no common external tariff or common commercial policy under the Paris Treaty, member states are free to protect their coal industries, or alternatively to import coal at world prices. To the extent that member states tended to import American coal, two effects were apparent. One was that countries such as the Netherlands and Italy, which had sited their steel plants on the coast, were in a good position to take advantage of these cheap supplies. On the other hand, West German iron and steel enterprises were highly dependent on the higher-priced domestic supplies. This distorted conditions of competition within the Community iron and steel market. The other effect was that cheap imported coal contributed towards a further erosion of the position of Community coal producers. The High Authority therefore proposed a subsidy for Community coking coal and coke. It was argued in justification that if no subsidy were given, intra-Community imports would dry up as industry switched to imported supplies, and that the subsidy would help to buttress the domestic industry. Opposition was encountered from the French, but in 1967 the Council of Ministers agreed to a subsidy system. Where coking coal and furnace coal produced in a particular member state was delivered to the steel industry of that state, the subsidies would be paid by the member state government concerned. For coking coal and coke entering into intra-Community trade a Community contribution towards the subsidy would be made.

Before we leave the subject of aids in connection with the coal industry it is necessary to note that subsidies for coal production generally and subsidies for coal and coke for the steel industry in particular have continued to be a feature of the Community energy scene. Even after 1973 when, as we shall see, the price of oil rocketed, the coal industry continued to receive subsidies. In recent years all the main-coal producing countries have subsidized their coal industries – the subsidy per tonne was least in the UK, higher in France and Belgium and highest in West Germany. The Paris Treaty concept of free competition unencumbered by state aids has been markedly absent from the coal sector for many years.

The 1968 initiative

In December 1968 the new fourteen-man Commission presented a memorandum to the Council of Ministers entitled 'First guidelines for a Community Energy Policy' (EC Commission, 1968a). This was an attempt to put new impetus behind the search for a common policy. The document was extremely detailed, and the following description should be taken as an account only of its most striking features. The policy sought to achieve the same aims as the Protocol. Apart from freedom of choice for consumers and fair competition between energy suppliers, the essential aims were stability, security and cheapness of supplies. The memorandum implicitly admitted that up to a point there was some conflict between these latter aims.

The Commission recognized the existence of distortions. It therefore proposed that the solution to this problem was the full implementation of the Rome Treaty in the energy field. Freedom of movement of supplies should be achieved within the Community; this meant the elimination of impediments, whether they were state monopolies or technical obstacles. Differences in taxes were one distorting factor; the specific solution was the harmonization of consumer taxes on energy products and of taxes on hydro-carbon fuel, in conjunction with the elaboration of the common transport policy. Whilst on the subject of the establishment of a real common market in the energy sector, we might note that the Commission called for the full implementation of the freedom of establishment and the freedom to supply services.

Security of supplies called for action in a number of energy fields, particularly coal and oil. The memorandum recognized that the domestic coal production necessary to ensure security could not be achieved without a coordinated import policy. In the light of past High Authority pronouncements this probably meant that the Community needed a common commercial policy which set quantitative limits to coal imports. The memorandum also noted the need for aids to the coal mines, while recognizing that production needed to be concentrated in the most efficient mines. It called for the introduction of Community aid arrangements (since Community coordination already existed this probably referred to the need for Community financing) and for better coordination of existing Community aid with national aids. In the field of oil, adequate stockpiles were one way to achieve security. The memorandum also called for a Community supply policy and programme. Undoubtedly the intention here was that the Community should watch the pattern of oil imports in order to guarantee that it was sufficiently diversified. If the Community was not satisfied with the pattern, the memorandum proposed that suitable procedures for remedying the situation should be evolved. The Community would also be constantly considering the supply possibilities open to it, the risks of interruption and the methods of coping with them.

The Commission also proposed that the ECSC principle of drawing up general objectives (i.e. forecasts of the evolution of demand) should be applied not only to coal but to the whole of the energy sector, particularly in order to guarantee that investment kept pace with the rapidly rising demand for energy. The ECSC principle of notification of investment projects (which has been operational since the inception of the Paris Treaty in respect of coal and steel) should also be generally applicable in the energy sector. Opinions should be rendered on investment projects, and Community control would be tightened if experience showed that recommendations were being ignored.

The Commission also saw the need to maintain competition in energy supply. Since some enterprises already occupied a dominant position in the market for oil, natural gas and nuclear fuels, the Commission proposed that there should be a notification system, together with a period of suspension of action, where mergers were contemplated. This would enable the Commission to voice an opinion. The possibility of preventive control was contemplated in this field. The Commission also suggested *a posteriori* notification of the prices obtaining in the market for energy. This was, no doubt, particularly intended to put the oil industry on a par with the coal industry which, under the Paris Treaty rules, was required to publish its price lists.

In November 1969 the Council of Ministers approved the basic outlines of the 1968 memorandum and asked the Commission to submit the most pressing proposals as soon as possible. In practice not a great deal emerged. In December 1968 the Council adopted two directives requiring member states to hold oil stocks equal to 65 days' consumption. (The Commission proposed that this should be increased to 90 days as from 1 January 1975.) National governments, and not the Commission, can commandeer these stocks if a crisis arises. In December 1970 the Commission submitted a draft directive to the Council designed to bring into line taxes on petroleum fuels in the various states. This has not yet been adopted. In January 1972, as a result of the pressure of oil-producing countries for substantially higher prices, the Council adopted two regulations under which member states were required to notify the Commission of investment plans for oil, natural gas and electricity, and of import programmes for oil and gas. The Commission sought direct notification, but in practice, other than in periods of crisis, the process takes place through the member states. These two regulations did not give the Commission any power of action in the energy field but they were designed to provide the necessary information on which a common policy could be built – given the goodwill of the member states. These were the main fruits of the 1968 initiative.

The oil shocks of 1973 and 1979

Even before the crisis of 1973 there were signs that a new energy situation was about to emerge. This was apparent from the activities of the oil producers organized in the Organization of Petroleum Exporting Countries (OPEC) who, as we have noted above, were pressing for a higher price for oil. This posed a danger to the Community since it had become increasingly dependent on imported oil. By 1971 the Six derived only 20 per cent of their energy from coal and 60·8 per cent from oil. (The position of the Nine at the time of the first enlargement was very similar, the figures being 24·8 per cent and 58·4 per cent respectively.)

It was, however, the Yom Kippur War of 1973 which precipitated the crisis. The war involved the Arabs using their control over oil supplies as a weapon to force other states, including the Nine, the United States and Japan, to bring pressure to bear on Israel. Supplies of oil were reduced, and in the case of the Netherlands (and the US) supplies of Arab oil were totally cut off. This precipitated a crisis within the Community, since the threat was that if the other eight countries supplied the Netherlands and undermined the blockade they themselves were likely to be exposed to blockade treatment. The conception of a free market in oil and oil products within the Community was a major victim of the Middle East conflict. The answer of the Nine seems to have been not to call the bluff of the Arab oil suppliers by openly declaring their intention to supply the Dutch, but rather to adopt what may be termed a 'low profile' policy – it was anticipated, particularly by the French and British, that patient diplomacy would be more productive of a satisfactory resolution. It is noticeable that the Nine, in their November 1973 statement on the solution to the Israeli–Arab conflict, adopted a stance which was distinctly favourable to the Arab cause.

The use of supply cuts as a political weapon was accompanied by dramatic increases in the posted price of crude oil. Between 1 January 1973 and 1 January 1975 the price of Arabian light crude rose by over 475 per cent (Weyman-Jones, 1986, p. 20). Initially this was taken to be a temporary problem – a device to secure a satisfactory settlement in the

Middle East after which prices would return to normality. However, it soon transpired that these new price levels were to be maintained in the long term. The argument ran that this was a fair price – oil had not previously kept pace with the inflation in the price of industrial goods produced by countries in Western Europe, North America and Japan. It was the fact that major OPEC producers (the Middle East alone possesses about three fifths of the world's proven oil reserves) intended to maintain permanently this high price level which constituted the revolution in the facts facing energy policy-makers in the Nine. At the same time the view gained ground that the whole world was in any case moving into a period of energy shortage – even oil had a limited life as a major source of energy. It should be added that some of the factors which had helped to create the glut of oil in the sixties were no longer operative. For example, the US was now a net importer of oil.

This was not the final episode in the shift to a new reality in oil prices. In the late seventies a second oil shock occurred which was coincident with the Iranian revolution. Between 1 January 1979 and 10 January 1981 Arabian light crude prices rose by 134 per cent. This oil, which had cost as little as $1·39 a barrel in 1970, was priced at $34 a barrel in 1981, whilst higher-quality crudes commanded as much as $41 on the Rotterdam spot market (Weyman-Jones, 1986, pp. 20–21).

At this point it is worth noting how well-founded the EC Commission's concern about import dependence – particularly dependence on the politically unstable Middle East – had been. Two wars – the Six Day War and the Yom Kippur War – had vindicated the fear of vulnerability. What had been less clearly foreseen was the possibility of being in the hands of a cartel in the shape of OPEC. Given the magnitude of the challenge, it was not unreasonable to expect that the Community would feel that it was best tackled by a common response. At last a common energy policy would emerge. What might its shape be? Did it indeed happen?

Clearly it was worth considering whether it was possible to match the monopoly power of OPEC by some form of equivalent buying (i.e. monopsony) power. If that was impossible it was at least important to create a dialogue between oil users and oil producers in which the need for security of supplies and price moderation and stability were top of the agenda.

A prime feature of the common policy would presumably be a drive to become less energy-intensive and in particular to become less dependent on imported energy – most notably oil. The price rise itself would contribute to such an end, since it could induce a shift to other cheaper energy sources including indigenous supplies and it would create an incentive to save energy. It would also be possible to further stimulate such a shift and saving by imposing a tax on imported energy. Indeed a proposal for a Community tax was made in 1979. This idea had a number of virtues, since apart from giving rise to a shift and to saving it was also argued that it would reduce the price received by OPEC producers,[1] would provide an own resource for the Community budget and, by inflating the price of British North Sea oil, would help to compensate for the UK's budget imbalance.

Clearly it was important to develop indigenous supplies of energy. One source was solid fuel, of which the most obvious was coal. Here we must note the fundamental change which had taken place. The facts of the sixties were that oil was getting cheaper and coal dearer, in absolute and relative terms. A central feature of energy policy was the subsidizing of coal, and the emphasis in Community policy was on the harmonization of subsidies to avoid distortions, at least gross distortions, of competition. This did not prevent coal production in the Six from falling, contrary to what the West European coal producers (with their forecast of a world energy shortage in the mid seventies) wanted. Coal production fell from 239 million metric tonnes in 1960 to 165 million in 1971. Nevertheless, the policy of subsidization helped to limit the decline of coal production and the associated increasing dependence on imported energy. In the new circumstances, a policy designed to stabilize, and if possible to increase, the output of coal was likely to be on the agenda. Financial aid from the Community in order to make the coal industry more efficient and thus to enable it to increase its penetration of the market was well worthy of consideration.

It would be necessary to stimulate the use of other indigenous sources of energy. There was an obvious need for a substantial exploration programme in order to find more oil, more natural gas and more hydroelectric power in Europe. A massive investment would also have to be made in the actual process of extraction. There was also a need to consider largely unexploited renewable sources such as solar energy, geothermal energy and wave power. Here again a substantial research and development programme was called for. If more domestic energy sources were to be developed in Europe it could be argued that it would be necessary to safeguard such supplies from undercutting. For example, North Sea oil was a high-cost source of energy which could be undermined if, deliberately or otherwise, the world price of oil were to drop.

1. Economic analysis predicts that the imposition of an indirect tax will *normally* raise the price to consumers but lower the price received by producers

Investment in oil, etc., extraction was likely to be encouraged if a floor price was guaranteed. This was also likely to be a precondition for a willingness to share energy in an emergency.

Atomic power as a basis for producing electricity is an obvious alternative to imported oil. This, however, raised the question of foreign dependence. Uranium has to be imported, and in the past some producers (notably Canada) had refused to export it. However, the world market was sufficiently well supplied, with some producers being tied to member states, so that the import dependence factor was not regarded as a matter for great concern. It should also be pointed out that continued access to imported uranium supplies was only a problem in the case of the existing generation of nuclear reactors. The new generation of fast breeders only require an initial priming of uranium. Thereafter they work on plutonium and produce further plutonium via a recycling process. Thus they constitute a kind of renewable energy source. There is one major problem attached to uranium and plutonium reactors, namely accidents, as Three Mile Island, in the US, and Chernobyl, in the USSR, were to prove. Plutonium is a particularly nasty substance, and there is an added security risk in that, with the aid of quite elementary technology, it can be used to produce hydrogen bombs. Both these factors mean that there is a real problem of public acceptability. In the longer term it will probably be possible to produce electricity by atomic fusion rather than fission, but that is still a long way off.

A common energy policy would also call for the creation of emergency procedures and facilities for dealing with situations such as a reduction or cutting off of external supplies. Such procedures would involve methods of sharing and reducing the use of short supplies. The holding of adequate stocks of oil and coal would also be a crucial facility. The 1968 decision to hold stocks of oil equal to 65 days' consumption (later raised to 90 days') was undoubtedly well conceived.

Clearly it was important that every effort should be made to diversify the geographical source of imported energy supplies. This was crucial in the case of oil but was also important in the case of natural gas. Coal was much less of a problem.

The Community's response has been a fourfold one, consisting of (a) the adoption of Community energy targets and balance sheets; (b) the implementation of policies which give rise to the rational use of energy; (c) the elaboration of emergency procedures; and (d) the use of all the Community's financial instruments to provide grants and loans to the energy sector with the aim of reducing import dependency. We will consider them in that order.

Quite quickly after the 1973 shock, the Community decided to introduce targets designed to reduce dependency on imported oil. Thus in 1974 the Commission called for a series of policy initiatives which would reduce the imported component of energy consumption from approximately 60 to 40 per cent. Late in 1974 the Council of Ministers adopted a Resolution on the objectives of Community energy policy for 1985. It set the somewhat more conservative target of changing the pattern of energy demand and supply so that by 1985 the Community's import energy dependence would fall from 63 per cent (the actual figure for 1973) to below 50 per cent and if possible to 40 per cent. At the Bremen summit of 1978, the Heads of State and of Government added another element to the 1985 objectives when they agreed that oil imports in that year should be held down to the 1978 level. The process of producing objectives has been a continuing aspect of Community energy policy. Table 23 shows the 1985 energy objectives for 1995. It is important to stress that the purpose of these objectives is to set member states a

Table 23. Community [1] primary energy balances 1985 and 1995 (million tonnes oil equivalent)

	1985	1995[2]	1995[3]
1. Total primary demand	1048	1136	1205–1255
Components of total primary demand			
(a) Oil	484	470	520–560
(b) Natural gas	184	190	195–205
(c) Solid fuels	238	287	265–295
(d) Nuclear	124	165	179–185
(e) Hydro, etc.	18	24	22–23
2. Total domestic production			
Components of domestic production			
(a) Oil	148	113	100
(b) Natural gas	126	110	not estimated
(c) Solid fuels	173	196	not estimated
(d) Nuclear	124	170	179–185
3. Net oil imports (i.e. 1(a) − 2(a))	336	357	420–460

Notes: 1. Including Spain and Portugal.

      2. Forecasts made before the fall in oil prices in 1986.

      3. Assuming the low oil prices of 1986 continue to operate, thus increasing demand and reducing domestic production.

Source: EC Commission, *Energy in Europe*, No. 6, 1986, p. 17.

collective target which, if achieved, will ensure that by 1995 the Community energy situation is secure. The action necessary to fulfil these targets lies with the member states, although Community financial assistance can help – see below. If member states fail to act in conformity with the plan then in the final analysis there is nothing to compel them to mend their ways. The Commission will of course monitor trends and will draw the Council of Ministers' attention to any signs that the Community is drifting off the target path.

The data in the two left-hand columns of Table 23 indicate that between 1985 and 1995 Community primary energy demand will rise from 1048 million tonnes oil equivalent (Mtoe) to 1138 Mtoe. All the components of energy demand will rise except for oil (item 1(a)) which will fall by 14 Mtoe. Items 2(a) to 2(d) indicate the likely growth of domestic supplies. There are some obvious shortfalls. Community oil production will drop – a reflection of North Sea trends. This is one reason why net oil imports (item 3) will rise from 336 Mtoe to 357 Mtoe. Natural gas production will likewise fall and the gap will have to be bridged by increased imports – some of it via the pipeline from Russia. Solid fuel production will have to rise, and there will have to be a very big increase in nuclear power. Without the planned growth of these two items, the position on net oil imports will be correspondingly worse. If the targets are met then oil consumption will be kept down to 40 per cent of total energy consumption. Clearly the public acceptability of nuclear power will be a crucial factor.

As we indicated earlier, Community energy policy does not merely consist of drawing up targets. An important feature of the policy has been the encouragement of rational use of energy. This has partly manifested itself in the form of measures to encourage energy saving. For example, the Council in 1979 adopted a Recommendation on the improvement of the thermal efficiency of buildings. Money has also been voted for demonstration projects on energy saving – see below. The other aspect of rational use of energy has been concerned with energy pricing. The Council of Ministers has on several occasions endorsed the principle of realistic energy pricing – this really implies that prices should be based on marginal cost. According to the Commission, such correct pricing will:

– further energy efficiency and conservation by ensuring that consumers' decisions are based on prices which take full account of the costs of energy supply;
– lead to effective decisions on fuel choice, again by ensuring that consumers take account of real costs in their investment and purchasing decisions;

- similarly, help to ensure optimal allocation of each particular fuel according to its value in each type of use;
- promote security of energy supply by assuring the necessary revenues to underwrite investments in production or long-term supply contracts. (EC Commission, 1984b, p. 3)

The third strand of the common energy policy is concerned with emergency measures. The decision of the community to hold oil stocks equal to 90 days' consumption has already been mentioned. Member states must also ensure that electricity producers maintain sufficient stocks at thermal power stations to ensure a supply of power for at least 30 days. In 1976 the Council agreed to a mechanism for sharing scarce oil supplies in an emergency, and in 1977 this was followed by agreement on methods of reducing oil usage in times of difficulty. At the Rome Summit of 1975 the UK appeared to secure the Community's agreement to a minimum floor price for oil. This would ensure the survival of North Sea oil in the face of a fall in the world price. However, the European Council does not make Community laws and no decision on this topic was subsequently taken by the Council of Ministers.

Fourthly, we need to note that the Community's financial mechanisms – the Community budget, the New Community Instrument and the European Investment Bank – have between them channelled large amounts of grant and loan money into the energy sector. Thus the Community budget has made a large number of grants towards demonstration projects concerned with energy saving, the development of renewable energy sources and the promotion of alternatives to oil and gas (both of which are heavily imported). The budget has also met 80 per cent of the cost of the JET (Joint European Torus) project. This is concerned with atomic fusion which we mentioned earlier. If successful, it will in the very long run provide abundant supplies of relatively safe energy. JET is actually organized as a joint undertaking in accordance with Articles 45 to 50 of the Euratom Treaty. The balance of the investment has been subscribed by the member states, Switzerland and Sweden. The borrowing powers of the New Community Instrument and the European Investment Bank have between them been heavily involved in financing the rational use of energy and the development of non-imported sources of energy – e.g. atomic power.

Whilst it is possible therefore to point to some significant developments in the field of energy policy, it is also necessary to point out that no instruments similar to the price support mechanisms of the CAP have been introduced. The idea of a Community imported energy tax was considered but dismissed.

The oil shock of 1986

We have thus far presented the post-1973 picture in terms of high and uncertain supplies of imported oil. We now have to take account of the fact that oil prices reached their peak on the world market in 1982. The effect of those high prices was to induce consumers to save energy and switch away to other sources and to bring additional sources of high-cost oil on stream. As a result, the supply/demand balance on the world market changed. Prices weakened and the inflation of the price of manufactures produced by oil-importing economies also helped to erode the real price of oil – i.e. the quantity of imported manufactures which oil producers could command with each barrel of oil. Nominal and real prices began to drift down, and in 1986 the OPEC price system collapsed. Roughly speaking, oil prices halved in 1986. They then staged a limited recovery, but how effective the OPEC recovery strategy will continue to be is difficult to forecast. The price collapse does of course have implications for Community energy policy. Its beneficial effect is to reduce the Community's import bill. The reader may feel that this is an unambiguous benefit. However, the Commission does not see it in these terms. It points out that continued low oil prices would make users less concerned about the need to conserve energy. They would also inhibit the shift to non-oil energy sources. As a result, the Community would become more dependent on uncertain supplies of imported oil. This the Commission regards as dangerous. The effect on net oil imports of continued low oil prices is shown in the right hand column of Table 23. Apparently, high prices are bad but so are low prices.

9 Regional and Social Policy

Introduction

The reader of Chapters 4 and 5 could be forgiven for forming the view that the EEC is essentially an exercise in economic integration based on the economics of Adam Smith. That is to say, the course of economic events is to be determined purely, or largely, by the play of free trade and free competition. The word largely is perhaps more appropriate since the CAP is hardly a product of free-market thinking! However, the EEC is not purely Smithian. Within the *present day* Community there are provisions designed to counteract and compensate for the effects of competition – notably these are the European Regional Development Fund and the European Social Fund. Whilst their capacities are limited, they do at least represent a recognition of the need to provide a balanced approach to the integration problem.

Regional policy

Rationale

Let us begin by asking what arguments have been adduced in favour of regional policy within the context of the European Community. The reader will at once recognize that the above question has been framed in a way which leaves open the question whether regional policy ought to be at national level, Community level or both. Some clues as to what the answer may be will, however, be found below.

A major justification has been that large disparities existed when the Community of Six was created and that disparities have continued to exist. For example, Professor Levi Sandri, writing in 1965 but referring to 1958, indicated that the *per capita* income of the most favoured region in the Community (Hamburg) was about seven times that of the least favoured Italian region (Calabria) (Levi Sandri, 1965). It was no doubt with this in mind that the preamble to the Rome Treaty included a declaration that the contracting parties were:

anxious to strengthen the unity of their economies and to ensure their harmonious development by reducing the differences existing between the various regions and the backwardness of the less favoured regions.

It was also because of this that the treaty explicitly called for the creation of the European Investment Bank (EIB) and that first on the list of the bank's objectives was the provision of loans for the assistance of the less-developed regions. Without that requirement, Italy would have found the EEC a much less attractive prospect – we say more about the Bank below. Subsequent enlargements only served to continue the state of disparity. This was clearly the case when the UK, Ireland and Denmark joined the Community. Thus the Commission has pointed out that, taking an average of the years 1977, 1979 and 1981, gross domestic product per working person in various Danish regions was in the range of either 100–115 per cent or 115–130 per cent of the Community average, whereas in the various British and Irish regions it was either 70–80 per cent or less than 70 per cent of the Community average (EC Commission, 1984c, p. 2). Greek, Spanish and Portuguese membership has brought into the Community regions whose living standards (on a *per capita* gross domestic product basis) are for the most part less than 72 per cent of the Community average (EC Commission, 1984b, p. 10). One of the main Community instruments for dealing with the regional problem is the European Regional Development Fund (ERDF). The Commission has pointed out that Article 3 of the 1984 ERDF regulation declares that the Fund's prime purpose:

is to contribute to the correction of the principal regional imbalances within the Community by participating in the development and structural adjustment of regions whose development is lagging behind and in the conversion of declining industrial regions. (EC Commission, 1986, p. 5)

Clearly, the absence of a commitment to correct regional imbalances would severely undermine Community solidarity and would discourage weaker economies from participating in any further advance towards economic and political unity.

Up to now we have been discussing the regional inheritance of the Community. But in addition we have to take account of the fact that Community membership can itself give rise to regional problems: when a country becomes a member it has to conform to the rules concerning external protection (tariffs and quotas), and these may give rise to structural changes which manifest themselves in a regional form. For example, a member state has to replace its external protection by the common external tariff together with the CAP external protection régime. Quantitative restrictions may also have to be modified. If the Community arrangements are more protective than the old national ones then domestic activities will flourish, but if the Community system is less protective, then third-country competition is likely to give rise to the contraction of certain sectors. Community membership will also require the dismantling of all forms of protection against partner economies. Relatively efficient industries will then expand, but the relatively inefficient will be forced to contract. The actual way in which all these adjustments manifest themselves will vary from economy to economy, but the possibility that they can have an adverse regional impact is not in doubt. If the effect of membership is to cause an overall deterioration in the balance of payments, then monetary measures (e.g. an exchange-rate depreciation) may be necessary. Whilst they may bring the external account back into balance, it does not follow that the economy will be able to escape from industrial adjustments which have regional implications.

Harvey Armstrong and Jim Taylor have pointed out that Community membership can also give rise to problems in border regions (Armstrong and Taylor, 1985, p. 230). They distinguish between external and internal borders. External border areas (i.e. those at the periphery of the Community) may, prior to the creation of the customs union, have traded heavily with contiguous third-country economies. However, when Community protection régimes are instituted, those trading opportunities may be significantly reduced. Thus areas of West Germany bordering the German Democratic Republic (GDR) were forced to re-orient trade away from the GDR to the rest of the EEC. Internal border areas are those which are external when member states are separate but which become internal to the EEC when member states form a customs union. Such areas may have made a good living out of border formalities and processes, but such opportunities should disappear in a true internal market.

Another factor which has received considerable attention has been the possible tendency for industrial activity to gravitate towards the centre of the Community to the detriment of regions at the periphery. A glance at the map of gross domestic product *per capita* by region clearly demonstrates the existence of a central block of economic activity and prosperity which stretches from south-east England, Denmark and the Netherlands in the north, through central and north-east France and much of West Germany (other than certain eastern regions) to south-east France and northern Italy. Economists point to the pulling power of industrial locations at the centre. Firstly, they draw attention to economies of scale – i.e. the lower unit costs which *individual* firms enjoy as a result of producing large outputs. Since the bulk of the consuming public is close at hand, transport costs will be low. This in turn keeps prices low, which stimulates demand and in turn gives rise to scale economies. Secondly, economists have identified certain external economies – i.e. economies which depend on the size of the output of an industry (as opposed to the output of an individual firm). Thus when an industry concentrates in a region, it stimulates the emergence of firms within the region which benefit the industry. Firms may set up to process the industry's by-products or to supply it with specialist financial and commercial services. Transport and other costs may, however, mean that only firms in the centre will be able to benefit to the full from these facilities. Thirdly, economists have identified certain agglomeration economies which arise from the general concentration of economic activity in a region. Thus transport and telecommunications facilities may emerge which are only viable if used very intensively. These polarization factors may be accompanied by counterbalancing dispersal forces – i.e. industry might be driven out towards the periphery as a result of the shortage and consequent high price of land and labour. However, the general view seems to be that without a powerful regional policy centralizing forces will tend to predominate.

Another set of reasons why regional policy has been deemed to be necessary is connected with the adverse regional impacts which can arise from Community policies. One of the main reasons why the ERDF was set up was because it was felt to be an indispensable concomitant of the plan to achieve economic and monetary union by 1980 (see Chapter 7). The argument appeared to run as follows. Suppose that industrial unions in the UK sought Community pay levels, but at the same time UK productivity lagged behind that of the Community. The UK would become uncompetitive in the Community market – exports would tend to fall and imports to rise. Both these factors would tend to create unemployment. Prior to the union this problem could be alleviated by a devaluation. But once an economic and monetary union was achieved this line of policy would be precluded. Exchange rates would quite possibly be fixed prior to the creation of a common currency. Within the Community, the UK, for example, would be placed in the same position as Northern Ireland currently is within the UK. Northern Ireland has not been able to alleviate its unemployment problem by making its goods more competitive in the UK market by means of a devaluation against Great Britain. It has in fact had to rely on generous levels of regional aid in order to offset its locational disadvantages.

Equally, within the union the UK would have to rely on Community aid.

Regional problems can of course arise as a by-product of policies other than monetary union. Thus if the CAP is modified in a way which hits certain kinds of farms (e.g. small farms) or the producers of certain products (e.g. milk), then regional problems may arise if such farms are, or the production of such products is, concentrated in certain areas. Then again a decision to enlarge the Community can have a very considerable impact on certain regions. The admission of the Iberian members is, for example, expected to hit the Mediterranean regions of the Community quite hard – particularly the producers of Mediterranean agricultural products. It is because of this that aid schemes in the form of Integrated Mediterranean Programmes have been agreed. Under these programmes the Community plans to spend 6600 million ECUs over a seven-year period which began in 1986. About 4100 million ECUs will come from the Community budget – the other 2500 million ECUs will take the form of loans from the European Investment Bank and the New Community Instrument. These loans may attract interest subsidies. The aim will be to improve the production of crops not in surplus, to modernize and restructure fishing fleets, to create new industrial, service, and tourist activities and to promote training schemes.

A Community regional policy can also be justified on the grounds that it can make national policies more effective. For example, it can prevent competition between member states in the giving of aids. As we noted in Chapter 4, when discussing state aids, such competition may enable the richer countries to outbid the poorer ones in attracting foot-loose investment, and it may mean that aid is not concentrated in the regions where it will produce the maximum benefit. A Community regional policy may also facilitate the coordination of national efforts – a problem region may in fact straddle national frontiers. Community regional policy could of course take the much more radical form of transfers from the richer to the poorer members of the Community. We discussed that idea in Chapter 4 when we considered possible longer-term developments of the Community budget.

Community regional instruments – the first phase

When we consider policies such as agriculture and transport, we see that there are separate Titles (i.e. groups of articles relating to a policy problem) within the Rome Treaty devoted to these subjects. The Titles call for common policies (in some cases detailing their nature) and provide powers for their implementation. But the *original* Rome Treaty contained no separate Title relating to the regional problem and made no explicit call for a common regional policy.

There were, and still are, provisions scattered throughout the treaty which bear upon the regional dimension, the most important of which is Article 92 relating to state aids. The general posture of Article 92 has already been discussed in Chapter 5. Basically it says that aids for regional development may be permitted (this is a derogation from the general principle that state aid is prohibited) and that the Commission shall exercise a general supervisory role. As we saw in Chapter 5, the Commission has used its powers under Articles 92 to 94 to control the level of regional aid and also the kind of aid instruments which may be employed. In the first case, grant ceilings have been prescribed for the various regions, and in the second, aid instruments have themselves been subject to scrutiny.

Article 92 therefore seems to suggest that the original role of the Community in the area of regional policy was to be largely negative. The Commission would vet aids, but it would not be involved in the giving of them – the latter would be a national responsibility. Ironing out the initial regional disparities and coping with the regional impact of integration was a job for the member states. But in fact this view is only partly true. Even in the earlier days three institutions had been established whose assistance had some impact on the regional problem. One of these was the European Investment Bank. This was established under the provisions of Articles 129 and 130 of the Rome Treaty. The Bank was devised to grant loans and guarantees on a non-profit-making basis within the Community for (according to Article 130) the following purposes:

(a) projects for developing backward regions;
(b) projects for modernizing or converting undertakings; or for developing fresh activities called for by the progressive establishment of the common market, where such projects by their size or nature cannot be entirely financed by the various means available in the member states;
(c) projects of common interest to several member states which by their size and nature cannot be entirely financed by the various means available in the individual member states.

Originally, the activities of the Bank were confined to the territories of the member states, but subsequently its sphere of operations was widened to cover countries which had come to have association or other agreements with the Community. These currently include Turkey;[1] African, Caribbean and Pacific (ACP) countries – these are ex-colonial dependencies of the original Six and the UK; certain Overseas Countries and Territories (OCTs);[2] a group of Mediterranean countries – the Maghreb Countries (Algeria, Morocco and Tunisia), the Mashrek Countries (Egypt, Jordan, Lebanon and Syria) plus Israel, Cyprus, Malta and Yugoslavia.

The subscribers to the Bank are the twelve member states. The capital subscribed by them amounts currently to 28·8 billion ECUs, of which about 9 per cent is actually paid up. The unpaid capital acts as a guarantee. Although some of the resources are thus provided by the Twelve, the bulk is raised by borrowing on the international capital market. In addition there are three other sources of funds. One is the New Community Instrument (NCI), or Ortoli Facility, which we mentioned in Chapter 3. Although the Commission uses this mechanism to raise money on behalf of the Community, the funds are made over to the EIB. The other two sources are the Community budget and direct financing by the member states.

The EIB has been engaged in lending on a very considerable scale see Table 24. Between 1959 and the end of 1985 it extended loans and guarantees amounting to 45 692 million ECUs. Most of the money – 89 per cent – was devoted to internal purposes. The great bulk of the internal assistance is devoted to the development of backward regions by way of infrastructure and productive enterprise investments. In 1985 regional development projects enjoyed some 60 per cent of the Bank's lending from its own resources together with those of the NCI. Most of the regional lending has been directed towards the poorer countries. In 1985, 79 per cent of lending for regional purposes from the Bank's own resources (but not including those of the NCI) was directed towards Italy, Greece, Ireland and the UK.

Whilst it is legitimate to regard the EIB as a regional policy instrument, it is important to note that regional assistance normally takes the form of capital grants, rebates of interest, subsidies to inputs, etc. Clearly this kind of activity is outside the scope of the EIB, which has to lend at interest. However, the fact that the EIB has an 'AAA' credit rating, the highest there is, means that it can borrow on keen terms and reflect those keen terms in the interest rates it charges to its customers.

1. Greece, Spain and Portugal also received assistance prior to full membership.
2. Not yet independent.

Table 24. EIB financing [1] 1959–85

	Total	%
Loans from EIB own resources and guarantees		
Within the Community	35 464	77·6
Outside the Community	3 966	8·7
Total	39 430	86·3
Financing provided from other resources		
Within the Community		
– New Community Instrument	5 070	11·1
Outside the Community		
– Community budget and member states	1 191	2·6
Total	6 262	13·7
Grand total	45 692	100·0
Within the Community	40 535	88·7
Outside the Community	5 157	11·3

Note: 1. million ECUs.
Source: EIB, *Annual Report 1985*, Luxembourg, 1986, p. 9.

Two [1] other bodies also made a contribution (and indeed continue to do so). One was the European Social Fund, which we shall discuss in more detail later in this chapter. The Fund makes money available for a variety of purposes including retraining and increased mobility of unemployed workers. The other fund which has made a contribution has been the EAGGF. It has, for example, contributed towards the cost of programmes designed to improve the incomes of hill farmers in certain less-favoured regions. We should also note that the Brussels Commission has since 1967 been responsible for operating the relevant provisions of the Paris Treaty. Redevelopment policy has consisted of loans made available to develop new sources of employment in areas where employment in the coal and steel industry has contracted. Readaptation policy has been directed towards making grants to tide workers over until they could find new jobs, to assist with resettlement and to contribute to the cost of retraining.

1. For completeness we should note that, although it came after the inception of the ERDF, the EMS has also given rise to interest subsidies on EIB and NCI loans. These were directed to Italy and Ireland and were designed to enable them to cope with the challenge posed by participation in the EMS exchange rate mechanism.

The European Regional Development Fund

Since the inception of the EEC, the Commission has been striving towards a policy which would deal effectively with the regional problems of the Community. The Action Programme of 1962, and the Memorandum of Regional Problems of 1965 (with its stress on development poles such as that created at Taranto-Bari), were expressions of that concern. It was not, however, until 1969 that the Commission came into the open with the idea that it should itself play an active part in the process of aid-giving and not just be concerned with negative controls (under Article 92) and studies of the general problem. In documents attached to the 1969 Memorandum on Regional Policy (EC Commission, 1969c) it proposed the creation of a Regional Development Rebate Fund which would make grants by way of abatements of interest on loans for regional development purposes. This particular proposal was not implemented, but in the same year another proposal was made which eventually led to the creation of the ERDF. We are of course referring to the Hague Summit of 1969, which called for the creation of an economic and monetary union by 1980. The Werner Committee, in its final report of 1970 (EC Commission, 1970), recognized that Community-financed regional interventions would be necessary, but it did not describe in detail the exact reasons why. We have, however, already considered the kind of thinking which almost certainly lay behind the Werner proposal. The next step occurred in 1972 at the Paris Summit, when the British, who were just about to enter, were successful in pressing for the establishment of what came to be called the ERDF. Whilst the kinds of consideration just referred to inspired this move, undoubtedly there was another motivating factor at work. As we saw in Chapter 3, the terms of entry secured by the UK were such that, compared with other members of the Community, its ultimate contribution to the Community budget was likely to be high in relation to the benefits it was likely to receive. The idea of a regional fund financed from the Community budget was therefore seen as a means of correcting the imbalance – that is to say it was expected that, given the problems of its economy, the UK could look forward to being a major beneficiary. The regional fund would do for the UK what the EAGGF had done for the agricultural surplus producers!

The ERDF formally came into operation on 1 January 1975, and its operations between then and 1985 are summarized in Table 25. The ERDF has operated under three sets of rules – those operating up to

1979, those operating from 1979 to 1985 and those which have applied since the latter date.

The ERDF of course derives its resources from the Community budget. Up to 1979 the ERDF money was allocated to member states in the shape of fixed national quotas rather than being allocated to specific projects on the grounds of economic criteria such as unemployment rates, per capita income, etc. Whilst it is true that the original quota shares appeared to broadly reflect the relative seriousness of each state's problem, critics argued that the quota system was too crude and that fund money would be aimed at curing problems of markedly differing severity. It should be added that quota money could only be used to (partially) assist investment in industrial, handicraft, service and infrastructure projects which were located in regions which member states had themselves scheduled for regional assistance. Moreover, fund money could only be used to support projects which were being assisted by member states. In short, quota money flowed in directions determined by the existing regional aid policies of member states. Since the possible projects which could benefit from aid far outstripped the funds available, member states had to sift through possible beneficiary projects in order to submit a limited number which would match the national allocation. It was a cardinal principle of the fund's activities that fund assistance should add to member state efforts. If a member state reduced its regional aid spending because it expected to receive funding from the ERDF, then the additionality principle would be breached.

The Commission was never happy with the concentration of all the resources in the quota section. In its view the fund ought to have been divided into two – the quota section would have facilitated national regional aid efforts and a non-quota section ought to have been created to deal with the consequences of existing and future *Community* policies. In 1979 the Council of Ministers agreed to such a division, although the allocation of only 5 per cent of the fund monies to non-quota uses was a grave disappointment to the Commission. Non-quota funds were to be used to overcome problems which were associated with (a) Community decisions in other fields (e.g. agriculture or external trade), (b) changing world-wide economic circumstances (e.g. steel, textiles and shipbuilding) and (c) frontier regions. The first batch of non-quota measures were agreed in 1980.

In 1984 a new fund regulation was agreed by the Council of Ministers. It began to operate in 1985 and currently governs the operation of the ERDF. The main features are as follows.

Firstly, instead of spreading the ERDF money thinly over the

Table 25. ERDF operations 1975–1985

Commitment appropriations[1]

Year	Quota	Non-quota	Total	Annual increase (%)	Share of Community budget (%)
1975	—	—	257·6[2]	—	4·8
1976	—	—	394·3[2]	53·1	5·6
1977	—	—	378·5[2]	−4·0	4·9
1978	—	—	581·0	53·5	4·6
1979	900·0	45·0	945·0	62·7	6·1
1980	1 106·8	58·2	1 165·0	23·3	6·7
1981	1 463·0	77·0	1 540·0	32·2	7·3
1982	1 669·0	90·5	1 759·5	14·3	7·6
1983	1 909·5	100·5	2 010·0	14·2	7·6
1984	2 025·0	115·0	2 140·0	6·5	7·3
1985	2 174·9	115·0	2 289·9	7·0	7·5

Notes: 1. Million ECUs. 2. 300 million UA in 1975, 500 million UA in 1976, 500 million UA in 1977 – all converted to ECUs at January 1978 rate.
Source: EC Commission, *Eleventh Annual Report (1985) to the Council by the Commission – European Regional Redevelopment Fund*, COM (86), 545 final, p. 9.

Community, it will be much more concentrated. It is indeed intended that the bulk of the resources should go to between 25 and 30 per cent of the Community's population.

Secondly, the quota/non-quota distinction has been abolished. Instead, money is allocated to member states on a more flexible basis which involves indicative ranges. The indicative ranges as from 1 January 1986 are as follows:

	Lower Limit (%)	Upper Limit (%)
Belgium	0·61	0·82
Denmark	0·34	0·46
West Germany	2·55	3·40
Greece	8·36	10·64
Spain	17·97	23·93
France	7·48	9·96
Ireland	3·82	4·61
Italy	21·62	28·79

	Lower Limit (%)	Upper Limit (%)
Luxembourg	0·04	0·06
Netherlands	0·68	0·91
Portugal	10·66	14·20
United Kingdom	14·50	19·31

These limits have been designed to reflect the severity of national regional problems as revealed by productivity and unemployment levels. The lower limits are the amounts which the member states are guaranteed, and if adhered to would leave an unspent margin of 11·37 per cent of all ERDF resources. The margin which is actually left over is available to the Commission to allocate as it sees fit, thereby giving it more discretion over the way in which regional aid is distributed.

Thirdly, programme financing is to assume a much bigger role. Prior to the 1984 regulation there was no programme financing other than the relatively modest amounts of money earmarked for non-quota specific Community measures. It is now intended that programmes should be expanded progressively so as to absorb at least 20 per cent of ERDF resources. There will be two kinds of programme. (a) Community programmes will be undertaken at the initiative of the Commission. They are intended to deal with serious problems affecting the socio-economic situation in a region or in more than one region. Normally they will involve the territories of two or more member states. They will take the form of consistent multi-annual measures which serve Community objectives and the implementation of certain Community policies. Money for these programmes does not have to be spent in national assisted areas. (b) National programmes of Community interest are submitted to the Commission by member states and pursue national objectives. At the same time they must also contribute to the realization of Community goals and policies. Assistance under this heading will only be available in areas benefiting from national regional aid.

Fourthly, more emphasis is being placed on what is called internally generated development. This means that rather than relying on development emanating from outside a region, an attempt will be made to stimulate the untapped possibilities which exist within the region.

Fifthly, the ERDF fund is, as previously, limited to providing only a proportion of the cost of projects and programmes – the limit varies from 50 to 55 per cent. The new regulation reiterates the need for additionality. It also reflects an anxiety to shift more of the ERDF money towards industrial, craft and service investments as opposed to infrastructure improvements.

Whilst all this represents a welcome improvement, the ERDF will only have a major impact when its share of the Community budget is significantly increased above present levels. Unless Community budget resources are increased, that can only come about if the EAGGF enjoys a smaller share of the cake.

The Single European Act

Earlier we noted that the Rome Treaty, as originally drafted, did not provide for a Community regional policy. The Commission now claims that the Single European Act of 1986 has changed all that. In defence of that position it points to the fact that the Act has given rise to an amendment of the treaty. There is now a new Title which is headed Economic and Social Cohesion. A series of supporting articles have also been inserted into the Treaty. Whilst they do not in so many words call for the creation of a Community regional policy, they do declare that the aim of the Community shall be to reduce disparities between the various regions and the backwardness of the least-favoured regions. This really involves bringing one of the preamble declarations into the body of the Treaty. This is followed by a declaration to the effect that the ERDF is designed to redress the principal regional imbalances by participating (a) in the development and structural adjustments of regions whose development is lagging behind, and (b) in the conversion of declining industrial regions.

Social policy

The basic provisions

There are four strands to Community social policy. The first is really contained in Article 2 of the Rome Treaty, which lays down the tasks which the Community has to achieve. These are said to be the promotion of

... an harmonious development of economic activities, a continuous and balanced expansion, an increase in stability, an accelerated raising of the standard of living ...

A major preoccupation of the EEC is the enlargement of the Community cake. Such an enlargement has social as well as economic implications. The question of the distribution of the cake, and in particular the question of the level of social services and the like, is largely left to the member states in the first instance. In the longer term the influence of harmonization may be felt; this is discussed below.

The second strand of social policy relates to factor mobility. As we have already noted, under the Rome Treaty social policy is not confined to those spheres of activity which involve financial hand-outs. It also covers those policies which enable people to better themselves by virtue of the removal of restrictions on their freedom. The establishment of conditions in which, for example, a worker can move from one member state to another without loss of social security benefits and so forth, is an act of social policy. In a significant number of individual cases such opportunities almost certainly provide a more powerful means of social improvement than mere doles to the unemployed. The subject of freedom of movement of labour and the right of establishment have, however, been dealt with in Chapter 6, and we shall not discuss them further here.

The third aspect of social policy is to be found in Articles 117 to 122. Their central theme is social improvement and social harmonization. Article 117 looks to the need to promote a better standard of living. The latter is to be defined broadly and thus takes in not only wages and salaries but also many other social factors. Article 118 indicates that these social factors include matters relating to employment, labour law and working conditions, basic and advanced vocational training, social security, prevention of occupational accidents and diseases, occupational hygiene, the right of association, and collective bargaining between employers and workers. The essential message of Articles 117 and 118 is that it is desirable that social standards should rise and that *pari passu* they should be harmonized. For the most part no specific targets are set and no timetables are laid down. Nevertheless, it is assumed that harmonization will progressively occur, partly as an inevitable by-product of the creation of the Common Market, partly through the power to approximate laws contained in Article 100, and partly by virtue of the Commission bringing the member states together to study social policy issues.

The reader will have noticed that social security is one of the factors in the above list. The harmonization of it was a feature of the negotiations leading up to the Paris and Rome Treaties. The reason for this was that within the Six employers bore a heavy burden of social security contributions. Because the burden on French employers was particularly severe the French Government attempted, at the time when the Paris Treaty was being negotiated, to include provisions for the immediate harmonization of social costs of production. In practice, the High Authority was not given the power to harmonize social conditions, and Article 3 merely refers to the general intention to harmonize conditions in an upward direction. In negotiations leading up to the Rome Treaty the issue was again raised by the French. They argued that the higher rate of social security contributions – very approximately 50 per cent on top of wages – raised their costs of production and placed them in a competitively vulnerable position. They also cited other examples of exceptional burdens, such as the law on equal pay for equal work and paid holiday schemes. Once again the French did not succeed in obtaining an explicit agreement to harmonize social security burdens within a given time span.

With regard to the question of equal pay for equal work, it should be noted that the French secured what they no doubt regarded as a success. Article 119 of the Rome Treaty required that during the first stage each member state would introduce the equal pay for equal work system. The reason why the French pressed the equal pay for equal work point is obvious enough. In industries where the wages of women were raised above the level they normally would have been in the absence of the law governing equal pay, French industry would be at a competitive disadvantage in relation to member states which did not have such a law. The general espousal of equal pay under the Treaty therefore amounted to agreeing to the proposition that equalization would remedy distortions which would otherwise be caused by different legal provisions. It should, however, be pointed out that equal pay is a social and not an economic principle. Even if equal productivity is forthcoming this does not justify equal pay. According to conventional wage theory, the productivity of workers relates only to the demand side of the labour market. An entrepreneur will be prepared to take on a different quantity of labour at each wage rate, the actual amount being determined by the rule that the marginal revenue product of labour should be equal to the wage rate. Given equal productivity of male and female operatives an entrepreneur would be indifferent as between the two. However, on the supply side at each and every wage rate the amount of female labour offering itself might be significantly different from the amount of male labour on offer. The absolute equalization of wages paid to males and females could therefore give rise to the unemployment of female labour. This loss would have to be set against the elimination of distortions discussed above.

The French also seem to have made some progress on the holiday pay issue in the sense that Article 120 of the Rome Treaty required the member states to maintain the equivalence between the existing paid holiday schemes.

The fourth strand of Community social policy relates to the European Social Fund. Like the European Investment Bank, which we discussed earlier, the creation of the ESF was specifically required by Article 3 of the Rome Treaty. The basic Treaty provisions are to be found in Articles 123 to 128. Their general thrust is concerned with retraining and resettlement of the unemployed and the maintenance of jobs whilst enterprises convert their activities. The most recent detailed constitution was laid down by the Council of Ministers in 1983.

The Fund is fed by the Community budget. In 1986 Fund spending was about 7 per cent of total Community budget spending.[1] The budget reimburses up to 50 per cent, but in some cases 55 per cent, of certain forms of national expenditure. The eligible forms of spending are as follows. Firstly, there is that concerned with vocational training and guidance. Secondly, the ESF can grant subsidies for up to one year for job creation of young or long-term unemployed. These jobs must offer stable prospects. Thirdly, the Fund can help to meet the expenses incurred in connection with geographical mobility of workers. Finally, the ESF can assist in the provision of services and technical advice concerned with job creation. In 1983, in order to make the Fund more effective, the Council of Ministers decided that 75 per cent of ESF spending should go towards training and employment of the under-25s. It also decided on a geographical concentration of expenditure. Seven zones have now been designated as having an absolute priority. The under-25s do not get all the money. The Council has emphasized that, in respect of the rest of the Fund spending, priority should be given to (a) assistance for the unemployed (especially long-term), (b) women wishing to return to work, (c) handicapped persons who want to work, (d) migrant workers, (e) workers who need to retrain because of technological change, and (f) persons working in the field of employment promotion.

1. This is calculated on a commitment basis.

New bearings in social policy

The Paris Summit of 1972 was significant for its concern with what may be termed the 'image' of the Community. The Summit noted that economic expansion was not an end in itself: social considerations were also important. Disparities in living conditions should be reduced, and this should be achieved with the participation of all the social partners. The quality of life as well as the standard of living should be improved, particular attention being given to intangible values and to the protection of the environment. All this has been described as giving the Community a human face – to replace the faceless economic machine centred in the Berlaymont Building in Brussels. The Summit called for an action programme, and the Commission subsequently obliged by publishing in 1973 its Social Action Programme. The document contained a long list of areas where action was needed, some being matters of priority; we shall not attempt to list them here. The programme of action, in a somewhat amended form, was accepted by the Council of Ministers in January 1974. The detailed actions fell into three categories – those related to the attainment of full and better employment; provisions concerning the improvement and upward harmonization of living and working conditions; measures which would increase the involvement of management and labour in the economic and social decisions of the Community, and of workers in the running of their firms. We shall not attempt to review all the achievements which arose out of this new initiative but merely highlight a few of the significant steps.

On the employment front, a good deal of attention has been devoted to the plight of young people. In 1976 the ministers of education adopted a resolution concerning measures to improve the preparation of young people for work and to facilitate their transition from education to working life. In the following year the Commission addressed recommendations to the member states on the vocational preparation of young people under twenty-five who were unemployed or threatened with unemployment. In 1978, following a declaration of the European Council at Bremen, the Council of Ministers took a new step when they extended ESF funding to include the creation of new jobs for unemployed persons under twenty-five. An important institutional development occurred in 1977 with the opening in Berlin of the European Centre for the Development of Vocational Training.

The Community has been quite active in respect of the improvement of living and working conditions, notably in the case of women. In the case of equal pay for equal work the Commission found that the member states had been dragging their feet. Therefore in 1975 the Council issued a directive requiring the principle to be adopted within one year. In 1976 there followed another directive on the principle of equal treatment for men and women as regards access to employment, vocational training and promotion and in respect of working conditions. In 1978 a directive was also adopted on the subject of equality of treatment for men and women in matters of social security. The Community has also sought to achieve a stronger protection of all workers' interests. In 1975 Council adopted a directive on the approximation of laws concerning mass dismissals. In 1977 it issued a directive on the approximation of laws relating to the safeguarding of rights of employees in the event of transfers of undertakings or parts thereof. In 1980 a directive was also adopted on the protection of employees in the event of the insolvency of their employer. In 1975 the Commission addressed a recommendation to the member states on the subject of the length of the working week and paid holidays. Important institutional developments include the setting up of the European Foundation for the Improvement of Living and Working Conditions, in Dublin in 1976, and the decision of 1974 to establish the Advisory Committee for Industrial Safety, Hygiene and Health Protection.

The Community has less to show on the participation and industrial democracy fronts. Institutional changes have occurred which give employers and workers a close involvement in policy matters, and the Commission has put forward a proposal for a fifth directive on the approximation of national company laws which would, if adopted, give workers a say in the running of companies. More will be said about this topic in the next chapter. Mention must also be made of the Vredeling proposal, named after the Commissioner who introduced it in 1980. If approved this would, for example, require a parent company in one member state to supply the management of its subsidiaries in other member states with key information. The latter would cover the company's financial position, prospects and likely developments. This information would then be communicated to the workforce in the subsidiaries.

The impression which emerges is that since about 1980 much of the steam has gone out of the social action programme other than in those areas concerned with tackling the unemployment problem. It is the growth of the latter which has increasingly held the centre of the stage. Within the Twelve, unemployment was 8·7 million in 1980, but by 1985 it was over 16 million. A good deal of the work of the Council of Ministers has been concerned with making recommendations about approaches to various aspects of the unemployment problem. To a large extent the implementation of these proposals has been in the hands of member state governments.

Education

The social policy actions discussed above have tended to focus on employment and the work-place. But a discussion of social policy also allows us to take into account the Community's impact on education, notably higher education. Space does not permit us to detail all the Community actions, but four need to be highlighted. As early as the Messina conference of 1955 the idea of extending European integration into the fields of teaching and research was under consideration. At the Hague Summit of 1969 the Heads of State and of Government expressed interest in the idea of a European University.Thanks to pressure by the European Parliament, the European Institute of Florence was established in 1976 by a special convention signed by the Nine. It focusses on research and post-graduate teaching and is financed by the member states together with a subsidy provided by the EC Commission. The Community has for a number of years financed joint study programmes, which have involved student and staff exchanges in different member states. In May 1987 the ministers of education of the Twelve launched an intensified programme designed to increase such student and staff mobility. It is called ERASMUS. The Community has of course supported university-level research on a considerable scale. As we shall see in Chapter 10, the Community's science and technology programme, by being concentrated at the research end, has provided considerable funds to support research in higher education institutes. The European Documentation Centres, financed by the Community, have also presented scholars with a valuable research facility.

10   Industrial Policy

The present scope of Community industrial policy

The main focus of this chapter will be industrial policy in the EEC. The industrial policy provisions of the ECSC treaty are significantly more *dirigiste*, and we will discuss them later. Industrial policy in the EEC can be presented under four headings. (a) The first is concerned with the creation of a European industrial base. We have referred to this previously in terms of completing the internal market. (b) Considerable attention has been given to the need to facilitate business integration in the Community. This has given rise to a variety of proposals. One has related to the creation of a European company. Others have been concerned with measures which wordfacilitate cross-frontier mergers, and other forms of cross-frontier cooperation, and which would better enable parents and subsidiaries to organize themselves on a Europe-wide basis. In connection with the above, emphasis has been laid on the need to deal with the specific legal and fiscal impediments to cross-frontier arrangements. The desire to make business integration a reality has also led to proposals for the harmonization of national company laws. (c) There has been a long standing, and in recent years a growing, concern about the technological gap between the EEC and countries such as the US and Japan. Suggestions as to how the Community could catch up have taken two forms. One has been highly *dirigiste*. For example, the EEC should treat its high-tech sector as an infant industry which should be protected from import competition until it can stand on its own two feet. The less *dirigiste* approach has been to propose that individual states are too small to mount the necessary R & D efforts across the board. Rather, critical areas should be identified and national R & D efforts should be pooled. (d) Specific policies have been devised to deal with problem industries which have been encountering structural difficulties.

The policy emerges – slowly

We have to begin by recognizing that there was no call for an industrial policy in the *original* Rome Treaty. There were, however, provisions scattered through the Treaty which related to aspects of industrial policy, and in the early days the Commission had to rely on them for a number of policy proposals. The word proposal is very relevant here, because this is a field of activity where the ratio of draft directives (concerned with the internal market and business integration) to those actually adopted has, to say the least, been extremely high.

It is also true to say that up to 1970 the prime concern of the Six was to construct the Community as it was envisaged in the 1957 Treaty. As we noted in Chapter 1, it was only when the twelve-year transition period had come to an end that the Community could afford to give consideration to further goals, and one of these was industrial policy.

An important step was taken in 1970 when the Commissioner concerned with industrial affairs, Guido Colonna, put forward a memorandum on industrial policy. The memorandum was an ambitious document. Firstly, it envisaged the creation of a single European market or base. Secondly, it emphasized the idea of companies organizing themselves on a European scale. For this to happen certain legal developments were called for including the adoption of a European Company Statute, the approximation of national company laws, the introduction by all member states of legislation relating to corporate groups and the possible introduction of new forms of business cooperation. On the fiscal front there was a need to eliminate the discriminatory tax treatment accorded to cross-frontier mergers when compared with that applied to internal amalgamations. The third part of the memorandum was more *dirigiste* in character. The Commission, recognizing the need for the Community to catch up on matters of technology, saw the trans-national firm as being the vehicle which would enable this to be achieved. It therefore suggested that the Community should introduce development contracts with a priority being given to firms that were willing to carry out technological development on a trans-national basis. The reader should appreciate that although the EEC had been in existence for twelve years, businesses had been remarkably slow to merge across frontiers. Section four emphasized the importance of economic adaptation – new industries would have to be developed to create new jobs as existing industries declined. The emphasis was laid on the new industry element, and stress was placed upon the importance of labour mobility, the application of new technologies and the improved effectiveness of business management. The specific techniques to be applied to industries in decline were not discussed, although the need to deploy the resources of the Community (e.g. those of the European Social Fund) so as to facilitate change was referred to. We shall see that in due course the detailed problems involved in coping with industries in decline or in difficulty became a major preoccupation of Community industrial policy. The fifth and final section called for the extension of Community solidarity into the field of external relations.

The memorandum was discussed by the Council of Ministers, but considerable difficulties were encountered. Whilst the French were willing to contemplate a *dirigiste* approach, the Germans in particular were opposed and favoured a free market as opposed to an active industrial policy. However, at the Paris Summit of 1972 the Commission was supported by the Heads of State and of Government. The communiqué at the end of the summit called for the establishment of a single industrial base, a concept for which the UK claimed some credit, the elimination of barriers of a fiscal and legal kind which hindered mergers and closer links between firms, the rapid adoption of the European Company Statute, and the promotion of a European scale of firms which were competitive in high technology. The communiqué also referred to the transformation and conversion of declining industries under acceptable social conditions – a reference no doubt to the use of Community instruments such as the European Social Fund and the newly agreed European Regional Development Fund. Reference was also made to the need for fair competition within and without the Community – this seemed to pick up the point made in the fifth section of the Colonna Report.

In 1973, in the light of the Paris Summit, the Commission submitted a new memorandum on industrial policy. It was a toned-down version of the Colonna memorandum, and on the basis of it a programme of future action was adopted by the Council of Ministers later that year.

1972 was also an important year for internal scientific and technological collaboration. The Paris Summit communiqué expressly called for a common policy in the field of science and technology. There duly followed in 1973 a Commission memorandum setting out a scientific and technological policy programme which stressed the need for (a) coordination of national science and technology policies; (b) joint execution of projects of Community interest; (c) a more effective flow of scientific and technical information; (d) technology forecasting, and (e) the creation of an effective organizational structure – the latter was a crucial element. Early in 1974 a programme of action on these lines was adopted by the Council of Ministers.

Unfortunately, the progress which the Community made towards achieving these goals was rather disappointing. Actions which helped towards the creation of a European industrial base did follow, as we have seen in Chapters 4 to 6. But the fact that in 1985 the Commission was able to draw attention to a host of proposals that had not been adopted, and that according to the Single European Act the internal market will not be created until 1992, indicated that much more needed to be done. We shall discuss these matters in this chapter only briefly, since the nature of what has been done and needs to be done has already been indicated in Chapters 4 to 6. In respect of business integration, a variety of proposals were tabled by the Commission, but as yet relatively little has been achieved. We discuss this topic in more detail below. In the case of science and technology, the Community did subsequently devote relatively limited amounts of budget resources to R & D purposes but not on a scale calculated to prevent the technological gap from widening and certainly not enough to cause it to narrow. In the early 1980s, however, the need for a more dynamic response to the technological challenge posed by the USA and Japan led to an important reappraisal of Community R & D policy. We also discuss this below. The Community has also adopted policies in respect of industries experiencing structural difficulties, and we round off our account of industrial policy by considering two cases.

European industrial base

Significant progress has been made towards this end thanks to internal tariff and quota disarmament and the attack on NTBs – see Chapters 4 and 5. Much yet remains to be done if the Community is to take advantage of the force of competition and the economies of scale that a true European market could offer. Here the Commission places great emphasis on the completion of the internal market by 1992 as foreshadowed in the Single European Act.

The Commission has drawn attention to the critical importance of pressing forward with the process of standardization, both in respect of traditional products and also high-tech products – e.g. those concerned with information technology and telecommunications. It also emphasizes the absolute necessity of pressing ahead with the opening up of public procurement to Community-wide competition. The Commission also points to the need to take action in the field of industrial and commercial property rights (e.g. patents), since these place barriers in the way of the Community's technological efforts. The Commission, whilst noting the crucial importance of maintaining competition, is also disposed to favour cooperation in R & D, specialization and joint ventures, in so far as such collaboration promotes technical progress.

Business integration

In the early days of the Community great stress was laid upon the need to create larger firms. Data were assembled to prove that in a number of important industries the size of firm in the Community was significantly smaller than in the US. This, it was argued, put the Community at a disadvantage, since there are economies of large-scale production and distribution which might only be fully reaped by large firms, and in addition R & D was an activity characteristic of large enterprises and beyond the means of small ones. Although this view was evident within the Community, it would be dangerous to say that it was the Community view (if such a thing can in any case be said to exist). The idea that bigger firms were desirable was most strongly held by sections of industry. For example, the Community's federation of national industrial associations, the UNICE, was strongly in favour of it and so was the Patronat Française. The French Government was particularly favourable to the greater-size thesis. A prime aim of the Fifth Plan was to reduce the number of independent enterprises by creating larger groups. In some cases it was envisaged that only one or two firms should constitute the industry. The Commission, on the other hand, seemed in the earlier days to take a more cautious view. Clearly the larger market provided the possibility of greater size without the problems of concentration which would arise at the national level. Cross-frontier mergers would also help to cement the Community together, and international companies with subsidiaries in several member states were extremely adept at providing mobility of capital (and know-how) which the Rome Treaty obviously sought to achieve. But the Commission's original stance was guarded – the aim of the policy was not simply the pursuit of larger firms but the introduction of greater neutrality in respect of those factors which determined firm size. It aimed to eliminate those factors which artificially encouraged or impeded concentration.

The Commission focused particular attention on the fields of taxation and company law as ones in which conditions of neutrality should be brought about. In the fiscal field, the most obvious distortion was the artificial stimulus to vertical concentration presented by the multi-stage or 'cascade' type of turnover taxes. Originally, these existed in all the member states of the EEC except France, being particularly prominent in Germany. As we have seen, the 'cascade' system involves imposing a turnover tax upon raw materials, semi-finished products, or bought-in component parts every time they are sold by one firm to another. The result is that the taxes imposed in the earlier stages of manufacturing a product that passes through several stages are compounded in the final selling price of the product, which is thus higher than it would be but for the multiple incidence of tax. Under these circumstances, it is not surprising that industries in Germany should have chosen to avoid this multiple incidence wherever possible by vertical integration. In a completely vertically integrated concern that extends right back to the sources of raw materials, taxes are imposed only once at the final stage of production. The implications for the economy as a whole of this artificial inducement to vertical concentration are that the real economic advantages of specialization are less likely to be achieved, since the firm is encouraged to spread its activities for purely fiscal reasons, and vertical integration may in some circumstances make it possible for a vertically integrated concern to embarrass its non-integrated competitors, even if they are more efficient, by denying them raw materials, components or markets. The Commission always held, therefore, that the solution to this problem lay in the adoption of the value-added system which had been operational in France. This form of tax neither encouraged nor discouraged vertical concentration, and this is one reason why the Community adopted VAT.

The other area where, as we have seen, the Commission sought to make progress was in the field of cross-frontier mergers and cross-frontier business organization.

In respect of cross-frontier mergers two problems arose – one fiscal, the other legal. Let us take the fiscal point first. For a true merger to occur, a legal liquidation would have to occur in one country followed by a legal reconstruction in another. Unfortunately, when a company was liquidated, some countries imposed a liquidation tax on the difference between the book value and the actual value of the company's assets. In addition, in most countries capital gains arising at the time of liquidation were subject to taxation. If the tax liability was substantial, it might make the cost of an amalgamation prohibitive. Within each of the member states of the EEC, therefore, the fiscal authorities made certain concessions to companies in these circumstances, perhaps by levying the tax at a reduced rate or by permitting the payment to be phased over a number of years. But this understanding attitude on the part of the authorities usually vanished when cross-frontier amalgamations were under consideration. In particular, the possibility of phasing the tax payment over a number of years became unattractive to the official mind when the company on which the tax was levied was due to disappear from the national scene. Thus economically desirable mergers might be impeded. On the legal side, the problems were often quite stark. Dutch law, for example, did not provide for mergers between domestic companies, so mergers with companies in other member states were quite clearly impossible. German law too posed a problem, since it precluded mergers between German and foreign companies.

Before we turn to the solutions proposed in respect of mergers, it is necessary to note that fiscal problems also arose where companies were organized on the basis of a parent in one member state and subsidiaries in others. In particular, the possibility of double taxation of dividends was a real one. Even at the national level the fiscal systems of the Six only went part of the way towards eliminating this double taxation. In Germany, the Netherlands and Luxembourg, only when the degree of participation of the parent in the subsidiary was at least 25 per cent did companies enjoy the *Schachtelprivileg*, under which they were regarded by the fiscal authorities as part of a self-contained group, and double taxation of the subsidiaries' dividends was thus avoided.

To deal with the legal problems of cross-frontier mergers, three developments were proposed. The first was an international convention on mergers which would modify national laws so that international mergers were possible. Such a draft convention was submitted to the Council of Ministers in 1973 but has now been abandoned in favour of a directive aimed at harmonizing national company laws (see below) so as to facilitate cross-frontier mergers. This tenth directive has not yet been adopted. The second was to establish, side by side with national laws, a system of Community company law which would enable a European Company or *Societas Europea* to be formed. Such a statute was submitted to the Council in 1970, and a modified version was tabled in 1975. It too has not yet been adopted – in its proposals leading up to the Single European Act, the Commission looks to its adoption by 1990. Seven company-law harmonization directives have so far been adopted. It should be noted that this harmonization process is complementary to the European Company Statute, because the less the differences between national laws the easier it would be for the member states to accept the statute. For example, German law allows workers to participate in the running of a German company (*Mitbestimmung* or co-determination) but not all national company laws adopt that principle. The Commission has proposed that the fifth draft directive, which deals with this problem, should be adopted by 1988.

On the fiscal side, certain developments were required both in respect of mergers and in the case of the parent–subsidiary relationship. If liquidation taxes were eliminated on domestic mergers, they should be dropped in respect of the cross-border variety also. Capital gains taxes on liquidation should be as liberally applied to cross-border mergers as they were to internal amalgamations. In some cases, means of eliminating double taxation were needed. Again the Commission has produced draft directives to deal with such problems. For example, in 1969 two draft directives were sent to the Council concerning double taxation and the treatment of hidden reserves arising during merger operations: neither has yet been adopted. In 1985 the Commission indicated that these must have a very high priority in the drive to complete the internal market.

The reader will recollect that the Colonna Report referred to the desirability of introducing other forms of business collaboration which would foster cross-frontier cooperation. In 1973 the Commission submitted a draft regulation to the Council designed to create a European Economic Interest Grouping. This would not be a company as such but would provide a legal basis for cooperation. It would be available to persons as well as companies, would have a cross-frontier character and would be particularly helpful to small and medium-sized undertakings. A modified proposal was submitted in 1978, and happily this was adopted in 1985.

From what has gone before it will be apparent that the business integration cupboard is still largely bare. The only positive achievements are a handful of company harmonization directives, the measure relating to the European Economic Interest Grouping and the Business Cooperation Centre. The latter was established in 1972. It acts as a marriage bureau for small and medium-sized firms and advises them on the economic, tax and financial aspects of cross-frontier cooperation and integration.

Science and technology

In the light of the 1974 programme of action in science and technology, the Community did devote limited amounts of budget resources to R & D. However, by the early 1980s the Community had begun to realize that it was suffering from a loss of competitiveness on world markets and that a more dynamic response to the technological challenge posed by the US and Japan was needed. In 1981 the Commission addressed a communication to the Council of Ministers on the need to develop a genuine European dimension in responding to this challenge and that appropriate financial instruments should be devised to support such an initiative.

Two alternative strategies were suggested. When the European Council met at Copenhagen in 1982, the Commission presented a package of proposals designed to establish Europe as a world industrial power. Firstly, it called for the removal of barriers within the Community in order to generate greater efficiency through competition and scale economies. This was not new or controversial. Secondly, and very controversially, it argued that protection would be necessary for at least five years if European advanced-technology industries were to attain international levels of competitiveness (Pearce and Sutton, 1985, p. 5). In 1983 the French Government reacted in a similar way when it produced a memorandum which called on the one hand for protection, on infant-industry grounds, and on the other for collaborative R & D and the opening up of public procurement. The French were also critical of the way in which domestic anti-trust policy frustrated the cross-frontier mergers which were necessary if the competition of the US and Japanese industrial giants was to be challenged successfully. This was in fact a reaction to the proposed merger between Thomson-Brandt of France and Grundig of West Germany, which was forbidden by the German cartel office. The French were critical because they felt that the West Germans were looking at competition in too narrow a context. If national markets were protected then mergers between firms which were previously competitors could be dangerous. But in the more open trading environment of today there was plenty of outside competition to keep merged firms on their toes.

This protective approach did not commend itself to the Community as a whole. Instead, the approach adopted has been based on the following ingredients. (a) The areas of technology where the Community is at risk need to be identified. (b) Having identified them, the Community should seek to meet those R & D challenges on a collaborative basis. This the Community has done – see, for example, the ESPRIT programme below. (c) The proportion of the budget's resources devoted to Community R & D efforts should be increased. At the Fontainebleau Summit of 1984 this was agreed. (d) Community collaborative activities should be set within multi-annual framework programmes. This too had happened. The first ran from 1984 to 1987. The second will run from 1987 to 1991 and the Commission has asked[1] for 7735 million ECUs. (e) R & D collaboration should also

1. The actual allocation was reduced to 5396 million ECUs.

include cooperation with other European countries. (f) The Rome Treaty should more explicitly address itself to the research and technology challenge. A little more needs to be said on these last two points.

The idea of collaboration with other European countries is not in fact new. A body known as COST (Committee on European Cooperation in the Field of Scientific and Technical Research) was established by the Council of Ministers as far back as 1970. It has been a vehicle for involving other European countries in collaborative research projects on a case-by-case basis. COST currently comprises the Twelve and seven other countries. Between 1970 and 1985, fifty-five cooperative projects were carried out within the COST framework. What the American and Japanese challenge did was to place even greater emphasis on the urgency of achieving such wider European collaboration. In 1985 a European Technology Conference was held in Paris, and this in turn gave rise to EUREKA. This body currently brings together the Twelve, six EFTA countries and Turkey. Its object is to increase the productivity and competitiveness of European industry on the world market by means of cooperation in the field of advanced technology. In contrast to the Community's own research efforts and those of COST, which are largely concerned with pre-competitive research, EUREKA will be concerned with projects which are closer to the market. EUREKA will therefore tend to involve collaboration between firms, whereas Community research tends to focus more on universities and public-sector research bodies.

The idea of injecting an explicit commitment to research and technology in the Rome Treaty is a product of a memorandum which the EC Commission addressed to the Milan Summit in 1985. The memorandum was entitled *Towards a Technology Community* (EC Commission, 1985c). It was endorsed by the European Council and became one of the background documents which led to the Single European Act. As a result of the latter, the Rome Treaty has been amended. A new Title VI has been added which is headed Research and Technological Development. The ensuing articles state that the Community's aim should be to strengthen the scientific and technological base of European industry and to encourage it to become more competitive at the international level. To this end the Community will encourage firms, universities and research centres in their research and technological development activities. It will also help firms to exploit the Community's internal market through the opening up of public contracts, standardization and the removal of fiscal and legal barriers to cooperation. Although the multi-national R & D framework programmes will be decided on the basis of unanimity, individual items will be decided by majority vote. This is a most important development.

We turn now to the Community's internal R & D efforts. These are divided into two main categories – direct and indirect. Direct action is carried out by the Community's own Joint Research Centre. Indirect action consists of projects which are carried out under contract by universities or industrial firms. Generally, the Community will pay half the cost – the rest being put up by the contractors.

The following are three examples of the more important indirect programmes. We mentioned the Joint European Torus (JET) project when discussing energy policy. It is concerned with nuclear energy produced by fission as opposed to fusion. As an exception to the rule, the Community contribution in this case was 80 per cent. Another programme which has attracted considerable publicity has been the European Strategic Programme for Research and Development in Information Technology (ESPRIT). This arose out of the Commission's investigations into areas where the Community was falling behind the USA and Japan. Information technology was agreed to be such an area. As a result, a ten-year programme was launched in 1984 involving twelve major European companies, hundreds of small and medium-sized firms as well as research centres and universities. The first five years were planned to cost 1500 million ECUs, of which 50 per cent would come from the Community budget. Another project, entitled Research and Development in Advanced Communications Technologies for Europe (RACE), was launched in 1985. This is concerned with the development of the technological base for a network of integrated broad-band telecommunications systems using optical fibres. Between 1985 and 1986, the research priorities were defined. Between 1987 and 1992, the precompetitive research work will be carried out, and between 1992 and 1996 the actual equipment will be developed. The second phase was held up by a funding dispute but was finally given the green light in September 1987.

Problem industries

In the post-transition period, a new element began to emerge in industrial policy. The Community was forced to address itself to what may be termed problem industries, that is to say industries which had begun to exhibit structural weaknesses, often as a result of foreign competition, although the recession which began in 1974 aggravated the situation.

Three industries have frequently featured in this context – textiles, steel and shipbuilding. We will concentrate on the first two, since in both cases quite clear policies were developed which had a good deal in common.

It should be emphasized that whilst industries may be in difficulty, and whilst chronic excess capacity may exist and a need to slim down and modernize may be apparent, the EC Commission is not empowered to step in and carry out the rationalization process. This latter role has to be discharged by the firms themselves, no doubt aided and encouraged by governments. That does not mean, however, that the Commission is powerless to act. It can in fact intervene in two ways. (a) It can control state aids in order to ensure that they are directed towards restructuring as opposed to merely propping up inefficient structures which have no prospect of longer-term viability. (b) It can also control imports from outside the Community, thus giving the industry a breathing space within which to adjust. In the case of the steel industry, which comes under the more *dirigiste* Paris Treaty, the Commission can also intervene in order to set a limit to internal competition and ruinous price wars – again the object is to give the industry a breathing space.

In the case of textiles, the Commission began to define its policy as early as 1971. In that year it published its *Framework for Aid to the Textile Industry* (EC Commission, 1971b). The Commission recognized that the textile industry would have to face a situation in which it was increasingly open to cheap imports. Production within the Community was likely to shrink. It was equally likely that member states would seek to protect their industries by giving aids. These, if uncontrolled and uncoordinated, would distort competition within the Community. The Commission therefore laid down a series of rules which not merely sought to prevent internal distortions but were designed to facilitate the orderly readaptation of the industry. In issuing these rules, the Commission was not in any way seeking to indicate that aid-giving was necessary, but it did recognize that in certain acute situations it might be inescapable. What it did say was that aids which merely consisted of subsidies to price were unacceptable – they would merely prop up industries which in fact might have no prospect of independent viability. In so far as aids were permitted, they should not add to capacity – there was likely to be too much already. Rather, aids should reduce existing excess capacity (thus giving the remaining capacity a chance to survive) and should facilitate diversification away from the areas of acute competitive pressure. Aids to existing activities were to be permitted, but they should be designed to enable the industries to become competitive.

Had the last element not been present, the rules would have been exclusively designed to facilitate the contraction of the industry. The aid rules were revised in 1976, but some of the essential features of the 1972 system were retained. Thereafter, the Commission continued to monitor aids. By 1985 the Commission was able to report that substantial restructuring had taken place, that the industry had largely regained the competitiveness required for its survival and that it could no longer be regarded as a crisis industry. Clearly, the Commission was signalling that it would therefore be disposed to regard aid-giving as unjustified. In the case of man-made fibres a critical excess capacity problem emerged in the 1970s. The problem became so acute that in 1977 the Commission requested member states to refrain from giving any aid that would have the effect of adding to man-made fibre capacity. Aids were, however, approved where they would reduce capacity, and later the Commission also agreed to a cartel designed to scrap capacity. This section of the industry appears to have continued to present problems, and even as late as 1985 the Commission was stressing the need to maintain an active aid-monitoring system.

On the external side, the original posture of the Community towards textile imports from the third world was quite generous. This was reflected in the Arrangements Regarding International Trade in Textiles, more familiarly known as the Multi-Fibre Arrangements (MFA), the first of which was negotiated in 1973 and ran until the end of 1977. It related not only to textiles but also to fibres and clothing. The parties to it were the developed countries such as the EEC, US and Japan, which were major markets for the above products, and a large number of supplier countries which for the most part could be called developing or newly industrializing countries (NICs). It did not allow the penetration of developed industrialized markets to proceed in a totally unregulated manner but did, subject to certain exceptions, allow for a liberal growth in imports of 6 per cent a year.

However, by 1977, when the negotiations for the second MFA were beginning, the mood of the importing countries had changed. The penetration of the NICs and recession had taken their toll. The attitude of the EEC and the other importing parties stiffened. Discussions within the EEC in 1976 revealed considerable pressure at national level for a more restrictive arrangement. In the event, although the second MFA (to run until the end of 1981) maintained the import growth ceiling at 6 per cent, it also provided for a 'most-sensitive product' range where there was to be virtually no growth. Just how restrictive this could be was demonstrated by the UK, where the most-sensitive product range accounted for 61 per cent of imports. The third MFA, which ran from the end of 1981 until the end of July 1986, continued the much tighter approach, but in the fourth MFA (to run until July 1991) the Community adopted a more relaxed approach – no doubt in the light of the improved viability (see above) of the Community textile industry.

Iron and steel is an industry for which the Community has a special responsibility because, along with coal, it is, as we noted earlier, subject to the special régimes laid down under the Paris Treaty. Specific rules and procedures, described below, are prescribed which effectively call for competition but impose conditions in respect of price, output and investment decision-making.

(a) Cartels and Dominant Positions are subjected to control in ways broadly similar to Articles 85 and 86 of the Rome Treaty. A specific power to control mergers (including a requirement to notify) is provided.[1]

(b) Rules are laid down which govern the pricing offers which can be made. These rules call for price publicity. Prices must also be related to a geographical basing point, and quotations to customers take the form of the publicized basing point price plus transport costs (the latter are supposed to be transparent, i.e. publicized and thus known to all possible suppliers) from the basing point to the customer. There is, however, considerable scope for competition. Under conditions of boom, steel firms will probably be able to charge the full basing point price plus transport cost. But if there is a recession in sales they can align their prices down. They can indeed align them down to *match* the lowest delivered price which any other producer within the Community could offer. Such an offer does not have to be made – it is sufficient that it could be made. In other words, knowing all the basing point prices of all other producers and knowing the transport charges of all other producers to the customer in question, any particular producer can push his quotation down to the lowest of those theoretically possible delivered prices. It is of course always open to a producer to notify a cut in his own basing point price, in which case he can make lower offers. Equally well, if some producers notify cuts in their basing point prices then other producers have more scope to align down to match them. Here we are referring to internal alignment – competition against other Community offers. In addition Community producers can align down to meet (actual) offers from non-Community sources. This is referred to as external alignment. During recessions, the Community steel industry has proved

1. Such antitrust rules also apply to coal.

to be highly competitive. List prices have been cut and the alignment possibility has been used to the full as Community producers scrambled to obtain a share of diminished Community orders; this has been particularly noticeable when the export market has also been depressed. They have also competed vigorously against non-Community offers which in depressed world market conditions have come in at low, even artificially low, price levels.

(c) In conditions of manifest crisis the Commission can step in and fix prices, production quotas, etc. In other words, although price competition, subject to rules, is to be the order of the day, if it gets out of hand intervention is possible with a view to limiting the price fall. Given that before the Second World War the European steel industry was cartelized and had little experience of competition, it is hardly surprising that when faced with the prospect of free competition it should be felt prudent that a safety net be provided.

Procedures, which can also be viewed as a safety net, are prescribed for investment. Here the fear presumably was that free competition might lead to the creation of excessive productive capacity with a consequent possibility of ruinous pressure on prices. Provision was therefore made for the exercise of official influence on the volume and direction of investment. A forecast of the likely evolution of demand is made, and the Commission then attempts to keep investment in productive capacity in line with that development. This is referred to as the General Objectives system. Excessive investment can be discouraged (but not prevented) by adverse official opinions on reported projects and by the withholding of a Community contribution to investment financing.

As we have observed, the Community steel industry has proved to be highly competitive, much more so than the U K industry, which has been shielded from internal competition – either it operated price-fixing cartels, took the officially prescribed maximum prices (under the old Iron and Steel Board) as minima, or has been nationalized. Not surprisingly, the Community steel industry was stimulated to increase efficiency. Thus in 1976 the West German industry required 18 man hours to produce a tonne of steel whilst the U K figure was 30. But on the other hand, although relatively efficient by U K standards, the steel industry of the old Six did not keep pace with developments in countries such as Japan. In 1976 the Japanese industry needed only 4 man hours to produce a tonne of steel!

From 1974 onwards, the steel industry of the Nine was in difficulties.

The recession in the Community, and in the world market, greatly intensified internal competition. Community producers also had to contend with low offers from outside (e.g. Japan). During the height of the recession prices on occasions fell between 30 and 50 per cent below list levels, and the industry worked at as little as 60 per cent of its production capacity.

All this has led the Community to introduce measures to deal with the factors which were driving companies towards bankruptcy. (In 1977 the British nationalized industry was reported to be losing getting on for £2 million per day.) This first led the Commission in 1976 to introduce the Simonet Plan. Henri Simonet was then the Commissioner responsible for steel. The plan began to operate at the beginning of 1977 and consisted of voluntary cooperation between the Commission and producers, whereby delivery programmes were suggested which would in effect prevent the market from being swamped, thus helping to pull prices back up. In 1977 Viscount Etienne Davignon took on the industrial portfolio. Under his guidance more drastic measures (called the Davignon Plan) were introduced. In the spring of 1977 (under Article 61 of the Paris Treaty) prices were prescribed for concrete reinforcing rods, and guidance prices were also laid down for a number of laminated products. Then in January 1978 minimum prices were also prescribed for merchant bars and coils, and for the first time steel stockholders were required to obey these minima. The Commission also negotiated agreements with foreign steel-supplying countries whereby they were required to restrain their exports to the Community market. In the interim, minimum reference prices were laid down for steel coming into the Community, and a penal duty was placed on shipments sold below these minimum levels.

All this served to improve the profitability of the steel industry. In 1978 and 1979 prices improved. However, in 1980 the voluntary restraint on output collapsed. There was a scramble for orders, prices fell and the Commission was forced to declare a manifest crisis and impose mandatory output and sales quotas. The Commission had in fact assumed a monopolistic control of the industry.

Not surprisingly, the difficulties of the steel industry led member states to grant aids to their industries. As in the case of textiles, the Commission has had to control these. In 1981 the Commission persuaded Council to adopt a new aid code. Undertakings benefiting from aids had to be engaged in implementing a systematic and specific restructuring programme. Such programmes should lead to an overall reduction in production capacity and should not add to capacity in areas for which there is no growth market. Aids should be progressively reduced – the code envisaged the final phasing out of aid-giving by the end of 1985. In the interim, the Commission was given the task of supervising the application of the code.

In fact the Commission did decide that from the end of 1985 a new aid code should operate. This prohibited all operating aids and all aids intended to finance investment. However, aid towards protection of the environment, for R & D and for closures was to be permitted but under strict conditions. In 1985 the Commission also persuaded the Council to make a start on removing the quota system which had been instituted back in 1980. In 1986 it endeavoured to persuade the Council to complete the dismantling of quotas. However, the Council agreed to take only limited steps and to defer action in order to give consideration to the views of the industry, which wanted to delay the liberalization process. The steel industry had in fact offered to make voluntary capacity cuts provided the quota system was extended until 1990. In March 1987 the Council of Ministers returned to the issue of quotas but decided yet again to defer action, arguing that the cuts offered by the industry were not sufficient to deal with the excess-capacity problem. By June 1987 it was apparent that the steel industry was unable to find the necessary cuts in capacity, and the Commission was left with the extremely difficult task of producing a plan for capacity reductions which would pave the way for a free market. Subsequently, the Commission was able to secure a number of undertakings to close excess production capacity. On the basis of those undertakings the ministers of industry were able, later in 1987, to agree to the progressive phasing out of quotas. Steel quotas should be finally abolished by 1990.

Fisheries

A discussion of industrial policy provides as relevant a location as any for a brief review of policy in respect of the fishing industry. A common fishing policy has been on the agenda for a long time, but it was not until 1983 that final agreement was achieved. Having said that, we should also note that the original Six were able to achieve a common position as early as 1970. Regulations were adopted, operative from the beginning of 1971, which were based on the principle of free and equal access for all EEC fishermen to Community fishing waters and a free market for fish within the Community. Exceptions were, however, provided. The Six in fact managed to put this agreement together rather conveniently, in that four countries with significant fishing interests were about to join. Indeed, the fact that something of a *fait accompli* seemed to exist was one reason why Norway finally decided not to join. Arrangements were, however, made for the three new members. These included a general exclusive six-mile zone for fishermen of the coastal states, together with a twelve-mile exclusive zone in some areas. But unless the common fishery policy was reviewed these exclusive areas would become Community waters after 1982. This was not an acceptable long-term solution as far as the new members were concerned – they were giving up a lot and getting little in return.

There was therefore scope for possible future discord, but for a time the focus of concern switched to the international level. Between 1974 and 1976 the third United Nations Conference on the Law of the Sea (UNCLOS III) was in session, and in its deliberations the question of the extension of national fishing limits to 200 miles figured prominently. Prior to the conclusion of UNCLOS III, some of the Nine were in favour of going ahead with such an extension. It was, however, decided to await the conclusion of the conference. In fact, a binding international agreement failed to emerge from the final session and, following the Canadian, Norwegian and US announcements to the effect that they intended to extend their limits to 200 miles, the Community decided to do likewise. This agreement, reached at The Hague in October 1976, was also partly precipitated by threats of unilateral action, most notably from the UK. The extension was to take effect from the beginning of 1977. The Commission was also charged with carrying on negotiations with non-members, Clearly, in the absence of specific agreements the 200-mile limit would exclude countries which had previously fished in what was now being referred to as the Community pond. If they were to be allowed to fish then questions arose as to how large a catch they could be allowed and whether they would reciprocate in respect of their own waters. The Commission identified three categories of third-country negotiations. There were countries where reciprocity was possible, e.g. Iceland and Norway. There were countries with little or no interest in Community waters but with possible surpluses in their own waters to which access might be allowed, e.g. US and Canada. Finally there were those who had an interest in the Community pond but had little to offer in return, e.g. Eastern European states.

By 1976 the internal problem now began to loom up again. Was it really going to be a Community pond with completely free access or would states be able permanently to enjoy exclusive zones? Alternatively, or perhaps in conjunction with such an arrangement, would the Community opt for some overall catch, perhaps reduced on conservation grounds, which would be allocated between states on a percentage basis? Since the common 200-mile limit meant that countries such as the UK and Ireland lost access to important fishing grounds (e.g. Iceland), what, if any, kind of compensation would be allowed within the pond allocation?

The UK set out by regarding the 12-mile limit as quite inadequate. Its initial policy stance was to demand a 100-mile exclusive zone, although this was subsequently dropped to 50 miles. Subsequently, the idea of a solution based purely on exclusive zones was given less emphasis, and more attention was paid to the idea of an absolute catch level divided into national quotas. In late 1977 the Commission suggested possible quotas, the UK figure being almost 30 per cent. This did not match her demands (45 per cent), which in part reflected her desire for compensation for lost access elsewhere.

In the final analysis, the agreement eventually achieved in 1983 consists of a mixture of zones and quotas. All waters within the 200-mile zone are in principle open to all Community fishermen. However, member states are allowed to retain limits of up to 12 miles for their own fleets and those enjoying historic rights. A conservation box has been established around the Orkney and Shetland islands, and a limited number of Community licences will be issued in order to avoid over-fishing of endangered species. These limits will run for an initial period of ten years. The conservation of Atlantic and North Sea fish stocks is to be achieved partly by annually fixing total allowable catches of various fish. Some of the catch is earmarked for non-member countries. The remaining EEC share is allocated to various member states. Conservation measures also include the prescribing of net mesh sizes. A market organization reminiscent of the CAP is also provided for. If fish prices fall, producers can withdraw supplies from the market and will be compensated from Community funds. Community funds will also be available to finance structural improvements in the industry.

The European Community has some form of trade or economic cooperation agreement with virtually every country in the world. Sometimes they are concluded with country groups, as in the case of the Lomé Convention which currently takes in sixty-six developing countries. Sometimes the agreements are with individual countries, as in the case of the framework trade agreement of 1978 and the trade and economic cooperation agreement of 1985 with the People's Republic of China. Some arrangements are narrow, as in the case of agreements with Romania, Hungary, Poland, Bulgaria and Czechoslovakia which focus on textiles, steel and some agricultural products. Sometimes the relationship is widely based, as in the case of the agreement with EFTA, which has created a free trade area in industrial goods between it and the Community. It would be tedious indeed to recount the detail of this multiplicity of agreements. Rather, what we shall endeavour to do is to sketch the broad outlines of the Community's trade and aid relationships with the rest of the world using particular instances to illustrate the various kinds of connection. This chapter should be read in conjunction with Chapters 1, 4, 8 and 9.

The structure of Community trade

The structure of Community trade in 1985 is shown in Table 26. The following key points emerge. About 55 per cent of member state exports were directed towards other member states – from which it inevitably follows that Community exports to the rest of the world represented about 45 per cent of total exports. The Community had a sizeable trade deficit with the rest of the world, whereas intra-Community imports and exports must of necessity balance. The Community had a balance-of-trade surplus with other industrialized economies in Western Europe. It also had a surplus with other industrialized countries excluding the US and Japan. It had a substantial surplus with the US – this was part of the well-known US trade deficit. The Community had a trade surplus with state trading nations other than those in Eastern Europe. By contrast it had a trade deficit with developing countries – only in the case of the Mediterranean Basin was there a broad balance. It had a significant deficit with Eastern Europe and a large and persistent deficit with Japan. The deficit with the OPEC oil exporting countries was even greater than that with Japan.

Table 26. The trade [1] of the Twelve in 1985

	Imports from	Exports to	Balance [4]
World	874 523	849 923	− 24 600
Intra-EC	466 649	466 581	—
Extra-EC	406 357	378 647	− 27 710
EFTA	81 988	84 770	2 782
Other West European	8 683	12 909	4 226
US	68 934	85 524	16 590
Japan	28 577	10 474	− 18 103
Other industrialized countries	23 781	24 266	485
ACP [2] plus overseas departments and territories	30 633	22 168	− 8 465
Other developing countries	125 296	106 742	− 18 554
Eastern Europe (state trading)	33 971	23 540	− 10 431
Other state trading	4 495	8 255	3 760
Miscellaneous	1 516	4 694	3 178

Trade with specific country groups included in extra-EC category above

	Imports from	Exports to	Balance [4]
Mediterranean basin	44 260	44 086	− 174
OPEC	72 208	48 600	− 23 608
Latin America	29 872	14 627	− 15 245
ASEAN [3]	10 376	9 916	− 460

Notes: 1. Million ECUs. 2. Lomé Convention countries – i.e. ex-colonial dependencies. 3. Association of South East Asian Nations. 4. Exports minus imports.
Source: Statistical Office of the European Communities, *External Trade Monthly Statistics*, 1986, no. 12.

The Common Commercial Policy

The Rome Treaty (Articles 110 to 116) requires the EEC to develop a Common Commercial Policy (CCP) – which should aim to contribute to the harmonious development of world trade and to the progressive removal of barriers. The centre-piece of the CCP is the Common External Tariff (CET). As we indicated in Chapter 4, all member states must apply the CET – unilateral changes are ruled out. In any GATT (General Agreement on Tariffs and Trade) negotiations concerned with the level of the CET, the negotiating mandate will be laid down by the Council of Ministers. The actual negotiations will be carried out by the Commission, which will be advised by a special committee set up by the Council. The final agreement will be ratified by the Council. The CCP also requires member states to bring their *quantitative* restrictions into line, and negotiations about quantitative limits (e.g. the Multi-Fibre Arrangements discussed in Chapter 10) are conducted by the Commission, on behalf of the members, against a similar organizational background. The CCP also requires the member states to establish common principles in respect of (a) the systems under which aid is given in relation to exports to third countries (some implementing steps have been taken), (b) export policy (see Chapter 4 for an account of the New Commercial Policy Instrument) and (c) protection from unfair import competition (see Chapter 4 for anti-dumping rules, etc).

Let us look a little more closely at the centre-piece – the CET. At the end of the Second World War, when the major economic powers were seeking to devise a new world economic order, they envisaged two international bodies. One was to deal with monetary matters, the other was to be concerned with trade. The IMF was the product of the first aspiration. It was anticipated that an International Trade Organization (ITO) would be responsible for the second. In fact the ITO never came into being. Nevertheless, negotiations concerning tariffs were held in Geneva in 1947, and these led to the signing of the GATT. The GATT system has continued to be the focal point of international trade bargaining. GATT gave rise to rules concerning international trade matters. These required that tariff bargaining should be based on reciprocity and should not give rise to discrimination. The latter was particularly important in the context of EEC trade policy. It implied that if a country offered to cut its import duties on goods coming from country A, then it should also apply that treatment to all other countries – this is called most-favoured-nation treatment. The reader may wonder how the Community was able to form a customs union and still stay within

GATT rules. Obviously, a customs union is discriminatory – import tariffs on partner goods are eliminated but are maintained on goods coming from third countries. The answer to that question is quite simple. GATT provided an exception in the case of customs unions (and free-trade areas). Various rules were devised, including the requirement that in the case of a customs union the CET should on the whole be no higher than the general incidence of the duties which the parties had imposed prior to the union. The EEC drew attention to the fact that the CET was based on an arithmetical average of the previous national duties and that therefore it had not breached GATT rules.

If the EEC had left matters at that then there would be little more to discuss. As far as tariffs are concerned we would merely have to record that all non-members have had to face the CET. In fact, matters did not end with a non-discriminatory CET. Rather, the EEC chose to conclude a variety of trade agreements in which different groups were treated differently, and within given groupings (e.g. developing or industrialized economies) different treatments were accorded. To the evolution of this situation we now turn.

Part Four Association

The Part Four Association provisions are to be found in Articles 131 to 136. They were devised in order to accommodate the interests of the dependent or formerly dependent territories of the member states. Countries which benefited from Part Four Association arrangements came to be the most favoured third countries.

During the negotiations leading up to the Rome Treaty, the French vigorously pressed the idea of associating overseas territories. The Spaak Report (Spaak, 1956) made no mention of them, and it was only at the Venice meeting of foreign ministers in May 1956 that France, by making association a condition of going ahead with the scheme for a common market, got the subject on the agenda. The French had good reasons for taking this line. Firstly, they regarded the overseas territories as an extension of France, but a customs union of the Six would definitely discriminate against them. Secondly, France bore a considerable burden both in the form of aid and relatively high prices for colonial raw materials. She felt that the Six should be placed on a more equal footing by taking on part of the financial responsibility. This was further emphasized by the fact that countries such as Germany were investing in commercial enterprises in the French dependencies and therefore derived much advantage from French expenditure on the necessary infrastructures. The overseas dependencies were listed in Annexe IV and included French West Africa, French Equatorial Africa, the French Trustee territory in the Cameroons, Madagascar, a range of other French overseas settlements and Togoland, the Belgian Congo and Ruanda Urundi, the Italian Trustee territory of Somalia and Netherlands New Guinea. The Netherlands Antilles was added in 1964.

The original basis of association was concluded for five years. Thirty-one countries were covered – all of them were dependencies. These latter were referred to as Overseas Countries and Territories (OCTs). The broad thrust of the association arrangements, which had a double character, was as follows. The Community undertook to reduce its tariffs on goods coming from the dependencies in line with internal tariff disarmament. This was a vital concession in so far as the primary products supplied by non-associated states faced the Community's common external tariff. The dependent territories were required to reciprocate but could, however, retain protection needed for their development, industrialization or revenue, provided they extended to all member states the preferences they had previously extended to the mother country. The Treaty also brought into existence the European Development Fund (EDF) which was to channel aid to the associated territories. Such EDF aid is a notable feature of association under Part Four. The Six agreed that over the first five years they would make available $581·25 million. France and West Germany subscribed $200 million, Italy $40 million, Belgium and the Netherlands $70 million each and Luxembourg $1·25 million. French territories obtained no less than $511·25 million of this aid. It should perhaps be added that owing to administrative and technical difficulties there was a considerable delay in disbursing this money.

By 1960 many of the OCTs had become independent, and a new basis for association was required. Therefore in 1961 and 1962 negotiations took place, and these in turn led to the Yaoundé Convention. Yaoundé I ran from 1 July 1964 and Yaoundé II came into force on 1 January 1971. The signatories of the former were eighteen in number and were described as the Associated African States and Madagascar (AASM). In Yaoundé II the eighteen were joined by Mauritius. Trade and aid arrangements were also devised in respect of the remaining OCTs. Broadly speaking, Yaoundé I and II were concluded on the following lines. Tropical products entered the Community free of duty. In some cases where competition arose, duty-free quotas were prescribed. In the case of industrial products, preferential access to the EEC was allowed but they might be subjected to quotas. There was no requirement for the AASM to reciprocate in respect of the Community's exports – they could if necessary introduce or maintain protective duties and quotas. Aid was also provided. Under Yaoundé I, 666 million UA was made available by the EDF together with 64 million from the EIB. Under Yaoundé II, the aid level was raised to 828 million UA from the EDF and 90 million from the EIB. In addition an institutional framework, including a Council of Ministers, was established.

Inevitably, the preferences granted to the associated states gave rise to criticism. The Latin American states in particular called upon the EEC to abolish its preferential system, and as a result the EEC agreed to reduce the CET on tropical products from third countries generally. As a consolation, the AASM were allowed to benefit from a reduction in the defences enjoyed by Community agricultural producers under the CAP. The AASM too began to find the Yaoundé system less beneficial. This arose from the fact that the Community decided to grant preferential access to other groups. In 1971 it introduced the General System of Preferences (see below), and from 1972 it decided to develop a global Mediterranean Policy (see below). It was partly in order to compensate for these changes that the Community decided to step up the level of convention aid.

As Yaoundé II neared its end, the question of its successor fell due for consideration. Two factors suggested that the formula was in need of modification. Firstly, there was the decline in the value of preferential access – a point we have just made. Secondly, as a result of the 1973 enlargement a lot of other ex-colonial dependencies were now in the queue for association benefits – i.e. those of the UK.

The solution was the Lomé Convention of 1975, which was hailed as a breakthrough in the relationships between the developed and the developing. It brought together the nineteen AASM – the original Yaoundé states plus Mauritius – and twenty-one less developed Commonwealth countries. In addition there were five outsiders and Guinea, thus making forty-six in all who collectively were called the African, Caribbean and Pacific States (ACP). Lomé I was followed in 1981 by Lomé II, and in 1986 Lomé III entered into operation. Lomé III takes in sixty-six ACP states – they constitute more than one third of the countries represented in the UN.

What are the essential features of the present Lomé system? Firstly, the ACP states enjoy tariff preferences for their exports to the Community. Indeed, over 99 per cent of the ACP exports entering the Community market do so free of tariff and quota. It should be mentioned that the ACP countries depend on the Community market for some

40 per cent of their exports. Secondly, a relatively generous approach has been adopted by the Community in respect of ACP exports of agricultural produce. In particular, price and purchasing guarantees exist in respect of traditional exports of sugar from the ACP. However, the importance of all this should not be overrated, since only about 0·5 per cent of ACP exports fall into the category of agricultural products subject to CAP import levy protection. Thirdly, in respect of EEC exports to the ACP, the Community does not demand reciprocal tariff preferences. All that the Community requires in return is non-preferential and non-discriminatory most-favoured-nation treatment – a concept we discussed earlier. Fourthly, the current convention envisages the provision over a five-year period of 8500 million ECUs by way of aid. The EDF will provide 7400 million ECUs, and the EIB will make available a further 1100 million ECUs. The EDF contribution will be broken down as follows – 4860 million ECUs in grants, 600 million ECUs in loans, 600 million ECUs in the form of risk capital, 925 million ECUs for STABEX and 415 million ECUs for SYSMIN. The latter two require some explanation.

STABEX was introduced under Lomé I. Under this arrangement, funds are provided for ACP countries to cover shortfalls in earnings brought about by fluctuations in the price or output of agricultural products exported to EEC countries. There is also a provision whereby countries which by virtue of their geographical position do not have the EEC as a main outlet can have their exports to all destinations taken into consideration. The number of commodities covered by the STABEX scheme was progressively increased, and under Lomé III forty-eight are covered. STABEX aid usually takes the form of grants, but in the case of the more developed ACP states it may consist of interest-free loans. SYSMIN (Special financing facility for ACP and OCT mining products) was introduced under Lomé II. It is directed towards ACP states which are heavily dependent on mining exports to the Community and is designed to remedy harmful effects on their incomes caused by serious temporary disruptions affecting the mining sector. Assistance in this case usually takes the form of loans.

A number of OCTs still exist – e.g. St Helena, the Netherlands Antilles and New Caledonia. Similar types of arrangement have been made for them – the terms are goverened by Council Decision 383/86 of 30 June 1986.

As we have indicated, the ACP states and OCTs enjoy a privileged status. They do not of course constitute the whole of the developing world. Nor do they take in all the developing countries of the

Commonwealth – the reader will not have noticed any reference to India or Pakistan, to cite but two examples.

Association under Article 238

So far, the discussion has been about the association provisions which were designed in the first instance for the benefit of the colonial dependencies of the Six. In addition, Article 238 provides for association generally. The Community may indeed conclude with a third country, with a group of third countries or with an international organization an agreement which gives rise to an association involving reciprocal rights and obligations. We will illustrate this possibility with respect to two sets of countries: those within the Mediterranean Basin and those who still remain within EFTA.

The Mediterranean policy is an interesting one because it has concerned developing countries who have enjoyed relatively privileged access to the Community market even though they did not fall into the same ex-colonial category as the ACP. The EC Commission put forward proposals for a global Mediterranean policy in September 1972, and the policy was agreed in principle at the Paris Summit in October that year. The Council of Ministers agreed on the main guidelines the following month.

The essential features of the Mediterranean policy in its most generous form were to be as follows. The Mediterranean countries would enjoy tariff-free entry to the Community market for their industrial goods. The Community would not demand reciprocity but would be content with most-favoured-nation treatment. Agriculture would have to be treated in a different way, since the CAP precluded free access for imported agricultural produce. However, tariff reductions could be accorded to imported Mediterranean agricultural produce. But this concession would in practice be a limited one, since the most important form of protection was minimum import prices, and that would not be dropped. Financial assistance in the form of grants and loans, together with other forms of cooperation, would be made available.

The Maghreb agreement of 1976 (Algeria, Morocco and Tunisia) and the Mashrek agreement of 1977 (Egypt, Lebanon, Jordan and Syria) were examples of the above approach. It should be noted, however, that recession and foreign competition forced the Community to impose restrictions on imports into the Community. Whilst some of these related to products which were not of importance to Mediterranean producers, some, such as textiles, were. Even if the quotas were generous, they were bound to inhibit plans for industrial development based on the expectation of absolutely free access. It must also be pointed out that the relatively generous picture which has been painted is one which really applies to southern Mediterranean countries. In other cases, such as Malta and Cyprus, the Community has looked to ultimate reciprocity regarding industrial trade, although the impression emerges that these northern Mediterranean countries have been successful in dragging their feet on this issue.

The EFTA countries are a good example of privileged status within the industralized-economy category. Privileged in this context refers to tariff-free access to the Community market. The situation is relatively simple. When the UK and Denmark joined the Community, the latter agreed to reciprocal free trade in industrial goods as between the enlarged EC and the diminished EFTA. Later we will contrast the position of other industrialized countries with that of EFTA members.

Outsiders

Not all developing countries have enjoyed the same privileged access to the Community as those who have participated in Lomé and in the Mediterranean arrangement. Earlier we pointed out that countries in Latin America had been particularly vociferous in calling for an end to the preferential system operated by the EEC. At the second United Nations Conference on Trade and Development (UNCTAD) in 1968, the Six showed a general willingness to shift ground. This brings us face to face with the idea of a generalized preference system, which was raised at the first UNCTAD in 1964. The general implication of this idea for the Community was that it should give a generalized preference to developing countries rather than be selective. If developing countries were to expand their output of manufactured and semi-manufactured goods, they would need outlets in the markets of developed countries. The outlets would in fact take the form of a tariff preference for developing countries in respect of these goods – that is to say, in the case of the EEC it would levy a lower rate of duty on imports from developing countries than from developed ones. At the second UNCTAD the idea of generalized preferences was formally accepted and the rich nations agreed to make offers.

Negotiations followed, and a generalized preference plan was worked out. In March 1971 the Six agreed that in July 1971 it would introduce generalized preferences. They were in fact to run for ten years. In December 1980 the Council of Ministers agreed to extend the arrangement for a further ten years – 1981 to 1990 – and to modify the conditions.

Under the Generalized System of Preferences (GSP), imports into the Community from developing countries are exempted from customs duties, although the quantity of goods is not unlimited but is subject to ceilings or quotas. The Commission has explained (a) that the GSP is generalized in that the preferences are granted by the majority of industrialized countries, (b) that the preferences are non-discriminatory, (c) that they are autonomous (do not have to be negotiated), and (d) that they are non-reciprocal.

Whilst the GSP sounds fine in principle, it clearly is not a substitute for the more generous access arrangements which have been accorded to other groups. Robert Hine, in a very penetrating study of EEC trade arrangements, has argued that it has been a very disappointing exercise. This he says is a result of an amalgam of factors. Firstly, the impact has been small because of the exclusion of some products from the scheme. Secondly, in respect of products which are included, strict quantitative limits have been applied to the tariff-free treatment – this was obviously bound to be so in the case of 'sensitive' products such as textiles where the Multi-Fibre Arrangement was at work. Thirdly, a high share of the benefits tended to go to a relatively small group of the better-off NICs. Fourthly, the scheme has been complex in operation – unnecessarily large stocks have had to be held, and some of them have not ultimately been able to benefit from the scheme (Hine, 1985, pp. 196–211).

The Community has also established cooperative contracts with both South-East Asia and Latin America. In the case of the former, it concluded a cooperation agreement with the Association of South-East Asian Nations (ASEAN) in 1980. The members of ASEAN are Indonesia, Malaysia, the Philippines, Singapore and Thailand. Apart from some limited financial aid, and other forms of cooperation, the main element of the arrangement is the possibility of benefiting from the GSP. In the case of Latin America, the Community signed cooperation agreements in 1983 and 1985. Again apart from financial aid and food aid (see below), the other benefit held out was participation in the Community's offer under GSP.

The Community is a substantial provider of Food Aid. The idea of food aid for poorer countries originated in 1967. It arose out of the Food Aid Convention which was created as part of the Kennedy Round of GATT tariff negotiations. Community food aid efforts, as distinct from member state efforts, began in 1969. In 1986 Community gifts included 1 247 000 tonnes of cereals, 82 900 tonnes of milk powder,

20 000 tonnes of butter oil and financial aid equivalent to 71 000 tonnes of grain.

The GATT, Japan and US

As we indicated in Chapter 4. the Community has not been reluctant to engage in GATT negotiations designed to reduce the level of the CET. The tariff reductions resulting from the Dillon Round (1961–2) and the Kennedy Round (1964–7) were discussed in Chapter 4. The Tokyo Round (1973–9) led to further cuts but was also important because it involved negotiations on NTBs. Codes of practice were agreed on technical standards, public procurement and subsidies, among other things. As a result, some modifications were made to EEC directives concerning these matters – e.g. public procurement. In 1985 an international conference was held at Punta del Este in Uruguay, where it was agreed that a new round of negotiations should be launched. This will be known as the Uruguay Round. It will cover not only the conventional topics, such as tariffs and NTBs, but also agriculture. The CAP is therefore bound to come in for some close scrutiny. The negotiations will also break new ground, since it is intended that matters such as the piracy of patents and trademarks and trade-distorting investment policies (e.g. local content rules) should also be on the agenda.

The tariff reductions of the Tokyo Round can easily give rise to a mistaken impression of the international trade atmosphere in the 1970s and 1980s. They could be taken to imply that the period has been one of trade liberalization. However, this is not so. It has in fact been one characterized by what has been called the 'New Protectionism'. Whilst member states have discussed tariff reductions and have indeed instituted such measures, other and newer forms of protection have been introduced. Some of the protectionist measures were discussed in Chapter 10 – e.g. the Multi-Fibre Arrangement and the restriction of steel imports into the Community. These were Community measures. But in addition there has emerged a range of nationally negotiated (either by governments or industries) voluntary export restraints (VERs) whereby countries have been asked to restrain their exports of particular goods to the Community. It has been argued that this form of protection has exploited a grey area between what is legal and what is illegal under GATT rules (Hine, 1985, p. 259). Japan has been a key target of such arrangements, and exports from Japan of cars, fork-lift trucks, colour TV sets and tubes, video-cassette recorders, motor cycles, audio-cassette recorders, quartz watches and machine tools have all been subjected to this treatment. In addition, countries in Eastern Europe and countries such as Taiwan, South Korea and Brazil have between them had to exercise restraint over exports of footwear, radios, cutlery, ceramics and TV sets (Pearce and Sutton, 1985, p. 44).

The trade relationship between the Community and Japan has been under particular strain because of the persistent and chronic trade imbalance between the two. As we saw in Table 24, Japan's imports from the EC in 1985 were only 35 per cent of its exports to it. The accusation has been levelled at Japan that it has failed to open its market whilst taking full advantage of the more open trading conditions in Western Europe. The history of EEC–Japanese relations in recent years has been one of (a) Community pressure on the Japanese to open their market, (b) repeated promises and limited actions to that end, and (c) VERs elicited by member states together with a growing Community involvement in the same kind of activity. Thus in 1983 the Commission presented the Japanese Government with a list of commodities for which VERs had already been agreed. It asked for restraint in respect of them and also negotiated VER in connection with video-cassette recorders. Cars have been a particularly sensitive issue. Despite repeated warnings by the Japanese Ministry of International Trade and Industry, Japanese car manufacturers have continued to increase their penetration of the Community market. By 1986 the figure had risen to 11·7 per cent. This gave rise to angry protests from EEC car producers and to a demand in 1987 for a Community freeze on car imports.

At the beginning of 1987, trade relations between the Community and Japan became even more tense. There were three reasons for this. Firstly, some countries were angered by Japan's refusal to open up specific markets. Notable among these was the UK, which threatened to deny Japanese financial institutions continued entry to British financial markets as operating enterprises if the Japanese Government refused to open its domestic telecommunications market to the UK firm Cable and Wireless. Secondly, in March 1987 the US decided to impose penal import duties on a wide range of Japanese electronic goods because of Japanese dumping of semiconductors. The Community feared that the Japanese electronic products would be diverted to the European market and therefore began to make preparations to keep them out. Thirdly, the Community itself began to prepare retaliatory measures against Japan because of its long-standing failure to open up its domestic market.

Trade relations with the US have also been difficult, although in this case the trade balance in recent years have been distinctly favourable to the Community, as the data in Table 25 show. As we noted earlier, the

Community's favourable balance is a part, but only a part, of the large US trade deficit which has given encouragement to protectionist elements in the US. The US would no doubt argue that Europe has not itself been free of such manifestations. The merits of such rival claims are a matter we will not pursue. What is clear is that tensions have existed and they have revealed themselves in a number of sectors, of which agricultural products (including citrus fruit) and steel are examples.

The CAP has been a long-standing cause of conflict, since the growth of self-sufficiency within the Community has reduced the scope for US agricultural exports to the Community whilst the subsidized sale of EC surpluses on the world market has reduced the revenues from US sales elsewhere. Both these effects have been illustrated by trade disputes in the 1980s. In late 1986 and early 1987 a dispute blew up over the effect of Spanish accession which led to variable import levies being placed on Spanish imports of maize and soya under the CAP. The US objected because the expected effect of this action was a reduction of US exports of these products to Spain. It therefore threatened to retaliate by imposing duties of 200 per cent on EEC products including brandy, gin, certain white wines and cheese. At the end of January 1987 a compromise formula was found which averted a minor trade war. The EEC undertook to purchase specified quantities of maize and other cereals from outsiders, including the US, and in addition it reduced import duties on twenty industrial items. The sensitive nature of EC-subsidized exports is well illustrated by an episode in 1983, when the US Government signed two agreements with Egypt for the sale of large quantities of wheat flour, butter and cheese at subsidized prices. The Community took exception to these sales at a loss, since they were taking place in what is regarded as one of its traditional markets. In truth it was really a case of the US recovering by subsidized sales a market which had been previously captured by the EEC by means of subsidized sales!

Steel has been the subject of trade disputes since 1982, when the US Department of Commerce initiated a series of anti-dumping and anti-subsidy investigations in connection with steel imported from Community countries. Two thirds of Community steel exports to the US were thereby put at risk. It would be tedious to recount the details. These episodes have usually led to threats and retaliations by the EEC, after which a restricted level of exports to the US market has been negotiated.

This is rather a sad topic on which to end a book about an institution which the US did much to encourage in the early days. The hope must be that the European Community and the US, who are each other's main trading partners, will be able to avoid a trade war which would be greatly damaging to both and greatly divisive.

Epilogue

The reader will be aware that by 1986 the Community was once more moving into a state of financial crisis. The extra Community budget revenue agreed at Fontainebleau in 1984 – see Chapter 3 above – was proving to be inadequate. Two summit meetings in 1987 gave consideration to the EC Commission's request for extra resources – the proposal is discussed in Chapter 3. The main sticking point was the refusal of the UK to agree to any further budgetary resources until a programme had been agreed which would put an end to the mounting expenditure on agricultural surpluses.

The Heads of State and of Government met again at Brussels in February 1988 in an atmosphere of high tension. The Community budget was running out of funds, and in addition it had not been possible to agree a budget for 1988. As a result the Community was forced to fall back on the emergency procedure whereby it was only allowed to spend each month one twelfth of what it had spent in 1987.

Extremely tough negotiations ensued in which the UK and the Netherlands demanded strong curbs on agricultural over-production. In this connection two particular issues gave rise to controversy. Firstly, what kind of device should be used to control output – see Chapter 8 for a discussion. West Germany favoured set-aside measures – i.e. farmers should be compensated for taking land out of surplus production. The UK, however, favoured stabilizers. Under such an arrangement an output threshold would be agreed, and if output exceeded that limit then price cuts would be introduced as a deterrent. Secondly, if stabilizers were introduced then the level of the output threshold was absolutely crucial. The British argued for a low threshold, but this was opposed by France and West Germany. Measures had already been introduced in respect of the milk and beef surpluses – see Chapter 8 – and these seemed to be having the desired effect. A major residual problem was the surplus of cereals. The UK therefore proposed an annual cereal threshold of 155 million tonnes – West Germany and France wanted 160 million tonnes.

The summit meeting at one stage seemed to be heading for complete collapse, but fortunately a last-minute compromise was arrived at on the issue of agricultural curbs. It was agreed that the main emphasis in agricultural control should be placed on stabilizers, although set-aside measures would also be provided for and the Community would contribute to the cost thereof. It was agreed that for the agricultural seasons 1988–89 to 1991–92 a cereals threshold of 160 million tonnes would be employed. If output went beyond this level, price cuts of 3 per cent would be applied. If output consistently overshot the target, the price cuts would cumulate. A somewhat similar penalty system was agreed for oilseeds. In agreeing to the budget package as a whole, the UK and the Netherlands indicated that their agreement was contingent upon similar stabilizer arrangements being applied to a range of other products.

The agricultural control issue having thus been disposed of, the way was then open for an agreement on a new budgetary regime. A ceiling on budgetary expenditure was agreed. As a proportion of Community GNP it should not exceed 1·2 per cent on a payments basis or 1·3 per cent on a commitments basis. It was also agreed that the growth of agricultural spending should not exceed 74 per cent of the growth rate of Community GNP. Structural spending (e.g. the spending of the ERDF and ESF) should by contrast grow relatively rapidly. It was decided that by 1993 structural spending would be increased by 100 per cent on the 1987 level. In addition, structural spending should be more concentrated on the poorest regions, and indeed spending on them should be doubled by 1992. All this was a clear gain for countries such as Spain, Portugal and Greece.

A revenue-enhancing system was agreed. The three existing budget revenue sources – food import levies, the external tariff and the VAT – are to be retained. The VAT rate ceiling will stay at 1·4 per cent. Commission President Jacques Delors had suggested that the 10 per cent deduction which member states are allowed to cover collection costs should be dropped, but this was not agreed to. Most importantly, a fourth revenue source has been added. This will involve each member state paying a given percentage of its GNP. This is different from the Delors proposal – see Chapter 3 – which had envisaged that this levy should be applied to the difference between the VAT base and GNP. It should also be noted that in calculating a member state's VAT contribution it will be assumed that the VAT base does not exceed 55 per cent of GNP.

The UK succeeded in renewing its budget rebate. In 1984 it was agreed that this rebate should be 66 per cent of the difference between the UK's VAT related payment and its budget expenditure benefits. This system will now apply to the difference between its VAT and GNP related payments and its benefits.

Abbreviations

AASM	Associated African States and Madagascar
ACP	African, Caribbean and Pacific Ocean Countries
Benelux	Belgium, the Netherlands and Luxembourg Customs Union
CAP	Common Agricultural Policy
CCP	Common Commercial Policy
CEEC	Committee for European Economic Cooperation
CET	Common External Tariff
Comecon	Council for Mutual Economic Assistance
COPA	Committee of Agricultural Organizations (Comité des Organisations Professionelles Agricoles de la CEE)
Coreper	Committee of Permanent Representatives (Comité des Représentants Permanents de la CEE)
COREU	Correspondance Européenne
COST	Committee on European Cooperation in the Field of Scientific and Technical Research
EAGGF	European Agricultural Guidance and Guarantee Fund (FEOGA)
ECC	European Communities Commission
ECE	Economic Commission for Europe
Ecosoc	Economic and Social Committee
ECSC	European Coal and Steel Community
ECU	European Currency Unit
EDC	European Defence Community
EDF	European Development Fund
EEC	European Economic Community
EFTA	European Free Trade Association
EIB	European Investment Bank
EMCF	European Monetary Cooperation Fund
EMF	European Monetary Fund
EMS	European Monetary System
EMU	Economic and Monetary Union
EPC	European Political Community
ERDF	European Regional Development Fund
ESF	European Social Fund

ESPRIT	European Strategic Programme for Research and Development in Information Technology
EUA	European Unit of Account
Euratom	European Atomic Energy Community
EUT	European Union Treaty
FEOGA	Fonds Européen d'Orientation et Garantie Agricoles
GATT	General Agreement on Tariffs and Trade
GDP	Gross Domestic Product
GNP	Gross National Product
IGC	Inter-governmental Conference
IMF	International Monetary Fund
JET	Joint European Torus
MCA	Monetary Compensating Amount
MFA	Multi-Fibre Arrangement
MTFA	Medium-Term Financial Assistance
NATO	North Atlantic Treaty Organization
NIC	Newly Industrializing Country
NTB	Non-Tariff Barrier
OCTs	Overseas Countries and Territories
OECD	Organization for Economic Cooperation and Development
OEEC	Organization for European Economic Cooperation
OOPEC	Office for the Official Publications of the European Communities
OPEC	Organization of Petroleum Exporting Countries
R & D	Research and Development
RACE	Research and Development in Advanced Communications Technologies for Europe
SEA	Single European Act
SEDOC	Système Européen de Diffusion des Offres et Demandes d'emploi et de compensation internationale
STABEX	Stabilization of Export Earnings Scheme
STMS	Short-Term Monetary Support
SYSMIN	Special financial facility for ACP and OCT mining products
TVA	Taxe sur valeur ajoutée
UA	Unit of Account
UN	United Nations
UNCTAD	United Nations Conference on Trade and Development
UNICE	Industrial Confederation of the European Community (Union des Industries de la Communauté Européenne)
VAT	Value Added Tax
VER	Voluntary Export Restraint
WEU	Western European Union

References

Armstrong, H., and Taylor, J. (1985), *Regional Economics and Policy*, Philip Allan.

Bloomfield, A. (1973), 'The Historical Setting' in Krause, L. B. and Salant, W. S. (eds), *European Monetary Unification and its Meaning for the United States*, Brookings Institution.

Christie, H., and Fratianni, M. (1978), 'EMU: Rehabilitation of a Case and Some Thoughts for Strategy', in M. Fratianni and T. Peeters (eds), *One Money for Europe*, Macmillan.

Coffey, P., and Presley, J. R. (1970), 'Monetary Developments within the European Economic Community: 1970 – A Year of Achievement', *Loughborough Journal of Social Studies*, no. 10, November.

Dahlberg, K. A. (1968), 'The EEC Commission and the Politics of the Free Movement of Labour', *Journal of Common Market Studies*, vol. 6, no. 3, pp. 310–33.

Dennis, G., and Nellis, J. (1984), 'The EMS and UK Membership: Five Years On', *Lloyds Bank Review*, October, pp. 13–31.

EC Commission (1968), 'First Guidelines for a Community Energy Policy', *Bulletin of the European Communities*, Supplement no. 12, OOPEC.

EC Commission (1969a), *Memorandum on the Coordination of Economic Policies and Monetary Cooperation within the Community*, COM (169), 50.

EC Commission (1969b), 'Memorandum sur la reforme d l'agriculture dans la Communauté Économique Européenne' (Mansholt Plan), *Bulletin of the European Communites*, Supplement no. 1, OOPEC.

EC Commission (1969c), 'Memorandum on Regional Policy', *Bulletin of the European Communities*, no. 12, OOPEC.

EC Commission (1970), 'Economic and Monetary Union in the Community' (Werner Report), *Bulletin of the European Communities*, Supplement no. 7, OOPEC.

EC Commission (1971a), *Regional Development in the Community*, Brussels.

EC Commission (1971b), *Framework for Aid to the Textile Industry*, SEC (71) 2615 final.

EC Commission (1972a), *First Report on Competition Policy*, OOPEC.

EC Commission (1972b), *Fifth General Report*, OOPEC.

EC Commission (1973), *Second Report on Competition Policy*, OOPEC.

EC Commission (1975a), *Ninth General Report*, OOPEC.

EC Commission (1975b), *Report of the Study Group, Economic and Monetary Union 1980* (Marjolin Report), DOC 11/675/3/74.

EC Commission (1976a), 'European Union' (Tindemans Report), *Bulletin of the European Communities*, Supplement no. 1, OOPEC.

EC Commission (1976b), *Tenth General Report*, OOPEC.

EC Commission (1977a), *Eleventh General Report*, OOPEC.

EC Commission (1977b), *The Role of Public Finance in the European Communities*, vols. 1 and 2 (MacDougall Report), OOPEC.

EC Commission (1980), 'Reflections on the Common Agricultural Policy', *Bulletin of the European Communities*, Supplement no. 6, OOPEC.

EC Commission (1981a), 'Report from the Commission of the European Communities to the Council pursuant to the mandate of 30 May 1980', *Bulletin of the European Communities*, no. 1, OOPEC.

EC Commission (1981b), *Communication from the Commission to the Council on the State of the Internal Market*, COM (81) 313 final.

EC Commission (1982), *Sixteenth General Report*, OOPEC.

EC Commission (1983), *The Future Financing of the Community*, COM (83) 10.

EC Commission (1984a), *Five Years of Monetary Cooperation in Europe*, COM (84) 125 final.

EC Commission (1984b), *The Application of the Community's Energy Pricing Principles in Member States*, COM (84) 490 final.

EC Commission (1984c), *The Regions of Europe*, European File 15/84, OOPEC.

EC Commission (1985a), *Completing the Internal Market*, COM (85) 310 final.

EC Commission (1985b), *Perspectives for the Common Agricultural Policy*, COM (85) 333 final.

EC Commission (1985c), *Towards a Technology Community*, COM (85) 530 final.

EC Commission (1986), *Eleventh Annual Report (1985) to the Council by the Commission: European Regional Development Fund*, COM (86) 545 final.

EC Council of Ministers (1970), 'The Problem of Political Unification' (Luxembourg Report), *Bulletin of the European Communities*, no. 11, OOPEC.

EEC Commission (1961), *Memorandum on the General Lines of the Common Transport Policy* (Schaus Memorandum), VII COM (61) 50 final.

EEC Commission (1962a), *Report of the Fiscal and Financial Committee* (Neumark Report), Brussels.

EEC Commission (1962b), *Programme for the Implementation of the Common Transport Policy*, VII COM (62) 88 final.

EEC Commission (1965), *Concentration by Firms in the Common Market*, SEC (65) 3500.

EEC Commission (1966), *The Development of the European Capital Market* (Segré Report), OOPEC.

Hine, R. (1985), *The Political Economy of European Trade*, Wheatsheaf.

HMSO (1971), *The United Kingdom and the European Communities*, Cmnd 4715.

HMSO (1974), *Renegotiation of the Terms of Entry into the European Economic Community*, Cmnd 5593.

HMSO (1975a), *Membership of the European Community*, Cmnd 5999.

HMSO (1975b), *Membership of the European Community: Report on Re-negotiation*, Cmnd 6003.

Josling, T. E. (1973), 'The Reform of the Common Agricultural Policy', in D. Evans (ed.), *Britain in the EEC*, Gollancz.

Kruse, D. C. (1980), *Monetary Integration in Western Europe: EMU, EMS and Beyond*, Butterworths.

Levi Sandri, L. (1965), 'The Contribution of Regional Action to the Construction of Europe', *Third International Congress on Regional Economics*, Rome.

Llewellyn, D. T. (1983), 'EC Monetary Arrangements: Britain's Strategy', in A. M. El Agraa (ed.), *Britain Within the European Community: The Way Forward*, Macmillan.

Lundgren, N. (1969), 'Customs unions of industrialized West European countries', in G. R. Denton (ed.), *Economic Integration in Europe*, Weidenfeld & Nicolson.

Maillet, P. (1982), *The Economy of the European Community*, OOPEC.

Marsh, J. S. (1977), 'Europe's Agriculture: Reform of the CAP'. *International Affairs*, vol. 53, no. 4, pp. 604–14.

National Coal Board (1962), *Meeting Europe's Energy Requirements*.

OEEC (1956), *Europe's Growing Needs of Energy – How Can They Be Met?* (Hartley Report).

Palmer, M., Lambert, J., Forsyth, M., Morris, A., and Wohlgemuth, E. (1968), *European Unity: A Survey of the European Organizations*, Allen & Unwin.

Pearce, J., and Sutton, J. (1985), *Protection and Industrial Policy in Europe*, Routledge and Kegan Paul.

Presley, J. R. (1974), 'Progress Towards European Monetary Union', *Economics*, vol. X, part 3, winter 1973/4.

Spaak, P. H. (1956), *Comité Intergouvernmental créé par la Conférence de Messine, Rapport des chefs de délégation aux Ministres des Affaires Étrangères* (Spaak Report).

Strange, S. (1967), *The Sterling Problem and the Six*, PEP and Chatham House.

Tsoukalis, L. (1977), *The Politics and Economics of European Monetary Integration*, Allen & Unwin.

Tsoukalis, L. (1981), *The European Community and its Mediterranean Enlargement*, Allen & Unwin.

van Ypersele, J. (1979), 'Operating Principles and Procedures of the European Monetary System', in P. H. Trezise (ed.), *The European Monetary System: Its Promise and Prospects*, Brookings Institution.

van Ypersele, J., and Koeune, J. C. (1985), *The European Monetary System*, OOPEC.

Wageningen Memorandum (1973), *Reform of the European Community's Common Agricultural Policy*, Trade Policy Centre, London, and Agricultural University of Wageningen.

Weyman-Jones, T. G. (1986), *Energy in Europe: Issues and Policies*, Methuen.

Zis, G. (1984), 'The European Monetary System 1979–84: An Assessment', *Journal of Common Market Studies*, vol. 23, pp. 45–72.

Further Reading

ALLEN, D., RUMMEL, R., and WESSELS, W. (1982), *European Political Cooperation*, Butterworths.

ARMSTRONG, H., and TAYLOR, J. (1985), *Regional Economics and Policy*, Philip Allan.

BOLTHO, A. (ed.) (1982), *The European Economy*, Oxford University Press.

BUCKWELL, R. (1982), *The Costs of the Common Agricultural Policy*, Croom Helm.

BUTTON, K. J. (1984), *Road Haulage Licensing and EC Transport Policy*, Gower.

CAMPBELL, A. (1980), *EC Competition Law*, North Holland.

CAMPS, M. (1964), *Britain and the European Community 1955–1963*, Oxford University Press.

CLOUT, H. (1984), *A Rural Policy for the EEC*, Methuen.

COFFEY, P. (1979), *The Economic Policy of the Common Market*, Macmillan.

COHEN, C. D. (ed.) (1983), *The Common Market: 10 Years After*, Philip Allan.

COLLINS, D. (1983), *The Operations of the European Social Fund*, Croom Helm.

COSGROVE-TWITCHETT, C. (1981), *A Framework for Development: The EEC and ACP*, Allen and Unwin.

COSGROVE-TWITCHETT, C. (1982), *Harmonisation between Britain and the European Community*, Macmillan.

CURZON PRICE, V. (1981), *Industrial Policies in the European Community*, Macmillan.

DIEBOLD, W. (1959), *The Schuman Plan*, Praeger.

DOSSER, D., GOWLAND, D., and HARTLEY, K. (1982), *The Collaboration of Nations*, Martin Robertson.

EC Commission (1980), *The European Community's Transport Policy*, Office for the Official Publications of the European Communities.

EC Commission (1981), *Grants and Loans from the European Community*, Office for the Official Publications of the European Communities.

EC Commission (1981), *The Social Policy of the European Community*, Office for the Official Publications of the European Communities.

EC Commission (1982), *The Economy of the European Community*, Office for the Official Publications of the European Communities.

EC Commission (1983), *The European Community and the Energy Problem*, Office for the Official Publications of the European Communities.

EC Commission (1986), *The European Community's Budget*, Office for the Official Publications of the European Communities.

EL-AGRAA, A. M. (ed.) (1985), *The Economics of the European Community*, Philip Allan.

ERDMENGER, J. (1983), *The European Community Transport Policy*, Gower.

European Investment Bank (1983), *European Investment Bank, 25 Years 1958–1983*, EIB.

FENNELL, R. (1979), *The Common Agricultural Policy of the European Community*, Granada.

GEORGE, S. (1985), *Politics and Policy in the European Community*, Clarendon Press.

GOYENS, M. (ed.) (1985), *EC Competition Policy and the Consumer Interest*, Cabay.

GROEBEN, H. VON DER (1987), *The European Community: The Formative Years*, Office for the Official Publications of the European Communities.

HALL, G. (ed.) (1986), *European Industrial Policy*, Croom Helm.

HARRIS, S., SWINBANK, A., and WILKINSON, G. (1983), *The Food and Farm Policies of the European Community*, Wiley.

HILL, B. (1984), *The Common Agricultural Policy – Past, Present and Future*, Methuen.

HINE, R. C. (1985), *The Political Economy of European Trade*, Wheatsheaf.

HODGES, M., and WALLACE, W. (1981), *Economic Divergence in the European Community*, Allen & Unwin.

KRUSE, D. C. (1980), *Monetary Integration in Western Europe: EMU, EMS and Beyond*, Butterworths.

LASOK, D. (1980), *The Law of the Economy of the European Communities*, Butterworths.

LASOK, D., and BRIDGE, J. W. (1982), *Introduction to the Law and Institutions of the European Communities*, Butterworths.

LUDLOW, P. (1982), *The Making of the European Monetary System*, Butterworths.

MCLACHLAN, D. L., and SWANN, D. (1967), *Competition Policy in the European Community*, Oxford University Press.

MARSH, J. S., and SWANNEY, P. J. (1980), *Agriculture and the European Community*, Allen & Unwin.

MATTHEWS, A. (1985), *The Common Agricultural Policy and the Less Developed Countries*, Gill and Macmillan.

PEARCE, J. (1981), *The Common Agricultural Policy*, Routledge and Kegan Paul.

PEARCE, J., SUTTON, J., and BATCHELOR, R. (1985), *Protection and Industrial Policy in Europe*, Routledge and Kegan Paul.

PELKMANS, J. (1984), *Market Integration in the European Community*, Nijhoff.

ROBSON, P. (1980), *The Economics of International Integration*, Allen & Unwin.

SHEPHERD, G., DUCHÊNE, F., and SAUNDERS, C. (1983), *Europe's Industries: Public and Private Strategies for Change*, Pinter.

SHONFIELD, A. (1973), *Europe: Journey to an Unknown Destination*, Allen Lane and Penguin.

STEGEMANN, K. (1977), *Price Competition and Output Adjustment in the European Steel Market*, J. C. B. Mohr (Paul Siebeck).

STEVENS, C. (ed.) (1981), *EEC and the Third World: A Survey 1*, Hodder & Stoughton.

STEVENS, C. (ed.) (1982), *EEC and the Third World: A Survey 2*, Hodder & Stoughton.

STEVENS, C. (ed.) (1983), *EEC and the Third World: A Survey 3*, Hodder & Stoughton.

STRASSER, D. (1981), *The Finances of Europe*, Office for Official Publications of the European Communities.

SWANN, D. (1983), *Competition and Industrial Policy in the European Community*, Methuen.

TSOUKALIS, L. (1977), *The Politics and Economics of European Monetary Integration*, Allen & Unwin.

TSOUKALIS, L. (1981), *The European Community and its Mediterranean Enlargement*, Allen & Unwin.

TUGENDHAT, C. (1986), *Making Sense of Europe*, Viking.

VANDAMME, J. (ed.) (1985), *New Dimensions in European Social Policy*, Croom Helm.

WALLACE, H. (1980), *Budgetary Politics: The Finances of the European Communities*, Allen & Unwin.

WALLACE, H., WALLACE, W., and WEBB, C. (1983), *Policymaking in the European Communities*, Wiley.

WALLACE, W. (ed.) (1980), *Britain in Europe*, Heinemann.

WISE, M. (1984), *The Common Fisheries Policy of the European Community*, Methuen.

WEYMAN-JONES, T. G. (1986), *Energy in Europe: Issues and Policies*, Methuen.

VAN YPERSELE, J., and KOEUNE, J. C. (1985), *The European Monetary System*, Office for the Official Publications of the European Communities.

Index

FOR THE BEST IN PAPERBACKS, LOOK FOR THE

In every corner of the world, on every subject under the sun, Penguin represents quality and variety – the very best in publishing today.

For complete information about books available from Penguin – including Puffins, Penguin Classics and Arkana – and how to order them, write to us at the appropriate address below. Please note that for copyright reasons the selection of books varies from country to country.

In the United Kingdom: Please write to *Dept E.P., Penguin Books Ltd, Harmondsworth, Middlesex, UB7 0DA.*

If you have any difficulty in obtaining a title, please send your order with the correct money, plus ten per cent for postage and packaging, to *PO Box No 11, West Drayton, Middlesex*

In the United States: Please write to *Dept BA, Penguin, 299 Murray Hill Parkway, East Rutherford, New Jersey 07073*

In Canada: Please write to *Penguin Books Canada Ltd, 2801 John Street, Markham, Ontario L3R 1B4*

In Australia: Please write to the *Marketing Department, Penguin Books Australia Ltd, P.O. Box 257, Ringwood, Victoria 3134*

In New Zealand: Please write to the *Marketing Department, Penguin Books (NZ) Ltd, Private Bag, Takapuna, Auckland 9*

In India: Please write to *Penguin Overseas Ltd, 706 Eros Apartments, 56 Nehru Place, New Delhi, 110019*

In the Netherlands: Please write to *Penguin Books Netherlands B.V., Postbus 195, NL–1380AD Weesp*

In West Germany: Please write to *Penguin Books Ltd, Friedrichstrasse 10–12, D–6000 Frankfurt/Main 1*

In Spain: Please write to *Longman Penguin España, Calle San Nicolas 15, E–28013 Madrid*

In Italy: Please write to *Penguin Italia s.r.l., Via Como 4, I-20096 Pioltello (Milano)*

In France: Please write to *Penguin Books Ltd, 39 Rue de Montmorency, F-75003 Paris*

In Japan: Please write to *Longman Penguin Japan Co Ltd, Yamaguchi Building, 2–12–9 Kanda Jimbocho, Chiyoda-Ku, Tokyo 101*